Illinois Central College
Learning Resource Center

RUSSIAN RESEARCH CENTER STUDIES 51

POLAND'S POLITICS:

Idealism vs. Realism

POLAND'S

POLITICS: Idealism vs. Realism

Adam Bromke

Harvard University Press
Cambridge, Massachusetts · 1967

The Russian Research Center of Harvard University is supported by a grant from the Ford Foundation. The Center carries out inter-disciplinary study of Russian institutions and behavior and related subjects.

This volume was prepared in part under a grant from the Carnegie Corporation of New York. That Corporation is not, however, the author, owner, publisher or proprietor of this publication and is not to be understood as approving by virtue of its grant any of the statements made or views expressed therein.

To the memory of my mother
who taught me the grammar of Poland's politics

PREFACE

Now that this book is complete it is my pleasant duty to express gratitude to all those who helped me. Several institutions and persons assisted in the preparation of this volume.

My first debt is to the Russian Research Center of Harvard University, where I held a research fellowship in 1960–1962. The stimulating atmosphere of the Center made my stay there not only profitable but also most enjoyable. I am also greatly indebted to the Canada Council for providing me with the travel grants which made possible a visit to Poland in March and April of 1961 and again in June 1964.

Turning from institutions to persons, I would like to express warm gratitude to several of my friends who agreed to read either in its entirety or in part the manuscript and offered valuable comments. These were: Professors Merle Fainsod, Adam B. Ulam, Melvin Croan, and Wiktor Weintraub of Harvard University; Professors M. Kamil Dziewanowski and Andrew Gyorgy of Boston University; Professor William E. Griffith of the Massachusetts Institute of Technology; Professor John W. Strong of Carleton University; Mr. Benedykt Heydenkorn of Toronto and Mr. Zbigniew Łasiński of New York. Many of their suggestions have been incorporated into the final version of this study but I, of course, bear full responsibility for all statements and conclusions.

To Professor Philip E. Uren of Carleton University, Mr. R. H. Dickie, and Miss Grace Powell I am grateful for the preparation of the map. To the editors of *East Europe, Problems of Communism,* and *Survey,* I am obliged for permission to use parts of my articles which previously appeared in their publications. I would also like to extend sincere thanks to Mrs. Helen W. Parsons of the Russian Research Center for her wonderful administrative and technical assistance. Mrs. Barbara Smith, Miss Robin A. Remington, Mrs.

Deirdre Ryan, Mrs. Wendy Jones and Miss Elizabeth Gryger helped me in research and in the editing of the various chapters.

Last but not least, I would like affectionately to thank my wife, who not only remained at my side during all the ups and downs of writing the manuscript, but even typed the first version. Adam Robert, who arrived in the midst of the eighth chapter, and Alexander Richard, who just made it in time for the final revision, provided many enjoyable moments of distraction.

ADAM BROMKE

Ottawa, Ontario,
September 1965

CONTENTS

POLAND'S POLITICS:

Idealism vs. Realism

INTRODUCTION

The title chosen for this book emphasizes the antithesis between political idealism and political realism in Poland's politics. Amid all the crisscrossing currents of international politics, social processes, and ideological trends, the conflict between these two schools of political thought stands out as the single most pervasive phenomenon in modern Polish political life.

The conflict between political idealism and political realism in Poland is at bottom a psychological one. It stems from the universal roots of man's security dilemma; the "uncertainty and anxiety as to his neighbors' intentions."[1] As such, the controversy between the two schools of political thought in Poland is basically the same as is found in any other country. The uniqueness of the Polish conflict is rooted in the fact that throughout the last two centuries the security dilemma has plagued the Poles with unusual persistence and exceptional ruthlessness. Wedged between Germany and Russia, Poland has been repeatedly threatened by its neighbors, eager to deprive it of its very existence.

Ever since Poland's decline as a great power during the seventeenth and eighteenth centuries, it has not been able to adjust peacefully to a new station in European politics. Geography has prevented the Polish nation from taking the position of a middle power, which by virtue of its human and material resources it could have expected to attain. Power in international politics being relative, Poland has been reduced to the virtual status of a small country and, indeed, for well over a century was denied the right of an independent existence.* Facing preponderant power whether they looked toward

* At that stage of European history, Poland was not the only great power on the decline. Its case was, nevertheless, unique. While the countries located on the periphery of the European continent, such as Sweden, Spain, or Turkey, all suffered loss of territory, they retained their independence; but Poland, because of its central geographic position, was totally dismembered by its neighbors.

Russia or Germany, the Poles have battled desperately to continue as a separate political identity.

The only way the Poles could improve the adverse balance vis-à-vis either one of their neighbors has been by securing external allies. The geographical position of the country, a prominent Polish historian observed early in this century, "has made it necessary to seek support from without in any attempt to rise from decline." [2] Foreign policy, thus, has become the fundamental issue in Polish politics, overshadowing all other matters. Indeed, in the course of recent history, probably no other nation has been so consistently and so passionately engaged in debating its foreign policy as has Poland.

In the endless debate over the course of their foreign policy, the Poles have split along psychological lines between "those who imagine the world to suit their policy, and those who arrange their policy to suit the realities of the world." [3] The discrepancy between Poland's potential and actual position in the international sphere has generated a tension between the political order as people think it *ought to be* and as it *is*. In short, the Poles have been divided into political idealists and political realists.

The political idealists, in line with their psychological predilections, have taken a rigid, moralistic stand. They have claimed that to deprive Poland of its place in the international sphere was an unjust act and they have insisted that this should be corrected. They have argued that restoring Poland to what they consider its rightful place is not only in line with Polish national interests, but indispensable for upholding moral order in international politics. Until this can be achieved, they have pledged to carry on a relentless battle to overthrow the existing political order, counting on assistance from nations sharing their ideals. The political idealists, thus, clearly have considered Poland's freedom as their major goal and have been ready to undergo large sacrifices to attain it. They have espoused heroism as the highest national virtue.

On the other hand, the political realists, in accordance with their own psychological inclinations, have adopted a more pragmatic attitude. Viewing Poland's situation in the international sphere at any given time, they have tried to make the best of it. They have believed that the only way Poland could improve its power position was by increasing its internal strength. The political realists have repudiated a struggle against the existing political order for reasons of principle; they have felt that this would weaken rather than strengthen the Polish nation and, instead, they have advocated a modus vivendi with their more powerful neighbors. The primary objective of political realists, thus, has been to protect the nation from any further blows and to secure for it as much opportunity for normal internal development as possible. The realists have praised prudence as a supreme national virtue.

Conflicting programs of foreign policy, reflecting these two different approaches to politics, crystallized in Poland as early as the eighteenth century. From political idealism developed the program of "independence and insurrection, directed primarily toward shaking off the yoke from the East." The method advocated was "military action supported by assistance from France." From political realism emerged "the program of seeking Russian support, which in the first place was directed toward defense of the territorial integrity of the Commonwealth against the two German courts and was expected to accomplish the most urgent reforms under Russian protection." [4]

In this way the rivalry between political idealism and political realism acquired a unique place in Polish politics. Ever since the eighteenth century, adherence to one or the other programs of foreign policy has divided the Poles into two opposing camps. Political movements traditionally have formed and split, not over domestic issues, but over the course of Poland's foreign policy.*

Precisely because of the special role of these two programs in Polish politics, they both developed a capacity for absorbing within their ranks individuals and groups espousing a wide range of political views. Over a period of time, the leading exponents of either political idealism or political realism have represented a broad spectrum of divergent and, indeed, at times, conflicting views on internal political and social reform. Both programs have enjoyed the support of political movements ranging from the extreme right to the extreme left. Thus, at different stages of Polish history, the programs of foreign policy advocated by political idealists and political realists, respectively, have become entwined with various political ideologies and social philosophies — usually representing a complex amalgam of all these strands.

Yet, despite the fact that both political idealism and political realism have become entangled within a maze of ideological trends and social processes, it is still possible to observe a continuity in these political traditions from the eighteenth century until today. Indeed, throughout these two hundred years, the rivalry of these two traditions for the hearts no less than for the minds of the Poles represents the most constant thread in Poland's history.

* The importance which the Poles attached to the selection of allies is underlined by the fact that they have coined a special expression to depict their preference for one or the other alliance. They call it an "orientation" in foreign policy, a term which has often been used in political debates in Poland.

The reason for the remarkable continuity is simple. The security dilemma which has plagued the Polish nation for the past two centuries has not yet been solved. The major concern in the minds of all politically conscious Poles remains the relative vulnerability of their country in the international sphere. In this respect there is no essential difference in the situation of the ancient Commonwealth of Poland in the eighteenth century and that of the Polish People's Republic in the middle of the twentieth century. In Poland the towering political reality is still its location between Germany and Russia.

PART I

Political Idealism and Political Realism

There is a tendency in history for people to swing from one extreme to the other. Having done so, they look for reasons to explain their actions.

William John Rose, *The Rise of Polish Democracy,* 1944.

Either with the Germans or the Russians: no third possibility exists.

—Roman Dmowski, *Przegląd Wszechpolski,* 1901.

I

THE EARLY POLITICAL REALISM

From the eighteenth century, when the two schools of political thought crystallized, until the 1860's, political idealism and political realism existed side by side in Poland. Yet, on the whole, idealism commanded the greater influence. Poland was dismembered in 1795 only after the Poles had lost a war against Russia, and a last-ditch insurrection against the occupying Russian troops had been suppressed. During the Napoleonic wars, the Poles identified their cause with that of France and fought on Napoleon's side in most of his campaigns. With the assistance of the French emperor, they temporarily restored an independent, though substantially smaller Polish state, only to lose it again after Napoleon's downfall. At the same time, however, some Polish statesmen, among whom the most prominent was Prince Adam Czartoryski, strove to promote Poland's cause by cooperation with Russia. The autonomous Kingdom of Poland, which was established in the Polish central provinces under the rule of the Russian tsar in 1815, came into being largely because of Czartoryski's efforts at the Congress of Vienna.

Although weakened by the defeat of Napoleonic France, the idealist school predominated on the Polish political scene for another half a century. It was in this period that idealism came to be known in Poland as "romanticism." The term was adopted under the influence of the romantic movement in Western Europe. The literary works of Lessing and Schiller, and Scott and Byron, and the philosophic writings of Kant and Schelling had had a broad impact in Poland. Their appeal to emotion rather than to reason was acclaimed by the Poles. "Measure your powers by your purpose, not your purposes by your powers," the great Polish poet, Adam Mickiewicz, taught his compatriots. In this romantic vein, the Poles identified their national interests with those of progressive forces in the West. Hopes for the reemergence of the Polish state focused on an anticipated liberal revolution in Europe. A large number of Polish emigrés, who commanded some sympathy and even political influence in Western Europe, particularly in France, provided a link between the revolutionary movement in the West and in Poland. Meanwhile, the realists, although generally on the defensive, were by no means inactive. Under Russian protection, Prince Ksawery Drucki-Lubecki successfully carried out a program of internal reform in the Kingdom of Poland. The insurrection against Russia in 1830–31, which led Tsar Nicholas I to abolish the autonomy of the Kingdom, however, for the most part destroyed the fruits of Lubecki's work. It was only in the late fifties that Margrave Aleksander Wielopolski attempted to reactivate the precepts of political realism.

MARGRAVE ALEKSANDER WIELOPOLSKI

Wielopolski embraced political realism early in his life. He was in his twenties when he was sent in 1830 as an emissary of the Polish revolutionary government to London to plead for assistance from Britain. The failure of the mission convinced him that it was futile for Poland to count upon support from the West. "We repudiate the deceptive sympathy, cheap slogans, and everything that pompous people label as the rights of nations," he cried in 1845, "those rags thrown us by European charity which cover neither our wounds nor our scars." [1] As a result of his experience, Wielopolski also rejected revolutionary tactics. He took advantage of the amnesty granted by the tsar to political refugees and returned to Poland where he soon became a leading exponent of political realism.

In trying to promote Polish interests through an alliance with one of the occupying powers, Wielopolski at first hoped for cooperation with Austria. The events of 1846, however, when Austrian officials, in reprisal for the Cracow insurrection, instigated the peasants to a bloody slaughter of the Polish gentry in Galicia, led to his disillusionment with that country as well. He then turned into a staunch supporter of association with Russia. Wielopolski, as a true conservative, placed his hope in gaining the favor of the tsar. "We come to you, as the most magnanimous of our enemies, to give ourselves up," he addressed Nicholas I. "We were your slaves by the right of might . . . Today you acquire a new right to rule over us. We surrender to you as free men."[2] He also strongly stressed the Slavic bonds between the Poles and the Russians and, last but not least, the common danger posed by the Germans. In return for his unreserved loyalty to the Romanov dynasty, Wielopolski hoped to regain Poland's autonomy and carry out internal reforms. Nevertheless, he realized that, after the insurrection of 1830–31, a return to the *status quo ante,* restoration of the full autonomy of the Polish Kingdom, was not feasible. Consequently, he put forward a more restricted program of reforms. Thus, instead of aiming at a major constitutional remedy, he advocated a series of practical steps which would give the Poles a large degree of self-government.

Wielopolski's chance to put his program into practice came in the early sixties. Following the Russian defeat in the Crimean War and the death of Nicholas I, the Poles once again gained confidence. Conspiratorial activities greatly intensified, and in the early sixties, a revolutionary mood swept the country. This tension provided Wielopolski with an opportunity to press for concessions at St. Petersburg and his program was accepted by Tsar Alexander II. Polish autonomy was somewhat extended and several significant internal reforms were launched. Wielopolski's work, however, was cut short by the ill-fated uprising of 1863–64. Wielopolski himself was partially to blame for the failure. His arrogance and harshness in carrying out his plans alienated the Poles and contributed to the upheaval. Although it is doubtful that his program could have succeeded had he adopted a different attitude toward his compatriots, the gap between Wielopolski's realistic program and the romantic aspirations of the Poles was all but unbridgeable. "He was in conflict with the whole nation, whose aims were independence and restoration [of Poland's] borders from before 1772."[3] Nothing short of achieving these goals could have satisfied the Poles in 1863.

The 1863 insurrection was a milestone in Polish history between the era of political idealism and that of political realism. "The year 1863 represents one of the most fundamental watersheds [in Polish history]. None of the defeats so profoundly uprooted life in Poland and none affected so strongly the minds of at least the next two generations."[4] The results of the uprising were disastrous. The Russians retaliated with stern reprisals. In the Polish provinces a ruthless policy of assimilation and Russification was undertaken. Even small and purely formal manifestations of separate state existence were eradicated. The very name of the Polish Kingdom was changed to "By-Vistula Land."

Still more serious than the marked deterioration of the internal situation were the consequences of the insurrection in the international sphere. The outbreak in Poland was ably exploited by Bismarck for his own ends. By helping the tsarist government to quash the Polish rebellion, he gained Russian gratitude. Thus, having assured Russia's neutrality, he was free to move against Austria and then against France. The outcome of the Franco-Prussian War, in turn, had far-reaching repercussions in Poland. The very foundations on which the plans of the romantic school rested, namely, anticipated assistance from France, were demolished.* France lost all interest in supporting Polish aspirations to independence; indeed, she sought an alignment with Russia, which culminated in a formal alliance in 1894. Moreover, Poland not only lost an ally but gained an enemy. Confident of their power, the Germans soon launched a policy of repression against the Poles in German provinces, a policy which was to continue virtually uninterrupted until World War I.

The changes in the international sphere had a severe effect in Poland. Under the combined impact of three factors — a crushing military defeat, disillusionment with France in particular and with the West in general, and an emerging German threat — the romantic program rapidly declined. The Polish emigrés soon lost their former significance. They desperately clung to romanticism, but deprived of influence in Western Europe, and especially in France, they soon ceased to play any important political role. The reaction among the Poles at home was different but no less profound. In the early 1870's "hopelessness spread among the broad strata of politically conscious society. Only now did they realize that the epoch of insurrections, the epoch of romantic policies definitely and irrevocably had come to an end." [5]

POSITIVISM AND ORGANIC REFORM

After the 1860's, for at least the next three decades, the school of political realism prevailed in Poland. At first, the reaction of the Polish people was directed against costly and futile revolutionary tactics, on the principle of *sauve qui peut!* The reaction was often no less emotional than the revolutions themselves. Driven by despair, some writers moved as far as they could from the romantic position. They professed that nothing remained to be done but to abandon Polish nationality and to dissolve in a Russian sea. "Only through sincere association with the Russian nation," cried a dis-

---

* In line with their program of supporting revolutionary movements in Western Europe, more than a hundred Polish emigrés participated in the Paris Commune of 1871 — a few in positions of military leadership. This contributed considerably to the decline of their popularity in France.

tinguished former collaborator of Wielopolski, Kazimierz Krzywicki, "can we hope for significant social achievements." [6]

Soon, however, a more reflective mood emerged. A critical inquiry into the past was continued, climaxed by a thoroughgoing reexamination of the entire modern history of Poland by the Cracow historical school. "After its grim experiences," wrote one of the leading exponents of the school, Michał Bobrzyński, "our society lost confidence in past historiography. Finding in it nothing but the description of noble deeds with which our history allegedly abounds, the generation after the last uprising was apt to ask why these had not produced the same fruits as in other nations." [7] Consequently, the Cracow historians pursued a merciless struggle against "myths" in Polish historiography. Instead of ascribing Poland's misfortunes to external circumstances, they sought to uncover the errors of the Poles themselves. They bitterly criticized the followers of political idealism, and praised the early proponents of political realism. Projecting their analysis of the past into the future, the Cracow historians advanced their own political program. "Its essence was the preservation of traditional culture, the abandonment of conspiracy and the struggle for independence, and the adoption of reason and discipline." [8]

Along with the sharp scrutiny of Poland's history by the Cracow scholars, a group of young writers in Warsaw expressed harsh criticism of the more immediate past. These men passionately attacked the older generations. "All ties between us are severed," [9] exclaimed their leading exponent, Aleksander Świętochowski. They repudiated the insurrectionist political program, denouncing it as a romantic illusion. While rejecting Polish traditions, the young writers turned to contemporary Western thought for inspiration. They adopted the scientific theories of Darwin, Buckle, and Haeckel, the social teachings of Mill and Spencer, and the positivist philosophy of Comte. Using Comte's philosophy as a basis, they evolved their own theory of positivism. Since for Comte "positive" meant "real," in that it was opposed to something imaginary, the Poles used this distinction for their own purposes, reifying the concept into a social and even political positivist program. In Poland, positivism was not a philosophic concept, as in Comte's writings, but "an approach to practical problems, above all, social problems . . . For the generation of Poles who opposed the romantic ideology to seek guidance in something that was real, and not imagined in the minds of utopians, obviously represented positivism. Positivism, thus, represented a reaction to romanticism in all its manifestations." [10]

The positivist program, therefore, was by definition, thoroughly realistic.

The warning which Tsar Alexander II had given the Poles in 1857, *point de rêveries,* was now scrupulously observed by them. At the root of political realism was the acceptance of foreign rule as unchangeable. "Historical necessity," wrote one of political realism's most outspoken exponents, Antoni Wrotnowski, "makes it impossible for the Poles to continue striving for their independent state. This goal could not be attained even through the greatest sacrifices." [11] Within this framework, improvements in the lot of the nation were sought. Any activity in the field of foreign policy was ruled out. "There is no room today for a Polish external policy," claimed a prominent writer and former romanticist, Józef Kraszewski. "Among the peoples of Europe, apart from the open or concealed enemies, there are none who would fraternally sympathize with us." [12] Under such circumstances, the only path seemed to be a return to Wielopolski's program of reconciliation with Russia.* "We have to adjust to reality," declared an anonymous author. "The largest part of Poland belongs to Russia. Each attempt at liberation only weakens the nation, so let us try to reach agreement with the Russian government and nation. This is not a disgrace, for negotiation with a greater power is a normal course of diplomacy." [13] Thus, all possible avenues of *rapprochement* with Russia were tried. In the late 1870's and early 1880's, when the wave of terrorist activity conducted by *Narodnaya Volya* (People's Will) swept through the tsarist empire, the positivists stressed their solidarity with the government in its efforts to wipe out the revolutionaries. The common bonds of Pan-Slavism, especially as directed against Germany, were often emphasized. Repeated assurances of unreserved loyalty to the dynasty were made. In 1877, on the eve of the Russo-Turkish War, and again in 1880, on the occasion of the twenty-fifth anniversary of the reign of Alexander II, addresses to this effect were sent to the tsar by the cream of Polish aristocracy.

By this time, however, it was too late to revert to Wielopolski's program. The Polish uprising of 1863 had brought about a nationalist reaction in Russia. Danilevsky denounced the Poles as traitors among the Slavs for their

* A similar program of reconciliation with the foreign ruler was simultaneously launched in the Austrian provinces where, after 1866, it was highly successful. The conservative movement managed to win from the Austrians a large degree of autonomy for Galicia. Until the end of the nineteenth century and largely even until World War I, Polish conservatives not only dominated the political scene in Galicia, but also played an important role in Austrian politics. In the German provinces, the program of reconciliation was almost entirely stultified by the government's anti-Polish policy, which gradually intensified in the years 1872–1914. As a result of this German policy, on the eve of World War I, there existed among the Poles in the Prussian provinces considerable pro-Russian sentiment.

Western culture. Katkov claimed that the Polish nation no longer existed, for its fate had been sealed through military conflict. Count Muravycv, who had repressed the Poles in Lithuania, was a popular figure in Russia. Nor was Tsar Alexander II more favorably disposed. For the remaining years of the reign of Alexander II as well as throughout the entire rule of Alexander III, no political concessions to Poland were made.

Under these circumstances, the Poles renounced political activity, turning their whole attention to socioeconomic reforms. After forty years of preoccupation with revolutionary activity, Poland required a good deal of work in this area. The Poles soon evolved a constructive plan of action. Borrowing the term from Spencer, they advanced a so-called program of "organic reform," * directed at the moral, educational, and economic rejuvenation of the nation. "We believe," wrote Kraszewski, "neither in revolution nor in radical utopias which profess to change society overnight and to cure all its social ills by means of some panacea . . . We believe in slow and gradual progress [which] through reforming individuals, increasing enlightenment, encouraging work, order, and moderation should accomplish the most salutary revolution, or rather evolution in the social system." [14]

In accordance with the philosophy of organic reform, the Poles greatly intensified their efforts in the socioeconomic sphere. They concentrated their attention on everyday practical problems. They retreated into private life, primarily looking after their own welfare. Furthermore, the *laissez-faire* system, which prevailed in the country at the end of the nineteenth century, extended into Polish politics as well as economics. There existed almost perfect harmony between private and national goals; the distinction between the public and private spheres of life was clearly drawn. Concentrating on economic rather than political activity, then, was doubly attractive. It not only provided an individual with a rewarding outlet for his energies, but also increased his independence from the state. Since the state represented a foreign oppressor, the liberal slogan of *enrichissez vous* was virtually turned into a patriotic program.

The effects of organic reform in Poland were commendable. Within a few decades, great strides were made in every field. In the territory of the former Polish Kingdom by 1900, the population increased almost twofold; the value of industrial output rose thirtyfold over the level of 1860.[15] Economic progress in turn accelerated far-reaching social changes. "The ancient Poland of landed gentry was transformed into an all-class society . . ." [16]

---

* The literal translation of the Polish term is "organic work."

In the cities, the industrial proletariat grew rapidly. A badly needed, viable middle class emerged, providing the nation with vigorous and enlightened leadership. At the same time, through determined educational efforts, the gap dividing urban and rural areas was considerably reduced. The peasants, who on the whole had remained passive during the insurrection of 1863, now were becoming conscious of their nationality. At the close of the nineteenth century, the modern Polish nation was clearly in the making.

NATIONAL DEMOCRACY: ROMAN DMOWSKI

Despite widespread adoption of its basic tenets, in the 1890's positivism was on the decline. Two factors contributed to this development. First, the policy of reconciliation with Russia brought about no visible improvement in the political situation in Poland. The abandonment of Russia's anti-Polish policy, hoped for when Nicholas II came to the throne, did not materialize. There were no significant changes in the Russian attitude. On the contrary, the almost complete acquiescence of the Poles to Russian rule made many Russian officials believe that a policy of repression was the most effective method for dealing with them. Secondly, the positivist program was self-contradictory. Paradoxically, the very success of organic reform worked against it. Consolidation of the nation's economic and social strength led to the revival of its political aspirations. Thus, the old program, with its renunciation of political activity no longer satisfied the Poles. In particular, the younger generation, which did not remember the disaster of 1863, began to look for new political solutions.

The National Democratic movement, which played the major role on the Polish political scene from the beginning of the century until World War I, was rooted in a patriotic reaction. The National Democrats, after an initial period of intense searching for new means by which to advance Poland's position, embraced a modified version of political realism. To a very large extent, their program was formulated by the party's most outstanding leader, Roman Dmowski. "Although Dmowski belonged to a generation which opposed the ideology of Warsaw's positivism, he was nevertheless strongly influenced by this nonromantic trend, the trend of temperance and political realism." [17] Dmowski's political realism, however, was more sophisticated than that of the preceding generation and even that of Wielopolski. In several respects Dmowski's program moved nearer to political idealism — in a way it strove to effect a synthesis between romanticism and positivism.

Dmowski was highly critical of the past, yet his criticism was of a constructive nature. His objective, which he emphasized in the title of his major theoretical work, "The Thoughts of a Modern Pole," published in 1903, was to transform the Polish nation into a completely modern one. Dmowski's program was not restricted but all-embracing in character. He did not depreciate the importance of organic reform; on the contrary, he called for intensifying national efforts in the economic and social spheres. At the same time, however, he stressed the significance of political action. Indeed, his was a political program *par excellence*. Furthermore, Dmowski's attitude was not defensive but offensive. Rejecting the revolutionary method because he did not believe it could be effective, he encouraged the nation to engage in constant political battle. He was fully aware that concessions from foreign rulers could be gained only under pressure. "Struggle is the foundation of life," he exclaimed in a strongly Darwinian manner in 1903. "Nations morally degenerate and decay whenever they cease struggling." [18]

Dmowski was "a sober politician: he possessed [political] insight, had a good grasp of existing reality and the limits imposed by it, and was well aware of the fluidity of life in general and politics in particular." [19] His political program, therefore, rested on an analysis, carried out with almost scientific precision,* of the current international situation. It was within this framework that he sought to improve the lot of the nation. Although it has been occasionally questioned by his adversaries, there is little doubt that Dmowski's eventual aim was to regain the independence of Poland. For an ardent nationalist, this was a natural aspiration. Being also a political realist, however, he distinguished between ultimate and immediate objectives. Dmowski saw little chance of rebuilding the Polish state in the near future.** Consequently, he decided to advance Poland's cause by an alliance with one of the occupying powers. Since Dmowski considered Germany the archenemy of Poland, he regarded Russia as Poland's potential partner.

Dmowski took this stand because, in line with his modern nationalism, he repudiated the prepartition idea of Poland as a multinational union, em-

* Dmowski's education in the natural sciences may well have contributed to his outlook. Before entering politics, Dmowski studied biology and zoology at the University of Warsaw, where in 1891 he received the degree comparable to the doctorate at West European universities.

** Dmowski conceded this fact even after the Polish state had actually come into existence. He attributed this development to the singularly favorable — for Poland — outcome of World War I, which brought about the simultaneous disintegration of the three occupying powers. See *Świat powojenny i Polska* (Warsaw, 1931), p. 165.

bracing instead the concept of an ethnically unified state. From this angle, it was far more important for him to retain Poland's western provinces, which, in addition to being the cradle of the Polish nation, still had a majority of the Polish population, than to hold the eastern territories to which the Poles had moved fairly late in their history and where, as a whole, they represented a minority among various other nationalities. In Dmowski's eyes the policy of systematic suppression of the Poles in German provinces was threatening the Polish nation with the loss of those lands which were essential for its survival. Thus, he called for an unrelenting effort on the part of the Poles to resist the German *Drang nach Osten*. In his book, "Germany, Russia and the Polish Question," published in 1908, he wrote: "everything and everywhere that things are done for the strengthening of Poland, in the last instance, represents the struggle against the Germans." [20]

Dmowski anticipated the forthcoming conflict between Germany and Russia. This, however, only strengthened his view of the necessity of a Polish alliance with Russia. In the case of a German victory in a conflict with Russia, he reasoned, the situation of Poland would not improve but worsen. The western provinces definitely would be lost. In the rest of Poland, the most that could be expected would be the establishment of some sort of a buffer state under virtual German rule.* On the other hand, Dmowski believed that in the event of Russian victory in such a conflict, the position of Poland would considerably improve. Not only would the threat of Germanization of the Polish western provinces be removed, but the unification of all Polish lands under tsarist rule would inevitably lead, initially, to a large measure of self-government and, ultimately, to Polish independence. The Russians, who had not been able to enforce effectively a policy of Russification in the central Polish provinces, obviously would not be able to conduct such a policy on a national scale.

The cornerstone of Dmowski's program of *rapprochement* with Russia was the conjuncture of Polish and Russian interest vis-à-vis Germany. He hoped that the sharpening rivalry with the Germans would make the Russians seek a modus vivendi with the Poles. As had political realists in the past, however, Dmowski explored other possible avenues of understanding with the Russians. At one stage, he tried to exploit the issue of Pan-Slavism for this purpose. He also strongly opposed all brands of social-

---

* Dmowski, unlike some other Polish politicians who hoped to achieve unification of Poland under the Hapsburg dynasty, also rejected alliance with Austria. He did this because he anticipated that Austria-Hungary would be utterly dependent on Germany in the event of a victory of the Central Powers over Russia.

ism. Indeed, in the years 1905–1906, the National Democrats in Poland countered force with force to suppress the revolutionary movement fomented by the socialists.

The Russians certainly did not make it easy for Dmowski to carry out his program. The National Democrats' demands for restoration of the autonomy of the Polish Kingdom fell upon deaf ears in St. Petersburg. Despite the steadily widening rift between Russia and Germany in the international sphere, the Russian government continued its anti-Polish policies until World War I. The apparent failure of Dmowski's policies caused much agitation even within the ranks of the National Democratic movement itself. Discouraged by lack of tangible successes, several groups, often composed of the best of the younger generation, left the party. This, however, did not undermine Dmowski's confidence that his course was the right one. At the outbreak of the war, the National Democrats declared themselves unequivocally on the side of Russia against Germany.

The unexpected course of World War I forced Dmowski to revise his program; he moved closer to political idealism. In accord with his expectations, the Central Powers lost the war, but Russia did not win either.* This created a vacuum in Central Eastern Europe which provided Poland with an opportunity to regain her independence. In such circumstances, the classic policy of the romantic school, namely, to rely on Poland's own military strength assisted by an alliance with the Western countries and particularly France, was once again revived. Dmowski himself embraced the romantic program. He moved to Western Europe where he founded the Polish National Committee, which represented Poland on the side of the Western allies, and which organized the Polish army that fought under the French on the western front. Through these activities, culminating in his signing the Treaty of Versailles on behalf of Poland, Dmowski contributed greatly to rebuilding the Polish state.

In the interwar period, even though he continued to support Poland's alliance with France, Dmowski did not abandon the view that Russia was of principal importance to Poland. He had little doubt about Russia's increasing stature in the international arena. "Russia is approaching the foremost role in world affairs," he wrote in 1931. "The Russian problem, irrespective of the political system in today's Russia, is so profound that it re-

---

* Dmowski admitted in 1925 that the outbreak of the revolution in Russia had taken him by surprise. He explained sarcastically that he had failed to perceive the role played by the vital "revolutionary element, namely, the Russian government." Roman Dmowski, *Polityka polska i odbudowanie państwa* (Hanover, 1947), I, 194.

quires serious thought not only on our part, as Russia's neighbors, but on the part of the whole world." Consequently, Dmowski fully appreciated the importance of Poland's relations with Russia. "Russia . . . as future events will prove, represents our most important neighbor . . . here is the crux of Poland's future." [21]

In spite of the vast difference between his strongly accentuated nationalism and Soviet Communism, Dmowski was convinced that an independent Poland should maintain proper, if not friendly, relations with the Soviet Union. In 1920, he bitterly opposed Piłsudski's military venture into the Ukraine. Again, in 1930, he wrote a series of articles strongly denouncing proposals for Poland's participation in military intervention in the Soviet Union.[22] In subsequent writings, he kept hammering on the same theme: "In our position," he warned the Poles, "in view of the threat from the West, we cannot afford the luxury of being involved in intervening in the East." [23]

At that stage, however, Dmowski's views were of little practical political consequence. In the interwar period, except for a few short intervals in the early 1920's, the National Democrats did not participate in the Polish government. After he returned to Poland from the Paris Conference, Dmowski, aging and ill, had little strength left to fight for power. His writings, especially after the late twenties, lost a good deal of their early analytical perception. They were increasingly given to xenophobia and anti-Semitism. Dmowski's efforts to rebuild the National Democratic movement, which had been greatly weakened through defections during World War I, were at best a qualified success. The attempts in the late twenties to attract the younger generation, brought about in the thirties new splits in the National Democratic ranks. Some splinter groups embraced semi-fascism and sought accommodation with the dictatorship of the followers of Marshal Piłsudski.

2

THE DECLINE OF POLITICAL REALISM

The Marxists were not exempt from the traditions of Polish politics. The cleavage between political realism and political idealism also divided their ranks. Polish socialists repeatedly split into opposing factions; the major issue between them was not social revolution but foreign policy. As a whole, the romantic tradition prevailed. The growth of the socialist movement in the late nineteenth and early twentieth centuries, therefore, paved the way for a decline of political realism in Poland.

The first interest in Marxist thought in Poland in the 1870's coincided with the golden era of positivism. Despite their entirely different social precepts, there existed a degree of affinity for positivism among the early Marxists. In the sense that past Polish traditions were repudiated and inspiration sought abroad, both Marxism and positivism represented a reaction of the younger generation against romanticism. The difference, of course, was that the positivists turned to Western liberalism, and the socialists to Marxist internationalism. Thus "uncritical acceptance by the first socialists of . . . cosmopolitan socialism," a prominent Polish historian observed, "may be explained in psychological terms by [their] aversion to patriotic 'phraseology.'"[1] Indeed, the emotional revulsion of the early socialists against the romantic tradition was so strong that they persisted in denouncing it even in defiance of Marx himself. They explicitly ignored Marx and other Western socialists who had emphasized the contribution of the Polish insurrections, including that of 1863, to the cause of European revolution.* When the first clandestine socialist group, the "Proletariat," was founded in Poland in 1882, its program was consistently internationalist. There was no thought of making an issue of independence for Poland. Like the positivists, the early Polish socialists favored reaching some understanding with the Russians. The difference was that while the positivists strove for cooperation with the tsarist government, the socialists sought to establish close bonds with the Russian revolutionaries. Still, this difference was not so great as it might appear. Since the founding of the Proletariat coincided with the height of the terrorist activities conducted by Narodnaya Volya, the Polish socialists believed that the "rise to power in Russia by the revolutionaries [was] imminent," [2] and, therefore, assumed that they were dealing with the future Russian government. In fact, in 1884, an agreement providing for the close cooperation between Proletariat and Narodnaya Volya, although on an autonomous basis, was concluded. The agreement, however, proved to be of little consequence, for soon thereafter Narodnaya Volya was suppressed in Russia. The Proletariat survived a little longer, but after 1884, when several of its leaders were arrested by the tsarist police, its activities declined. By 1886, for all practical purposes, the group ceased to exist.

The association between the early Polish socialist group and Narodnaya Volya, however, was not without influence on the development of the socialist movement in Poland. In at least two respects, it pushed the Polish socialists away from political realism. First, the collapse of their hopes for an early revolution in Russia forced the Polish socialists to rely on their own strength after the suppression of Narodnaya Volya. This in turn gave the socialist movement in Poland a distinctly national character. Second, by adopting the Russian method of spreading revolution through conspiracy and armed terror, the early Polish socialists moved in the direction of the romantic tradition. "Even though in the ideology of the first Polish socialists one can easily trace the influence of the [positivist] trends prevailing in the entire society, [positivist] in the sense that their program was both divorced

* A characteristic incident took place at the meeting organized by the Polish socialists in Geneva in 1880, on the fiftieth anniversary of the uprising of 1830. The letter addressed to the meeting by Marx, Engels, and other former leaders of the General Council of the International praised Polish revolutionary tradition and ended with the words *"vive la Pologne!"* The speech by the Polish socialist leader Ludwik Waryński expressed exactly the opposite view, however: "When the next uprising takes place," he declared, "it is not the slogan 'long live Poland!' but one battle cry common to all proletarians that will be heard — 'long live social revolution.'" Quoted by Feldman, *Dzieje polskiej myśli politycznej,* 2 ed. (Warsaw 1933), p. 221.

from romanticism and sought inspiration in scientific theory, the very act of founding a political party both conspiratorial and revolutionary in nature, was essentially incompatible with the nonpolitical ideas of organic reform." [3]

The rapid growth of the industrial proletariat, which from 1870 to 1897 increased more than four times[4] in the Russian provinces alone, provided fertile ground for socialist political propaganda. At the same time, the decline of positivism and the patriotic revival in the younger generation caused the resumption of conspiratorial and revolutionary political activities.* Especially in the Russian provinces of Poland, where no possibility for an open socialist party existed, a fusion of the conspirators, those for social revolution and those for national independence, seemed a logical development.

Thus, when a new socialist party, the Polish Socialist Party, was formed in 1892, it was strongly committed to the goal of Polish independence. The party program advocated a "close union of social and political struggles; the struggle for improving the fate of the working class and the struggle for political liberation of the country. The ideas of socialism and national independence became inseparably linked." [5] The Polish Socialist Party was a clandestine organization confined to the Russian provinces of Poland. It did not reject cooperation with the Russian socialists in the common struggle against the tsarist government, but was willing to cooperate with the Russians only on the basis of complete independence and equality. This stand was supported by the argument, in itself flavored with nationalism, that social conditions in Poland were more advanced, and chances for carrying out a socialist revolution were better in Poland than in Russia. Therefore, instead of emphasizing close relations with Russian revolutionaries, the Polish Socialist Party developed strong ties with Polish socialists in Austria.

The union of the social revolution and the struggle for independence in the program of the socialist party were largely responsible for its rapid growth. The Polish Socialist Party attracted not only people who were interested in the socialist program, but also many who were merely anxious to wage a battle against the Russian rulers. Indeed, the latter group soon seemed

* Since the socialist movement and the National Democracy both stemmed from the same roots of patriotic reaction, there existed a close bond between the two in their formative stages. It was only in the early 1900's and, particularly, during the revolutionary ferment of 1904–1905 that the two movements definitely parted, the National Democrats embracing a modified version of political realism, and the major wing of the socialists drifting toward political idealism.

to overshadow the former. This composition of the party was reflected in its leadership, where "the dominant type was a man to whom Marxism was primarily a rationalization of his own moral revolt against social as well as national injustice. But abstract, doctrinaire Marxism had for him little appeal unless adapted to the realities of the country and integrated with the native revolutionary tradition." [6]

The shift from internationalism to nationalism was not unanimous, however. In 1893, a group of socialists who continued to adhere to the internationalist tradition of the Proletariat organized their own party, the Social Democracy of the Kingdom of Poland. In 1898, they were joined by some socialist groups from Lithuania, whereby the party assumed the name, Social Democracy of the Kingdom of Poland and Lithuania. The Social Democrats bitterly opposed combining social revolution with the struggle for national independence. They regarded the program of restoring the Polish state as "a complete renunciation of effective political struggle and a departure from the goals of the proletariat." [7] In line with the Marxist concept of the primacy of economic factors in the historical process, the Social Democrats considered that the existence of an independent Poland was made impossible by her close economic bonds with Russia.* An elaborate argument to this effect, the so-called theory of "organic incorporation" of the Polish Kingdom into Russia, was put forward by the party's leading theoretician Rosa Luxemburg. [8]

Starting from these theoretical assumptions, the Social Democrats were not interested in working with Polish socialists from other provinces, but strove for the closest possible cooperation, and, indeed, integration with Russian socialists. Consequently, in the early 1900's negotiations were undertaken with a view to merging the Social Democracy of the Kingdom of Poland and Lithuania with the Russian Social Democratic Workers' Party. The actual merger, however, did not take place until 1906. Paradoxically, the chief issue in the negotiations was the emphasis of the Russian Social Democrats on the right of secession from the Russian state of various national minorities. The Polish Social Democrats, influenced by the views of Rosa Luxemburg, found this objectionable. Only under the impact of the revolution of 1905, despite their continued reservations regarding Lenin's doctrine of self-determination, did the Polish Social Democrats decide to join the

---

* Rosa Luxemburg's argument that Poland's continued association with Russia was economically beneficial, incidentally, in several respects, came close to the reasoning of the "positivists," especially to that of Świetochowski.

all-Russian movement.** From then on, even though as a result of their con-spiratorial character the complete integration of the two parties was never actually accomplished, the fortunes of the Social Democratic Party of the Kingdom of Poland and Lithuania were closely linked with those of the Russian Social Democratic Workers' Party. In this way, the Polish Social Democrats became involved in the struggle between the Bolsheviks and the Mensheviks. They tried to steer a middle course between these two wings of the Russian party, but as a whole, came closer to the Bolshevik positions.

Despite the fact that in its early stages the Social Democracy of the Kingdom of Poland and Lithuania was merely "a self-styled vanguard of a hardly existing mass movement," [9] its split with the Polish Socialist Party represented a serious blow to the fortunes of socialism in Poland. It led to the recurrent division of the socialist forces. Ever since the end of the nineteenth century "the dispute over the issue of national independence [had persisted] not only between the Polish Socialist Party and the Social Democracy, but also on several occasions [has reappeared] within the ranks of the Polish Socialist Party which [has oscillated] between giving priority to the principles of independence and that of class struggle." [10]

The abortive revolution of 1905–06 accelerated the next crisis in the Polish Socialist Party. At that time the group led by Józef Piłsudski had gained predominant influence in the party. Piłsudski and his collaborators represented the new type of party leader who had little interest in Marxism as a program of class struggle. They were attracted to the Polish Socialist Party primarily because it espoused the goal of Polish independence and offered opportunities for conspiracy against the Russians. Piłsudski himself "was a follower of this [trend in Polish political thought], which linked the political and armed struggle against foreign rule with social revolution. As such, he was a successor of political romanticism . . . [He] thought that the Polish state could be restored . . . only through armed insurrection." [11] Thus, Piłsudski viewed the outbreak of the Russo-Japanese War in 1904 and the revolutionary ferment in Russia which followed as providing Poland with a chance to attempt to cast off Russian rule by means of an armed insurrection.

Piłsudski's original plan was based on the classic romantic concept, namely, an insurrection backed up by military assistance from abroad. In 1904, he

---

** The stand of Polish Social Democrats, denying even the implication of Poland's right to independence (like that of the Proletariat in the 1880's), ran contrary not only to the views of Lenin, but also to those of other leading figures in the international socialist movement, such as Liebknecht, Kautsky, and Plekhanov.

went to Tokyo to solicit Japanese support for such a venture against the Russians. His mission was frustrated by Dmowski, however, who followed him to Tokyo and persuaded the Japanese that cooperation with the Polish socialists was doomed to military failure. Despite his inability to secure any effective assistance from abroad, Piłsudski proceeded with his plan for an uprising in the Russian provinces of Poland. He established the Military Organization of the Polish Socialist Party, which in 1905–06 carried out spectacular attacks against the tsarist authorities.* Again, however, Piłsudski's plans were scuttled by Dmowski. The National Democrats not only came out strongly against terrorist tactics, but formed their own worker's units, which on a few occasions came to blows with the socialists. The masses followed the lead of the National Democrats, turning their backs on the socialist call to arms.

The fiasco of the 1905 revolutionary attempt led to a new cleavage in the Polish Socialist Party. In 1906, the policy of Piłsudski's group was severely censured by the left wing of the party. Reckless terror was denounced as not only politically ineffective but also as exposing the party and the working class to heavy losses. The wisdom of trying to achieve Poland's independence through fomenting armed uprising was questioned. In its place was advocated the exploiting of avenues for gradual reform which appeared to have opened within the tsarist empire at that time. To that end, cooperation with the Russian socialists to promote further democratic transformation of the Russian political system, and, if possible, to gain autonomy for the Polish Kingdom, was proposed. At that stage, the left wing prevailed in the Polish Socialist Party. Consequently, the Piłsudski-led right wing split from the party, assuming the name of the Revolutionary Faction. Once disillusionment with the meager scope for reform in the tsarist empire spread throughout Poland, the right wing regained sufficient ground to claim that they represented the majority, and, therefore, in 1908 reverted to the name of Polish Socialist Party. But the split between the two wings never healed. The right wing continued to give priority to Piłsudski's program of national independence over that of social reform; Piłsudski and his closest collaborators gradually turned completely away from socialism.

---

* The Social Democracy of the Polish Kingdom and Lithuania was also active in 1905–1906 but, in line with its program, it put its hopes in the success of a revolution in Russia. Much as the party was interested in fomenting revolution in Poland, it opposed the plans for restoring independence by means of an anti-Russian insurrection. Consequently, it played a far less effective role than the Polish Socialist Party in the armed resistance against the tsarist authorities.

The left wing, which in time assumed the name of the Polish Socialist Party Left, continued, in spite of unsuccessful attempts to promote reforms within the Russian state, to give priority to social change. Although it never formally joined the Russian Social Democratic Workers' Party, this group maintained close connections with the Russian socialists. As such, it moved toward the position of the Social Democracy of the Kingdom of Poland and Lithuania. Cooperation between the two parties gradually tightened, leading to their merger into the Communist Party of Poland in 1918.

THE MILITARY MOVEMENT: JÓZEF PIŁSUDSKI

The group of men led by Józef Piłsudski, originating as a faction of the Polish Socialist Party but gradually losing its socialist character, completely reverted to the tradition of romanticism in the years immediately preceding World War I.

Józef Piłsudski was born in 1867 and brought up in the eastern borderlands of Poland, where the impact of Warsaw's positivism was weak and the legend of the insurrection of 1863 was very strong. In his early life, he was never exposed to the influence of political realism. In an autobiographical sketch published in 1903, Piłsudski describes the atmosphere surrounding him in his childhood: "Mother, an irreconcilable Polish patriot, did not even attempt to conceal from us her sorrow and disappointment over the defeat of the uprising; on the contrary, in bringing us up she stressed the necessity of continued struggle against the enemy of our country . . . At that time, all my dreams focused around the struggle against the Muscovites." [12]

Piłsudski never abandoned his early dreams. Throughout his adult years, he remained under the spell of the legend of the 1863 insurrection. In a study written in 1924, he praised the uprising: "The year 1863 gave us an unknown greatness . . . the greatness of an effort of collective will." [13] Even if the insurrection was a military failure, in Piłsudski's opinion it had had important political consequences. The memory of heroic battles against the foreign oppressor prevented the Poles from adopting a submissive attitude of *Treuga Dei* (avoiding the military struggle) and made them continue their struggle to cast off foreign oppression. This admiration of Piłsudski for the uprising of 1863 played a very important part in shaping his political outlook.

At least two essential elements of Piłsudski's political program seem to be rooted in the impact upon him of the legend of the insurrection of 1863. The first was his profound hatred of Russia. From his early childhood in the 1870's, he despised "the Muscovites . . . with his whole heart." The persecution of the Poles by tsarist officials, particularly harsh in Poland's eastern borderland, soon affected Piłsudski himself. His years in school, during which, as a Pole, he was exposed to chicanery by Russian teachers, were for him "a sort of penal servitude," causing his "hatred for the tsarist administration [to grow] with every year." [14] At the age of twenty, Piłsudski actually was sentenced to five years in Siberian exile, charged with complicity in a plot to assassinate Tsar Alexander III, a conspiracy of which he was ignorant.* This increased Piłsudski's hatred of the tsarist system even more, "that Asian beast, concealed behind a European façade." [15] Upon his return from Siberia, Piłsudski resolved to undertake an active struggle against Russia, which he clearly regarded as the archenemy of Poland.

The second element of Piłsudski's program, rooted in the legend of 1863, was his conviction that armed force was the only effective way to struggle against Russia. His bitter personal experiences only intensified his desire for all-out conflict. "Without a fight and a fight with the gloves off," he exclaimed in 1908, "I am not even a fighter, but a beast submitting to a stick or a knout." [16] In line with his appraisal of the effects of the insurrection of 1863, Piłsudski was convinced that reverting to the tradition of military struggle against foreign oppression would be useful and, indeed, indispensable for the Polish nation. In his opinion, uprising, irrespective of its outcome, was a duty of each generation of Poles. "Each generation," he asserted, "must demonstrate with its blood that Poland is alive and that she is not reconciled to foreign bondage." [17] The uprising would release the nation's strength and revive international interest in Poland. Consequently, Piłsudski wanted "Poland, who had forgotten the sword so rapidly after 1863, to see it flashing once again in the hands of her own soldiers." [18] He was determined to concentrate all his energies on preparing a new Polish insurrection against Russia.

Having derived the anti-Russian and insurrectionist character of his political program from the experiences of 1863, Piłsudski needed only one more element in order to revert fully to the classic romantic tradition, namely, faith in assistance from abroad. It was precisely in seeking this missing ele-

---

* It was one of those coincidences of history that this event critically influenced the views not only of the future leader of Poland but also that of Russia. It was for participation in this plot that Lenin's brother, Alexander Ilyich Ulyanov, paid with his life.

ment that he first turned to socialism. Following in the footsteps of early romanticists, who in the first half of the nineteenth century pinned their hopes for the reemergence of the Polish state on the victory of a liberal revolution in Europe, Piłsudski tried to promote Poland's independence by linking it with the fortunes of the international socialist movement. At that point, he "could not enter into an alliance with any foreign power, so he sought an alignment with the only force willing to accept it, namely, international socialism." [19] As soon as he saw the chance of obtaining support from some foreign states engaged in rivalry with Russia, however, Piłsudski lost his interest in socialism and tried to enter into agreement with them. His abortive attempt to interest the Japanese in military assistance for Poland in 1904, a step clearly motivated by nationalist and not socialist ideology, exemplified this. From 1908, when friction began to grow between Russia and Austria, Piłsudski turned his attention to cooperation with the Austrians.

Cooperation with Austria had important advantages for Piłsudski's incipient struggle against Russia. In the Austrian provinces of Poland, he found a territorial base where he could train his military forces. The Austrian authorities appreciated the military value of such a force in case of conflict with Russia and, consequently, tolerated Polish paramilitary movement in Galicia. Piłsudski eagerly exploited this opportunity, and from 1908 devoted all his energies to building up a nucleus of Polish armed forces. In the early stages, this military movement was still secretly subordinated to the political leadership of the Polish Socialist Party. Piłsudski provided the link between the political and military branches, but he increasingly identified himself with the latter. In 1912, when the program of alignment with Austria against Russia gained the support of some other political groups, the political leadership was recognized; whereby the Polish Socialist Party became only one of several parties jointly exercising supervision over the military movement headed by Piłsudski. The political control over the military, however, was a fairly loose one. Thus, for all practical purposes, Piłsudski gained an instrument with which he could realize not only military but also his own political plans.

The military movement led by Piłsudski openly claimed the romantic political tradition. The Polish units trained in Galicia were presented as direct successors of those who had fought in the insurrections of 1863 and 1830. The young men who joined the movement were taught to espouse the soldierly virtues of discipline, honor, and, above all, heroism. The moral strength of the Polish units was to compensate for their relative physical weakness, and thus enable them to overcome all obstacles standing in the way of Polish independence. Piłsudski himself, in the vein of the romantic poet Adam Mickiewicz, subscribed to the motto that "the art of overcoming obstacles is the art of not regarding them as such." [20] One of Piłsudski's closest collaborators, Tytus Filipowicz, in a pamphlet entitled "A Political Dream," derided the political realists, "who believed that a nation should adjust its goals to the existing conditions." [21]

The cooperation with Austria, however, also presented several pitfalls for Piłsudski''s program. It was obvious that in the approaching European conflict, Austria was to be allied to Germany in her struggle against Russia. This meant that cooperating with the Austrians left the Poles open to serious perils. It not only excluded any possibility of Poland's regaining her provinces from Germany, but, indeed, cast a shadow over the prospect of restoring a Polish state even in Poland's Russian provinces. In view of Germany's interest in expanding to the east, it was doubtful if the Germans would tolerate the existence of a truly independent Polish state on their eastern border after they defeated Russia. To make matters worse, the power discrepancy between Germany and Austria suggested that in the event of victory over Russia, the Germans, and not the Austrians, would be decisive in determining the fate of Poland.

Piłsudski and his followers were aware that after the defeat of Russia, Germany was likely to emerge as the major power in East Europe. Yet they still felt that cooperation with Austria would best promote Polish interests.* The argument in favor of such a course was put forth by Piłsudski's close political associate, Witold Jodko-Narkiewicz. In case of a conflict between Austria and Russia, Jodko-Narkiewicz argued, Poland's goal should be to

---

* Piłsudski and his followers were, of course, under strong attack from Dmowski who accused them of ignoring the German danger. This was true in the sense that they clearly regarded Russia as Poland's main enemy. In the words of a prominent Polish historian and, incidentally, a follower of Piłsudski: "There is little doubt that some supporters of the pro-Austrian line, following the example of several previous generations, tended to push the Polish-German antagonism into the background" (Wilhelm Feldman, *Dzieje polskiej myśli politycznej*, 2 ed., Warsaw, 1933, p. 354). On the eve of World War I, however, Piłsudski voiced an opinion that the best possible outcome of a European conflict for Poland would be for Russia to be defeated by Germany, and Germany to be defeated in turn by France. Since this is precisely what happened, some writers claim that Piłsudski "predicted" the result of World War I. See Alexandra Piłsudska, *Piłsudski* (New York, 1941), p. 211; Henryk Cepnik, *Józef Piłsudski*, 3 ed. (Warsaw, 1935), p. 99. Actually Piłsudski viewed such a development merely as one of several courses which the war might take. See Marian Kukiel, *Dzieje Polski porozbiorowe* (London, 1961), pp. 493–494; Władysław Pobóg-Malinowski, *Najnowsza historia Polski* (Paris, 1953), I, 204.

separate from Russia the largest possible part of the Polish provinces with a view "to securing [their] independence, and if this would be impossible, [their] broad autonomy." This end was to be accomplished by "an inde pendent Polish military struggle against Russia carried out under the banner of independence of the Polish lands." The rationale behind such an action was, in the opinion of Jodko-Narkiewicz, that "a military struggle would arouse the enthusiasm of the entire nation and multiply as much as possible its strength." In this way, he continued, the Poles "would become an ally, who must be respected and to whom it would be worthy to offer con cessions . . . This would also represent the most effective way of counter acting the possible Prussian danger." [22]

It was precisely this policy of giving priority to the military struggle against Russia which Piłsudski's military movement followed in the early stages of World War I. In August 1914, the Polish troops under Piłsudski's personal command entered the Russian provinces from Galicia, to uphold "by word and sword the principle of independence" [23] of Poland. Piłsud ski seems to have hoped that the appearance of Polish soldiers would arouse such enthusiasm among the Polish population that they would join his movement en masse or perhaps even stage an uprising against the Russians. In 1914, however, Piłsudski's hopes were once again frustrated by Dmowski. Under the influence of the National Democrats, the Poles in the Russian provinces not only refrained from taking up arms, but, inded, re ceived coldly Piłsudski's legionnaires fighting on the Austrian and, what in the eyes of the majority of Poles was even worse, on the German side.

The nearly complete lack of response by the Polish people to their mili tary struggle against Russia severely disenchanted the young legionnaires. Largely due to the resolute leadership of Piłsudski, they continued to fight, and fight well. The difficult situation in which they were placed, however, led to a twofold reaction among the troops. On the one hand, they developed a contempt for the masses who, as their military song complained, failed to appreciate the soldiers' sacrifice, refusing to believe that "striving is the same as accomplishing." On the other hand, as a compensation for their alienation from the people, there grew among the legionnaires a strong personal attachment to their commander, the belief in their "beloved leader." [24] Gradually, this sentiment led them virtually to identify allegiance to Piłsudski with loyalty to the country at large.

As World War I continued and all the Russian provinces of Poland fell into the hands of the Central Powers, Piłsudski's plans for restoring an independent Polish state in that part of the country faded away. In view of her complete military and political dependence on Germany, the hope for effective support from Austria proved to be unfounded. The Germans, as had been expected, were not interested in restoring a truly independent Poland. Although toward the end of 1916 they did proclaim the establishment of a Polish state, this was to be "united in friendship and interests" with the Central Powers, in fact, a German protectorate.

Discouraged by the fiasco of his plans for cooperation with Austria, Piłsudski decided to change allies. In 1917, with Russia defeated, he could revert to classic romanticism and seek alliance with the Western powers, which he now hoped would overcome Germany. Consequently, he refused further political and military cooperation with the Central Powers. The Polish legions were dissolved and interned; Piłsudski himself was soon arrested and deported to Germany.

Piłsudski's *volte-face* worked well; everything played into his hands. His expectation of the Western allies' victory over the Central Powers proved to be correct. His resolute anti-German stand increased his popularity among the Polish people. His wartime reputation as an able military leader, and the loyalty he commanded among the troops, at a time when the building up of their own army was one of the most urgent tasks facing the Poles, enhanced his prestige even further. Consequently, upon his return from internment in Germany at the end of World War I. Piłsudski was entrusted with the leadership of an independent Polish state.

3

POLITICAL IDEALISM

(1918–1939)

The restoration of an independent Polish state in 1918 did not change the traditional nature of Polish politics. As a result of Poland's peculiar geographic location, her external and internal politics continued to be closely interconnected. The overriding concern of the Poles remained the issue of independence. However, while in the past the Poles had concentrated their energies on regaining an independent state, now they were preoccupied with maintaining its existence.

Throughout the interwar period Poland's position in the international sphere was precarious. From the outset, neither Germany nor Russia looked favorably on the restored Polish state; neither of them was reconciled to the existence of their present borders. In the west the German ambition to restore its 1914 boundaries threatened the Polish provinces of Pomerania, Silesia, and Poznania. Polish Pomerania, which separated East Prussia from Germany proper, represented a particularly explosive issue. Even though the population of Pomerania was overwhelmingly Polish, the Germans made it clear that they had no intention of abiding by the terms of the Treaty of Versailles, and would strive to regain what they labelled as the "Polish corridor." "Poland's existence is intolerable, incompatible with the essential conditions of Germany's life," General von Seekt, the arbiter of foreign policy during the early years of the Weimar Republic wrote in 1922. "Poland must go and will go," he exclaimed.[1] "No German government,

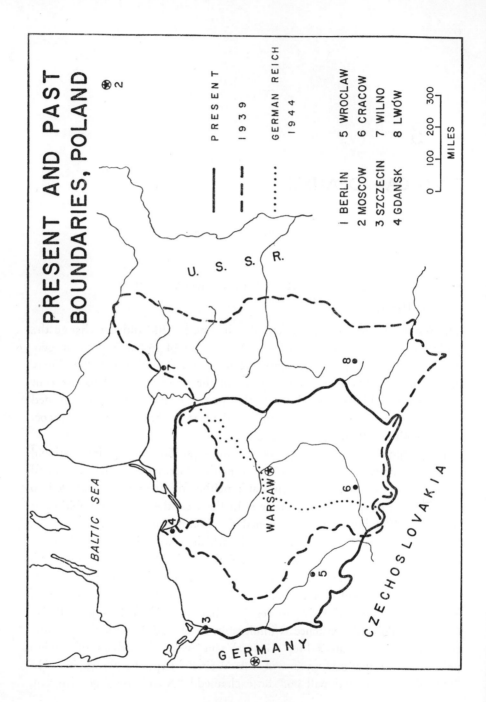

PRESENT AND PAST
BOUNDARIES, POLAND

PRESENT

1939

GERMAN REICH
1944

1 BERLIN   5 WROCLAW
2 MOSCOW   6 CRACOW
3 SZCZECIN   7 WILNO
4 GDANSK   8 LWÓW

0   100 200 300
MILES

U. S. S. R.

BALTIC SEA

WARSAW

GERMANY

CZECHOSLOVAKIA

from the nationalists to the Communists would ever recognize this frontier," asserted Germany's Foreign Minister, Gustav Stresemann, in 1925.[2]

Poland's eastern frontier was also insecure. The Soviet Union made no bones about its more than casual interest in Poland's eastern provinces, which were populated largely by Ukrainians and Belorussians. "By the Treaty of Riga," Chicherin, the Soviet Commissar for Foreign Affairs, wrote in 1923, "Russia and the Ukraine renounced the right to the territories situated to the west of the new Polish frontier; but this does not in any way imply that the fate of these territories is a matter of indifference to them."[3] The ideologies adopted by the Germans and the Russians, respectively, further aggravated their anti-Polish sentiments. The Russian Communists resented the existence of a "bourgeois" Polish state, which stood in the way of their carrying the proletarian revolution into the heart of Europe. The German Nazis, in power after 1933, looked down on the Poles as an "inferior race," first to be destroyed in their drive eastward.

Compared with her neighbors in the west and in the east, the restored Polish state was weak. This was the result of complex military, demographic, and economic factors. To begin with, there was a severe discrepancy in size. In 1939 the Polish population numbered 35 million; the German, 78.5 million; the Russian, 175.4 million.[4] Poland's strategic position was deplorable. Its borders were unnaturally long and twisted; there were no natural obstacles to hinder attacking armies either in the west or in the east. Gripped in German pinchers which extended from East Prussia in the north to the Silesian wedge in the southwest, the Polish position vis-à-vis Germany was particularly poor. The ethnic heterogeneity of its people posed another danger. Approximately one third of Poland's population consisted of various minority groups.[5] Several of the national minorities were not only out of sympathy with the Polish state but by aspiring to unite with their compatriots across the Soviet or the German border also threatened to subvert it from within. Last, but not least, the development of Poland's economy was far from satisfactory for purposes of national defense. The country was predominantly agricultural; the program of industrialization was slow. At first there was no armament industry. Subsequently, though still on a very small scale, one was developed.

The temporary weakening of both neighbors after World War I gave Poland a brief respite. In the thirties, however, when both Russia under Stalin and Germany under Hitler regained their strength, Poland's relative power position rapidly deteriorated. On the other hand, the deepening international crisis increased the danger of conflict in Europe. In view of Poland's central location, especially her geographic juxtaposition to Germany, it was obvious that she would be engulfed if war broke out. On the other hand, the overwhelming preponderance of military power of the Third Reich and the Soviet Union made Poland's defense against either of them, not to mention against a combined attack, virtually impossible. In this situation, only a very fortunate constellation of forces in European politics, which might have averted the outbreak of war, could have saved Poland from the approaching disaster. As on so many occasions in the past, the fate of the Polish state dangled upon developments in the international sphere.

THE PIŁSUDSKI MOVEMENT

In the interwar period the responsibility for Poland's foreign policy rested almost exclusively with Marshal Piłsudski and his followers. From 1918 to 1922 Piłsudski ruled the country as a chief executive with the approval of the Polish parliament. A few years out of public office, he was returned to power by an army coup d'état in 1926. Although relatively lenient, Piłsudski's rule was a dictatorship nevertheless.* After his death in 1935 until 1939, Poland's government remained in the hands of his close followers exclusively. Among them, Piłsudski's successor in command of the armed forces, Marshal Edward Śmigły-Rydz, soon emerged as a leading political figure. Responsibility for the course of foreign policy, however, rested largely in the hands of Colonel Józef Beck, personally selected by Piłsudski for the post of foreign minister.**

* It was at that stage that a final break between Piłsudski and the Polish Socialist Party took place. In the years 1918–1922, and, indeed, still during the coup d'état in 1926, the socialists, afraid of ascendancy of the forces of the right (notably, the National Democrats), half-heartedly supported Piłsudski. After the establishment of his dictatorship, however, when it became obvious that Piłsudski had no intention of promoting social reform, the socialists went into opposition. Piłsudski soon repaid in kind. Among the leaders of the opposition imprisoned by the regime in 1930 were several socialists.

** Śmigły-Rydz (1886–1943) gained the reputation of an able military commander, first as an officer in Piłsudski's legions during World War I, and, then when he led the Polish armies to Kiev during the Polish-Russian War. Prior to Piłsudski's death, however, Rydz never played any prominent political role so that his stepping into politics in the late thirties came as a surprise in Poland. Beck (1887–1944) served in Piłsudski's legions during World War I, and, subsequently, remained as a career officer in the army. He entered the field of foreign affairs only after Piłsudski's coup in 1926. Beck seems to have enjoyed not only the confidence but, indeed, the respect of Piłsudski. In 1928 the Marshal declared that Beck was a man "who will play a great role, attracting the attention of the world." Władysław Pobóg-Malinowski, *Najnowsza historia polityczna Polski,* vol. II (London, 1957), pt. 1, p. 544.

The Piłsudski movement remained essentially a military junta. Although on some occasions the Piłsudskiites tried to establish mass organizations, these never assumed the form of a political party. The major source of power was the armed forces. For all practical purposes, the military controlled the civilian authority. Many key positions in the government and state administration were filled by army officers. The armed forces, in turn, were dominated by former Piłsudski legionnaires. The highest posts in the army were almost exclusively in their hands. These legionnaires were held together by their devotion, bordering on hero worship, to Marshal Piłsudski. After his death, they remained united by loyalty to Piłsudski's political ideology and, increasingly, by their own self-interest.

The political ideology of the Piłsudski movement in the interwar period was based on a specific interpretation of Poland's history. In evolving this type of political ideology, the followers of Piłsudski were greatly assisted by the parallel trends in Polish historiography. During the war and especially after the restoration of an independent Polish state, historiography became closely linked to current political developments. "For four generations," wrote one of the leading exponents of the new historical school, Wacław Sobieski, "we denounced our past . . . Chained in slavery we dwelt upon the aims of our forefathers which had allegedly brought about the dismemberment of Poland . . . Today the times have changed. Having our own state, we look at the past in a different light." [6] Henceforth, a more forebearing and also more encouraging appraisal of Poland's past was adopted by the younger generation of historians.

The new historical school challenged the Cracow historians' evaluation of Poland's past. "The view that the cause of Poland's downfall has been rooted in our political system," argued a prominent representative of the new historical school, Oswald Balzer, "proved to be erroneous." [7] Other nations, he claimed, committed no lesser errors than the Poles; yet, they had not lost their independence. Poland's misfortunes, therefore, had not been rooted in the errors of the Poles themselves. Balzer's thesis was countered by the surviving followers of the Cracow school, notably Bobrzyński, but to little avail. New trends in Polish historiography were clearly ascendant. Several crucial stages of Poland's history were reexamined, explicitly with a view to undermining their critical appraisal by the Cracow historians. The picture of Poland's history which emerged from this analysis was largely the opposite of that which had prevailed at the end of the nineteenth century. The political programs and political leaders who had been particularly harshly dealt with by the older generation of historians were now vindicated. The followers of political idealism were praised; the supporters of political realism denounced.

The coincidence between the new trends in historiography and politics was best manifested in the writings that were historical in form but clearly political in nature. These works, in line with the principle of *historia est magistra vitae,* deliberately presented history as an example to be followed by the contemporary generation of Poles. Their authors, with little concern for scholarly objectivity, hailed the romantic tradition.

In a book translated as *The Spirit of Polish History,* Antoni Chołoniewski, advanced the thesis that Poland's misfortunes had their roots in the "moral superiority of the Poles over their neighbors near and far." [8] Poland before the partitions had been "morally, incontestably, in advance of the Europe of yesterday; and of the Europe today, by the whole length of her historic existence." [9] It was precisely because Poland was too progressive that her existence had been intolerable for neighboring countries. As a result they attempted to dismember her, and eventually succeeded. Yet, even after Poland had been dismembered, Chołoniewski continued, the Poles remained in the forefront of progressive forces in Europe. They continued to uphold their lofty ideals through their struggles for freedom both at home and abroad. A particularly important role had been played here by the "heroic type" of national leaders — notably, those who led the uprising of 1863 — whose example inspired the people to repeated efforts to cast off foreign bondage. The romantic program, argued Chołoniewski, precisely because of its moral values, which were predestined to prevail in the end, had been the most effective way to promote Poland's independence. "The alleged romanticism of our forefathers . . ." he asserted, "in fact represented a realistic and thoroughly sober program." Chołoniewski made it quite clear that he considered his book not merely a historical study, but a guide to Poland's future policies. "Today we know," he exclaimed, "that we can look at the past road of our nation not with a feeling of shame but that of pride . . . We now realize . . . that the political institutions and concepts which [Poland] developed . . . were based on courageous and noble ideals, ideals which have preserved their indestructible value until today." [10]

Piłsudski and his followers not only encouraged the new interpretation of Poland's past but carried it to the logical conclusion. They asserted that through their own achievements they had demonstrated the correctness of the romantic program. They developed the theory, ignoring the simultaneous defeat of both Russia and Germany in World War I, that the Polish state had been restored by their military struggle. In short, the Piłsudskiites claimed that they had proved the validity of their motto that "striving is the same as accomplishing."

By posing before the people as the redeemers of Poland's independence, the Piłsudskiites, of course, derived numerous political advantages. The enhancing of their past achievements enabled them to posture as a vanguard of the nation, entrusted with the task, as they themselves described it, of "moral renovation" of the country. This, in turn, legitimized their dictatorial rule in Poland. Political expediency, however, did not seem to be at the center of the Piłsudskiites' political ideology. The hard core of Piłsudski's followers became victims of their own myths. They were sincerely convinced that romanticism was the most effective way to promote Poland's interests. Since nothing succeeds like success they came to believe in the exaggerated version of their own role in Poland's history. Somewhere on their way up from the status of young legionnaires in 1914 to the generals' and ministers' posts which they occupied in the interwar Poland, the Piłsudskiites became overimpressed with their own importance.

As the years went by the logic of their political ideology pushed the Piłsudskiites to evolve still other historical myths. In order to justify staying in power, they had to safeguard their image as infallible political leaders. Consequently, they promoted the view that Poland's course under their rule abounded in successes, indeed, that they had turned Poland into a great power. In a pamphlet entitled precisely: "Poland is a Great Power" [11] Juliusz Łukasiewicz, succinctly presented the ideology of the successors of Piłsudski on the eve of World War II. "The last quarter of a century of our history," Łukasiewicz declared, "represents a constant chain of victories." "Poland's successes," he continued in the vein of Chołoniewski, "have been noble and lasting for they represent the victory of a just cause . . . for the policies of independent Poland [have been] based on the principle of the right of nations to freedom and respect." All the triumphs, Łukasiewicz claimed, Poland owes "to her creator and redeemer, Józef Piłsudski." It was he and his legionnaires, "who by a lonely, tragic effort . . . realized the dreams and hopes of our forefathers. It [was Piłsudski] who inspired the nation with a will to action and mapped the course of its historical progress. Finally, it [was] he who departing forever left at the helm of the Polish state the men of great stature, who faithfully and boldly realize his genius' testament." Under the leadership of Piłsudski's successors, asserted Łukasiewicz, the Polish nation has nothing to fear. Poland plays an important role in European politics. "Poland is a great power," he concluded, "representing the cornerstone of political order in Central Eastern Europe . . . The fate of contemporary Europe depends on the policies of Poland no less than on those of other great powers." [12]

The Piłsudskiites clung to their ideology until the outbreak of World War II. In June 1939 they turned down the offer of some opposition parties to join forces in defense of the country, boldly asserting that they alone were capable of steering the course of Poland's policies at this crucial stage of her history. Faced with the imminent danger of Hitler's aggression, the Piłsudskiites preserved at least an outward appearance of calm and confidence. Government propaganda repeatedly assured the people that the threat from Nazi Germany was not really a serious one, striving to create the impression that Poland was perfectly able to cope with a German military attack. The country is "strong, united, and prepared," it boasted. The Piłsudskiites' propaganda exerted a profound impact upon the Polish nation. The Poles, who for years had been assured of the strength of their country, were now easily lulled into believing that they could repel German aggression. On the eve of the war, thus, the mood in Poland was "thoroughly optimistic . . . The Polish nation believed in its own power, that it would suffice, at least, to withstand the initial assault of the enemy. [The Poles were] also firmly convinced of the military power of their allies to relieve Poland soon and secure ultimate victory." [13]

THE FOREIGN POLICY OF THE PIŁSUDSKI REGIME

In foreign policy the Piłsudski regime followed closely the romantic tradition, merely adjusting to the new situation prevailing in the international sphere. All the major elements of romanticism were present.

Piłsudski and his followers never abandoned their conviction that Russia was the archenemy of Poland. In their eyes the overthrow of the tsarist regime had made little difference. Piłsudski regarded Bolshevism as a "purely Russian disease," [14] and as a successor of the imperialist tradition of tsarism. Consequently, "in matters of foreign policy he represented the view that the major and principal danger to Poland came from the east, from the Soviet Union." [15]

Throughout the entire interwar period Poland's foreign policy was guided by this predilection of Piłsudski. In the years immediately following

World War I, he conceived a bold scheme for weakening Russia once and for all by tearing away from her the former western provinces of the tsarist empire inhabited by nationalities other than Great Russians and bringing them under Poland's influence. He wanted Poland to replace Russia as the strongest country in East Europe. In 1920 he openly declared that his goal was "to turn back the clock of history, so that the great Polish Republic would emerge as the strongest military as well as cultural power in the entire east." [16] Piłsudski hoped to achieve this by restoring Poland's pre-1772 border with Russia and reviving the ancient federation of Poland, Lithuania, and the Ukraine. The federation of those three countries, in turn, was to be linked with the Baltic countries in the north and the Caucasus countries in the south. He "visualized Poland associated with a Ukraine governed from Kiev and supported by a free Caucasus. Poland thus would be at the head of a long chain of anti-Russian nations spreading from the Gulf of Finland, from Tallinn, to the Caspian, Tiflis, and Baku." [17] Despite extensive internal opposition to his plans, Piłsudski proceeded to put them into effect. His attempt to conquer the Ukraine in 1920 was intended as the first step in that direction. The Polish military venture into Kiev not only proved a failure, however, but resulted in a nearly fatal Soviet invasion of Poland. Thus, with Poland's successful defense and the conclusion of the peace treaty of Riga with the Soviet Union in 1921, this phase of Piłsudski's policy toward Russia came to an end.

Although forced to change his tactics in subsequent years, Piłsudski continued to believe that the main threat to Poland was posed by the U.S.S.R. In 1934, shortly before he died, he discounted the opinion of his advisors that after Hitler's rise to power the major danger to Poland came from Germany. This view of Piłsudski's was shared by his successors. Throughout the most of the thirties Poland's defense was planned in anticipation of an attack from the east rather than from the west. The plan to defend Poland's western borders was drawn hastily only late in 1938 and early in 1939. Even when the danger to Poland from Nazi Germany became imminent, the Piłsudskiites were still reluctant to seek support from the Soviet Union. "With the Germans," Marshal Śmigły-Rydz was reported to have declared on the eve of World War II, "we will lose our freedom; with the Russians we will lose our soul." [18]

If the policy of the Piłsudski regime was anti-Russian, this does not mean that it was pro-German. The difference in attitude toward the Soviet Union and Germany, respectively, was of degree rather than kind. With their eye to the threat from Russia, the Piłsudskiites tended to underestimate the danger to Poland from Germany, but they were not unaware of it. The Polish-French alliance of 1921 had an overtly anti-German character. Upon Hitler's ascent to power in 1933, Piłsudski pondered the possibility of a preventive war against Germany. When German troops moved into the Rhineland in 1936, despite the fact that the Polish-German nonaggression treaty had been signed in the meantime, Poland declared her readiness to assist France in the event of war.

Even when Poland's foreign policy appeared to be closest to that of Germany, at the time of *Anschluss* and during the Czechoslovak crisis of 1938, no genuine rapport existed between the two countries. Beck's policy of that period appeared to be motivated partially by delusions of grandeur; partially by his need for the appearance of external successes — no matter how cheap they were — to strengthen the internal position of the regime; and partially by his hope, similar to that of many other European statesmen at the time, that in exchange for his courtesies, *noblesse oblige,* Hitler would leave Poland alone. His diplomacy was often shortsighted at times and, particularly during the Czechoslovak crisis, harmful; but, it was not deliberately pro-German. In the late thirties the Piłsudskiites did not mind flirting with the Germans, but not to the point of being left alone with them. They had learned from their experiences in 1916–1917 that Poland, in partnership with Germany, was bound to become virtually a German protectorate. Consequently, they turned down the repeated Nazi offers to join in a war against the Soviet Union and declined to be lured by the prospects of territorial gain in the east in exchange for concessions to the Third Reich in the west. When pressed to the wall, they went to war against Nazi Germany.

The goal of the Piłsudski regime, then, was not to lean on either one of Poland's two mighty neighbors, but to conduct a foreign policy independent of both Russia and Germany. In summing up Piłsudski's testament in this sphere, an ideologist of the regime declared: "The principal aim of Poland's [foreign] policy ought to be . . . not to trail other states . . . We ought to conduct our own policy — neither French, nor German, but Polish — which would secure for the Polish state complete independence and full freedom of movement, indispensable in Poland's position between Germany and the Soviet Union." [19] Piłsudski and his successors hoped that they would be able to secure such freedom of action by preserving a delicate balance between Germany and Russia. They strove to maintain proper relations with both Poland's powerful neighbors, while not aligning themselves with either. Precisely in order to achieve this, Piłsudski signed treaties of nonaggression with both the Soviet Union and the Third Reich in the early thirties. The balancing of Poland's position between Hitler's Germany and Stalin's Russia, remained the guiding principle of Beck's foreign policy until 1939. Only the Nazi-Soviet alliance of 1939 brought his balancing act to an end.

Piłsudski and his followers seemed to be aware that preserving a balance between Germany and Russia was a hazardous game in view of Poland's relative weakness. Consequently, as in the years immediately after World War I, they tried to strengthen Poland's hand by close cooperation with other smaller countries in Central Eastern Europe on the theory that, if united, these countries would be in a better position to match either Germany or Russia. Piłsudski "planned a union of all countries menaced by the common German and Russian danger . . . His eyes went from the snows of Sweden and Finland to the mosques of Turkey." [20] Beck continued this policy of Piłsudski on a less ambitious scale. He strove to organize a bloc of states along a Helsinki–Bucharest axis. Very little came of his efforts. Most of the countries in Central Eastern Europe, either due to a fear of aggravating their relations with Germany or Russia or simply because of their antagonism toward Poland, did not support the Polish plan. The animosity shown the plan by Czechoslovakia, the second most powerful state in the area, was particularly damaging. Thus, the only countries with which Poland managed to establish closer cooperation were Rumania and Hungary in the south, and Estonia in the north. This, of course, was a far cry from Piłsudski's original design. It did not change Poland's vulnerability vis-à-vis either Germany or Russia in any substantial way.

In the absence of any effective system of alliance in Central Eastern Europe, Poland was compelled — in the traditional vein of political romanticism — to seek an alignment with the Western European powers. The Polish–French alliance of 1921 thus became the cornerstone of Poland's foreign policy. Poland's alliance with France did not work too well, however. The geographic distance between the two countries was reflected in the different concepts of their national interests, and consequently, in fairly frequently diverging policies. France considered cooperation with Poland useful, but not indispensable. "In the minds of French politicians . . . the destruction of the Polish state was not strictly equivalent to a downfall of

France." [21] Actually, the Polish–French alliance was reinvigorated only in the spring of 1939, at the same time that a Polish–British alliance was concluded. Poland's alignment with France and Britain in 1939 was expected to serve as a deterrent to Hitler's aggression. In the event, however, that the alliance strategy should fail to achieve its purpose and Germany was to attack Poland, neither France nor Britain was prepared to give Poland effective military assistance. In July 1939 Lloyd George warned that the British guarantee to Poland was militarily meaningless should war break out, for Britain did "not possess the means to redeem it." [22]

In view of Poland's enmity toward both Russia and Germany, and her inability to improve her position effectively either through alliance with other small Central East European countries or with West European powers, the Poles could rely only on their own meagre resources throughout the entire interwar period. In these circumstances Piłsudski and his followers resorted to the familiar romantic theme stressing the moral force of the Polish nation. Indeed, the goal of the army coup d'état in 1926 had been to improve Poland's defenses by strengthening the country internally. Piłsudski had held the view that "in the peculiar geographic position of Poland, no traditional democracy could work; the people of Poland must find a new form of [political system] suitable to their own overwhelming tasks . . . and must endeavour to establish a greater coherence and unity, which can bear the full weight of coming events." [23] Consequently, the Piłsudskiites embarked on a program of what they called the "moral renovation" of the nation.

These principles of Piłsudski were strictly observed by his successors. The Piłsudskiites extolled the role of the army in national life. "The armed forces," exclaimed an ideologist of the regime, "represent the cornerstone of [Poland's] independence . . . The army, as a symbol of the strength of the whole nation, ought to enjoy the support and admiration of all the people." [24] Piłsudski's teaching also led his followers to continually emphasize the significance of the moral force of the country. In 1936, Śmigły-Rydz asserted that concern with Poland's defense should "release the moral and creative strength of the nation." [25] As the danger of military conflict increased, the superiority of moral over physical force was stressed more and more strongly. The moral strength of the Polish armed forces was to compensate for its physical weakness and carry it to victory. On the eve of World War II, the whole Polish nation was taught to espouse the same soldierly virtues which a quarter of a century before had been required of Piłsudski's legionnaires:

honor, discipline, and, above all, heroism. "The nation which wants to live in freedom," Łukasiewicz exclaimed, "must be determined to fight . . . it must be willing to pay the sacrifice of life, and to do it with enthusiasm." [26]

WORLD WAR II AND ITS AFTERMATH

When the German attack came on September 1, 1939, Poland proved to be no match for the gigantic Nazi war machine. The desperate fight of the Polish forces against the superior German armies only brought about heavy casualties among the Poles. "Horses against tanks," exclaimed an American who inspected the remnants of one of the battles. "Brave and valiant and foolhardy though they were, the Poles were simply overwhelmed by the German onslaught." [27] The Polish army was defeated in a matter of a few weeks. The entry of Soviet troops into eastern Poland on September 17th, in fulfillment of the Molotov–Ribbentrop agreement, sealed the fate of the independent Polish state.

Poland was partitioned by her two traditional enemies. The U.S.S.R. incorporated the eastern part of the country into the Ukrainian and the Belorussian republics (the district of Wilno was given to Lithuania). The western part was incorporated into the Reich — the Polish population was expelled from all these provinces. In the central part an exclusively German government was established. The Germans had no room in their plans for a Polish state, even a *Zwischenstaat* such as they had tried to establish in 1916. Their objective was to turn Poland into a German colony. "We have no plans for rebuilding Poland," wrote General Halder, "the Polish intelligentsia must be prevented from establishing itself as a governing class. The low standard of living must be preserved. Cheap slaves . . ." [28]

The crushing military defeat and the collapse of their independent state profoundly shocked the Poles but by no means destroyed their morale. All hope was not gone; the war was not yet over. Although Poland's allies, France and Britain, had failed to assist it in the initial military campaign, they fulfilled their pledges by declaring war on Germany. The Poles now pinned their hopes for the restoration of their state on the ultimate victory of the Western allies. In the meantime, however, they did not sit idle but continued to struggle against Nazi Germany, both with Allied troops abroad and in the underground at home. In these efforts the Poles looked for leadership to the Polish Government-in-Exile, set up first in Paris and, after the defeat of France, transferred to London.

The Polish Government-in-Exile consisted of the representatives of the major political parties which opposed the political ideology of the Piłsud-skiites before the war. This does not mean, however, that they rejected Piłsudski's political concepts *in toto*. The very logic of their position as a government-in-exile, allied with the Western powers and maintaining connections with their country only through conspiratorial means, pushed them toward political romanticism. The personal background of the leading figures in the government, many of whom had been linked with Piłsudski at one stage or another, contributed to this tendency.

Until 1943 the Government-in-Exile was dominated by its premier and also the commander-in-chief of the armed forces, General Władysław Sikorski. Before the war, Sikorski had been a staunch opponent of the Piłsudski regime. His opposition to Piłsudski developed only during World War I and especially in the early twenties, however. Although he had never belonged to the close circle of Piłsudski's followers, Sikorski had collaborated with him in establishing and directing the Polish military movement before World War I.* Thus, he certainly shared Piłsudski's belief in military struggle as the most effective means of promoting Polish independence. Furthermore, even when Sikorski was at its helm, several crucial posts in the Government-in-Exile remained in the hands of close followers of Piłsudski. Władysław Raczkiewicz,** a former high-ranking official of the Piłsudski regime, occupied the post of president. The Piłsudskiites also retained a great deal of influence at the lower levels of government, especially in two crucial organs: the army and the diplomatic service. Those who now came to the forefront were usually people who had been brushed aside by their leader at one stage or another. They had not been responsible, therefore, for the policies of the Piłsudskiites' regime in the thirties, but they had not opposed them either. Certainly they still adhered to many essential tenets of Piłsudski's political ideology. Last but not least, the younger generation of army officers and diplomats who had made good under the Piłsudski regime played an increasingly important role in the Government-in-Exile. These men, even if they were opposed to the older Piłsudskiites, thought in similar political categories. It was difficult for them to escape the influence of Piłsud-

* Sikorski, who was born in 1881, was considerably younger than Piłsudski; yet, as a reserve officer in the Austrian army, he had had better military training than Piłsudski, who was self-taught in military matters. In fact, it was Sikorski who trained the nucleus cadre of Piłsudski's military movement.
** Before the war, Raczkiewicz (1885–1947) was a high-ranking civil servant and speaker of the Senate for some time.

ski's political ideology, for it was the only one they knew well. All these groups derived their conception of Poland's policies in World War II essentially from the experiences of World War I. Above all, like Piłsudski in 1914, they attached great importance to the military effort of the Polish nation.

Under the direction of the Government-in-Exile, thus, the Poles continued to fight against Nazi Germany. After the defeat of their regular army at home in September 1939, they immediately resorted to conspiratorial struggle. They built up an underground force which at its peak in August 1944 stood at 380,000 men.[29] Throughout the early stages of the war, the Polish underground established an impressive record in propaganda, intelligence, and sabotage activities. In later years Polish partisan units, at times up to a division in strength, kept harassing the occupying German army. The Warsaw uprising in 1944 climaxed Polish underground activities. There, Polish freedom fighters engaged in a desperate battle, lasting for sixty-three days. On the German side five divisions including some crack armored units took part. The determination with which the Poles fought is described in a despatch from Warsaw by a British observer at the height of the uprising. "Warsaw today," he wrote, "is in a state of total warfare . . . Nearly the whole population is engaged in some sort of public work. Thousands of people have been mobilized to put out fires that are raging in many parts by day and night . . . The actual army is a queer mixture. Fighting in it are boys of sixteen years and old men of sixty years. Few have regular weapons to carry . . . Food is also a great problem." This picture is supplemented by the account of an American airman, who flew over Warsaw shortly before suppression of the uprising, which was unassisted by the Russian armies standing idle a few miles away. "Not much remained of the Polish capital," he reported, "of large districts of the town which had covered areas of several square miles nothing remained but heaps of rubble . . ."[30]

In conjunction with the struggle at home, Poles who made their way abroad fought side by side with Allied troops. Polish units up to a corps in strength participated in almost all the major campaigns in Europe and even in Africa. Toward the end of the war there were almost 230,000 Polish soldiers under British command in Western Europe.[31] The Poles abroad fought with no less determination than their brothers at home. They achieved several spectacular successes, the best known probably being the capture of a German stronghold at Monte Cassino in Italy in 1944. A distinguished British observer writes of the spirit permeating Polish troops in Italy, "It was an extraordinary sense of romance; not gaiety, exactly, but chivalry, poetry, adventure. It was more than a military formation. It was a crusade." [32]

The Polish soldiers fought with enthusiasm for they firmly believed that the cause of the Western allies was their cause, and that in shedding their blood for the West, they shed it for Poland. The Polish Government-in-Exile staked Poland's future on the victory of the Western powers. In the early stages of the war, when the Nazi-Soviet alliance strained relations between the Western democracies and the Soviet Union, the position of Poland was relatively simple. An alignment with the West carried with it promise, although the road to victory certainly appeared to be difficult — the defeat by the West of both Germany and Russia.*

With the outbreak of the Russo-German War in 1941, and the conclusion of at first the Anglo-Soviet, and, then the American-Soviet alliances, the situation changed. One of Poland's two traditional enemies became, to use the phrase by which the Poles often referred to the Soviet Union in the late war years, "the ally of their allies." Yet, in the early stages of the Russo-German conflict when its outcome was still in the balance, the need for a settlement in Polish-Soviet relations did not appear to be urgent. The Russians were thrown out by the Germans from the pre-war Polish territories. In 1941, thus, the Polish Government-in-Exile reestablished diplomatic relations with the Soviet Union and concluded an agreement providing for the release of Polish prisoners in Russia without resolving the territorial dispute. The problem of future Polish-Soviet relations loomed in the minds of the Poles only in 1943, after the decisive Soviet victory at Stalingrad. The U.S.S.R. immediately intensified its pressure for the recognition of its claims to Poland's eastern provinces and, after the mass graves of the Polish officers captured by the Soviets in 1939 were discovered by the Germans — clearly pointing to their premeditated murder by the Russians — relations between the Polish Government-in-Exile and the Soviet government deteriorated markedly, and soon were completely severed.

Although Russia's military victories greatly enhanced her chances of playing a significant role in Central Eastern Europe at the end of the war, the

---

* When France and Britain contemplated coming to the military assistance of Finland, defending herself against the Russian attack in 1939–1940, the Polish Brigade was included in the Allied expeditionary force being prepared to go to the Finnish front as a symbolic gesture of Poland's policy vis-à-vis the Soviet Union.

Polish Government-in-Exile continued to stake everything on its alliance with the West. It still hoped the ultimate outcome of the war would be the same as that of World War I *à rebours*. The Poles based their hopes on the assumption that Russia would defeat Germany and that Russia, in turn, would be held back from expansion in Europe by the West. In such circumstances, as in 1918, a truly independent Polish state could easily have been rebuilt. As late as 1944, the official position voiced by the publication of the Polish Government-in-Exile was that the Western allies would gain sufficient influence in Central Eastern Europe to safeguard Poland's independence as a result of the war. "Poland expects that both Britain and, thus, the British Commonwealth of Nations will take an active part in the organization of Europe . . . If this would be so, Poland will gain the strongest guarantee of her independence." This statement also expressed hope that the United States would "cooperate closely with Britain" [33] in carrying out this policy.

As the war went on and it became increasingly evident that the Western allies had little interest in opposing Soviet expansion in Central Eastern Europe, a crisis ensued in the Polish Government-in-Exile. Even under General Sikorski's leadership some friction developed in the ranks over the course of foreign policy. In 1941 the two leading Piłsudskiites, General Kazimierz Sosnkowski and August Zaleski,* resigned from the government in protest against the lack of explicit recognition of Poland's right to her prewar eastern territories in the Polish-Soviet agreement. The conflict came to a head only after Sikorski's death in mid-1943. Two opposing centers crystallized around his successors: General Sosnkowski, who became commander-in-chief of the armed forces; and Stanisław Mikołajczyk, a leader of the Peasant Party who took over the premiership.** Toward the end of 1944 both men were forced to resign their posts, but the split among the exiles persisted. Each group adopted a different tactic: one followed a hard line, the other took a more conciliatory posture toward the Communists.

---

* Sosnkowski, born in 1885, was one of the closest of Piłsudski's political and military collaborators from 1908 to the early twenties. During World War I, he was the chief of staff of Piłsudski's legions, and, subsequently, was detained with Piłsudski in Germany. After 1926, however, Sosnkowski was kept politically inactive by Piłsudski and his successors, although he continued to hold a high army post. Zaleski, born in 1883, was Beck's predecessor as foreign minister during the Piłsudski regime.

** Mikołajczyk, born in 1901, was a leader of the Peasant Party in his native province of Poznania, and a member of its national executive since 1933. His rapid climb to the post of premier of the Government-in-Exile was largely due to the fact that the more senior figures of the Peasant Party, such as Wincenty Witos, or Władysław Kiernik, remained in Poland during the war.

The Government-in-Exile, now headed by a veteran socialist, Tomasz Arciszewski,*** was dominated by supporters of the hard line. Realizing that, for all practical purposes, they were abandoned by the West, and seeing no possibility of defending Poland's independence from the Soviet Union on their own, the Government-in-Exile decided to take a purely moralistic stand, insisting on everything or nothing. They denounced the West for betraying the cause of Polish independence. "I consider it my duty to state," Arciszewski wrote to President Roosevelt after the decision of the Yalta Conference had become known, "that the resolutions of the Crimean Conference, as they were published, have been accepted by the Poles as a new partition of Poland, and as placing her under a Soviet protectorate." [34] They flatly refused to become a party to any international agreement sanctioning the Soviet annexation of Poland's eastern territories, and they repudiated any cooperation with the Communist-dominated government installed in Poland under the protection of the Soviet army toward the end of the war. Upon the withdrawal of recognition by the major Western powers in mid-1945, the Polish Government-in-Exile, in a defiant gesture, decided to continue its activities in London.

Underlying the decision of the Government-in-Exile to remain abroad seems to have been their belief that a conflict between the East and the West, which would validate the romantic tradition to which they adhered, was inevitable, if not imminent.* The Poles apparently assumed that Stalin's aggressive tactics would eventually compel the Western democracies to take arms against the Soviet Union. In such event, they thought, opportunities would arise to free Central Eastern Europe, and thus Poland, from Com-

*** Arciszewski (1887–1956) was one of the most prominent figures in the Polish Socialist Party. As a young man, he collaborated closely with Piłsudski in the socialist movement and served with Piłsudski's legions during World War I. In the twenties, however, he moved into the opposition to the Piłsudski regime. During World War II, Arciszewski was one of the leaders of the Polish underground and came to London through clandestine channels only shortly before assuming the post of premier.

* One of the leaders of the Polish underground relates in his memoirs his conversation in 1945 with an emissary of the Polish Government-in-Exile, which depicts the mood prevailing among the exiles in London at that time. "The emissary introduced himself as an officer of the Polish Armed Forces and declared that his task was to present [to the leaders of the underground in Poland] the views and plans of the most prominent Polish figures abroad. All those opinions without exception predicted a rapid conflict between the Western allies and Soviet Russia, leading to a war designed to push Russia to her prewar borders and to liberate East Europe . . . [The emissary] quoted the alleged statements of various persons mentioning their names. They differed only with regard to the date of the future war. The dates varied from two months to two years." Zygmumt Zaremba, *Wojna i konspiracja* (London, 1957), p. 334.

munist rule. "The trend of events that began with the German aggression against Poland on September 1, 1939," one of the foremost Polish exile leaders, General Władysław Anders,** wrote in 1947, "has not ended but only been interrupted . . . Poland was the first, but not the last, victim of horror coming from the east. This truth, scorned in 1945, and hushed up in 1946, and even still in the first half of 1947, is now becoming clear. The world drama is approaching its final scene . . ."[35] The Poles, of course, looked forward to a military conflict between the East and the West not merely because they wanted a new war. They had every reason to be more tired of the struggle than any other nation. It was simply that they saw no other possibility for regaining Poland's independence.

In anticipating such a trend of events it was not only the Government-in-Exile which felt duty bound to continue activities in London. The same expectation led roughly half a million Poles who had left Poland to remain abroad.[36] Even after the Polish forces under British command were disbanded in the late forties, many clung to the belief that ultimately they would again be called to arms to assist in liberating their homeland. Last but not least, the same hope caused the remnants of the anti-Nazi partisan units in Poland to turn to military struggle against the Communist regime. They battled desperately against Communist-led forces backed up by the Soviet occupying army until they were completely wiped out in the late forties.[37]

Mikołajczyk and his followers took a different course from that of the Government-in-Exile. Encouraged to do so by the Western leaders,* Mikołajczyk strove to find a modus vivendi with Russia. Although, at first, he tried to salvage at least a portion of Poland's eastern provinces, he eventually accepted their loss and merely pressed for as generous as possible compensation to Poland in the form of German territories in the West. He also agreed

** In the interwar period Anders, born in 1892, was a career officer but not a Piłsudskiite. Indeed, in 1926 he was chief-of-staff of the forces opposed to Piłsudski's rise to power. Anders emerged as a national figure only during World War II. Captured by the Russians in 1939, he became a commander of the Polish army formed in the Soviet Union in 1941. He led his troops out of Russia to Italy, where they gained considerable fame, notably in the battle of Monte Cassino. Toward the end of the war Anders, succeeding Sosnkowski, became acting commander-in-chief of the Polish armed forces.

* Churchill, eager to find a face-saving device which would release Britain from her commitment to uphold Poland's independence, insisted especially that Mikołajczyk should go to Poland to join the Communist-dominated government. In June 1945, mixing promises with threats, Churchill placed a virtual ultimatum before Mikołajczyk: "If you back out now, I'll wash my hands of the whole Polish case." Quoted in Stanisław Mikołajczyk, *The Rape of Poland: Pattern of Soviet Aggression* (New York, 1948), p. 119.

to joint Soviet and Western influence in Poland on the basis of what Church-ill outlined to him as a "fifty-fifty pattern." This meant that the Polish gov-ernment would be composed half of Communists and their followers, and half of Polish democratic leaders.[38] Mikołajczyk proceeded to Poland in mid-1945 in order to give such a government a try by joining the Com-munists in the Provisional Government of National Unity. "There was the danger," he said in subsequently explaining his motives, "that if independent Polish leaders did not participate in the work of the three Ambassadors [entrusted with the task of solving the Polish problem by the great powers at the Crimean Conference], the Polish people, and not the Big Three, would be blamed for the failure of Yalta." [39] Mikołajczyk, although he re-nounced the idea of military conflict between the Western democracies and the Soviet Union, pinned his hopes on Western diplomatic support. He led the Polish Peasant Party into open political struggle against the Communists, apparently expecting that at the crucial juncture the West would effectively intervene on his behalf.* The intervention, however, did not come. Thus, "Mikołajczyk behaved as a representative of . . . Anglo-American interest in Poland . . . [while] London and Washington had little real interest in the evolution of Polish politics, and in practice no possible means of in-fluencing it. He acted then, like an Ambassador without credentials." [40] Still the Polish Peasant Party put up a good fight. Throughout 1946 despite the intimidations, persecutions, and outright terror directed against its sup-porters, the party held on in opposition to Communism. Early in 1947, how-ever, after the general elections were forged by the Communists, when there was still no effective support from the West, all hope was lost. Mikołajczyk and a handful of other party leaders threatened with arrest escaped to the West.[41]

With defeat of the last of the wartime underground and the suppression of the open opposition led by the Polish Peasant Party, resistance to the Communist regime in Poland came to an end. After close to a decade the fighting in the country was over, and the Poles looked around to appraise its results. In the eyes of the overwhelming majority of the Polish people, World War II and its aftermath were disastrous. Poland had suffered tremendous

---

* Just before Mikołajczyk's departure from London for Poland, Churchill assured him of the complete support of Britain and the United States. "You must realize," he said "that behind you stand two mighty countries with all their resources." Quoted by Edward I. Rozek, *Allied Wartime Diplomacy: Pattern of Poland* (New York, 1958), p. 388.

losses. Over six million Poles had lost their lives in the war,* and Poland's national income in 1945 was only 38.2 percent of what it had been in 1938.[42] The ill-fated Warsaw uprising itself accounted for the loss of 250,000 people and the destruction of 55 percent of Poland's capital.[43] Losses incurred in the postwar armed resistance to Communist power were also heavy. At that stage over 20,000 Communists and several thousand police functionaries and soldiers were killed,[44] while the number of slaughtered partisans must have been considerably more. When one considers that the people who perished in the military struggle were usually from the most active and patriotic elements of the country, the losses, measured in terms of their national importance, were even more severe than the bare figures indicate. However, despite all their sacrifices, the outcome of World War II represented a bitter disappointment for the Poles. Poland's only gain was the land she received from Germany. At the same time almost half of the prewar Polish territory was incorporated in the U.S.S.R. and, with the establishment of a puppet Communist government, the entire country was turned into a virtual dependency of the Soviet Union. Indeed, in the late forties most Poles believed that for all practical purposes Poland had lost the war. Her fate was what one writer termed as "the defeat in victory." [45]

* Poland's losses were by far the heaviest among all the Allied nations. There were 220 out of every 1,000 Poles killed. Corresponding figures for Yugoslavia were 108; U.S.S.R., 40; Czechoslovakia and France, 15; the United Kingdom, 8; the United States, 1.4. However, only 664,000 Poles were killed in battle; the rest, and particularly over three million Polish Jews, died as a result of Nazi persecutions. Wydawnictwo Zachodnie, *Straty wojenne Polski w latach 1939–1945* (Warsaw, 1960), pp. 41–42.

4

THE RISE OF COMMUNISM

THE COMMUNIST PARTY OF POLAND

In the interwar period the Communists, both by virtue of their foreign policy program and their ideology, came nearer to the realist tradition than did any other political movement in Poland. After the Bolshevik revolution in Russia, the Polish Communists found themselves in a position similar in some ways to that of the positivists during the late nineteenth century or of the National Democrats in the early twentieth century. They represented the political group in Poland which not only stood for maintaining close bonds with Russia but also shared the outlook of the Russian leaders. Polish Communists, of course, derived comfort from developments in Russia. Social revolution in Russia was a reality. In order to carry out the testament of the Proletariat, providing for intimate cooperation between Polish and Russian revolutionary governments, all there remained to do was to bring about a revolution in Poland. Precisely with a view to promoting this goal, the Social Democracy of the Kingdom of Poland and Lithuania and the Polish Socialist Party Left joined in founding the Communist Party of Poland [1] in December 1918. At last, they thought, the dreams of the Proletariat were near to fulfillment.

The Communist Party of Poland, however, was never to accomplish its goal. Within the twenty years of its existence, at no time did it come near to carrying out a revolution in Poland. Indeed, it failed to become a political force of any significance. The party refrained from participation in open political life in Poland and remained a clandestine organization. Its membership was negligible.[2] Its activities amounted to instigating some scattered

strikes and engaging in a few acts of sabotage and terror. The front organizations which it set up did not fare much better. They gained very little
support from the working class,[3] far less than that enjoyed by the Polish
Socialist Party. All in all, throughout the whole interwar period, the role
of the Communist Party in Polish politics remained marginal.

The Communist Party itself was largely a self-made fiasco. The Polish
Communists neglected to take into account the changes which had taken
place in the country since the end of the nineteenth century, clinging rigidly
to Rosa Luxemburg's program of Social Democracy. They once again
ignored the advice offered them by leaders of the international Communist
movement, notably Lenin, who in 1919 urged them to consider the strength
of nationalist sentiments in Poland in planning their revolutionary strategy.[*]
The Polish Communists viewed the emergence of an independent Polish
state as incompatible with historical process in the world at large, and took
a purely negative attitude toward it. "In this epoch of international social
revolution which destroys the foundations of capitalism," declared the
resolution adopted at the founding meeting of the Communist Party of
Poland, "the Polish proletariat rejects every political solution that is con-
nected with the evolution of a capitalist world, solutions like autonomy,
independence, and self-determination." The Communists regarded an independent Polish state as merely a transition to Poland's submersion in "the
international camp of social revolution [where] there is no problem of
national borders."[4] Therefore, quixotically, they refused to have anything
to do with it. They opposed the establishment of a Polish army, and attempted
to sabotage its efforts to uphold Poland's frontiers. They boycotted the first
national elections in 1919 and later in the same year chose to continue as a
clandestine organization rather than to register as a political organization
with the duly constituted authorities of the Polish state.

The Communist policy of repudiating Poland's independence was hopelessly out of tune with the mood of the country. The Poles had adhered to
political realism in the late nineteenth century and largely still in the early
twentieth century, when there seemed no other choice. After 1918, however,
when an independent Polish state was in existence, to advocate Poland's

---

[*] In March 1919, at the Bolshevik conference in Moscow, Lenin openly acknowledged that
the Polish working class was being told by the bourgeoisie that the Great Russians were
striving to restore their domination of Poland under the guise of Communism, and urged
the Polish Communists to cope with this by promoting a revolution "in a different way than
the Bolsheviks." He also reported that when he offered this advice to the Polish Communists,
one of them retorted: "No, we will do what you did." V. I. Lenin, *Sochineniia*, XXIX (Moscow,
1950), 154.

union with Russia was anachronistic. In the eyes of the Polish people, such a political program was retrogressive, and they would have none of it.* The Communists' appeal in the name of social reform did them little good. The Polish working class did not feel that social revolution was necessarily linked to political union with Russia. The Polish Socialist Party offered them the alternative of social reform without a renunciation of their independence. In any case, intoxicated with the idea of ultimately winning their freedom from foreign rule, the Poles would rather have given up social revolution than independence.

The invasion of Poland by the Red Army in the summer of 1920 severely tested the Communist policy. The Polish Communists pinned all their hopes on a Russian victory. In the territory occupied by Russian troops, a provisional Communist government was set up to direct the Polish social revolution. The broad masses of the Polish people took exactly the opposite stand, however. They viewed the Red Army not as an emancipating force but as a foreign invader bent on depriving them of their newly won independence. Thus, the Poles closed ranks behind the government of national unity headed by the peasant leader, Wincenty Witos. It was truly by the efforts of all strata of the Polish nation that the Red Army was eventually pushed back from the gates of Warsaw.

The memories of events in 1920 weighed heavily against the Communist Party of Poland throughout its entire existence. The Red Army's invasion aggravated the Poles' animosity toward Russia, making them skeptical of the Communist program of close cooperation with the Soviet Union in the international sphere. Moreover, the Polish Communist support of the invading Red Army made their platform of social revolution also suspect. The Communist Party remained, for all practical purposes, an outcast in Polish politics. No respectable political group was willing to cooperate with it. The Communists' efforts to form a "united front" with the Polish Socialist Party and other parties on the left, made first in the early twenties and then in the late thirties, were turned down. The socialists' reasons for refusing to cooperate with the Communists were well put in 1923 by Mieczysław Niedziałkowski, a prominent leader of the Polish Socialist Party: "With you, gentlemen," said Niedziałkowski, "one never knows if you are geniune political workers

---

* This was indirectly admitted by Feliks Dzierżyński, who wrote in 1921: "Our mistake was in repudiating Poland's independence for which Lenin always rebuked us . . . As a result . . . we lost our struggle for an independent Soviet Poland." Quoted in Dziewanowski, *The Communist Policy of Poland* (Cambridge, Mass., 1959), p. 103.

or agents of the Russian government. In the past, as the Social Democracy of the Kingdom of Poland and Lithuania, you bitterly denounced the aspirations for independence. After Poland regained independence you opposed it ruthlessly. You led Cossack regiments against your own country." [5]

As a result, the Communist Party of Poland was caught in a vicious descending spiral. The less support Polish Communists had at home, the more they leaned on the Soviet Union; yet, the more heavily they relied on assistance from Russia, the less popularity they had in Poland. Throughout the whole interwar period the Communists never managed to escape this dilemma. Their feeble attempts to evolve a Polish brand of Bolshevism out of a synthesis of social revolution and national aspirations in the mid-twenties failed. The half-hearted repudiation of Luxemburg's program, which took place at the Party's Second Congress in 1923, came too late to improve its fortunes. With the increasing "Bolshevization" of the party in subsequent years, the Communist Party of Poland became totally subordinate to the Comintern which, in turn, particularly after Stalin's consolidation of power, was a tool of the Russian government.*

In the eyes of the Poles, the best evidence of the dependence of the Polish Communist Party on Moscow was its willingness to make sweeping concessions to both the Soviet Union and Germany at the expense of Polish territory. The Polish Communists, who in the past had so bitterly opposed the right of the Polish provinces to secede from Russia, now strongly supported this right for various national minorities within Poland. In the east the Communist Party of Poland advocated ceding those provinces populated largely by Ukrainians and Belorussians to the Soviet Union. "The Party," wrote its official organ in 1923, "whole-heartedly supports the liberation movement of national minorities in the eastern provinces, and their aspiration to join the neighboring Belorussian and Ukrainian Soviet Republics." [6] In the west, in order to strengthen the position of the German Communists, who were considered by the Comintern as more important than the Poles, the Communist Party of Poland was prepared to yield Pomerania

---

* Their subordinate status to the Russian Communists in the interwar period and, indeed, until 1956 is now admitted by Polish Communists. The theoretical journal of the Polish Communist Party acknowledged in 1961 that the relationship between foreign Communist parties and the Soviet Communist Party had meant in practice: "the imposition upon all parties of the views and opinions of one party, or to be more precise, the opinions and views of its leadership." "Kierunek odnowy i marszu do komunizmu," Nowe Drogi, December 1961, p. 48.

and Upper Silesia to Germany.* In a proclamation issued early in 1933, the Polish Communists declared that after victorious revolution the Polish proletariat would "renounce all the decisions of the Treaty of Versailles regarding Upper Silesia and the Pomeranian 'corridor,' and would grant to the people of those provinces the right of self-determination including their secession from Poland." [7]

Their readiness to offer Polish territory to both Russia and Germany, of course, even further decreased the popularity of the Communist Party among the Polish people. The Poles viewed this Communist policy as a treasonable design aimed at a new partition of their country. "The members of the Communist Party, with their insistence on joining the Soviet Republic outright and their willingness to give away Poland's western provinces to Germany, were considered simply as foreign agents who would once again turn their country into a Russian province." [8] Consequently, when the Piłsudski regime resorted to stern measures against the Communist Party of Poland in the thirties, the country showed little concern. The widespread arrest of Communist leaders was accepted as inevitable in order to protect the Polish state from the activities of what was generally regarded as a subversive group.

Without any following at home, the Polish Communists were also of little use to the Russians. Consequently, under the pretext of harboring Piłsudski's police spies and provocateurs, the Communist Party of Poland was abruptly dissolved in 1938.** At the same time, several hundred Polish Communists who had sought refuge in the Soviet Union, including almost all the party leaders, were summarily executed.† The only ranking Polish

* The readiness of the Polish Communists to make territorial concessions to Germany in the interwar period is rarely mentioned in Poland today. Nevertheless, since 1956 some indirect references have been made to this. "While writing these words," one writer digressed, "I recall an old comrade from the Communist Party of Poland, who did not agree with the concessions to the Communist Party of Germany concerning Upper Silesia." Władysław Machejek, "Na historycznym zakręcie," Życie literackie, October 28, 1956.

** In February 1956, on the eve of the initial denunciation of Stalin by Khrushchev, a joint statement of the various Communist parties was issued in which the charges against the Communist Party of Poland were declared to have been falsified and the decision to dissolve it groundless. Trybuna Luda, February 19, 1956.

† The reasons for Stalin's decision to liquidate the cream of the Polish Communists still remain veiled in mystery. The leading Western historian of the Polish Communist movement, Professor M. K. Dziewanowski, has advanced the thesis that Stalin, in anticipation of his rapprochement with Hitler, decided to get rid of the Polish Communists, whose presence could be embarrassing on such an occasion. See Dziewanowski, The Communist Party of Poland (Cambridge, Mass., 1959), pp. 149–154. For a similar view, see "Interview with an Ex-insider" Soviet Survey, July-September, 1960. It seems to be entirely possible, however,

Communists saved from death in Moscow, ironically enough, were those who were imprisoned in Poland at that time. One of them, then still a fairly obscure party member, was Władysław Gomułka.*

The years 1939–1941, in the words of a prominent Communist leader, represented "the most difficult period" for the Polish Communists. The dissolution of their party and the slaughter of their leaders in 1938 caused them "a feeling of pain and bitterness." [9] Thus, on the eve of World War II the Communist movement in Poland was disorganized and demoralized. The Soviet Union's alliance with Germany, and its participation in the attack against Poland in 1939, turned the position of the Polish Communists from bad to worse. Poland and Russia were now virtually in a state of war. "Nothing [is] left of Poland," boasted Molotov in October 1939, "this ugly offspring of the Versailles Treaty." [10] The persecution of the Polish population in Poland's prewar provinces incorporated into the Soviet Union was hardly less severe than that in the territories under German rule. Several hundred thousand Poles were deported to distant parts of Russia, many of them to labor camps. Many others were arrested and executed by the NKVD. In such circumstances there was little support in Poland for a political party whose entire program rested on close Polish-Russian co-operation. Indeed, in the years 1939–1941, the Communist movement came to a virtual standstill in Poland.

THE POLISH WORKERS' PARTY

The German attack on Russia marked a complete about-face, at least on the surface, in the Soviet attitude toward Poland. In line with the general course of Soviet foreign policy — stressing the need for a united war effort against the Axis — the harmony of interests between Russia and Poland in

---

that there was no explicit political reason for striking against the Polish Communists. Because of their close connections with the Soviet Communist party they might have simply been caught up in the convulsions of Soviet system at the time when it underwent the "great purges."

* Władysław Gomułka was born in 1905 in southern Poland of mixed peasant-worker stock. At the age of sixteen, soon after he started to work as a locksmith in the oil industry, he became active in trade unions and, subsequently, joined the Communist Party. Throughout the thirties Gomułka led the life of a professional revolutionary, at first working as a trade union organizer on behalf of the Communist Party of Poland. In 1932, during the strike in Łódź, he was severely wounded and captured by the police. He was sentenced to four years for subversion, but was released for health reasons after only two years. Then, he went to the Soviet Union where he studied at the International Lenin Institute in Moscow. Upon his return to Poland in 1936 Gomułka was arrested again, receiving a sentence of four and a half years.

a common struggle against Nazi Germany was now strongly underlined. Soviet leaders denied harboring any aggressive plans toward Poland or any intentions of interfering in her internal affairs. On the contrary, their avowed desire was, in Stalin's own words, "to see a strong and independent Poland after the defeat of Hitler's Germany."[11]

After the outbreak of the Russo-German war, two Polish Communist groups appeared almost simultaneously abroad and at home. Communist leaders who had fled to Russia established the Union of Polish Patriots. After diplomatic relations between the Soviet Union and the Polish Government-in-Exile were broken off in 1943, they posed as a counterpart of the Polish political leaders in London. Under their aegis the nucleus of a Polish army under Soviet command was formed to fight on the eastern front. At the same time, a new underground Communist party, called the Polish Workers' Party, was founded in Poland with Władysław Gomułka as leader.* The party formed its own partisan units which, although numerically insignificant,[12] posed as the vanguard of the Polish resistance movement's struggle against the German occupying forces. When the Soviet army pursuing the retreating Germans reached central Poland in July 1944, the two Communist groups, together with some small leftist political organizations, created the Committee of National Liberation, which claimed to be a provisional Polish government.

The platform of the Polish Workers' Party differed a great deal from that advocated by the prewar Communist Party of Poland. The new party emphasized strongly that it was not a direct successor of the traditions of the older movement. On the contrary, it explicitly underlined its disapproval of at least some features of the old Communist program. "We are a young party," exclaimed Gomułka in 1945, "because we have repudiated everything which in the past damaged the interests of the workers' class and the working masses."[13] In particular, the Polish Workers' Party rejected the Polish Communist movement's negative stand toward Poland's independence. Indeed, the Communist leaders openly admitted that ignoring Polish aspirations to independence had been responsible for the fiasco of the Social

---

* Gomułka was released from prison at the outbreak of World War II. After participating in the defense of Warsaw against the Germans, he moved to the southeastern part of the country where he remained in obscurity until 1941. Early in 1942 he joined the Polish Workers' Party, and in the summer of the same year he was appointed a secretary of its Warsaw branch. In this capacity he directed resistance against the German occupying forces. In December 1942 Gomułka became a member of the party's Central Committee. In November 1943, after two of his predecessors in the post had been killed, he became Secretary-General of the Polish Workers' Party.

Democracy as well as that of the Communist Party of Poland. The Communist Party of Poland, expounded Gomułka,

was burdened with the past errors of the Social Democratic movement on the national question . . . The cardinal mistake of the Communists was that, while they fully appreciated the problem of social revolution, they ignored the issue of independence. The Communists asserted outright that as long as the bourgeois-capitalist system prevailed, Poland's independence would in no way improve the position of the workers' class and the working masses. Consequently, in their opinion, the problem in Poland could be resolved only by revolution along the Russian pattern . . . It is obvious, that this stand [was] false and erroneous.[14]

Indeed, Gomułka not only castigated the attitude toward Poland's independence of Social Democracy and the Communist Party of Poland but approved the Polish Socialist Party position on this issue. Although he criticized the Polish socialists for being carried away by the struggle for independence to the point of abandoning the struggle for socialism, Gomułka made it clear that he considered their concern with Poland's independence correct. "The struggle for social emancipation," he exclaimed, "cannot be separated from the struggle for national liberation." [15]

While repudiating the early Polish Marxists' version of political realism, the Polish Workers' Party moved closer to the tradition of political idealism. Indeed, the party posed as a successor of the romantic tradition. "We are a party of the Polish nation," asserted Gomułka in 1944. "We have grown from its sorrows and suffering, from its blood and struggle, from its most patriotic and most revolutionary aspirations." [16] A year later Gomułka even more explicitly linked the Polish Workers' Party with romanticism. "In the struggle against the German invader," he said, "we reverted to the patriotic, insurrectionist traditions of the Polish people . . . Our partisan units followed the example of the best fighters for Freedom and Independence of the Polish nation . . . We have every right to regard ourselves as successors of the insurrectionist tradition." [17]

In line with the romantic tradition, the Polish Workers' Party combined the goals of social revolution and national liberation in its appeal. It rejected the old Communist program of union with Russia and upheld Poland's right to independence. "There exist two reasons," Gomułka elaborated in 1945, "why Poland cannot become a Soviet republic. First, the Polish nation does not want it; second, the Soviet Union does not want it." The Polish Workers' Party, he emphasized, "stands for Poland's sovereignty and independence." [18]

The program of the Polish Workers' Party, in line with its adherence to the principle of Poland's independence and sovereignty, advocated the specifically Polish nature of social transformation in Poland. The Polish Communists now seemed to follow Lenin's advice of 1919 and stressed that the Communist revolution in Poland should differ from the Russian one. Social changes in Poland were to be introduced in a milder and slower fashion, taking specific Polish traditions and needs fully into account. Last but not least, the Polish Workers' Party completely reversed the stand of the Communist Party of Poland on the territorial dispute between Poland and Germany. The Polish Communists now not only rejected territorial concessions but championed the recovery of the ancient Polish lands which had been a part of Germany for centuries. One of the major goals of the Polish Workers' Party, Gomułka asserted toward the end of World War II, is "to restore to Poland her borders, extending along the Oder, the Neisse, and the Baltic Sea." [19]

Yet, even though the Polish Workers' Party proclaimed itself a successor of the romantic tradition, it still remained far from the classic concept of political idealism. Several crucial aspects of its program were obviously derived from the tradition of political realism. Above all, the cornerstone of Communist foreign policy was close cooperation between Poland and Russia. The Polish Workers' Party also retained the stand taken by the Communist Party of Poland in the Polish-Soviet territorial dispute. It endorsed the annexation of Poland's prewar eastern provinces by the Soviet Union.

However, despite all the concessions on the part of the Communists to Polish nationalism and the pronounced leftward swing of Polish society under the equalitarian impact of the war, the program of the Polish Workers' Party failed to produce any substantial response. At the time the Communist-dominated provisional government of Poland was formed, the membership of the Polish Workers' Party was at 20,000.[20] Once the party assumed power in 1944–1945, its membership, as well as that of the different political groups linking their fortunes to those of the Communists, rose rapidly.[21] However, in the immediate postwar years, the Communist Party and its allies commanded no significant popular following in the country. The great majority of Poles remained loyal to the Polish Government-in-Exile and, subsequently, supported the opposition led by the Polish Peasant Party.*

* In 1956 Gomułka himself admitted that in the immediate prewar years the Polish Workers' Party had not commanded the support of a majority of the nation. *Przemówienia 1956–1957* (Warsaw, 1958), pp. 197–198.

The Communist regime in Poland was entrenched in power only after a prolonged and, at times, fierce struggle between the Polish Workers' Party, openly assisted by Soviet military might,* and the anti-Communist political forces supported by the overwhelming majority of the Polish people.

The bitter Polish resistance to a Communist regime was essentially nationalist rather than anti-socialist in nature. The relatively mild character of the social revolution advocated by the Communists, on the one hand, and the widespread support for social reforms among the Polish people, on the other, made the gap separating the two parties in the social sphere of secondary importance. In the years immediately following World War II, as in 1920, the Poles opposed the Communist Party's rise to power not because it advocated social revolution but because it was generally regarded as a tool of the Russian government. The Polish people simply did not believe the repeated assurances of the Polish Workers' Party that it did not take orders from Moscow. The whole tradition of the Polish Communist movement belied this. The party's consent to the annexation of Poland's eastern territories by the U.S.S.R. strained their credibility even further. Above all, the reliance of the Polish Workers' Party on Soviet support in its struggle for power was viewed by the Poles as conclusive evidence of its dependence on Russia.

To make matters worse for the Polish Communists in the immediate postwar years, their appeal to Polish nationalism — stressing the recovery of Poland's ancient lands from Germany — was not particularly effective. World War II had created a situation, rare in recent history, in which a defeated Germany was virtually eliminated from international politics and, thus, could pose little threat to Poland in the west. Moreover, in view of their consent to the removal of the German population from the prewar German territories acquired by Poland, it looked as if the Western powers considered the Oder-Neisse border between Poland and Germany a final one. Soviet support of Poland's right to this frontier, therefore, did not appear exceptionally significant to the Poles.

In such circumstances, the program expounded by the Polish Workers' Party compared unfavorably in the eyes of the Poles with that advocated by the anti-Communist opposition. The classic romantic concept of relentless struggle against Russia coupled with expectations of effective support from

* The assistance of the Soviet army in establishing the Communist regime in Poland has been openly admitted by the Polish Communists on many occasions. In 1948 Bierut said: "the presence of the Soviet army paralyzed our class enemies." *O Partii*, 2 ed. rev. (Warsaw, 1952), p. 207.

the West was still fully in line with the aspirations of the Polish nation. The goal was to save Poland from subjugation by Russia without weakening her position vis-à-vis Germany in any way.

GOMUŁKA'S "RIGHTIST-NATIONALIST DEVIATION"

In the years 1947–1948 a change took place in Soviet foreign policy. The thesis of the struggle between two global systems, capitalism and Communism, was brought out of wartime retirement. A general tightening of Soviet controls over East Europe soon followed. In September 1947 the Cominform was established to coordinate the activities of the various Communist parties under Russian guidance. In February 1948 the Communist coup d'état took place in Czechoslovakia. In the spring of the same year, when the Yugoslav Communists refused to accept Russian interference in their domestic affairs, the Soviet-Yugoslav dispute flared up. At the same time individual differences among the Communist states in East Europe were played down. The relevance of Soviet experience for all Communist-ruled countries was emphasized. "The Communist Party of the Soviet Union (Bolshevik), created and educated by the great geniuses of revolutionary theory, Lenin and Stalin," declared the official journal of the Cominform early in 1948, "serves as an example to all fraternal Communist parties." [22]

The new Soviet policy encountered unexpected opposition in the Polish Workers' Party from an influential group headed by the Secretary-General, Władysław Gomułka. Gomułka, in line with his program combining political realism with political idealism, seemed to be genuinely committed to upholding Poland's independence from Russia. He was "a fervent Communist . . . determined to see Poland become a Communist republic. [Yet] for all his Communism he [was] careful to emphasize that he was a Pole not a Russian puppet." [23] Gomułka's stand posed no problem in the years 1945–1947, when Moscow was willing to tolerate a considerable degree of diversity in the policies of various Communist parties in East Europe. At that stage he was "an effective and, even from the point of view of Russia, desirable leader of Polish Communism. His personality and behavior were such that he could arouse among the rank and file of the Polish Workers' Party . . . a degree of confidence and enthusiasm for him as a Polish Communist with a personality of his own." [24]

When the Soviet line began demanding strict uniformity in the policies of all East European Communist parties in 1947–48, however, Gomułka proved reluctant to follow the Russian lead. On several occasions he took a stand different from that of the Soviet Communists. When the Cominform was founded, Gomułka voiced his misgivings. When the Soviet-Yugoslav dispute erupted, Gomułka declined to come out against Tito strongly enough to satisfy the Soviets. Even in the aftermath of the Yugoslav affair, when Moscow emphasized the relevance of Russian experience for all Communist countries, Gomułka continued to push for Poland's right to evolve socialism in a manner different from the Soviet Union. In particular, he was opposed to the swift collectivization of Polish agriculture. All in all, "forgetful of the origin of his authority, Gomułka was beginning to have a policy of his own." [25] This, in the eyes of the Russians, represented a dangerous deviation which could not be tolerated; thus, Stalin marked Gomułka for removal from power. In view of its complete dependence on Russian support against the still rebelling Polish society, the Polish Workers' Party had little choice but to obey the Russian directive even though this might have been distasteful to some Polish Communists.

In the summer of 1948, therefore, the leaders of the Polish Workers' Party who enjoyed the confidence of the Russians launched an attack against Gomułka and his followers.[26] Gomułka was accused of "rightist-nationalist deviation," the essence of which was that he inadequately stressed the unique role of the Soviet Union and the Soviet Communist Party in the international Communist movement and the significance of the Russian revolutionary experience for Poland. Gomułka rejected the charges that he opposed close relations with the U.S.S.R., but he admitted that he was against Soviet interference in Poland's domestic affairs. "The core of my rightist, nationalist complex," he said, "must have been my attitude toward the Soviet Union, toward the Soviet Communist Party (Bolsheviks) . . . It never entered my head that Poland could progress along the way to socialism without being supported by the Soviet Union, but . . . it was difficult for me to shift my attitude toward the Soviet Union into the realm of interparty ideological relations." [27] The willingness of Gomułka in part to recant his mistakes did not help him much. He was replaced as head of the party by Bolesław Bierut,* who was trusted by Moscow. Soon Gomułka and his

---

* Bierut was born in 1892 in Central Poland. In 1912 he joined the Polish Socialist Party Left and, subsequently, the Communist Party of Poland. In the interwar period he was a Comintern agent engaged in revolutionary activities both in Poland and other countries. In 1927 and again in 1933 he was imprisoned in Poland. In 1939 he was released from prison and went into the Communist underground. When the Communist government was set up in Poland in 1944, he became the acting head of state. Early in 1947 he assumed the office of President of the Republic.

close collaborators were also removed from all high government and party posts. At the same time extensive purges, affecting one-fourth of the total membership, were carried out among the ranks of the Communist Party.[28]

Gomułka's punishment was not limited to removal from the leadership of the Communist Party, however. In accordance with Stalinist practices, he not only had to be deprived of any political influence but also personally disgraced. Consequently, toward the end of 1949, a new attack was launched against the former Secretary-General. This time the charges bordered on an accusation of high treason. In particular, Gomułka was charged with tolerating opponents of the Communist regime in responsible government and party posts, an accusation clearly designed to implicate him in an alleged conspiracy against the state. Realizing that his political career was over and that his life was probably at stake, Gomułka shifted his stand. He not only denied the charges against him in a dignified manner but, in turn, attacked his accusers. He boldly asserted that his ideological errors had been shared by all the leaders of the Polish Workers' Party. Gomułka's courageous defense, of course, did not help him. Within a few weeks he was expelled from party membership, headed for political oblivion. This disgrace, however, was still not considered severe enough. Consequently, in 1951 Gomułka was secretly arrested and subjected to an investigation obviously planned as a prelude to his public trial. In the atmosphere of Stalinist terror which reigned over all Eastern Europe at that time, this could lead to only one thing: Gomułka's physical liquidation.

In 1948–49, outside the Communist Party, Gomułka's downfall aroused relatively little interest in Poland. The great majority of the Poles remained indifferent to the struggle between Gomułka and the pro-Soviet faction in the Polish Workers' Party. They viewed it as an internal squabble, the outcome of which would not change their plight one way or the other. There was little sympathy for Gomułka among the people. The role which he had played in liquidating the anti-Communist opposition was still vivid in the popular mind. If anything, the spectacle of Gomułka's fall from power strengthened the Polish people in their conviction that Communism was bad *per se*. Their image of Russian Communism as a Moloch devouring its own children in constant thirst for blood only seemed to be confirmed.

As the years went by, however, the image of Gomułka among the Polish people underwent some change. Several factors contributed to this. With the elimination of the anti-Communist opposition, the attention of the Poles naturally began to focus on internal divisions in the ranks of the Polish

Communists. Contrasted to the line adopted by the Communist Party after his downfall, Gomułka's position compared favorably in retrospect. Differences between the two programs were accentuated beyond reality by the intense anti-Gomułka propaganda launched in the late forties and early fifties. Its objective, the usual Stalinist treatment of disgraced Communist leaders, was to publicly smear the whole record of the former Secretary-General. The effect was exactly the opposite. It increased Gomułka's popularity in the country. Denouncing Gomułka's views as anathema to everything that the Communist Party stood for created an image of him as genuinely opposed to an ideology that the Poles despised. Accusing Gomułka as a tool of nationalism identified him with values held by most of his countrymen.

An element of admiration for the disgraced Communist leader soon emerged. His courageous defense in 1949 gained him the respect; his persecution and arrest in 1951, the sympathy, of the masses. Once these emotions entered the picture, Gomułka's old image as a militant leader of the Communist Party faded into the background, supplanted by that of a martyr, a staunch opponent of the Stalinist system and a true defender of Poland's national interests. Thus, the popular legend of Gomułka grew. Indeed, among many people the belief spread, based on no concrete evidence but not devoid of some inherent logic, that under the impact of his experiences Gomułka had revised or even totally abandoned his belief in Communism.

THE POLISH UNITED WORKERS' PARTY (1949–1956)

The Polish Workers' Party merged with the Polish Socialist Party[29] into the Polish United Workers' Party shortly after Gomułka's downfall. The Unity Congress was held on the thirtieth anniversary of the foundation of the Communist Party of Poland in December 1948. From the outset it was obvious that the Polish United Workers' Party rejected the program of combining political realism with political idealism to which the Polish Workers' Party had adhered throughout most of its existence. The platform adopted by the expanded Communist Party clearly reverted to the hard-core realist traditions of the Communist Party of Poland and the Social Democracy of the Kingdom of Poland and Lithuania.

The political program which had been advanced by the leaders of the Polish Workers' Party and, particularly, by Gomułka in the early forties, was now harshly denounced. It had been erroneous, the head of the Communist Party, Bolesław Bierut, declared, to regard "the Polish Workers' Party as essentially a new party, cut off from its predecessors . . . a party representing an ideological synthesis between the tradition of 'struggle for independence' of the Polish Socialist Party and the tradition of class struggle of the Communist Party of Poland." [30] Such an approach, he elucidated, represents a distortion of the Communist program. Gomułka, Bierut continued, "had wanted to adopt not the Leninist but the Polish Socialist Party program as a foundation for the ideological platform of the united party." This was "a deviation from the principles of Marxism-Leninism, an opportunist and nationalist revision of Leninism, and, indeed, an actual surrender to the nationalist traditions of the Polish Socialist Party." [31]

There have existed two currents in the Polish workers' movement, Bierut explained, representing two diametrically opposed social ideologies. The Polish Socialist Party represented one current. It was extensively exposed to the "influence of bourgeois ideology . . . aimed at subjugating the workers' movement to the interests and the goals of capitalism." The other current has been represented by the Proletariat, the Social Democracy of the Kingdom of Poland and Lithuania, and the Communist Party of Poland. It has always remained faithful to Marxism and conducted a determined struggle against the "penetration of bourgeois ideological influence in the ranks of the workers' movement." [32]

The true Marxist current in the Polish workers' movement, Bierut pointed out, had opposed the bourgeoisie's nationalist influences and followed proletarian internationalism. In particular, it had maintained strong bonds with the revolutionary movement in Russia. Indeed, close cooperation with the Russian revolutionaries was the characteristic feature of this current of the workers' movement in Poland. The leaders of the Proletariat, even at the time, understood "that the overthrow of despotism could be accomplished only hand in hand with the Russian people." The Social Democracy of the Kingdom of Poland and Lithuania, continued Bierut, has been "educating the Polish workers in the spirit of close alliance with the Russian revolutionary movement." Finally, after the revolution had taken place in Russia, the Communist Party of Poland "from the outset carried on a relentless struggle for alliance, fraternity, and friendship between the Polish nation and the people of the Soviet Union." Indeed, impressed with the successes of Russian revolutionaries, the Communist Party of Poland "followed the organizational and ideological example of the Communist Party of the Soviet Union (Bolsheviks)." [33]

The stress on the internationalist character of what Bierut described as the truly Marxist current in the Polish workers' movement, was carried to its logical conclusion by Communist historians. In the various historical publications officially sponsored by the Polish United Workers' Party, not only close cooperation between the Polish and Russian revolutionaries but also their plans to preserve close political bonds between Poland and Russia after the overthrow of tsarism were strongly emphasized. Indeed, some historians went so far in their works as to expurgate or paraphrase the occasional statements by leaders of Social Democracy or the Communist Party of Poland which referred to the strength of nationalist sentiments.*

From the beginning, the Polish United Workers' Party presented itself as a successor of the internationalist current in the Polish workers' movement. Bierut admitted, by way of explaining the nationalistic slogans of the Polish Workers' Party as merely a tactic useful in seizing power, that at the different stages of its development this current had had to assume different forms. He strongly emphasized, however, the uninterrupted continuity of its essential ideological outlook. Indeed, he claimed that "from the moment of founding the first socialist, revolutionary party: the Proletariat, through all its subsequent transformations, until the contemporary Polish United Workers' Party," [34] the movement was essentially the same: the sole carrier of proletarian ideology.

The Polish United Workers' Party stressed its devotion to proletarian internationalism. "Deepening attachment to proletarian internationalism," Bierut asserted, "represents the first, the foremost, and the chief task of the party." The special significance of firm bonds with the Russian Communists was emphasized for the Polish United Workers' Party. "The best guarantee of the further successful program of our party," expounded Bierut, "is its insoluble tie with the famous . . . Communist Party of the Soviet Union (Bolsheviks)." Intimate relations between the two parties were not to be conducted on a basis of equality, however. The Polish Communists eagerly

* One of the examples of such a practice concerned the statement by Dzierżyński, quoted on p. 54. The original statement of Dzierżyński was: "our mistake was in repudiating Poland's independence for which Lenin always rebuked us." In Dzierżyński's selected works published by the Department of the History of the Party in 1951, this was changed into: "our mistake was in repudiating the right of nations to self-determination including that of secession for which Lenin always rebuked us." Zdzisław Najder, "Dług i Skarb," *Przegląd Kulturalny,* December 20, 1956.

conceded first place to the Russians. It is of the utmost importance, Bierut declared, to spread "the consciousness of the great, leading role of . . . the Communist Party of the Soviet Union (Bolsheviks)" [35] throughout the ranks of the Polish party.

The Polish United Workers' Party never formally abandoned the goal of upholding Poland's independence. It did not go as far as the Communist Party of Poland which had advocated turning Poland into a Soviet republic. The Polish United Workers' Party, however, stood in favor of maintaining intimate bonds between Poland and the Soviet Union. In relations between the two parties and also in cooperation between the two states, the Polish Communists readily granted leading place to the Russians. "Erecting the mighty structure of Communism and transforming nature to suit the needs of man," exclaimed Bierut, "the Soviet Union is a guiding beacon of mankind, showing it the safe road of further glorious progress." [36]

The close cooperation between Poland and Russia, according to the program of the Polish United Workers' Party, was not to be confined solely to external relations between the two countries but would also be reflected in Poland's domestic affairs. The new Polish Communist Party did not openly repudiate the specific character of social revolution in their country. Differences between the political and socioeconomic system in Poland and that in the Soviet Union were played down, however. "Our road," said Bierut in describing the changes in Poland, "represents merely a variation on the general Marxist-Leninist road." In what respects does the Polish road vary from the Russian road? The difference between the social revolution in the two countries, he explained, is that revolution in Poland is being carried out with Russian assistance. "At the basis of our variation from the Soviet Union," Bierut elaborated, "lies assistance and support . . . from the victorious dictatorship of the proletariat in the U.S.S.R. Owing to that we can accomplish the function of a dictatorship of the proletariat within the framework of a people's democracy." [37]

Indeed, the Polish Communists pledged loyalty not only to the U.S.S.R. but also to the Soviet Communist leader, Stalin, personally. Again and again, the special role of Stalin was reiterated in cultivating close ties between Poland and the U.S.S.R. The Polish Communists never tired of eulogizing the Russian leader as a great friend and benefactor of Poland. "The contribution of Joseph Stalin to Poland's liberation," Bierut expounded, "to the determination of her borders, to the strength and progress of the People's Poland, is enormous." [38] Stalin's keen interest in Poland, the Polish Communist leader assured his compatriots, had not ended with freeing her from the German rule and rendering his help in establishing the new political system. "Also today," Bierut asserted, "Poland profits . . . from the invaluable creative advice, personal assistance and friendship of Comrade Stalin." [39]

Thus, in the years 1949–1954, the Polish United Workers' Party openly espoused close ties to Moscow and subordinate status to the Russian Communists. It also abandoned all pretences of carrying out social transformation in Poland in accordance with the country's own needs. Instead, the Polish Communists attempted to bring Poland's political and socioeconomic system as closely as possible in line with the system existing in Russia. They simply "copied the methods of building socialism accepted in the Soviet Union." [40] Poland's political and economic institutions, including the compulsory collectivization of agriculture, were gradually fitted into the Russian pattern. In 1952 promulgation of the new Polish constitution, closely modeled on the Soviet constitution, climaxed this process.

Nevertheless, eagerness with which the Polish Communists sovietized their country, apparently still did not represent, in the eyes of the Russians, a sufficient guarantee of their hold over Poland. Consequently, various aspects of life in Poland were, for all practical purposes, excluded from the supervision of the Polish United Workers' Party and brought under direct Soviet control. In 1949 the Soviet Marshal Rokossovsky was put in command of the Polish armed forces.[41] Russians were also placed in many other crucial government posts, especially in the security apparatus. The Soviet ambassador in Warsaw assumed a role of virtual overseer of the Polish Communists, freely intervening in the party and government affairs. At the climax of the Stalinist period, a well informed defector to the West reported: "Poland is ruled exclusively by Moscow . . . Nothing can happen which would be contrary to Moscow's will, and the entire mechanism of state is regulated in the most minute detail by the plenipotentiaries of the Soviet Union." [42]

Thus, by the late forties, the circle of Poland's history was complete. The dreams of the founders of the Proletariat were cruelly distorted in the process of accomplishment. The men who claimed to be the successors of the early Marxists' revolutionary traditions were now in power in Poland as well as in Russia. They professed to be creating new socialist societies. They also averred to be working hand in hand toward common goals. And, yet, it was not true. Poland was not a free country but, as in the nineteenth century, a dependency of Russia. Stalin's totalitarianism was even more oppressive than tsarist despotism. The Communists surpassed the most docile positivists in their servility toward the Russians.

The Polish people, of course, were acutely aware of the gigantic lie. They cherished few illusions about Polish-Russian relations. They considered the slogans of the socialist revolution as a decoy leading to Russian subjugation of their country. The role played by the Polish Communist Party came as no surprise to the Poles. It only confirmed their image of the Communists as mere Soviet stooges. For the great majority of the people, therefore, the existing reality in no way conformed to the vision of the early socialists. If anything, in their eyes, the Stalinist rule in Poland resembled the worst years of Russian oppression after the uprising of 1863.

5

THE REVIVAL OF POLITICAL REALISM

AFTERMATH OF THE DEFEAT

As it became increasingly evident that Communist rule was there to stay, the traditional divisions reappeared on the Polish political scene. It was easy for the Polish emigrés to adopt a wholly defiant attitude toward the political reality prevailing at home. The people in Poland, however, even if their sentiments had been fully in line with those of the exiles, had no alternative but to put up with it. They had to search for ways to improve the nation's lot under Russian domination. In these circumstances, which strongly resembled those of the nineteenth century, the Poles naturally turned for inspiration to the political thought of that period. In this way the tradition of political realism was revived.

Political realism first advanced in the guise of historiographic arguments which were traditionally Polish. In 1947 Aleksander Bocheński's book, provokingly entitled "The History of Stupidity in Poland,"[1] appeared. As he himself freely admitted, Bocheński's work was not of a scholarly nature. It was a collection of historiographic essays with strong political overtones. In his book, Bocheński, in the vein of the Cracow historical school,* bitterly denounced the tendency of historiography in the interwar period to exonerate the romantic tradition. He bluntly accused the Polish historians of "consciously or unconsciously deceiving the [Polish] nation."[2] In their distortion of Poland's history, Bocheński claimed, the historians were victims of two

---

* Politically there is a direct connection between the Cracow historical school and Bocheński. Before the war, Bocheński, born in 1904, belonged to a small conservative movement which was a direct successor of the conservatives who had played such an important role in the Austrian provinces of Poland before World War I.

complexes. In one case, an unfounded superiority complex prevented them from admitting "that in comparison with big and powerful neighbors, we are a small and weak nation." In the other an inferiority complex made them believe that "without our own independent state or, at least, desperate armed attempts aimed at its restoration, we shall cease to be a nation." These two complexes, in Bocheński's opinion, warped proper perspective in Polish historiography. Throughout several generations, he exclaimed, "prudence was regarded as treason; and crime and stupidity as heroism." [3]

This view of Poland's history, Bocheński continued, was reflected in the evaluation of Poland's position in the interwar period. Poland regained its independence due to the unique situation created by World War I in which both of her mighty neighbors were simultaneously weakened. Yet, Bocheński asserted, the Piłsudskiites "in order to justify their rise to power . . . managed to convince the Poles that they owed their freedom . . . to the struggle of a handful of legionnaires." Until the late twenties Poland's position in the international sphere was relatively secure, Bocheński wrote, but in the thirties the balance of power shifted decisively in favor of Poland's neighbors. The prevailing political ideology in Poland, as well as her line of foreign policy, however, continued unchanged. At that time "in order to be [regarded as] a Polish patriot, one had to refrain from even considering the possibility of alliance with one of our neighbors in the case of war with the other." The result of this policy, Bocheński concluded, was disastrous. "After twenty years of being steadily stupefied by apologists of an insurrectionist tradition . . . during World War II, our nation fell into an abyss of new conspiracies and messianism." [4]

In his book Bocheński called for a drastic departure from the romantic tradition in Polish historiography. Unless the distortion of Polish history is "radically and once and forever brought to an end," he exclaimed, "we shall perish completely." The task of historians, Bocheński emphasized, is to tell the people the truth, no matter how unpleasant it might be. "Only the historiography which presents the complete, ruthless facts," he asserted, "might be useful to the nation . . . Only the truth can help the nation which is placed in such a difficult geopolitical position." [5]

Bocheński also strongly criticized the commitment to military action characteristic of romanticism. He claimed that educational progress plays a far more important role in upholding a nation's morale than desperate armed insurrections. At the same time he denounced any expectations of Western assistance. Bocheński argued that Poland's geographic position between Russia and Germany, excluded any possibility of a lasting alliance with the

Western powers. The West is interested in Poland only as long as there is no opportunity for playing off Russia against Germany or vice versa. Once such an opportunity is open to them, the Western powers are no longer concerned with Poland. On the contrary, they are willing to sacrifice Poland's interests to those of whichever neighbor-state is allied with them at that moment.

Rejecting political idealism, Bocheński declared himself in favor of political realism. He praised past exponents of this tradition, particularly Lubecki, Wielopolski, and Dmowski. Although he carefully refrained from discussing contemporary events, in the guise of historiographic arguments Bocheński succeeded in making his views with regard to the current political situation quite clear. He stressed that political circumstances might occur in which the only rational course for a small nation, "in order to preserve and increase its strength, is to give up its independence and seek an association with another state." Moreover, he pointed out, in Poland's position it is necessary "to seek fullest support from either Germany or Russia." [6] Under the existing circumstances, Bocheński obviously had Russia in mind. In short, Bocheński, like the nineteenth-century political realists before him, appealed to the Poles to rid themselves of all illusions, to accept Russian overlordship, and to try to make the best of it.

At the same time another pseudo-historical study appeared which advocated a program of political realism. This was a biography of Margrave Wielopolski[7] by a prominent Polish writer, Ksawery Pruszyński.* The book, written in Pruszyński's vivid narrative style, certainly was not a contribution to historiography. Essentially an apology for Wielopolski — exalting his merits and explaining away his mistakes — it made no pretence to scholarly objectivity. Despite this, the book was of some importance. Pruszyński had written the book at the end of World War II in London. His objective, as he openly admitted in the foreword, was to question the position of the exiles opposed to seeking some modus vivendi with Russia. He felt that by invoking the ghost of a staunch conservative such as Margrave Wielopolski in his cause, he could most effectively refute his right-wing adversaries. The book, therefore, is an interesting exposition of the author's political creed, presented as an historical study.[8]

Pruszyński's book emphasized those aspects of the tradition of political

---

* Pruszyński (1907–1950) enjoyed a considerable reputation as one of the outstanding writers of the younger generation before the war. He gained special fame for his reports on the Spanish Civil War, where he was a correspondent on the Republican side. His writings abroad during the war enhanced his prestige still further.

realism which he considered relevant for Poland in the middle forties. The greatness of Wielopolski, Pruszyński declared, was that he refrained from "indulging in illusions or being carried away by emotions." Wielopolski, Pruszyński asserted, had known the West well, and precisely because of this knowledge "he did not base his political plans on [cooperation with] it." Finally, the writer concluded, Wielopolski "realized the horror of the German danger . . . and despite all existing obstacles, understood the need for cooperation between the two greatest Slavic nations," Russia and Poland. [9]

In the immediate postwar years the books of Bocheński and Pruszyński aroused little interest in Poland. At that time the majority of the Polish people clung desperately to romanticism. They adopted a posture described as that of "internal emigrés," regarding the Communist regime as essentially a foreign administration. They looked forward to the day when the Communist rule would come to an end and, in the meantime, restricted their cooperation with the Communists to a bare minimum. In this atmosphere the efforts of the early exponents of political realism were doomed to failure. Indeed, Bocheński, Pruszyński, and the others who accepted the existing political realities as fundamentally unchangeable were viewed by a great many Poles as "quislings" ready to collaborate with the enemy.

THE LEFT-WING POLITICAL PARTIES

Despite the general hostility toward the Communist regime and the people who collaborated with it, an increasingly large number of individuals, and even some political groups, began to cooperate with the Communists as the years went by. Among the latter, the most important were the three left-wing political parties: the Polish Socialist Party, the Peasant Party, and the Democratic Party.*

The reasons the left-wing political groups linked their fortunes with the Polish Workers' Party were manifold. Sheer opportunism was certainly an

---

* The Piłsudskiites movement and the National Democratic Party were declared by the Communist regime to be "fascist" and were banned from openly resuming their political activities in postwar Poland. Largely as a result of this ban, the supporters of these two political movements formed the core of an anti-Communist underground in the years 1945–1947. At the same time, however, some individuals from among the prewar National Democrats and even the Piłsudskiites (such as a former leader of National Democracy, Stanisław Grabski, or the former vice-premier in the Piłsudski regime, Eugeniusz Kwiatkowski) extended their cooperation to the Communist regime and assumed fairly responsible posts in the government.

important element. The complete breakdown in the continuity of political life provided all sorts of obscure individuals with a golden opportunity to emerge on the political scene in postwar Poland. Among the leaders of the left-wing political parties were many unscrupulous carreerists who, in offering their services to the Communists, were simply driven by their ambition to climb rapidly to the intoxicating heights of political influence. There is little doubt, however, that opportunism was not the sole motive behind the alliance of the left-wing groups with the Polish Workers' Party. Among the politicians who embarked upon this course, in the words of a staunch anti-Communist observer, "there were many people who honestly and sincerely strove to serve the country." [10]

Ostensibly the three left-wing political parties cooperated with the Polish Workers' Party due to their agreement, either on doctrinal or pragmatic grounds, with the Communist program of social revolution. The desire for the socioeconomic transformation of Poland certainly represented a genuine factor prompting many leaders of these political groups to join hands with the Communists. Yet, by itself, social reform does not appear to have been the decisive factor. As always in the past, also in the postwar years, the issue of social reform did not represent the major dividing line in Polish politics.*

Although the element of political realism was not overtly emphasized, it undoubtedly weighed heavily on the minds of the leaders of the left-wing political parties who aligned themselves with the Polish Workers' Party. Seeing no changes forthcoming, these men considered open opposition to the Communists futile. *Faute de mieux* they decided to try to improve the lot of the Polish nation by seeking some compromise with the Communists within the framework of existing political realities. They attempted to salvage whatever still could be saved from the wreck of an independent Polish state.**

* In the social sphere the gap separating the political groups supporting the Government-in-Exile from those cooperating with the Communist regime was not very wide. On the one hand, the underground quasi-parliament, loyal to the London government, in March 1944 passed a resolution promising far-reaching socioeconomic reform in postwar Poland. On the other hand, the program of social revolution advanced toward the end of the war by the Polish Workers' Party was quite moderate. Indeed, it was so moderate that some left-wing socialists, as, for instance, Oskar Lange, did not find it radical enough.

** This attitude on the part of politicians who cooperated with the Communist regime is well illustrated by the memoirs of a socialist leader who was still in the underground in 1945. In a conversation between the author and one of the persons who decided to seek some modus vivendi with the Communists, the latter exclaimed with tears in his eyes; "The decisive influence over Poland is in Russian hands. One has to be blind not to see that everything else does not count." Z. Zaremba, *Wojna i konspiracja* (London, 1957), p. 327.

Political realism also led the Polish people to join the ranks of the left-wing parties. "Those parties" observed an anti-Communist writer, "had no authority in society." Yet, he continued, "life does not accept a vacuum. In a time of shortages a substitute is accepted as a product of full quality . . . The desire for peace and a return to normal life was too strong to prevent effectively or for long the people joining openly established political organizations. . . ."[11] Consequently, even though they still represented a relatively insignificant minority in Polish society, it did not take long for the three left-wing political parties to substantially increase their membership.

Among these left-wing political parties, the most powerful was the Polish Socialist Party. By no means representing a direct successor of the prewar party, the postwar Polish Socialist Party originated during the war as a splinter from the extreme left-wing of the socialist underground movement. At that stage, it was composed of a handful of virtually unknown individuals.[12] Toward the end of the war the group, assuming the name of the Workers' Polish Socialist Party, established close bonds with the Communist underground. In 1944, when the Communist-dominated provisional government was formed, one of the members of this socialist group, Edward Osóbka-Morawski, became its chairman.* At the same time the party, taking the name of the Polish Socialist Party, came into the open.

When the leaders of the genuine Polish Socialist Party tried to recreate their own party, their demands were turned down by the Communist government on the grounds that a socialist party was already in existence. Thereby the supporters of the prewar Polish Socialist Party divided into three factions. Some of them remained loyal to the Government-in-Exile headed by their old leader, Tomasz Arciszewski, and strove to continue underground activities.** Others, led by another prominent prewar figure in the party, Zygmunt Żuławski, joined hands with Mikołajczyk's Polish Peasant Party in openly opposing the Communists' rise to power. A third group entered the ranks of the pro-Communist Polish Socialist Party. Among them the most prominent figure was Józef Cyrankiewicz.†

* Osóbka-Morawski (born in 1909) before the war was an insignificant member of the Polish Socialist Party in Warsaw.

** At the same time, however, a few socialists who had stayed during the war in London, notably a veteran trade-unionist and a minister in the Sikorski government, Jan Stańczyk, returned home and joined the pro-Communist faction.

† Cyrankiewicz (born in 1911) was a leader of the Polish Socialist Party in Cracow before the war. During the war he spent several years in a concentration camp, where apparently he established close bonds with the Communists. Immediately after his release from imprisonment, he assumed the post of Secretary-General of the Polish Socialist Party. Some light is thrown on the motives which led Cyrankiewicz to cooperate with the Communists by a

In line with the general political developments in the country, the pro-Communist Polish Socialist Party soon prevailed over the other two factions. The socialist group which remained underground was forcibly suppressed and, seeing no further purpose in conspiratorial activities, simply disintegrated. Those openly opposed to the Communist regime suffered a decisive blow with the defeat of the Polish Peasant Party. For all practical purposes, then, by 1947 the only socialist group which remained in existence as an effective political force was the pro-Communist Polish Socialist Party led by Cyrankiewicz.

The new Polish Socialist Party did not claim to be a direct descendant of the prewar party. On the contrary, it strongly denounced several essential aspects of the Polish Socialist Party's interwar program. Above all, it cut itself off from what Cyrankiewicz described in 1948 as "the most dangerous deviation" in the Polish socialist movement, namely, excessive preoccupation with the issue of Poland's independence. This cardinal error of the Polish socialists, in the opinion of Cyrankiewicz, had made them uphold the Polish state irrespective of its social system and, in effect, abandon the program of social revolution. The prewar Polish Socialist Party, according to Cyrankiewicz, had been a political party "committed to parliamentary democracy, well suited to a Polish republic ruled by the gentry and the bourgeoisie." [13] While unequivocally rejecting the old socialist program, the postwar Polish Socialist Party proclaimed itself to be the successor of the truly Marxist and revolutionary current in the Polish workers' movement. It reverted to the tradition of the Polish Socialist Party Left. In line with the tradition which it selected as its own, the Polish Socialist Party declared its readiness to cooperate closely with the Communist Party.

The Polish Socialist Party, thus, followed a consistently pro-Communist course. In 1946 it formally agreed to cooperate with the Polish Workers' Party, a move destined to result in a merger of the two parties. Throughout the whole period of struggle against the anti-Communist opposition led by the Polish Peasant Party, the Polish Socialist Party sided with the Communists. Finally, early in 1948, the Polish Socialist Party declared its readiness to join the Polish Workers' Party in a single workers' party. The actual merger took place at a Unity Congress late in the same year.

------

conversation of his in 1945 with Zygmunt Zaremba, a leader of the pro-London underground faction of the socialist movement. In this conversation, Cyrankiewicz repeatedly stressed the necessity of "adjusting to the political situation in which Russia was the decisive influence in East Europe." He also emphasized that "after years of idleness, he was anxious to undertake broad political activity." Zaremba, *Wojna i konspiracja,* p. 332.

The pro-Communist course of the Polish Socialist Party was strongly opposed in the ranks. Many prewar socialists had joined the party in the hope that they would be in a position to influence its policies from within and, in this way, preserve at least a vestige of independence from the Communists. Of course, they strongly resented the fusion of the two parties. Indeed, by the middle of 1947, the opposition gained a considerable influence in the party. Early in 1948, however, the pro-Communist wing led by Cyrankiewicz prevailed, and an extensive purge of the opponents of merger with the Communists was carried out. After this the Polish Socialist Party proceeded to surrender its existence as a separate political organization.

From the outset it was obvious that the former socialists were to play second fiddle in the Polish United Workers' Party.[14] In 1948 Cyrankiewicz became titular joint head of the party, yet there was not a shadow of a doubt that the real authority lay with Bierut. In other top party organs Communists heavily outnumbered former socialists. As the years went by, former socialists were weeded from positions of power in the Polish United Workers' Party. Out of twelve full members of the Politburo three had been former socialists initially; by 1954 only Cyrankiewicz remained among the top party leadership, and even his prestige was dwindling. In these circumstances, in the years 1949–1955, the influence of the former socialists on the actual policy-making process steadily declined.

The position of the other two left-wing political parties which cooperated with the Communists, the Peasant Party and the Democratic Party, was more complicated than that of the Polish Socialist Party. They were not Marxist parties, but ostensibly supported the Communist program of social revolution on pragmatic grounds. The main popular appeal of these parties was precisely that they offered their members a place in the new political system without requiring the acceptance of Marxist doctrine. Political realism, thus, undoubtedly played an even greater role in the Peasant Party and the Democratic Party than in the Polish Socialist Party. Yet, despite the fact that their program was seemingly so well suited to the needs of the time, neither the Peasant Party nor the Democratic Party managed to become a political force of any significance. The two parties encountered serious resistance to their progress at first from the anti-Communist opposition and, then, from the Communists. In the late forties and the early fifties there was little room in Poland for "middle of the roaders."

The pro-Communist Peasant Party, which originated in 1944 by splitting from the main body of the peasants' underground, became handicapped by the establishment in 1945 of an anti-Communist Polish Peasant Party. The latter represented the true successor of the powerful prewar Polish agrarian movement in the eyes of the peasants. The position of the pro-Communist wing began to improve only after disillusionment with Mikołajczyk's policy of all-out opposition to the Communists permeated the ranks of the Polish Peasant Party. Various groups, some led by well-known figures in the agrarian movement, shifted from anti-Communist to pro-Communist positions. Finally, after Mikołajczyk's flight abroad toward the end of 1947, the main current of the Polish Peasant Party began to cooperate closely with the Peasant Party.* In 1949 the two peasant parties merged into the United Peasant Party.[15]

The Democratic Party was perhaps the most indigenous of the three left-wing political parties. It claimed to be a direct successor of a very small party of radical intelligentsia founded shortly before World War II. Indeed, several people from the prewar group were among the leaders of the postwar Democratic Party. After the war, the Democratic Party gained some support among the intelligentsia and the middle classes, but its over-all influence in the country was still negligible. It remained the smallest of the various political parties which joined to defeat the anti-Communist opposition.

While the Communists were fighting the anti-Communist opposition and clung to the program of carrying out social revolution in Poland in a different fashion from the Soviet Union, the Peasant Party and the Democratic Party were treated by the Polish Workers' Party as junior but nevertheless genuine political partners. Both parties were fairly liberally represented in the government. Their separate traditions and programs were respected by the Communists. They were also allowed to handle their internal party affairs relatively unmolested.

As the anti-Communist opposition was suppressed, the Communists adopted a program of blind imitation of the Soviet system. There no longer seemed to be any need for political parties other than the Communist Party in Poland. The situation of the United Peasant Party and the Democratic Party thus changed radically. In the years 1949–1955, their role greatly de-

---

* The motives for seeking cooperation with the Communists rather than abandoning any political activity were well described by a former leader of the wartime peasant's underground, Kazimierz Banach. "The idea of dissolving the party would hurt the peasant movement . . . It would mean turning away from reality and an internal withdrawal of millions of peasants back to their farms . . . The peasants should bravely face the new reality and participate in building the new life, regardless whether they like it or not." Stefan Korboński, *W imieniu Kremla* (Paris, 1956), p. 330.

clined. Representatives of the two parties were, for all practical purposes, eliminated from the government. Their separate traditions were played down and their programs reduced to virtual replicas of that of the Polish United Workers' Party. Their activities were also drastically curtailed. Indeed, at the climax of the Stalinist period, the United Peasant Party, and especially the Democratic Party, were threatened with outright suppression, seemingly to follow in the footsteps of the anti-Communist opposition.

THE CATHOLIC GROUPS

In addition to the various political parties, two Catholic groups — one centered in Cracow and the other in Warsaw — appeared in postwar Poland. The position of these Catholic groups in a Communist-ruled state was still more complicated than that of the non-Marxist left-wing political parties. The Catholics could not identify themselves with the objectives of the Marxists to the same extent as did the left-wing radicals. In their case, the important element which prompted the left-wing political parties to cooperate with the Communist Party, namely, the support of social revolution modeled after the Soviet Union, was missing. The motives which induced the Catholics to seek a modus vivendi with the Communists, thus, may be reduced to political realism or simple opportunism.

The Cracow Catholic group originated in the immediate postwar years when two Catholic periodicals were launched there under the aegis of the Metropolitan of Cracow, Cardinal Sapieha. One was a popular weekly, *Tygodnik Powszechny;* the other a more sophisticated monthly, *Znak.* Cooperating closely with one another, these two periodicals provided a rallying point for Catholic intellectuals. Originally the people who joined the group shared no uniform political views, representing even conflicting political traditions at times. As the years went by, however, the differences lessened. From among the editors and writers of *Tygodnik Powszechny* and *Znak* gradually emerged a closely-knit group of Catholic laymen with a similar political outlook.

Political realism clearly prompted these Catholics to undertake their work. Seeing no imminent changes in the political situation, they strove to at least preserve a forum for the expression of Polish Catholic opinion in a Communist-ruled state. Their primary attention centered on religious rather than social or political problems. Yet, in the same way as any group coming into the open in postwar Poland, they had to endorse the existing political system.

They did this in as reticent a fashion as possible. They declared their willingness to seek some modus vivendi with the Marxists on the basis of "exchanging unbiased opinions." At the same time, however, they reaffirmed their determination "to derive solutions to essential problems in individual and social life from the Catholic Truth." [16]

Throughout the years 1946–1955 the Catholics around *Tygodnik Powszechny* remained faithful to their principles. During the struggle between the Communists and the anti-Communists, they refrained from taking one side or the other. In the subsequent years of Stalinist repression, they declined to soften their stand toward Communism. In spite of chicanery and even persecution by the Communist regime, they clung to their beliefs. This led to outright suppression. In 1949 *Znak* was closed down. In March 1953, after its editors had flatly refused to commemorate Stalin's demise with an eulogy to the dead tyrant, *Tygodnik Powszechny* was taken away. This brought their open activity temporarily to an end.

The ostensibly Catholic group in Warsaw centered around a weekly *Dziś i Jutro*. It differed from the *Tygodnik Powszechny* group at the outset in that its nucleus was a closely knit political group. Most of its leaders came from the prewar "national radical" organization known as the "Falanga," which had originated in the middle thirties as a splinter group of the extreme right-wing of the National Democratic Party. Falanga, led by young and ambitious Bolesław Piasecki,* had been a quasi-fascist organization. Influenced, if not by German Nazism, certainly by Italian fascism, its program was anti-liberal, anti-Communist and strongly anti-Semitic. It had been radical, totalitarian, and extremely nationalistic. Although for a while Falanga had won favors from the Piłsudskiite government, which used the group as an instrument to split the ranks of the opposition, it had little following in Poland.

During World War II the group preserved inner unity by establishing a small underground organization of its own. It formed armed units which fought German and Communist partisans alike.** In 1944, when the Soviet Army moved into Poland, the units dispersed, while Piasecki fell into the

---

* Piasecki was born in 1915. He was a law student when he assumed leadership of Falanga.

** Some writers believe that Piasecki collaborated with the Nazis. For instance, see: F. A., "La Chiesa in Polonia: Apprenze e realta," *L'Osservatore Romano*, July 11–12, 1960. This seems very unlikely. Piasecki's flair for the grandiose political scheme virtually excluded the possibility of his being an *agent provocateur* of the Gestapo, and no other form of collaboration with the Germans existed in occupied Poland.

hands of Soviet security forces. In view of his past record, Piasecki's fate seemed to be sealed. Yet, not only his life was spared but he soon reemerged on the Polish political scene. After talks with Gomułka Piasecki founded the "progressive Catholics' " movement or "Pax," as the organization became known from the name of a publishing house which it subsequently founded.

The reasons behind the miraculous survival of Piasecki in 1945 are still veiled in mystery. The prevailing version is that Piasecki impressed his captors so much that they found it expedient to negotiate with him. Allegedly, the principal negotiator on the Soviet side was the notorious General Serov, chief of the NKVD in Poland at that time.[17] As to the price that Piasecki paid for his head, there exist widely divergent views. According to the former high-ranking official of the Polish Ministry of Public Security who defected to the West in 1953, Józef Światło, "Piasecki became an agent of the NKVD" assigned "to subvert the Church from within." [18] According to the well-known Polish Catholic writer Stefan Kisielewski, to accuse Piasecki of being an agent is oversimplification, for his conceptions "although mistaken and dangerous" represent a genuine "ramification of Polish political thought." [19] Irrespective of which opinion is correct, it is safe to assume — as one of the best informed Western observers does — that "the agreement reached was not of the type concluded between a lower police official and a paid agent." [20] More complex political motives were clearly involved on both sides.

What were the motives which made Piasecki side with the Communists against the overwhelming trend of popular sentiments in Poland in 1945? His decision may be relatively easily attributed to sheer opportunism. There is little doubt that opportunism played an important part in Piasecki's offering his services to the Communists. The natural desire to save his life must have weighed heavily in his calculations. Moreover, Piasecki revealed early in his career that he burned with political ambition and that he was not particularly discriminating in selecting the means by which to promote his goals. He certainly was not a man who would easily turn down a chance to continue his political activities in postwar Poland. Yet, to attribute Piasecki's decision entirely to political opportunism does seem to be an oversimplification. An element of political realism was also present.* Piasecki, apparently at an early stage, came to the conclusion that Soviet rule over Poland was there to stay, and, consequently, that it would be necessary to cooperate with

* The two main exponents of political realism: Bocheński and Pruszyński, both became associated with the group centered around *Dziś i Jutro.*

the Russians.* Indeed, he was so impressed with Russian might that he seems to have been convinced of Soviet victory in the global conflict. "We are against America," proclaimed one of Piasecki's chief lieutenants, "because we think that she is going to be defeated in the forthcoming struggle. We are for Russia because we believe she is going to win. As Polish nationalists we choose our place in the camp which, in our opinion, must ultimately be victorious." [21]

What were the reasons which made the Communists accept his offer in spite of Piasecki's record? In 1945, the Polish Communists sought allies who could be effective in subverting the opposition, as long as they were not able to build a strong popular following of their own. Piasecki's group fell right into this category. It could appeal to some segments of nationalistically minded youth as well as to certain conservative elements in the country. At the same time, due to their entire background and, not the least, to the mysterious circumstances by which they had come into being, the progressivists were unlikely to gain broad popular support, and thus could not pose a threat to the Communist Party. Quite possibly, the original Communist plans with regard to Piasecki did not go beyond these short-term objectives. Once his loyalty was tested, however, he was given new tasks. The Communists certainly had no reason to be dissatisfied with Piasecki. If he was not their agent, he did his best to act like one.

The progressivists' big chance came to prove their usefulness to the Communist Party only in the very late forties. In the Church-State dispute, which flared at that time, the progressivists sided firmly with the State. At every stage of the prolonged struggle, whether it was the restriction of the Episcopate's charitable activities, the confiscation of the Church's property, the removal of religious instruction from the schools, or the campaign of intimidation against the clergy, the "progressive Catholics" supported the Communist government and denounced the hierarchy. They did not intend these tactics to cut themselves off from the Catholic community, however. On the contrary, on every occasion they loudly affirmed their allegiance to the Church, stressing that they merely opposed the "political" stand of its leaders. By 1953 when the persecution of the Church reached its climax, Pax in contrast, enjoyed the most prosperous period of its existence.

* According to the well-informed sources, Piasecki had an opportunity to flee to the West in 1946. He turned it down on the grounds that the activities of political exiles were doomed to failure, and that despite all the difficulties it was necessary to engage in political activity in Poland.

Side by side with their assault upon the organization of the Church, the progressivists began intruding into the body of Catholic doctrine. Piasecki in his book, "The Essential Problems," [22] and his followers in the articles published in the weekly *Dziś i Jutro,* expounded their creed:

Reversing the hierarchy of values [they] elevated the cause of the Revolution over the worship of God. Religion instead of being the most noble and sublime means for the achievement of salvation was to become an intentional measure of securing for the Church a temporal existence in the revolutionary world. Consequently, they required all Catholics including bishops and priests to use Catholicism as a source of inspiration for the building of socialism and to devote most of their time and energy to the realization of social and economic goals, determined by the atheistic leaders of the state.[23]

This stand could not be tolerated by the Church, and, consequently, on June 29, 1955 Piasecki's book and the weekly *Dziś i Jutro* were condemned by a decree of the Holy Office. The condemnation by no means discouraged the progressivists; on the contrary, it provided them with a pretext to close their ranks even further and intensify their efforts.

The "progressive Catholics" were handsomely rewarded for their services. An ingenious device was found to provide them with substantial financial means: in a Communist country the existence of a virtually capitalist concern was permitted. Pax's commercial and industrial undertakings, while retaining from a "legal point of view . . . the character of private companies," were given "almost every kind of nationalized enterprise privilege." [24] Above all, they were taxed as if they were not private but state enterprises. Thus, in 1956 Pax made "a one-hundred-million zloty profit, of which thirty-eight million were spent to cover the deficits of socio-political enterprises." [25]

At the same time the political importance of the progressivists grew steadily. With the suppression of other Catholic groups, they gained a monopoly on "representing" lay Catholics in Poland. In March 1953, when the last group of Catholic intellectuals which centered around the weekly *Tygodnik Powszechny* was disbanded their newspaper was handed over to Pax. With the mounting aressts among the members of the Episcopate, the progressivists moved to consolidate their hold over the clergy. In October 1953, a month after the imprisonment of Cardinal Wyszyński, ties were established with the pro-Communist regime organization of the so-called "priest-patriots." In July 1955, a few weeks after the publication of the decree of the Holy Office, the two organizations merged under leadership of the lay "progressive Catholics." It appeared, then, that Piasecki had obtained an instrument with which he could undertake to realize his political ambitions. In Pax circles rumors were circulating of "future participation in the government." [26]

Thus, by the middle fifties, a paradoxical political situation existed in Poland. With all other political movements either suppressed outright or at best on the decline, only two political groups — neither having broad popular basis in the country — remained on the Polish political scene. One was the Communist Party, committed to a materialistic outlook and the establishment of socialism. The other was Pax, ostensibly Catholic and led by a former fascist. What these two political groups had in common was their unconditional subservience to Russia. From among the Polish political movements and political leaders, Stalin, with his unsatiated zest for power, tolerated only those who unreservedly and, indeed, fervently carried out his orders. In such circumstances, of course, there existed no possibility of seeking a rational modus vivendi between Poland and Russia. The Soviet Communists like their tsarist predecessors were not really interested in co-operating with the Poles. They treated Poland simply as a Russian dependency.

6

THE TRIUMPH OF POLITICAL REALISM

THE UPHEAVAL OF 1956

Following Stalin's death, and especially after Khrushchev's accession to power, changes in both the foreign and domestic policies of the U.S.S.R. had far-reaching repercussions in the Communist-ruled states of East Europe. In the mid-1950's the impact of the new Soviet line proved to be most profound in Poland. As on many occasions in the past, the internal shift in Russia sparked significant political trends in Poland, culminating in the 1956 popular upheaval which was directed first against the Communist regime and, then, against the Soviet Union.[1]

The changes in Poland came slowly, indeed, more slowly than in some other countries in East Europe. Malenkov's "new course" exerted little influence over the policies of the Polish Communist regime. No significant loosening of the tight political and economic controls over the country was visible. Nor were there any unusual signs of unrest among the people. In the first post-Stalin years, the Stalinist system in Poland ostensibly remained intact.

Beneath the surface, however, important political changes were already incipient. The fall of Beria and the restricting of the role of the Soviet security apparatus had far-reaching impact upon the Polish security organs. Soon the role of the security apparatus in Poland was greatly reduced. The defection to the West at the end of 1953 of one of its high officials, Józef Światło, accelerated its decline. Western propaganda media made Światło's detailed information on Communist terror widely known in Poland, arousing anger among the people and spreading confusion among the Communists.[2] Thus, when the security apparatus was reorganized late in 1954, its powers were drastically curtailed. At the same time, some victims of Stalinist terror were released from prison. Among them was Władyslaw Gomułka, who had been spared from trial by the death of Stalin.*

In 1954, following the example of the Soviet Union, the Polish Communist regime somewhat relaxed its rigid control over literature. Throughout that year the "thaw" in Poland seemed easily confined within the limits prescribed by the Communist Party. Early in 1955, however, matters took a definite popular turn. The weakening of the terror apparatus emboldened the Polish writers, who began to openly criticize various aspects of the Communist political system. In August 1955 Adam Ważyk's celebrated "Poem for Adults," bitterly denouncing the grim reality of life in Poland, was published in *Nowa Kultura*,[3] climaxing the early phase of intellectual discontent. Spokesman for the Communist Party severely admonished Ważyk, but no other sanctions against him followed. The Communist regime failed to silence the Polish writers.

In 1955 the Soviet-Yugoslav *rapprochement* took place. The declaration issued at the May 1955 meeting of Khrushchev and Tito in Belgrade explicitly endorsed the principle that "questions of internal organization, or difference in social systems and of different forms of socialist construction, are solely the concern of the individual countries." [4] In the spring of 1956, as a gesture of Khrushchev's good will for Tito, the Cominform was disbanded. In June 1956 new talks between the two Communist leaders took place in Moscow, whereby the principle of "multiplicity of forms of socialist construction" was emphasized even more strongly.[5] The Polish Communists followed the Soviet lead. In October 1955 the theoretical journal of the Polish United Workers' Party reverted to Lenin's thesis that socialist construction in the different countries would take different roads. As an example of such a difference in Poland, they pointed to the slower collectivization of agriculture.[6] Another article written by a Politburo member, Jerzy Morawski, in March 1956, elaborated still further those Polish features of socialist construction that differed from Soviet practice. In addition to the previously underlined slower

---

* Various reasons why Gomułka escaped public trial, and thus, in all likelihood, execution have been suggested. The main reason, however, seems to be that the leaders of the Polish Communist Party well remembered Stalin's slaughter of their comrades in the late thirties and were by no means anxious to add new names to the list of his victims. Thus, they stalled Gomułka's trial under various pretexts until Stalin died, at which time the pressing of at least the criminal charges against the former Secretary-General was no longer necessary.

program of collectivization, the article singled out the unique relations of the Polish Communist government and the Catholic Church.[7] In the summer of 1956, contacts between Polish and Yugoslav Communists were revived.

In the meantime Khrushchev's de-Stalinization campaign, early in 1956, gave new impetus to the intellectual ferment in Poland. Now the "thaw" turned into a flood. Permission to criticize Stalin allowed the Poles to level sharp attacks at the Communist system. Repeated demands for its reform were publicly voiced. Encouraged by the example of the intellectuals, the masses became restive. Toward the end of June 1956 a workers' demonstration in Poznań turned into open revolt. The army suppressed the Poznań workers, but this failed to frighten the Polish people. On the contrary, in the summer, political unrest grew throughout the country.

The de-Stalinization campaign coincided with a serious internal crisis in the ranks of the Polish Communist Party. Bolesław Bierut died unexpectedly in March 1956. He was succeeded as the First-Secretary of the Polish United Workers' Party by Edward Ochab.* Ochab tried to steer a middle course at first: offering some concessions to the people while preserving intact tight Communist control over the country. Stalin's errors and crimes were now denounced and the specifically Polish characteristics of the social revolution underlined. No essential revision of Communist policies was undertaken, however. A few particularly compromised Communist leaders were removed from their posts, while Gomułka was openly cleared of any criminal responsibility. His political line, however, was still branded as erroneous. Ochab explicitly pointed out that Gomułka's "nationalist deviation," centered about a repudiation of Marxist internationalism, represented a betrayal of true Communist ideology.[8]

Whatever hopes Ochab might have had of appeasing the Polish people by these half-hearted measures were rudely dispersed by the workers' outburst in Poznań. Faced with the mounting tension throughout the country, the Communist Party was clearly thrown off balance. Its leadership proved to be divided and weak. "Differences in the party leadership," subsequently admitted one of its members, "were so profound that they paralyzed

---

* Ochab, born in 1906, joined the Communist Party in 1926. Before the war, he was active in spreading unrest among the workers, and in the late thirties spent several years in prison on charges of subversive activities. During the war, he was in the Soviet Union, where he became the deputy chief in charge of political education of the Polish army under Soviet command in 1943. In the late forties he occupied various governmental posts in Poland. In 1950 he became one of the secretaries of the Central Committee of the Polish United Workers' Party and concentrated his attention exclusively on party affairs. In 1948 he became a deputy member and in 1951 a full member of the Politburo.

authority, spread confusion and hesitation."[9] The Polish United Workers' Party split into two factions over the issue of coping with the existing crisis. The first wing, which eventually crystallized into the so-called "Natolin faction,"[10] advocated stern measures for suppressing the opposition. The second wing supported the carrying out of at least some genuine reforms within the existing system as a means of striking at the root of popular discontent. At a meeting of the Central Committee of the Polish United Workers' Party held in July 1956, when Ochab and also Cyrankiewicz added the weight of their prestige to the scales, the second wing prevailed. The entire party line was reappraised and revised. It was decided not to use harsh sanctions against the workers imprisoned during the Poznań revolt. An extensive program of political as well as economic reforms, aimed at what was described as the "democratization" of life in the country, was adopted.[11]

At this point, however, even the basic revisions of the Communist Party program failed to calm the country. Emboldened by the wavering at the top, the masses pressed for further concessions. The program of popular reform was never formulated with a great degree of precision. It was an ad hoc political platform whose separate fragments were advanced by dispersed segments of Polish society. Its authors were the students and the workers, the intellectuals and the peasants, who openly voiced their complaints against the Communist system at countless spontaneous meetings and in the various discussion clubs which instantly sprang up, especially clubs of young intelligentsia and Catholic intelligentsia.* Its exponents were political writers, ranging from fervent Marxists to orthodox Catholics, who aired the grievances of the people in the press, searched for their sources, and suggested remedies. In the various spheres of life and throughout the different parts of the country, of course, the demands for reforms were expressed in manifold ways. What they all had in common, however, was the desire on the part of the masses to restrict the Communist monopoly of power and to increase the people's share in the government of the country.

At this stage, above all, the people demanded a change in the party leadership to prove the sincerity of the new line. "The nation expects from the party," observed a prominent Communist, "not only a new program of action, but also such changes in part leadership . . . which would guarantee

* The most famous of the discussion clubs was the Club of the Crooked Circle in Warsaw, in which many leading Polish intellectuals participated. For the review of the club's activities in 1956 by one of its participants, see Witold Jedlicki, "The Club of the Crooked Circle," *East Europe*, June 1963.

that the adopted program will be realized with full energy." [12] The people next demanded that Gomułka return to power. Under the existing conditions this was a natural reaction. Here was a Communist leader uncompromised by a complicity in the Stalinist system — who had opposed it to the extent of risking his political career, and, indeed, his life. What better safeguard against the return to Stalinist practices could be found, the Poles asked themselves, than placing Gomułka at the helm of the Communist Party?

Gomułka's return to power, then, acquired symbolic dimensions in Poland. His restoration to the post of First Secretary of the Polish United Workers' Party became identified with the overcoming of all past evil. Consequently, Gomułka was given a resounding endorsement by the masses, whose enthusiasm bordered on hero worship. "There was an enthusiastic, irrationally enthusiastic support of all [the people] for Gomułka," a prominent Polish sociologist retrospectively observed. "Few people listened to what Gomułka actually said. All of them placed their hopes in him and expected their fulfillment." [13] Faced with this situation, the party leaders, recognizing that short of civil war there was no way to overcome the crisis, acceded to the popular demands. Early in August Gomułka was readmitted to the membership in the Polish United Workers' Party, and soon also to the highest party council. Preparations were undertaken for his reinstatement as First Secretary at the meeting of the Central Committee scheduled for October 19, 1956.

The drastic shift in the course of the Polish United Workers' Party in mid-1956 was significant not only because Polish Communists were genuinely striving to meet popular demands half-way, but also because they did so without the encouragement and, indeed, against the explicit wishes of Moscow. If the policy changes introduced by the Polish Communist Party in the spring still closely followed the Soviet pattern, those adopted in the summer did not. On the contrary, they moved in an opposite direction to the Soviet line, which was once again hardening by early summer. Toward the end of June, the Russians, frightened by the forces which they had released in East Europe — notably, the workers' outburst in Poznań — decided to restrict the scope of de-Stalinization. The Soviet Communist Party issued a declaration defining the limits of criticism of Stalin, and even stressing some of his achievements. [14] The differences between Polish and Soviet Communist Party policies came into the open during Bulganin's visit to Poland in the second half of July. Bulganin publicly warned the Poles against letting de-Stalinization be used to undermine the foundations of the Communist political system.[15] Ignoring the Russian advice, however, the Polish Communists proceeded to adopt a program of extensive reform. The Polish Communist Party, for the first time in its history, revealed a mind of its own.

In response, the Russian Communist leaders decided to resort to direct intervention. On October 19, 1956, the day of the meeting of the Central Committee of the Polish United Workers' Party, a delegation from the Communist Party of the Soviet Union, including Khrushchev, Molotov, Mikoyan, and Kaganovich, unexpectedly arrived in Warsaw. The Russians were motivated, reported one of the Polish Communist leaders, by their "deep anxiety . . . over the developments in Poland."[16] At the appearance of the Soviet delegation, the meeting of the Central Committee was interrupted to allow a group of Polish Communist leaders, headed by Ochab but including Gomułka, to negotiate with the Russians. The debate between the Poles and the Russians, "was not infrequently temperamental on both sides."[17] At the same time Soviet troops began to move toward the Polish capital.[18] Immediately Polish units, commanded by one of Gomułka's followers, General Wacław Komar, took up positions outside the city. Workers and students in Warsaw were alerted and armed. Poland's capital was once again on the verge of a bloodbath.

In 1956, however, Warsaw and, indeed, Poland were spared another desperate military struggle. On October 20th the Soviet leaders left Warsaw, postponing a settlement of the controversial issues until some future date. At the same time the Russian forces withdrew to their bases without incident. The meeting of the Central Committee of the Polish Communist Party was resumed. The program of reforms was affirmed and Władysław Gomułka was elected First Secretary of the Polish United Workers' Party. For the first time in recent history, instead of plunging into an abyss of uprising, defeat, and even worse oppression, the Poles managed to win substantial political concessions from the Russians by peaceful means.

THE NATURE OF THE "POLISH OCTOBER" *

Internal as well as external political factors contributed to the changes in Poland in 1956. The dissatisfaction with many socioeconomic measures of the Communist regime, of course, was prominent. As is traditional in

---

* To emphasize the revolutionary nature of the upheaval in Poland in 1956, the Poles labeled it the "Polish October," in parallel to the Bolshevik revolution in Russia in October 1917. As far as this writer can ascertain, the term originated with two young Marxist journalists, Ryszard Turski and Eligiusz Lasota, who used it as a title of a leading article in *Po prostu* of October 28, 1956.

Polish politics, however, it did not represent the crucial issue. The Polish people did not seem to seriously question the generally socialist character of Poland's socioeconomic system. What they opposed was that socialization in Poland had blindly followed the Soviet pattern rather than a pattern based on Polish needs. The aim of the popular upheaval, then, was not merely to correct the particularly objectionable features of the existing socioeconomic system, but rather to strike at their roots, which in the eyes of the Poles was the subjugation of their country to Russia.* "In the first place," a Polish writer declared in 1956, "the ferment in our country is not a result of economic difficulties, but a sudden outburst of long suppressed national dignity." [19]

The essentially nationalist as opposed to socioeconomic character of the "Polish October" was confirmed by the significant role played by foreign policy. At two crucial stages, in its origin and at its outcome, the Polish upheaval was decisively affected by her relations with Russia. The initial political changes in Poland were influenced by the developments in the Soviet Union, above all, by the launching of Khrushchev's de-Stalinization campaign early in 1956. By mid-1956, primarily under the impact of the Poznań revolt, political processes in Poland had acquired a momentum of their own. The reforms which the Poles proposed under the guise of de-Stalinization far exceeded those undertaken in Russia. And with the direct intervention of the U.S.S.R. in the fall of 1956, once again the external factor became of paramount importance. The reforms in Poland could not be carried out without a successful defiance of the Soviet leaders first. This step meant a decisive change in the pattern of Polish-Soviet relations. In the last analysis, it signified that, at least to some degree, Poland had regained its independence from Russia.

Since the primary objective of the "Polish October" was shaking off the yoke from the East, it might appear upon a cursory survey to fall in line with the romantic tradition. Indeed, at various stages, the upheaval in 1956 came quite close to turning into an armed uprising against Russia.** Had the latter

---

* The outburst in Poznań, which originated as a wage dispute, also had strongly anti-Soviet overtones. The workers' slogans were not only "We want bread and freedom" and "Down with Communism" but also "Down with the Russians."

** In two stages, at least, the Poles were only a hairsbreadth from engaging in a battle with the Russians. The first stage, of course, was in the middle of October when Soviet troops moved across the country toward Warsaw. The slightest incident then could have sparked a military conflict. The second stage came early in November, when a wave of sympathy for the Hungarians, traditionally linked to the Poles by firm bonds of friendship, spread throughout the country. The situation in Poland, then, was openly described as "having reached a boiling point." Radio Warsaw, November 7, 1956.

come about, in all probability developments in Poland would have been similar to those in Hungary. The battle in Poland would have been fiercer and longer and its consequences in the international sphere more serious. It could even have sparked a general uprising against Soviet rule in East Europe which would have had grave international consequences. However, the final outcome would have been the same as in Hungary.* A Communist regime dependent on the Soviet Union and openly based on coercion would have been restored in Warsaw as it was in Budapest.** Thus, potential human losses and suffering aside, a resort to military struggle would have been devoid of any purpose. It could only have worsened, not improved, the lot of the Polish nation. Apparently realizing this, the Poles stopped short of a revolution. Indeed, despite fierce agitation in 1956, violence erupted very infrequently. Except for the riots in Poznań, no blood was shed.

Refraining from armed struggle, however, was only one of the features that distinguished the upheaval in 1956 from romanticism. The other, also strikingly in contrast with positions held at least since World War I, was the moderation which the Poles revealed in their political goals. They abandoned the "attitude of insisting on everything or nothing, and showed a surprising spirit of compromise, in this part of the world usually attrib-

---

* Apart from the sheer law of numbers which would have made suppression in Poland a more complex military operation than in Hungary, at least two other elements were involved. First, since many Polish military units were commanded by officers who supported Gomułka (notably the Corps of Internal Security commanded by General Komar), the Russians would have been opposed by the regular Polish forces from the very outset in the event of conflict. Second, since Soviet troops, in all likelihood, would also have had to be moved from the west to suppress the Poles an uprising in Poland could have sparked unrest in East Germany. This, in turn, could have led to the entanglement of West Germany and, thus, NATO. It was exactly in order to prevent such a chain reaction that an American newsman in Warsaw, Mr. Leslie Bain, advised caution to the Poles. "In a conversation (quite formal) with one of the members of the Executive of the Polish Union of Journalists . . . Leslie Bain declared: 'You have to appraise the situation in a realistic fashion; any conflict could end in a disaster. In case of conflict the United States would not risk one soldier in Poland's defense. Tell this to the people who need to know . . .'" Quoted in 6 lat temu (Paris, 1962), p. 8. It is interesting to observe how closely the advice given to the Poles by Mr. Bain in 1956 followed that which had been given to them in 1948 by another American friend of theirs, former Ambassador to Poland, Arthur Bliss-Lane. "The most grievous error," Bliss-Lane wrote, "that the Polish people could commit would be to attempt to overthrow the regime by force . . . such an attempt, doomed to be abortive in the face of overwhelming physical power, would give justification to the Soviet government to overrun Poland under the pretext of restoring order. This would render impossible, for many years, fulfillment of any hope for Polish independence." I Saw Poland Betrayed (Indianapolis, 1948), pp. 307–308.

** The Russians, of course, would have had no trouble in finding in Poland Communists ready to endorse Soviet military intervention in exchange for being placed in power in the country. Indeed, the Natolin faction, as was openly pointed out by its opponents, counted on precisely such an outcome of events in Poland.

uted only to the Czechs."[20] In the first post-Stalin years the Poles moved carefully. They exploited developments in the Soviet Union to alleviate Communist oppression, but abstained from a comprehensive program of reforms. It was only when, in the spring of 1956, several advantageous events coincided that the Polish people embarked upon a bolder course. Yet, even in the autumn, when the ferment in the country was at its peak, popular demands showed a great deal of self-restraint. The Poles pressed for freedom from Russian interference in their domestic affairs, but did not propose to drastically change their foreign policy. No move was made toward withdrawing from the Soviet bloc. They urged far-reaching reforms in the existing political system but did not attempt to revise its essence by removing the Communist Party from power. Indeed, to borrow the sparkling phrase of Ernst Halperin, the Poles did their best to camouflage their democratic aspirations under the cloak of totalitarianism.[21]

In its early stages the "Polish October" resembled the revolt against Russia in 1863. In both cases there was a loosening of Russian control over Poland following the death of a tyrant which resulted in steadily mounting demands for further concessions on the part of the Poles. The authorities wavered in the same fashion when confronted with popular pressure for reform. Last but not least, there were equally remote prospects for Poland's success should the situation get out of hand. Yet, in 1863, these events culminated in an insurrection, while in 1956 they did not.

To a large extent the difference in leadership was responsible for the different outcome. The Polish Communists did not, as had Wielopolski, make the mistake of alienating the population by harshness and arrogance. At the height of the turmoil, they refrained from resorting to drastic measures which could have only intensified tension, thus increasing the chances of a popular outbreak. On the contrary, they skillfully identified themselves with popular demands, even though this involved the risk of defying Moscow's will. In this manner, the Communist leaders retained an over-all control of political changes in the country and managed to steer away from any extreme expression of popular sentiment.

Adroit leadership combined with a still more important element to prevent the revolution incipient in 1956. The fact is that Wielopolski's program had been strikingly out of tune with the mood of the country, whereas the Communist program was not. In 1863 political idealism had predominated in Poland, while in 1956 political realism had prevailed.

THE RISE OF NEOPOSITIVISM

When, after several mute years, popular sentiment in Poland became articulate again in the late fifties it differed basically from what it had been in the late forties. A profound change had taken place in the political outlook of the Polish people during the intermediate decade. The spirit of militant resistance to Russian rule, ignoring the patent power discrepancy between the two nations, was gone. Also gone was the optimistic belief, disregarding the balance of power in international politics, in assistance from the West. The Poles had become more sober in appraising their position vis-à-vis the Soviet Union and in evaluating their situation in the international sphere. In short, political realism clearly was once again in the ascendancy in Poland.

The shift from political idealism toward political realism which occurred in the 1950's was accelerated by the conditions similar to those responsible for the rise of positivism in the 1870's. As in the past, now also, three major elements could be distinguished as influencing this trend. These were: revulsion against military struggle, aftermath of a crushing defeat; disillusionment with the West; and reemergence of the German threat.

The realization of the tremendous losses they had suffered during World War II led to the revulsion against military struggle. This was manifest in various ways. First of all, the Poles became extremely aware of their vulnerable geographic position. They were conscious of the fact that any major conflict in Europe would be bound to engulf their country, exposing them to new losses and sufferings. The destructive potential inherent in a modern military conflict made such a prospect even more repugnant. Thus, a genuine fear of war existed in Poland. These sentiments were astutely described by a Polish-Canadian journalist who visited the country in 1959:

> The nightmare of war is still very much present in all of Poland. It is difficult to find a place which does not bear some direct or indirect scar of the military operations. Nothing is pronounced here with greater fear than war . . . I have not met anybody, including the most embittered and unhappy people, opposed to the existing social and political system, who attach any hope to war. On the contrary, they strongly, though not without resignation, stressed that if basic changes can be accomplished only through war, then the attempts to bring them about should be given up.[22]

The Poles also lost faith in their ability to protect their independence by their own military strength. They were well aware that no matter how strong the Polish army might be, it could not by itself defend the country against an attack from either one of Poland's more powerful neighbors. Indeed, Poland's entire military tradition was subjected to shattering criticism. In the late fifties, the soldierly virtues of honor and heroism, which had been widely respected in the interwar period, were derided in the satirical theaters of Warsaw. Audiences applauded as pathetic lancers charged to meet their death on the stage of the students' cabaret "Stodoła." The belief in moral strength and the readiness to sacrifice one's life in defense of the country were sneered at in the press. "Our predecessors," declared an article written by two young writers, "used to die willingly and deftly for the homeland. They were stupid and ridiculous fools." [23]

The decline of militarism in Poland was also reflected in the greatly reduced prestige of the armed forces among the people. In terms of social prestige, army officers, who had been highly respected in the interwar period, were now one of the lowest rated professions.[24] Uniforms were looked down upon in Poland. Even the younger generation, traditionally under the strong spell of the military, lost the taste for it. A prominent Polish writer depicted the attitude of Polish youth:

> Our youth is sensitive to clothing and likes to change it. Yet . . . there is no attempt to wear any uniforms, everything is thoroughly civilian . . . The uniforms have no fascination now.[25]

Wartime underground experiences were reexamined in a critical light. In particular, the disastrous Warsaw uprising of 1944 was subject to censure. Although the memory of the fallen soldiers was revered throughout the country, the purpose of the uprising was widely questioned. Critical studies discussing both the political and military aspects of the uprising written by two former high-ranking officers in the underground, were published in the late fifties.[26] At least the major thesis of these writers, that the Warsaw insurrection had been ill-conceived, seemed to be shared by a majority of the Poles, including a large number of former members of the underground. This attitude was described by a young university teacher, who himself had participated in the upheaval, in conversation reported by an American visitor to Warsaw:

> Although he is anything but pro-Russian, he was not critical of the Russians for failing to intervene. He thought they recognized that the uprising was designed to anticipate them and was in a sense directed against them. Therefore, they had a right to keep their hands off. By contrast, he was critical of what he characterized as the romantic strategic concepts of the London Poles who

believed that such a seizure of power would give them a position of strength against the Russians.[27]

Last but not least, the Poles seemed to abandon revolutionary and conspiratorial methods of opposing the Communist regime. Scattered underground groups had persisted in Poland into the early fifties. By 1956 they apparently had dispersed, for no evidence whatsoever existed to indicate that underground organizations had participated in the turbulent events of that year. As easy as it would have been for even a small conspiratorial group to channel the sentiments of the masses into a revolutionary mood at that stage, no such attempts were made. The outbreak in Poznań in June 1956 and the demonstrations in the various Polish cities throughout October and November of the same year were quite spontaneous.[28]

In the 1950's as in the 1870's a strong feeling of disillusionment with the West existed in Poland. In the early fifties many Poles still believed that the West and the United States, in particular, would eventually gain sufficient influence in Central Eastern Europe to assist them in shaking off the yoke from the East. The bellicose atmosphere prevailing in world politics at the time of the Korean War had seemed to support the view that the outbreak of a major conflict was imminent. The death of Stalin and the subsequent lessening of international tensions greatly undermined this expectation. At the same time, the hopes placed in the American policy of peaceful liberation, enunciated by the Republican Party upon its succession to power in 1952, gradually dwindled. The inability of the United States to score any success in Eastern Europe, dramatically underlined by the outcome of the upheaval in East Germany in 1953, and, especially, by the fate of the Hungarian uprising in 1956,* dealt a heavy blow to political calculations based on the hope of Western aid. As a result, a general disillusionment with the West pervaded Poland. This was emphasized by a competent and, incidentally, strongly pro-Western observer:

There exists in Poland general and profound embitterment with the West . . . Having no possibility of appraising the international situation in an objective fashion, the people for a long time could not believe that they were left to their own fate. They were angered and irritated by the propagandistic speeches, but

* The failure of the West to come to the assistance of Hungary was openly exploited by Polish Communists to weaken the appeal of the opposition. "Let us remember," declared the theoretical journal of the Polish United Workers' Party, on the eve of the elections in January 1957, "that at the time of the Hungarian tragedy the foreign radio stations appealed for reason and restraint on the part of the Poles. The reactionary forces in Poland which would like to spread disorder ought to know that the Americans are reluctant to shed their blood." *Nowe Drogi,* January 1957, p. 48.

still awaited the facts which would substantiate their faith. The passive attitude of the Western great powers toward the Soviet military intervention in Hungary brought an end to this.[29]

The decline of the faith in Western political intervention in East Europe made many Poles feel that the United States was generally on the defensive in the global conflict with the Soviet Union. The technical strides of the U.S.S.R., as well as their political advances, in the early stages of Khrushchev's era had a considerable impact in Poland. Paradoxically, this was only intensified by the fact that the reverses of the West ran contrary to the wishes of the Poles, and, therefore, were received in a highly emotional manner. Thus, the news of the launching of the Sputnik by the Soviets was at first discounted by many Poles as Communist propaganda, but brought about an outburst of indignation at the Americans when confirmed.[30] Similarly, when the U-2 incident was revealed, it resulted in irritation with the Americans, not because they had carried out the aerial reconnaissance, but because it ended in such a fiasco.[31] Likewise, Gagarin's space flight was viewed in Warsaw not only as a Soviet success, but also as an American defeat.[32] All in all, American prestige in Poland seemed to have deteriorated markedly. This trend was pictured, though in a somewhat exaggerated form, by an American observer in Warsaw:

The United States is viewed [by the Poles] as a harried and futile King Canute commanding the Soviet seas to recede. Any successes it scores in the international conflict are usually dismissed as convulsive and abortive attempts to stem the tide. Any Socialist offenses have the sanction of inevitability . . . In this respect, if there is a significant difference of outlook between Party functionaries and overt anti-communist Poles it is not readily apparent.[33]

Paralleling the decline of the faith in the assistance from the West, the influence of the political leaders who remained abroad, although they still retained considerable moral authority, among the Polish people also diminished.[34] Various factors contributed to this process. The relative isolation of the emigrés estranged them from the Polish people.* The passage of years,

* The major means of communication between the political exiles and the people in Poland has been the radio and, particularly, the station sponsored by the American Committee for Free Europe, which since 1952 has broadcast to Poland from West Germany for eighteen hours a day. In 1955–1956 the Free Europe Committee also engaged in the dissemination of leaflets carried by balloons from West Germany to Poland. Almost fourteen million such leaflets were delivered before the operation came to an end when it was felt that it no longer served any purpose in October 20, 1956. A considerable influence among the Polish intellectuals, particularly in the immediate post-1956 years, was exercised by the emigré literary and political monthly, *Kultura,* published in Paris, but circulating in fairly large quantities throughout Poland.

inevitably turning exiled leaders more and more into figures of the past, exacted its heavy toll. The eternal plague of all political refugees, bickering over issues no longer relevant, reduced their authority among the Poles. Yet, above all, the fiasco of their political program, based on the classic concepts of political romanticism, cut away at the influence of the emigrés in Poland. Once it became evident that any military intervention by the West on behalf of Poland was not going to take place the major pillar supporting their political calculations shattered. Growing realization of this, in turn, only led to further quarreling and disintegration among the various exile groups.* A prominent Polish political writer abroad summed up developments among the emigrés in the following words: "We failed to evolve new political concepts. At first we counted upon war and returning home. When most of us in the back of our minds lost the hope of returning [to Poland] a crisis and breakdown ensued." [35]

Last but not least in the 1950's, as in the 1870's, the Poles were greatly concerned with the rise of German power. One of the major reasons for the unrelenting military struggle against Soviet rule in the late forties had been that Germany, weakened as a result of its defeat in World War II, could no longer pose a threat to Poland. Thus, at that time, for all practical purposes, Poland had had only one enemy. With the revival of the economic and military strength of West Germany and its reemergence in international politics as a prominent member in the Western alliance, the entire picture radically changed.

Undoubtedly there existed a tendency among the Poles to overestimate the German danger. This is by no means surprising. The memories of Nazi brutalities were still very much alive in Poland, and they will probably remain so as long as the generation which went through the gruesome experiences of the war is alive. Yet, this was only a part of the problem. The other

---

* In the late forties, and in the early fifties the political exiles split into three groups. The death of its president, Władysław Raczkiewicz in 1947 was followed by a split in the Polish Government-in-Exile in London. Eventually two opposing groups crystallized: the first retaining the name of the Government-in-Exile, headed by August Zaleski; and the second assuming the name of the Council of National Unity and enjoying the support of the majority of political leaders, including General Władysław Anders and, also, although not formally, of General Kazimierz Sosnkowski. In the late forties, after his escape from Poland, a separate political group was formed by Stanisław Mikołajczyk in Washington.

The changes in Poland in the mid-fifties resulted in further splits among the Polish emigrés. Serious differences over the political program demanded by the new situation were revealed in all three groups. Indeed, a few exiled political leaders, notably, Stanisław Mackiewicz, a prominent political writer and a former premier of the Government-in-Exile, renounced opposition to the Communist regime and returned home.

part was that the Germans provided the Poles with genuine reason for concern. It was not only that the government of the German Federal Republic refused to recognize the border along the Oder-Neisse as final, but a noisy campaign for its revision was conducted, frequently with the tacit approval of prominent German political leaders, by refugee organizations. Coupled with the revival of German military power, and especially the prospect of West German nuclear forces, these facts acquired alarming dimensions in Polish eyes.

The maintenance of the present border with Germany, however, was regarded by the Poles as literally a matter of life and death. They realized that to take away from Poland almost one third of her territory with roughly one fourth of her population and close to one third of her industrial production would be disastrous. Of course, the eight million people living in the western provinces — about half of whom had been born there and one quarter of whom had come from the prewar eastern territories acquired by the U.S.S.R. — would resent remaining under German rule, and, yet, they would have virtually no place to go. They could not possibly be absorbed in the central provinces. Their forcible transfer there — all the human suffering involved apart — would bring about an impossible population pressure on scarce resources, with crippling effects upon the entire Polish economy.

The realization of the utmost importance of the western territories for Poland was coupled with a psychological element of profound importance, which can be understood only against the background of Poland's unhappy recent history. Paradoxically, this factor was of even greater significance for the non-Communist than for the Communist Poles. In the eyes of non-Communists, Poland's sole gain in World War II had been the recovery of her ancient lands from Germany. Viewed in this light, the maintenance of the Polish border along the Oder-Neisse rivers acquired for them an intensely emotional significance. It symbolized that Poland was on the victorious side in the war and that its tremendous losses had not been in vain. German refusal to recognize the existing frontier as final was regarded as denial by the Germans of their own defeat and evidence that they still harbored aggressive designs on Poland. By the same token, the American refusal to recognize the Polish-German border until the conclusion of a peace treaty with Germany was viewed as a tacit support of German claims and as an ultimate betrayal by the Americans of their World War II alliance with Poland.

Needless to say, the fact that the Polish western border was not recognized as final by the United States, while it was upheld by the Soviet Union, provided the Communist regime with a persuasive argument for Poland's close bonds with the camp of socialism. Viewed from this angle, Poland's alignment with Russia became a genuine means of protecting Polish national interests. The significance of this fact was aptly expressed by a British writer on Poland:

The Oder-Neisse frontier is the key to Polish foreign politics. It is the tie which binds Poland to Russia, since only the Communist states have recognized this frontier. Even if Gomulka were a conservative, he would still be tied to Russia until such time as the Oder-Neisse frontiers are universally accepted, especially by the Germans.[36]

The existence of the Polish-German dispute was not without some advantage to the Communist regime in Poland. By assuming the mantle of defenders of Polish national interests against the German threat, the Communists greatly enhanced their prestige among the Poles. Consequently, there is little doubt that the German danger was emphasized and re-emphasized not only for the sake of external but also of internal policies.* Yet, to regard the policies of the Polish government vis-à-vis Germany as merely an attempt to divert the attention of the Polish people from domestic problems by creating a bogey of German revisionism would be a mistake. The problem went far beyond its propaganda aspect and touched upon the very core of the complex political situation in Poland. On the one hand, the Polish Communists were guided by a mixture of ideological and patriotic motives with regard to the German issue. On the other hand, many Poles who rejected Communist ideology supported the regime's policies toward Germany wholeheartedly. Indeed, with respect to the border dispute with Germany, the stand taken by the Communist government was endorsed by virtually all non-Communist Poles.**

---

* On October 24, 1956, the very day when the Soviet tanks went into action in Budapest, Gomułka, in a speech at a mass rally in Warsaw, and Cyrankiewicz, in an exposé before the Parliament, both strongly stressed the necessity of preserving Poland's alliance with the Soviet Union so as to defend Poland's western border against German revisionism. *Trybuna Ludu*, October 25, 1956.

** There exist several organizations which provide a means for close cooperation between non-Communist Poles and the Communist government in upholding Poland's rights to her western territories. These are the Western Institute in Poznań, the Western Press Agency in Poznań and Warsaw, and the Society for the Development of the Western Territories, with a network all over the country. It is interesting to note that the first two organizations originated during World War II as integral parts of the non-Communist underground and came into the open only in 1945. As such, they represent the only branches of the wartime underground

The existence of virtual unanimity between the Communist regime and the Polish nation over the German problem introduced a novel element into the political picture in Poland. After several years of almost complete estrangement, in at least one sphere, a meeting ground was found between the Communist government and the Polish people. Poland's policy toward Germany, however, is not an ordinary issue in Polish politics but the one which, more than anything else, has traditionally determined Poland's stand in international politics. The endorsement by the Polish people of the Communist government's stand vis-à-vis Germany, thus, was largely tantamount to its winning popular support for the major course of foreign policy.[37] Furthermore, taking into account the paramount role which foreign policy has always played in Poland, the agreement over her external relations has also had far-reaching repercussions in internal politics. Its over-all effect was a significant lessening of tensions within the country. Indeed, there seems to be little doubt that widespread approval of the Communist policy toward Germany contributed more than anything else to the evaporation of the spirit of militant opposition in Poland. The German problem, wrote a Polish-Canadian journalist after visiting the country in 1965, "on one hand neutralized the indifference or even the enmity toward the system . . . and on the other hand enabled [the Communist regime] to gain at first, confidence, and then, support of the people." [38]

Under the combined impact of various historical forces, among which reemergence of Germany played the foremost role, a profound shift occurred in the political outlook of the Poles in the fifties. The Polish nation once again embraced political realism. In numerous conversations held by an American journalist with Poles in 1957, he was told that they considered themselves as realists. "We know," they emphasized in the tone of the nineteenth-century positivists, that "we must rely on ourselves alone." [39] This was made even more explicit in a report from Poland by an astute British journalist in 1962. Poland, he wrote, "is now a nation interested only in

---

which have managed to continue the same work and, incidentally, to some extent have even preserved the same personnel.

An interesting unanimity also exists between the Communist government and the anti-Communist exiles abroad with respect to the German problem. A quarterly review, *Poland and Germany,* published by the emigré Centre on Polish-German Affairs in London, is as much in favor of the existing border as the most militant publications in Poland. A prominent member of the Council of National Unity, Mr. Jerzy Zdziechowski, even resigned from that body in 1959 to assume the editorship of a quarterly, *Cahiers Pologne-Allemagne,* published until 1964 in Paris, in which articles dealing with the German problem by exiles and by writers from Poland appeared side by side.

survival; a nation once famous for mad gestures and the elegant approach to death now conducts as severely practical a policy as any in history . . . [The Poles] are sober rather than high spirited in their approach to foreign affairs. Their diagnosis is as sophisticated and unemotional as that of any surgeon refusing to operate . . . Poland's position in the Russian orbit is accepted with cold realism." [40]

PART II

Political Realism and Communism

It is difficult to find another nation in the world which is so sensitive to its independence and sovereignty as Poland. The ten centuries-old tradition of the Polish state and over a century of foreign oppression are responsible for this national characteristic.

— Władysław Gomułka, 1956

Since World War II a significant change in the opinions of the Poles has taken place. This change is the victory of political realism. It means the end of illusions, the end of myths, and the end of Hamlet-like foreign policy.

— Stanisław Stomma, 1961

7

GOMUŁKA'S POLITICAL PROGRAM

The "Polish October" ended in an uneasy truce. The Russians abstained from trying to reestablish their direct rule over Poland by military intervention, while the Poles refrained from armed uprising in an attempt to shatter all Russian influence over their country. Open clash was averted, but the conflicting interests remained. Each side still hoped to improve its position through peaceful means. On the one hand, especially after the Hungarian revolution, Soviet policy toward Communist-ruled countries in East Europe hardened. Late in 1956 Soviet and Chinese theoreticians once again stressed the necessity for similar internal development in all socialist countries and emphasized the role played by the Soviet experience in mapping the direction of such development, although the existence of some individual differences among the Communist countries was not completely denied. Under the guise of preserving the unity of the socialist camp, the Russians were clearly striving to restrict the scope of internal change in Poland. On the other hand, many Poles became intoxicated with the freedom which they had not tasted for many years. Toward the end of 1956 and early in 1957, they continued their harsh criticism of the past and put forward bold proposals for reform. Under the cover of de-Stalinization, the Polish people endeavored to push the changes in their country even beyond those concessions that had been won already from the Communist regime.

The Polish United Workers' Party headed by Władysław Gomułka stood in the center of the Polish-Russian tug-of-war, caught between international Communism's ideological strictures and Polish national aspirations. The party, however, in Gomułka's own words, was "weak like a convalescent after grave illness." [1] It commanded no authority among the people. Gomułka was virtually its sole political asset.

In these circumstances Gomułka's own political program became the focal point of Polish politics. It was, above all, his task to preserve the uneasy balance between Poland and Russia, and, if possible, turn it into a more lasting accommodation. His program closely reflected his position as a mediator in the Polish-Soviet dispute. Like ancient Janus, it faced both ways. It appealed to the Poles in the pragmatic terms of political realism. It addressed the Russians in the doctrinaire language of Marxism-Leninism.

POLITICAL REALISM

Following his return to power in 1956, Gomułka revealed himself much more openly as a political realist than he had in the middle forties. He still occasionally praised the revolutionary struggles of the Polish working class against tsarist oppression as well as those of the Polish Workers' Party against the Nazis; as a whole, however, he no longer accented the Communist movement's connection with political idealism. On the contrary, he bitterly denounced the policies of the movements which had adhered to romanticism as muddled, and strongly stressed the sobriety of political programs espoused by the Communist Party of Poland and its successors.

In a fashion resembling that of the Cracow historical school, Gomułka took a critical approach toward Poland's past. He was not satisfied with attributing Poland's misfortunes solely to the impact of outside forces but believed that the Poles themselves contributed to the unhappy course of their history. "The reasons for our national tragedies," he exclaimed, "should not be sought only in the activities of foreign states. They were also rooted, and perhaps even mainly, in the weakness of Poland, the weakness caused . . . by her disastrous domestic and foreign policies." [2]

Gomułka's criticism of Poland's past, of course, was primarily directed at her romantic policies in the interwar period and during World War II. He never tired of denouncing the Piłsudskiites' foreign policy and was particularly critical of their attempts at balancing between Germany and Russia. In his opinion, this had led first to Poland's cooperation with Nazi Germany; and, then, when this policy had failed to appease Hitler, to Poland's alignment with France and England. And Gomułka, following in the footsteps of the early political realists, strongly objected to linking Poland's fortunes with distant Western powers, sarcastically labelled by him as a "moon alliance." [3] The policy of relying on assistance from France and Britain in 1939 had represented such an alliance because Poland had not been protected from the German attack either politically or militarily. At that time, "anyone who appraised the situation in a realistic fashion," Gomułka asserted, "had no illusions about the value of Poland's alliance treaties with France and England . . . There was no doubt that in the event of war against Germany, the Western powers would not render assistance to Poland." [4]

In Gomułka's eyes, the cardinal error of Poland's interwar policy was to ignore the importance of an alliance with neighboring Russia. This "grew from the essential political concepts of the Piłsudskiites' movement. It was, in fact, a continuation of the anti-Soviet policy which brought about the expedition to Kiev in 1920." [5] Poland's hostility toward Russia, Gomułka claimed, was deeply damaging, for it "needed an alliance and friendship with the Soviet Union just as it is necessary to breathe air to live." [6] An alliance with Russia, unlike the alignment with the West European powers, could have effectively protected her from Hitler's Germany.

Gomułka explained that Poland

could have been saved from the German aggression or she could have secured her victory in a war against Germany only through a defensive alignment with the Soviet Union. This most vital necessity for the Polish nation, however, was ignored by the ruling [Piłsudskiites] as well as the leaders of the rightist opposition parties.[7]

Poland's crushing defeat in 1939 clearly demonstrated from Gomułka's viewpoint that her foreign policy had been wrong. Yet, throughout World War II, the political movements participating in the Polish Government-in-Exile refused to change this policy. Their hostility toward the Soviet Union continued during the war years. They regarded Russia as an enemy second only to Germany. The Polish political leaders in London, according to Gomułka,

advanced the deceitful theory of the "two enemies" of Poland . . . Despite all all the internal differences within the so-called "London camp," the theory of Poland's "two enemies" represented its common political platform and inspired its activities both at home and abroad.[8]

In contrast to his criticism of the foreign policy of the Piłsudskiites' regime and, then, that of the Polish Government-in-Exile, as incompatible with Poland's interests; Gomułka praised the program advocated by the Communist Party of Poland and, subsequently, the Polish Workers' Party as being fully in line with Polish needs. Both parties realistically appraised Poland's situation in the international sphere, and both appreciated the great significance of Poland's alliance with Russia. In the interwar period the Communist Party of Poland was "the sole party which persistently strove to replace the anti-Soviet policy by one of friendship and cooperation with the Soviet Union." During World War II, the same stand was taken by the Polish Workers' Party. "The Polish Workers' Party advocated and through its struggle against Nazism also promoted a program of Polish-Soviet friendship and alliance. It linked its hope for the defeat of the occupying Nazi forces to the only feasible and, from Poland's point of view, the most advantageous development; namely, liberation of Poland by the Soviet Army." [9] Gomułka felt that history fully vindicated this policy:

> The course of events demonstrated that among all political parties active during the war only the Polish Workers' Party appraised the situation realistically. The proper grasp of contemporary realities was at the root of policies of the Polish Workers' Party. Perhaps the Polish Workers' Party did not have the support of a majority of the people . . . [Yet] it was right. And all the opponents of the Polish Workers' Party were not right. This has been proven by history.[10]

Gomułka considered the vindication of past Communist Party policies not merely as a matter of historical record, but also as an issue which had current relevance. Indeed, in his eyes there were several similarities between the political situation which existed in Europe in the thirties and that which prevailed in the fifties. In the revival of West German power, coupled with Germany's claims to Polish territory, he saw a grave potential danger to Poland:

> In West Germany, which is so close to our country, there takes place a rearming of those forces which not so long ago ruthlessly invaded and conquered the whole of Europe. The remilitarization of the German Federal Republic, the German revisionism, represent — as the gruesome historical experience indicates — a threat to Poland, to our borders, to our security.[11]

Gomułka thought that the danger which West Germany posed to Poland, especially the threat to Poland's western provinces, should play a decisive role in shaping Poland's foreign policy. "For Poland," he asserted, "the essential criterion of appraising the policies of other countries is their attitude toward Poland's borders and German revisionism." [12] The attitude of Western powers toward the Polish-German border, in Gomułka's opinion, was quite unsatisfactory. They "accept in silence Adenauer's demands for a revision of

Poland's Western borders." [13] At best, this is so because the Western powers do not want to offend the German Federal Republic which is an important pillar of the Atlantic Alliance. At worst, it is because in the West there exist some influential political groups which support the German objectives as intrinsically valid:

The West German militarists would not be in a position to achieve anything if they had no protectors in the West. It is with the latters' assistance that the revanchist and imperialist forces in West Germany were revived and grow in strength.[14]

Using the same yardstick toward the Polish-German border dispute, Gomułka contrasted the stand taken by the West with that of the Soviet Union. Unlike the Western powers, Russia recognizes Poland's Western frontier as permanent and, if necessary, is prepared to uphold Poland's rights to the territory east of the Oder and the Neisse rivers with armed force. Thus, according to Gomułka, the Soviet Union "represents a power which paralyzes the plans of the potential aggressors . . . and the decisive force which guarantees the inviolability of [Poland's] borders." [15]

The affinity between political realism and Gomułka's program, however, was not confined solely to the field of foreign policy. Another essential element of political realism — the carrying out of extensive domestic reform — was also very much on Gomułka's mind. Indeed, he was well aware of the interdependence of external policy and internal progress, as were the exponents of organic reform in the nineteenth century. Gomułka felt that Poland's position in world politics would be improved by increasing her internal strength. "Independence and sovereignty," he exclaimed, "are upheld in the workshops and in the factories, on the farms and in the research institutes — they are upheld by the people who through their work and their knowledge multiply the nation's wealth and advance its culture." [16] In Gomułka's opinion the main task confronting Poland at the present stage of history was to promote internal economic progress; indeed, he saw this as the only way by which the Polish nation could better its position in the international sphere:

The country which does not develop new methods of production . . . both in industry and agriculture, has only one prospect — the prospect of backwardness, poverty, and weakness. And the lesson of history is clear: the backward and weak are always beaten. The backward and the poor are the rubbish of history.

The major task confronting us and the whole Polish nation is to make Poland one of the economically advanced countries in the world.[17]

After he returned to power in 1956, Gomułka moved openly nearer to political realism, although he did not completely repudiate his earlier partial commitment to political idealism. In one critical aspect he still strove to combine the two. He made it clear that he expected Poland's close alliance with the Soviet Union to be coupled with the maintenance of her internal independence. In relations among the countries of the socialist bloc, he asserted, "every country should possess full independence, and the right of every nation to sovereignty in an independent country should be fully and mutually respected." [18]

MARXISM-LENINISM

Gomułka's emphasis on political realism in the years after 1956 did not mean that he had ceased to be a Marxist-Leninist. On the contrary, he also underlined his faithful adherence to Communist ideology. Thus, side by side with his political realism, there was the other side of his program which conformed to the precepts of Marxism-Leninism.

Gomułka subscribed to all the major principles of Marxist-Leninist doctrine. To him "the dynamic force of contemporary history . . . [was] the working class." The working class, guided by the teachings of Marx and Engels which were further developed by Lenin, has been striving for several generations to establish all over the world "the system of social justice, the system free from exploitation of man by man" — the socialist system. It won its initial victory in Russia, where, in 1917 under Lenin's leadership, a successful revolution "resulted in the foundation of the first socialist state in the world" — the Soviet Union. After World War II socialism prevailed in several other countries in Europe and Asia. "Today over a billion people live under the victorious banner of socialism . . . but the struggle still goes on." [19] In Gomułka's opinion, the ultimate outcome of this struggle was a foregone conclusion: "Socialism represents the direction of development of contemporary mankind . . . There is no doubt that sooner or later the peoples of all countries will move in this direction." [20]

As Gomułka presented its history, Poland was ruled by the bourgeoisie in the interwar period. This group both suppressed the working class at home, and took a hostile stand toward the first country of socialism, the Soviet Union. In 1920 the Polish bourgeoisie invaded the Soviet Union, and subsequently subscribed to the policy of the so-called *cordon-sanitaire,* aimed at preventing socialism from spreading to Europe. In taking this course the rulers of Poland concealed their true objectives under the cloak of the traditional struggle against Russia. It was, however, "their class hatred toward the first country of the workers and peasants," and their fear of the "social impact of the Soviet example on the Polish people" [21] which primarily inspired the Piłsudski foreign policy. During World War II, Gomułka declared, the Polish Government-in-Exile continued an anti-Soviet policy for precisely the same reasons:

At the roots of the political concepts of the Government-in-Exile, at the root of policy conducted by the organizations and parties linked with this government at home, there was the same social program, the same ideology, and the same policy which before September 1939 had been at the root of the [Pilsudskiites'] government.[22]

Even after World War II, the Polish bourgeoisie, supported by the West, opposed the establishment of socialism in Poland by all available means. The underground directed by London exiles undertook an armed struggle against the Communist Party. At the same time the open opposition led by Mikołajczyk was a "Trojan horse, undermining the People's Poland from within." [23] This time, however, the forces of the bourgeoisie were defeated. The Polish working class, led by the Polish Workers' Party, dispersed them and came out "with a new political program which provided both for the restoration of Poland's independence and its lasting security as well as for the overcoming of economic and social backwardness." [24]

In the postwar years, according to Gomułka, Poland — ruled by the working masses, led by the Communist Party — completely reversed its prewar course. In the realm of foreign policy Poland abandoned its anti-Soviet stand and, instead, developed close bonds with the Soviet Union and the entire socialist bloc: "Poland is tied to the Soviet Union and all socialist countries by firm bonds of fraternity, friendship, and mutual assistance. We are united by . . . the common goal and the common ideology of Marxism-Leninism." [25]

In the domestic sphere the entire political, socioeconomic, and cultural system of postwar Poland underwent drastic transformation. Capitalism was destroyed and in its place socialism gradually evolved. Significant strides were made in promoting the economic development of the country, especially industrialization. Poland's internal progress was important not only because it brought socialism nearer, but also because by this very fact it contributed to the global victory of socialism over capitalism. People's Poland, Gomułka declared,

participates in this struggle not only by [the course] of her foreign policy, but also by her economic and cultural progress, which, while increasing the strength and wealth of our country, at the same time, represents our contribution to peaceful competition with the capitalist world.[26]

From the time he returned to power, Gomułka also presented himself as a successor of the internationalist trend in the Polish Marxist movement much more openly than he had done in the forties. Above all, he revised his view of the roles played by the traditions of the Social Democracy of the Kingdom of Poland and Lithuania and the Polish Socialist Party, respectively. His formerly positive opinion of the contribution of the Polish Socialist Party was now greatly toned down.[27]

Gomułka, like Bierut, recognized that two currents existed in the Polish Workers' movement: one represented by the Polish Socialist Party, the other represented by the Social Democracy. Gomułka, as did Bierut also, felt that only the latter trend was truly Marxist. He clearly regarded the Social Democracy of the Kingdom of Poland and Lithuania and the Communist Party of Poland as the predecessors of the Polish United Workers' Party, for those parties consistently had subscribed to proletarian internationalism and had maintained strong bonds with Russian Marxists:

The principle of international proletarian solidarity, and, especially, the principle of internationalist unity with the Russian proletariat and its party, guided the Polish revolutionary workers and their party the Social Democracy of the Kingdom of Poland and Lithuania, and, subsequently, the Communist Party of Poland — the great predecessor of our party.[28]

The stress on the traditions of what Gomułka considered as the truly Marxist current in the Polish Workers' movement was carried to its logical conclusion by Communist historians. In 1959 the party historian, Tadeusz Daniszewski, expounded the official position of the Polish United Workers' Party concerning this crucial historical controversy in the ranks of the Polish Marxist movement. The view that the Social Democracy of the Kingdom of Poland and Lithuania and the Communist Party of Poland correctly emphasized the class struggle, while the Polish Socialist Party rightly stressed the struggle for independence, Daniszewski declared, is erroneous and, indeed, represents a revision of Marxism:

If the Social Democracy of the Kingdom of Poland and Lithuania adopted an incorrect and non-Leninist position on the national question, it by no means follows that the Polish Socialist Party had taken the correct attitude. Quite the reverse. The experience of the Polish working movement shows clearly that the Polish Socialist Party . . . approached the national question not from proletarian but from petit-bourgeois positions.

We certainly cannot agree with the oft-repeated suggestion made by revisionist elements that the Polish Socialist Party's contribution to the cause of independence should be inscribed in the annals of the Polish United Workers' Party.[29]

Once his stand on the basic dispute permeating the ranks of the Marxist movement in Poland was clarified, Gomułka's assessment of the following stages of history of the Communist Party became relatively simple. Emphasis on the novel character of the Polish Workers' Party, although not completely eliminated, lessened. Gomułka now presented the party as a direct successor of the Proletariat, the Social Democracy of the Kingdom of Poland and Lithuania and the Communist Party of Poland, merely "born in a new historical epoch which required new ideas and new methods in its work." [30]

This agreement also enabled the Polish United Workers' Party to find a satisfactory formula for explaining away Gomułka's "rightist-nationalist deviation." In a speech delivered at the Party's Third Congress, held in 1959, the Politburo member, Jerzy Morawski — undoubtedly with Gomułka's personal blessing — minimized the significance of the party split in the late forties. He claimed that with regard to the principal direction of party policy, there had existed no differences among its leadership. The differences were limited to the choice of the most effective means by which to achieve a common end. However, Morawski explained, "in the political climate which prevailed at that time . . . these differences were not only exaggerated, but they were presented as an essential split over the principles of party policy as well as its ideological foundations.[31]

At first the view that there had been a fundamental split over policy, Morawski continued, was accepted by rank-and-file party members at face value. Yet, as time went by and it became evident that the means adopted by the party in 1949–1955 were unsatisfactory, the attitude of its members toward "rightist-nationalist deviation" gradually underwent drastic transformation. The opinion began to prevail that the line represented by those accused of a "rightist-nationalist deviation" was not a departure from Communist ideology; indeed, it was correct. Morawski asserted that "history has resolved beyond doubt the problems over which the controversy in the party revolved. And on the basis of historical experience we can assert today: there was no rightist-nationalist deviation in our party." [32]

Once the party disposed of the thorny problem of "rightist-nationalist deviation," it was able, in turn, to appraise the 1949–1955 party line in a fashion satisfactory both to Gomułka and to his former opponents. At the Third Congress of the Polish United Workers' Party, in accordance with the scheme submitted by Morawski, the means which the party had used in the Stalinist period were described as wrong, while the principal direction of its policies was presented as correct. "We have every right to assert," Morawski declared, "that in 1949–1955 the principal line of the party, representing the essence of socialist revolution and socialist construction, was correct." [33]

The resolution of the major historical controversies in the ranks of the Polish Communist Party, in favor of the internationalist tradition over the nationalist one, enabled Gomułka to unequivocally endorse the principles of proletarian internationalism. The Polish United Workers' Party, he said in his speech at the Third Congress, is "faithful to the principles of proletarian internationalism. [It] professes its steadfast solidarity with the entire Communist movement." [34]

POLAND'S OWN ROAD TO SOCIALISM

Even though Gomułka adhered to the trend in the Polish workers' movement which consistently upheld the principles of proletarian internationalism in general and the tenet of close cooperation with Russian Marxists in particular, his attitude toward Polish-Soviet relations still differed from that of Bierut. The position which Gomułka assumed after 1956 fell somewhere in between the line which the Polish Workers' Party trod in the immediate postwar years and the course which the Polish United Workers' Party followed in the years 1949–1955.

Gomułka's stand has been aptly described as "Leninism applied to Polish conditions." [35] For Gomułka's program was inspired not only by the platforms of the Social Democracy and the Communist Party of Poland, but also by Lenin's critical appraisal of these platforms. He fully subscribed to Lenin's censure of the Polish Social Democrats, and particularly Rosa Luxemburg,* for their stand on the national issue. Lenin, Gomułka declared, "understood the tasks of the Polish proletariat with regard to the national question better than many Polish Marxists." [36] On several occasions,

* Gomułka himself has abstained from censuring Rosa Luxemburg by name, but the critical appraisal of her program is implicit in his various pronouncements. The party historian, Tadeusz Daniszewski, however, explicitly referred to "the erroneous views of the Social Democracy . . . and its spiritual leader, Rosa Luxemburg." See "Under the Banner of Proletarian Internationalism," *World Marxist Review: Problems of Peace and Socialism*, January 1959, p. 52.

Gomułka pointed out, Lenin rebuked the Polish social democrats "for underestimating the tasks of the working class as leader of the [Polish] people in the struggle not only for socialism but also democracy and national liberation." [37] In contrast to the programs of the Social Democracy and the Communist Party of Poland, especially in the early stages of their existence, Gomułka looked favorably on the attempts of Polish Communists to evolve a synthesis between social revolution and national aspirations in the middle twenties. This chapter in the history of the Polish Communist movement was presented by party historians as resulting from Lenin's just criticism, and, as "the victory of Leninism in the Polish workers' movement." [38]

On the basis of what he regards as the true Leninist tradition in the Polish Communist movement, Gomułka proposed to evolve a new pattern of Polish-Soviet relations after 1956. In two important statements — one at the meeting of the Central Committee of the Polish United Workers' Party in May 1957 (the first post-October 1956 meeting); the other in an article published in *Pravda* on November 5, 1957 (during the meeting of Communist leaders in Moscow) — Gomułka described the "Polish road to socialism." [39] In line with Lenin's teaching, he tried to reconcile proletarian internationalism with the Polish national aspirations. Gomułka's concept of the Polish road to socialism, therefore, was presented in truly dialectical fashion.

On the one hand, the concept of the Polish road to socialism completely endorsed the principle of proletarian internationalism, of close bonds among socialist countries. It also recognized both the unique role of the Soviet Union in the socialist bloc and the special place of the Communist Party of the Soviet Union in the international Communist movement. Indeed, it considered some Soviet experiences valid for all countries engaged in constructing a socialist system. The Polish road to socialism "cannot imply rejection of universal laws and general principles derived from the experiences of socialist construction in the Soviet Union. Such a rejection would actually lead to the destruction of socialism." [40]

On the other hand, the concept of the Polish road explicitly implied a distinction between "the road of socialist construction in [Poland] and that road which the Soviet Union trod in constructing socialism." The rejection of this distinction would also be harmful for it "would hinder and distort socialist construction, and as a result would turn the working masses against socialism." [41]

Gomułka bridged these two contradictory aspects of his argument by making a subtle distinction between the general and the specific principles of socialist construction. The general principles were binding upon all socialist countries without exception. Unless they were observed, socialism could not be accomplished. By definition, the general principles were discovered by the first socialist country, the Soviet Union. The specific principles were determined by the concrete historical situation (both external and internal) under which socialism was being constructed, as well as by the national peculiarities of the people in a given country. According to Gomułka, the two sets of principles were not contradictory but supplementary:

> Each national road, and, thus, also the Polish road, to socialism must follow the general principles common to all countries and in this sense it represents an international road. In turn, this general international road to socialism contains a national substructure peculiar to each country and in this sense we talk of a national road to socialism.[42]

Gomułka was fairly vague — it seems intentionally vague — on the subject of the exact nature of the interrelationship between the general and the specific principles of socialist construction. He not only failed to enumerate these principles in any systematic fashion but emphasized that their precise application could be determined only pragmatically: "The general principles of the transition to socialism never and nowhere appear in a pure, abstract form. Everywhere they assume concrete historical content." [43]

In Gomułka's exposition there was a significant exception. He emphasized one characteristic of the Polish nation affecting the nature of the Polish road to socialism over and over again. The Poles, Gomułka asserted, attach great importance to the independence of their country:

> The specific feature of the Polish nation determined by its history is . . . the unique sensitivity to its independence. This is the result of the partitions, the centuries of oppression of the nation whose tradition is a millenium long.[44]

The concept of a Polish road to socialism as expounded by him in 1957 represented the quintessence of Gomułka's political program. It was important because it probably came as close as any to a genuine expression of his political creed, and as such reflected the program which he would have actually implemented had he remained in power after 1948. The significance lay, above all, in the crucial role of this concept for Polish-Soviet relations. It was the only aspect of Gomułka's political program which was weighted in favor of the Poles rather than the Russians in the Polish-Soviet tug-of-war. On all other issues — for reasons flowing from political realism, Marxism-Leninism or both — Gomułka conceded to the Russians. In the name of Polish national interest, he justified the close political, military, and economic bonds between Poland and the Soviet Union, and, indeed, the Communist system in Poland. In the name of Communist ideology, he advocated a Polish foreign policy essentially in line with that of the entire socialist bloc, and a domestic policy largely adhering to the Russian pattern. The only area where he refused to give ground was in upholding Poland's right to her own road to socialism.

Poland's right to her own road to socialism differing in some respects from that in Russia, had far-reaching implications, however. It provided Gomułka with a restricted but nevertheless genuine freedom from Moscow. Its single articulated aspect as well as its general ambiguity gave him some room for political maneuver vis-à-vis Soviet leaders. Stress on the sensitivity of the Polish nation to foreign rule served as a warning to the Russians that an attempt to restore the *status quo ante* of direct control over Poland would turn the Polish masses against them. In other words, it emphasized that Poland could be governed only by Polish Communists. The vaguely defined relationship between the general and the specific principles of the concept of the different roads also aimed to restrict indirect Russian influence in Poland. These ambiguities could be exploited by the Poles in two ways. In the first place, they left room for various and, at times, even conflicting interpretations of the existing limits. As such they enabled the Polish Communists to follow policies different from the Russians without appearing to cross the precarious borders of ideological unity. In the second place, the very fact of this ambiguity assumed that diverse interpretations were to be reconciled by means of a mutually satisfactory formula. This permitted the Polish Communists to enter into genuine negotiations with the Soviet Union over disputed issues.

Gomułka's interpretation of the concept of the different roads to socialism, thus, left the Polish Communists in a position vastly superior to their pre-1956 situation. They no longer were obliged to take their orders from Moscow but were entitled to have views of their own and even to attempt to impress them upon the Russians. The Polish United Workers' Party now clearly strove to attain the rank of a junior but nevertheless genuine partner of the Communist Party of the Soviet Union.

POLITICAL REALISM VS. MARXISM-LENINISM

The two sides of Gomułka's political program — his arguments borrowed from political realism and those derived from Marxism-Leninism — showed a large degree of similarity in their ultimate conclusions. Although for different reasons, they both took a highly critical view of Poland's past course, and they both pointed out a similar direction for Poland in the future. In foreign policy they advocated maintaining close bonds with Russia and in the domestic sphere, promoting economic progress.

The close affinity between political realism and Communism in Gomułka's program was by no means accidental. For him the distinction between the two did not exist. When he joined the ranks of the Communist Party of Poland in the twenties, he became a political realist and a Communist at the same time. After he took over the reins of the Polish United Workers' Party in 1956, political realism and Communism were still inseparably interwoven in his eyes. He was convinced that in Poland's present situation Communism was the most effective and, indeed, the only feasible way to accomplish the goals of political realism. Contemporary Polish patriotism, Gomułka asserted, "is inseparably linked to the socialism which restored Poland's freedom and sovereignty, gave her peace and security, and led to the dynamic development of the country." [45]

In terms of foreign policy, Communism was advantageous to Poland as an extremely important facet of her alliance with Russia. Indeed, Gomułka made it patently clear that he considered the existence of Communism in Poland as a *conditio sine qua non* of Polish-Soviet friendship. Consequently, in the electoral campaign in January 1957, he appealed to the Poles to support the Communist Party in the name of their national interest. Gomułka's reasoning was simple. By voting against the Communist Party one impaired the Communist system in Poland. By destroying Communism in Poland one endangered the Polish-Soviet alliance. And by breaking Poland's alignment with Russia, one injured Polish national interest. In a dramatic broadcast on the very eve of elections, Gomułka summed up this argument:

The enemies of the People's Poland would like to push our country into an abyss of chaos and anarchy . . . They are well aware that only socialist Poland can remain on the map of Europe as an independent and sovereign state. They are well aware that the Polish United Workers' Party is the guarantor of her independence . . . the guarantor of fraternal neighborly Polish-Soviet relations, which are in line with the most vital interest of the Polish nation. To [turn against] the candidates of the Polish Workers' Party is tantamount to destroying socialism in Poland . . . destroying the independence of our country, erasing Poland from the map of Europe.[46]

Communism, however, was not seen as only a tool of Poland's interests in the international sphere. According to Gomułka, it also fulfilled her domestic needs. Above all, unlike capitalism, the Communist system effectively promoted Poland's economic progress, and, especially her industrialization. In this way Communism also contributed to strengthening the country's defensive potential:

> The bourgeois state could secure for Poland neither the proper opportunities for her progress nor the indispensable defense potential . . . There has been only one way to overcome Poland's backwardness . . . to secure the development of her resources and to uphold her independence . . . the overthrow of capitalism and Poland's revival through socialism.[47]

Gomułka hoped that by coming out with the program which combined Communism with political realism, he would be able to reach a lasting accommodation between Russia and Poland. On the one side, he thought that the more flexible post-Stalinist Soviet leadership would find his formula of Poland's own road to socialism compatible with their version of Communist doctrine. On the other side, he believed that the Polish people, inspired by the precepts of political realism, would be satisfied with the restricted but nevertheless genuine autonomy inherent in it. Gomułka, thus, proceeded to convert his plan of a Polish-Russian modus vivendi into practice.

8

POLAND AND THE SOVIET UNION

THE POLISH-SOVIET DISPUTE (1956–1957)

The Soviet leaders found Gomułka's proposal for a new pattern of Polish-Russian relations,[1] based on his concept of Poland's own road to socialism, worthy of exploration. They entered into negotiations with Gomułka and, indeed, offered him various concessions. The Russians did not try to restore the direct rule over Poland abolished in 1956. They conceded that the Polish government should remain in the hands of the Poles. A formal agreement to that effect was concluded in Moscow between the Polish delegation, headed by Gomułka, and the Soviet leaders on November 18, 1956. It declared that relations between the two countries must be conducted "on the basis of complete equality, respect for territorial integrity, national independence and sovereignty, and non-interference in internal affairs."[2] An important aspect of the agreement, which was further elaborated in a separate military convention of December 17, was that it gave the Polish government formal control over the movement of Soviet troops in Poland. At the same time the Russians acquiesced in the removal of various inequities imposed on Poland during the Stalinist period; notably they agreed to compensate Poland to the amount of half a billion dollars for losses suffered in past trading relations. Last but not least, they consented to repatriate the Poles held in the Soviet Union.[3] The agreement of November 1956, thus, undoubtedly represented a significant improvement of Poland's position vis-à-vis Russia. According to Gomułka, it based Polish-Soviet relations on "Leninist principles of full equality, mutual respect, independence, and sovereignty."[4]

With the sanctioning of a new pattern of relations by the November 1956 agreement, the last vestiges of direct rule by the Russians were removed. Soviet overseers in the Polish government were relieved of their posts. Marshal Rokossvsky and most of the Russian officers in the Polish armed forces returned home. Except for a few (essentially technical) posts, which they continue to hold, there has been no overt evidence of any Russians in the Polish administration since 1956. In addition, the role of the Soviet ambassadors has been restricted to diplomatic functions. Ponomarenko, who backed the Natolin faction in blocking the adoption of the program of reform in 1956, left Warsaw in 1957. His successors, Abrasimov and Aristov, abstained from interference in Polish internal affairs. Furthermore, the Polish-Soviet military agreement has apparently worked well. Russian troops stationed in Poland have remained confined to their bases, and, except in the immediate vicinity of the bases, their presence has been hardly noticeable.

After 1956, Poland's government was in the hands of the Poles, but its independence was still greatly restricted. Poland continued to be ruled by a Communist government, which openly proclaimed adherence to the Soviet version of Marxism-Leninism. Close ideological ties between the two countries were preserved, and have provided the Russians with an opportunity to restore their influence indirectly.

As seen from Moscow, the criterion of adherence to Marxism-Leninism was, above all, Polish acceptance of the tenet that the broad features of Soviet experience in constructing socialism are valid for all Communist states. The greatest significance of the Bolshevik revolution, asserted an authoritative Soviet source on ideology, is "that it has shown that the general features of that revolution must inevitably be repeated in any country."[5] The necessity for the other Communist states to copy the Soviet model, which would also have affected Poland was, after 1956, no longer as urgent as it had been in the Stalinist period. To some extent it was modified by the recognition of the peculiar character of socialist construction in each country — the concept of different roads to socialism. According to an official Soviet statement on ideology, in realizing their goals, Marxist-Leninist parties "do not strive to accomplish them in the same form and through one and the same method everywhere. They take into account the concrete conditions and the national peculiarities existing in the respective countries."[6] The Russians were quite explicit, however, that the general principles charted by the U.S.S.R. were to take precedence over the specific ones evolved in any other country. Khrushchev himself asserted that "one must not inflate the importance of the [specific conditions], exaggerate them, and fail to see the main general path of socialist construction charted by the teaching of Marx and Lenin." [7]

There seems to be little doubt that Soviet stress on the universal significance of their experience was largely designed to restore their influence in Poland. The Russians strove to replace their direct rule over Poland with a more subtle, but no less effective, tight ideological control.

Gomułka went a long way to satisfy Soviet ideological demands on Poland. He explicitly recognized the universal validity of the general principles of socialist construction in the Soviet Union. This gave the Russians a powerful lever with which to impress their own policies on the Poles. Both by narrowing the specific principles which allow individual nations to digress from the general pattern and by widening the interpretation of general principles which are binding upon all the Communist countries, Moscow would be able to tell Warsaw not only what policies it should abstain from, but also what policies it should adopt. If carried to an extreme, such a relationship would have resulted in Poland's becoming a mere puppet of the Soviet Union.

Gomułka differed with the Russians over the method of interpreting the general principles of socialist construction. He made it clear that he was not prepared to accept Moscow's unilateral interpretation of the general principles as binding on Poland. Although he refrained from coming out with an alternative version of the general principles, he continued to emphasize the specific features of Poland's road to socialism. In comparison with the broad area of agreement between Gomułka and the Soviet leaders, this matter might seem trivial but it was in fact of profound importance. It encompassed within itself a broad range of problems, touching upon the heart of both interparty and interstate Polish-Soviet relations, and thus led in 1956–1957 to a serious dispute between the two parties and between the two Communist governments.

In the controversy over the method of interpreting general principles of socialist construction, the Russians, in line with their political objectives, attempted to retain the maximum influence in formulating common policies for the whole socialist camp. They played down the role of the smaller Communist parties, including the Polish party. Gomułka was prepared to go quite far to secure Soviet approval of the Polish United Workers' Party's orthodoxy, but at the same time he had no intention of abdicating the modest degree of independence which the Polish party had won from Moscow in 1956. He kept insisting that the Polish Communists should be treated perhaps as junior, but nevertheless as true partners by their Soviet comrades. Consequently, with respect to the method of interpreting general principles of socialist construction, Gomułka took a stand largely opposite to that of the Russians. He tried to reduce the Soviet part in determining policies binding upon the entire Communist bloc as much as possible, and to increase the scope of independent decision-making by the Polish United Workers' Party.

This tug-of-war between the Soviet and Polish Communists over the method of interpreting the general principles of socialist construction was clearly manifested in their divergent statements of 1957 and of early 1958. The Russians underlined their leading place in the international Communist movement, implying that this entitled them to the position of arbiter in the matters of ideology. They also emphasized their preference for multilateral over bilateral ties among Communist countries. The Soviet leaders were well aware that in multilateral contacts, as a result of their ascendancy over most of the Communist parties — and, above all, as a result of the backing of the Chinese Communist Party — they could easily muster an overwhelming majority to decide controversial ideological issues in their favor. Indeed, in 1957, the Russians apparently considered the possibility of formalizing multilateral bonds among the different Communist parties by setting up a new international to replace the Cominform. This, of course, would have provided Moscow with a most effective instrument with which to influence the policies of foreign Communist parties.

Gomułka adopted a different stand on each of these issues. Although he did not explicitly challenge the Soviets' leading role in the international Communist movement, he failed to confirm it. Instead of hailing the role of the Soviet Union as the "leader" or "head" of the socialist camp — the phrases which at that time were used by the other Communist parties — he continued describing the Soviet Union in a matter-of-fact fashion as the "first and the most powerful socialist state." At the meeting of the Communist leaders in Moscow in November 1957, apparently under heavy pressure from the delegates of other parties, Gomułka agreed to join in a declaration which described the Soviet position in the Communist bloc as its "head," but also as "the first and the most powerful state." Upon his return to Warsaw, however, Gomułka emphasized that his signing the declaration did not necessarily imply a change in his stand on this issue. Indeed, he explained away the significance of endorsing the phrase to which he objected as arising out of semantic difficulties. "The declaration is written in a political language" used by twelve parties, he said, "and this language is not identical for all parties with respect to all problems." [8] At the same time Gomułka stressed that the "cooperation among the Communist parties assumes the full political and organizational independence and the real sovereignty of each party. This essential principle enables each party to evaluate the situation existing in its country and to map the line of its political activities." [9]

Gomułka also strongly emphasized his preference for bilateral over multilateral bonds among Communist parties. Bilateral forms of cooperation, he said, "permit the broad exchange of information and experience . . . [and] ought to be more widely developed." In line with this view he failed to attend the meeting of the Communist leaders in Budapest in January 1957. He did attend the meeting held in Moscow on the occasion of the fortieth anniversary of the Bolshevik revolution, but after returning home he questioned the right of such a gathering to interfere in the internal affairs of any party without its consent. "The internal problems of each party," he said, "cannot be determined at interparty meetings." [10] Last but not least, Gomułka strongly resisted the reestablishment of a new Communist international. At the meeting in Moscow he agreed to the founding of a common Communist theoretical journal, but he opposed the restoration of an international Communist organization. He criticized the record of both the Comintern* and the Cominform and asserted that their experience demonstrated that "the practice of directing all Communist parties from one center . . . is not always advantageous and frequently is even harmful." [11]

Along with the controversy over the method of interpreting the general principles of socialist construction, a dispute was taking place over the actual observance of those principles in Poland. In ideological terms the latter quarrel was basically a corollary of the former. Since the Russians believed that they were entitled to formulate policies in common for the entire socialist camp, they could reasonably expect that as a socialist country Poland also would adhere to these policies. Gomułka rejected the Soviet right to determine policies for all Communist countries, and naturally did not feel bound by them. Instead he kept emphasizing the various specific

---

* Significantly, as an example of harmful policies of the Comintern, Gomułka singled out the dissolution of the Communist Party of Poland in 1938.

features of socialist construction in Poland which enabled her to digress from the pattern of policies, external as well as internal, prevailing in other Communist states. From the point of view of practical politics the second dispute touched upon the heart of the differences between Moscow and Warsaw, namely, how to determine the exact limits of Poland's own road to socialism.

The conflict over the exact scope of Poland's independence was manifested on the various occasions from late 1956 until early 1958 when the Polish Communist government took a stand different from that of the Soviet Union. In the realm of foreign policy, the first serious disagreement between the Polish and Soviet Communists was revealed in their evaluations of the 1956 revolution in Hungary. On October 28, 1956, *Pravda* wrote: "The events in Hungary made it crystal clear that a reactionary counterrevolutionary underground, armed and thoroughly prepared for decisive action against the people's government, had been organized with outside help." The Poles took an altogether different position. On the same day, the organ of the Polish Communist Party, *Trybuna Ludu,* published its own version of what was happening in Hungary. The source of the Hungarian tragedy, declared the Polish newspaper "should not be sought in the simplified version about 'alien agencies,' nor in looking for counterrevolution at each step . . . It must be sought, first of all, in the errors, distortions, and even crimes of the past Stalinist period." The Polish Communists clung to their opinion on the nature of the Hungarian revolution even after the uprising was suppressed. Indeed, Poland took a step hitherto unprecedented for a member country of the Soviet bloc. The Poles failed to support the Soviet position in the vote on the admission of United Nations' observers to Hungary and, instead, abstained from voting as did the Yugoslavs. Gomułka, however, did not press his opposition to Moscow too far. By mid-March 1957, following the example of all other Communist parties, he reversed his position and openly referred to the events in Hungary in 1956 as a counterrevolution.

Late in 1956 and early in 1957, the Polish Communists seemed to believe that they might count on the support of the Chinese in their differences with the Russians. They interpreted the Chinese declaration on relations among the socialist countries of November 1, 1956 — warning the Soviet Union of the error of "big-nation chauvinism" — as explicit approval of the changes in Poland. Indeed, the Poles hopefully drew a parallel between the "hundred flowers" course in China and the reforms in Poland. "Since

October 1956," argued a writer who visited China at the end of that year, "Poland has accomplished the same things which China had realized before." [12] Even after Chou En-lai's January 1957 visit to Warsaw, on the occasion of which he strongly stressed the need to preserve the unity of the socialist camp under Soviet leadership — and even after the abrupt abandoning of the "hundred flowers" policies by the Chinese Communists in mid-1957 — the Poles continued to praise China as Poland's ally in liberalizing the Soviet bloc. "The position of the Chinese Communists," declared a Polish weekly on the eve of Moscow conference, "continues to assist in the struggle against dogmatism and conservatism and helps to affirm the Leninist thesis of different roads." [13] However, the stand of the Chinese at the conference of Communist leaders in Moscow in November 1957 finally dissipated Polish hopes. Apparently, at the meeting, differences over the issue of the independence of individual Communist parties resulted in a clash between Gomułka and Mao Tse-tung. Toward the end of 1957 Polish-Chinese relations visibly deteriorated. Mao's visit to Poland, widely hailed in the Polish press early in 1957, never took place.

The attitude of Poland and the Soviet Union toward Yugoslavia also differed. Soon after Gomułka's return to power, Poland developed close bonds with Yugoslavia. Throughout the winter of 1956–1957, when the revolution in Hungary strained Soviet-Yugoslav relations, Polish-Yugoslav relations remained quite warm. The Poles not only did not denounce the Yugoslav system as had many other Communist parties, but in some respects, especially in the economic sphere, tried to copy it. The climax of Polish-Yugoslav cooperation came in September 1957, when Gomułka visited Belgrade. The declaration issued at the end of the visit was an unusual document. It explicitly endorsed the concept of "active coexistence," which stands at the center of Yugoslav neutralist foreign policy and which condemns all military alliances: the Atlantic Alliance and the Warsaw Treaty alike. The implication of this declaration was eagerly seized upon by some Polish newspapers. "For the first time on the Polish part the concept of 'active coexistence' was employed," commented a weekly devoted to international affairs. "What is the difference between 'active coexistence' and the 'peaceful coexistence' which guides our policy? The common elements are: the desire to liquidate the opposed blocs and to create a system of collective security." [14] Poland maintained close relations with Yugoslavia even after the Yugoslavs clashed with the Soviets over the interpretation of policies vis-à-vis the West at the meeting of the Communist leaders in Moscow in

November 1957. When the Yugoslavs refused to sign the final declaration, which contained a formulation of the concept of coexistence unacceptable to them, Gomułka attempted to bridge the gap by issuing a joint peace manifesto. Moreover, upon returning home, Gomułka noted the differences between the Yugoslav and other Communist parties, but played down their importance, stressing that Yugoslavia still "belongs to the family of socialist countries." [15]

It was not only in relations with the other Communist countries, but also with the West that serious differences between Warsaw and Moscow were revealed. Poland's request for U.S. economic assistance toward the end of 1956 was clearly viewed with suspicion by the Russians. In April 1957, at a meeting with Cyrankiewicz in Moscow, Khrushchev warned the Poles that by accepting a loan from the West they might find themselves in "bondage to the capitalist countries." [16] In June Gomułka admitted that there existed a political aspect to Poland's receiving American credits, but defended it by stressing that there were no strings attached to the aid. In the same month the Poles accepted a $95 million loan extended them by the United States.* The matter was apparently raised at the conference of Communist leaders in Moscow in November 1957, for upon his return Gomułka once again took a reassuring stand vis-à-vis the Soviets. He explicitly asserted that "Poland's policy, neither external nor internal, will be determined by foreign credits." [17] These political considerations notwithstanding, in February 1958 Poland accepted another $97 million from the United States.**

There was also a sudden burst of Polish diplomatic activity in Central Europe early in the fall of 1957. On September 9 (on the very eve of his visit to Yugoslavia) Gomułka launched the idea of the neutralization of the Baltic region as a precondition for closer cooperation among the countries in that area, in an interview with a Danish newsman. On October

---

* This amount was a disappointment to the Poles, who apparently had expected much more extensive economic assistance from the United States. In his address on the New Year's Eve of 1957, Gomułka half-jokingly mentioned $500 million as the amount of foreign assistance which would solve Poland's economic problems. *Trybuna Ludu,* January 1, 1957.

** Another aspect of Polish-American relations which might have worried the Russians was the development after 1956 of extensive cultural ties between the two countries. In 1957 the Ford and Rockefeller Foundations came out with a program for assisting Polish scholars who wanted to familiarize themselves with scientific achievement in the West. As a result, in 1957 and 1958, approximately three hundred Poles visited various Western and in particular American universities and research centers; at the same time, Western scholars went to teach or conduct research in Poland.

2, Polish Foreign Minister, Adam Rapacki* brought his plan for banning nuclear weapons from both Germanies, Poland, and Czechoslovakia before the General Assembly of the United Nations. On February 14, 1958 Rapacki's proposal was formally submitted to the governments of all countries concerned. The plan was cleared, though reportedly "only after months of quiet persuasion," [18] with the Soviet Union before it was submitted to the Western countries. On March 3, 1958, it received Moscow's warm endorsement. Since one of the main features of Rapacki's plan — as he openly admitted in his speech in the United Nations — was to prevent the nuclear arming of West Germany, it was natural that the Russians found it essentially in line with their policy. There seems to be little doubt, however, that the advantages of the Rapacki plan for Poland outweighed those for the Soviet Union. In view of the relative vulnerability of their country, the Poles had more reasons to be concerned about the growing military strength of West Germany than the Russians. Acceptance of Rapacki's proposal would have also brought Poland closer to the West. By reducing tensions and introducing even a restricted system of collective security in Central Europe, Poland's isolation from an outside world would have been largely overcome. That this was one of its goals, was confirmed by Gomułka, who in November 1958 stated that the Rapacki plan was also aimed at preventing the widening division of Europe "which neither Poland nor anyone desiring peace can wish for." [19] In December, in an exposé before the parliamentary committee on foreign affairs, Rapacki presented his plan as a part of a broader design of "constructive coexistence" intended to gradually reduce tensions between the two opposing blocs.

If the Russians had any reservations about the Rapacki plan, they were spared the effort of voicing them openly, because the Polish proposals were promptly rejected by the Western powers. Within a week after the Polish memorandum was submitted to the Western governments, the West German Minister of National Defense, Franz Joseph Strauss, denounced it as aimed at the weakening of the German Federal Republic,

---

* Rapacki was born in 1909 to a family with long intellectual and socialist traditions. His father was a university professor and a prominent leader of cooperative movement. Before the war Rapacki studied in Poland and Western Europe and was active in the socialist youth organization in Warsaw. He spent the wartime as a prisoner of war in Germany. Upon his return home in 1945 he joined the pro-Communist Polish Socialist Party and soon emerged as one of the closest associates of Cyrankiewicz. After the party's merger with the Communist Party in 1948, he entered its Politburo. Demoted to a candidate member in 1954, he was restored to full member in 1956, and in the same year took charge of the Foreign Ministry.

and questioned the wisdom of negotiating with Poland as a Soviet satellite. On May 3, 1958 the American Ambassador in Warsaw, Jacob D. Beam, delivered a courteous, but negative reply from the United States. In the American note the plan was characterized as providing "no method for balanced and equitable limitations of military capabilities" and accepting "the continuation of the division of Germany."[20] Rapacki tried to meet Western objections by revising his proposals. On November 4, 1958 he came out with a modified version of his plan, but without much hope for its success. The modifications he correctly predicted, "probably would not be acceptable to the opponents of our initiative."[21]

In 1956–1957 the differences between the Polish and Soviet Communists were not confined to foreign policy. At least three major aspects of Poland's internal policies — the economic reforms, the tolerance of relatively broad religious liberty, and the freedom of the written word — also came under fire from the Soviet and other Communist parties.

The Soviet-style management of the Polish economy was subjected to harsh criticism at a meeting of Polish economists in Warsaw in June 1956. Throughout 1956 and a good part of 1957 there were public discussions on how to evolve an economic system suited to Poland's own needs. Some of the participants even suggested establishing a system of economic planning, combined with a free market for producers' goods. They were obviously inspired by the example of the decentralized, planned economy in Yugoslavia. Most of the economists did not go that far, but they agreed upon the necessity of introducing some safeguards against the arbitrary decisions of the central planners.

Late in 1956 several reforms along these lines were carried out.[22] In October, the State Planning Commission — a highly centralized body which had run the entire Polish economy with a heavy hand in the Stalinist period — was replaced by a smaller advisory planning commission subordinate to the cabinet. In November, industrial establishments were given wider autonomy. In the same month, the workers' councils, which had come into being spontaneously in many factories, received formal sanction. Clearly inspired by the example of their counterparts in Yugoslavia, the councils were regarded as a form of genuine economic self-government aimed at the "strengthening of socialist democracy in Poland."[23] Integration of all workers' councils into a single organization, with a hierarchy separate from the state administration, was envisaged. In May 1957, a special commission, appointed to recommend the revision of the economic system, came out with proposals for even further decentralization of the economy. These were formally approved by the government.

At the same time there was a marked revival of private enterprise, particularly in agriculture. In the cities, during 1956–1957, the number of private small-scale production and commercial enterprises grew by 40 percent.[24] In the countryside the changes were still more profound. After Gomułka's rise to power, there was a general breakdown of collective farming and a return to private land-ownership. Close to 85 percent of the collective farms which existed in 1955 were disbanded.[25] By 1957 less than 2,000 collective farms were left in Poland, and their total share in the national agricultural production of that year was only 1.3 percent.[26]

Several reforms in the Polish economic system were viewed with considerable suspicion in Moscow. The workers' councils in Poland were never directly denounced, but the articulate criticism of their Yugoslav counterparts left no doubt concerning Moscow's disapproval. The revival of private ownership in Polish agriculture, which stood in striking contrast to the situation in the other Communist countries where collectivization was not only maintained but as in Hungary accelerated after 1956, was attacked by the Soviet and other East European Communists. On both of these issues Gomułka took a defensive stand. He tried to minimize the political significance of the workers' councils and presented them primarily as a means of eliminating bureaucratic inefficiency in factories. He also denied abandoning the ultimate goal of collectivizing Polish agriculture. At the same time, he repeatedly pledged that he was not going to promote collectivization by force, which amounted to saying that it was to be postponed for an indefinite period of time. Gomułka was obviously trying to avoid an open conflict with the Soviets over this issue, but without changing his policy.

The second internal matter which upset the Soviets was the broad religious freedom in Poland. Soon after Gomułka's return to power, the Catholic Church was freed from persecution and won several important concessions from the Communist regime. On October 28, 1956, Stefan Cardinal Wyszyński* and other clergymen were released from prison and

* Stefan Cardinal Wyszyński was born in 1901, the son of a church organist and a village school teacher. From the early stages of his ecclesiastical career he showed a keen interest in social issues, earning his doctorate in social sciences from the Catholic University of Lublin and further pursuing his studies in Western Europe. Already before the war his participation as a counsel in labor disputes and his writings on labor problems had earned him a reputation as the "workers' priest." His association with the wartime underground enhanced his prestige even further. In the postwar years he rose rapidly in the ranks of the Catholic hierarchy, being elevated to bishop in 1946, Archbishop and Primate of Poland in 1948, and Cardinal in 1953.

were allowed to resume their functions. In December an official agreement was concluded between the representatives of the government and the episcopate, providing for the reinstatement of religious instruction in the schools. Two Catholic periodicals, *Tygodnik Powszechny* and *Znak,* were revived, and five members of their editorial boards were put up as the official Catholic candidates in the forthcoming elections to the parliament. In return, the hierarchy threw its support behind the candidates of the Polish United Workers' Party.

The compromise between the State and the Church did not mean that the Communist Party had dropped its atheistic outlook. In May, 1957, Gomułka emphasized that the ideology of the Polish United Workers' Party is based on "dialectical materialism and is opposed to the idealist outlook." He also made it clear that he regarded the modus vivendi with the Church as merely a matter of expediency.* The party, he said, recognizes

that the idealist outlook will persist alongside the materialist one for a long time. Thus, there will be side by side the believers and nonbelievers, the Church and socialism, people's government and the Church hierarchy. This is obvious. From this fact we must draw the conclusions.

In its policy [the Communist Party] cannot apply administrative pressure toward the believers, ignoring the fact that the old quarrel with the Church had repelled millions of people from socialism.[27]

Other Polish Communists interpreted the *rapprochement* between Communism and Catholicism less narrowly than Gomułka. Many party members viewed it as the abandonment of all struggle against the Catholic religion and as an attempt to reconcile the two doctrines. Such views even made their way into the theoretical journal of the Polish United Workers' Party. Its May 1957 issue saw the State-Church compromise as more than a matter of sheer political expediency. There exists in Poland, it declared,

powerful religious fanticism . . . But there exists also among the atheists equally dangerous fanaticism . . . The slogan of the day should be tolerance.

The cooperation [between the Communists and the Catholics] is possible and is needed not only in the sphere of political activities, but also in creating such political, economic, and social relations which would facilitate the realization of the universal moral values.[28]

* The problem of religious freedom in Poland is primarily that of the Catholic Church. In contrast to the prewar period, in the postwar years the overwhelming majority of the Polish population was Catholic. If in 1939 the Catholics represented roughly 75 percent, after the war, due to the ruthless extermination of the Jews by the Nazis, the loss of various national minorities predominantly Orthodox in the east, and the removal of the German Protestants in the west, the proportion of Catholics in Poland rose to about 96 percent. Oscar Halecki, ed., *Poland* (New York, 1957), pp. 199, 201.

The Soviets never came out openly against the policies of the Polish Communist regime toward the Catholic Church. There seems to be little doubt, however, that they did not find such policies to their liking. The contrast between Poland and the other Communist countries — notably Czechoslovakia and Hungary, where the persecution of religion continued unabated after 1956 — was too striking not to cause concern to the Russians. There is strong reason to believe that this matter was taken up at the conference of the Communist leaders in Moscow in November 1957.

The relatively broad freedom of the written word was the third facet of the controversy with the Soviets over Poland's domestic affairs. Polish newspapers published articles which openly questioned Moscow's interpretation of several tenets of Marxism-Leninism late in 1956 and during a good part of 1957. The dissenters wrote in the weeklies: the young intelligentsia paper, Po prostu, and the more sophisticated Nowa Kultura. In the latter, a young philosopher, Leszek Kołakowski, in January and again in September 1957, published brilliant essays denouncing the very essence of historical materialism.[29] "You analyze history," Kołakowski addressed the orthodox Marxists,

approaching it with a ready-made scheme, and at the end of the inquiry you announce triumphantly that the same scheme emerged from your analysis — forgetting to add that you yourself put it there first . . . Maintaining that you, for the first time in history, are free from limitations which are imposed on man's perspective by his eyes, you fall victim to the same mystification which you rightly notice about your predecessors.

The Russians clearly were upset with the leadership of the Polish Communist Party for permitting the appearance of such statements in print. Late in 1956 and early in 1957, various pieces in the Polish press were selected for open attack by the Soviets and their faithful supporters: the Czech, East German, and even French Communists. The Polish writers were accused of deviating from Marxism-Leninism.[30] In the spring Po prostu was ordered to suspend its publication for the summer; Kołakowski's writings were singled out by Gomułka for public criticism as an example of attempted revisionism. These measures neither silenced the Polish critics nor appeased the Russians, however. In September 1957 the authoritative Soviet quarterly Voprosy Filosofii launched a direct attack upon Kołakowski. The article also sounded a warning to Gomułka. "The consequences of tolerating thoughtless treatment of ideological problems," it declared, "are clearly illustrated by the events which took place in the autumn of last year in Hungary." [31] Gomułka acted swiftly, and in October *Po prostu* was denied permission to resume publication. The student demonstrations which ensued in Warsaw were broken up by the police. In January 1958 there was a drastic purge of the editorial board of *Nowa Kultura*.

Early in 1958 the Soviet Union intensified its efforts to bring Poland back into line with the rest of the socialist camp. In January a mysterious meeting between Gomułka and Khrushchev took place in the Białowieża forest on the Polish-Soviet border. The exact nature of their talks was not disclosed, but it was revealed that they dealt with the internal situation in Poland, where Khrushchev found that there existed "not insignificant difficulties." [32] In April Voroshilov visited Warsaw and upon his return to Moscow criticized Poland for lagging behind in the collectivization of agriculture. "Polish agriculture," he declared, "has not as yet placed itself completely on the socialist road. There is much to be done [in this sphere] by the Polish Communist Party." [33] In May the Soviet press charged that accepting economic aid from America amounted to a betrayal of socialism. The charges were actually directed against Yugoslavia, but they were phrased in such a manner as to serve as a warning to Poland. "The imperialists do not give anything to anyone for nothing," expounded *Pravda*. "Everybody knows that American aid . . . leads in one form or another to economic and political dependence." [34]

In the spring of 1958 a new Soviet dispute with Yugoslavia flared up. The Poles refrained from joining the press campaign of vituperation against Yugoslavia undertaken by the other Communist countries. In April, two prominent members of the Polish Communst Party, Ochab and Morawski, went to Belgrade in an abortive effort to mediate in the Soviet-Yugoslav quarrel. When the League of Communists of Yugoslavia, however, came out with a program highly critical of the Soviet Union, in turn provoking a storm of attacks from the Russians and their allies, it became obvious that the Poles could no longer remain neutral in the matter. Then the execution of Nagy was announced on June 17, 1958, as if to demonstrate the inevitable end of the Communist leaders who strayed from the path approved by Moscow. The significance of this Soviet move could hardly be lost on Gomułka. Nagy's execution clearly meant that the lines had been drawn and sides had to be taken. Gomułka was now faced with the supreme test of his loyalty to international Communism.

Poland's position was very difficult. With Hungary suppressed, Yugoslavia expelled from the socialist camp, and all other Communist countries, including China, solidly backing the Russian line, Gomułka realized that he could not oppose Moscow alone without crossing the precarious limits of ideological unity. He may well have felt that "to rupture his relations with the bloc for the sake of Yugoslavia . . . or for the principles of a man already dead, even though the Polish leaders privately expressed their abhorrence of the execution, would be to engage in an idealism which he as a Polish Communist could ill afford." [35] Consequently, he decided that the time had come for a major retreat. Although later than the other Communist leaders and in terms more reticent, Gomułka, in a speech in Gdańsk on June 28, 1958, supported the Russians both in condemning Tito and supporting Nagy's execution. He denounced the Yugoslav "erroneous revisionist theories . . . which injured the united forces of the socialist countries and the whole international workers' movement"; and Nagy as a "revisionist . . . who step by step surrendered before the counterrevolution." [36]

By disassociating himself from both the Yugoslav and Hungarian forms of opposition to the Soviet Union, Gomułka clearly marked the limits beyond which he was not prepared to go in upholding Poland's right to her own road to socialism. As long as there existed some alternatives, which enabled him to digress from the Russian line without the impairing of ideological unity, he was willing to explore them. When pressed to the wall, however, he bowed to Moscow's will in the name of both Marxism-Leninism and political realism.

GOMUŁKA-KHRUSHCHEV AGREEMENT (1958–1961)

The year 1958 marked a turning point in Poland's relation with the Soviet Union. On the one hand, by that time Khrushchev had finally defeated his opponents and had emerged as an undisputed leader in the U.S.S.R. After the necessity of resorting to force in Hungary and the fiasco of his policy vis-à-vis Yugoslavia, Khrushchev was anxious to demonstrate that his East European policy was successful in Poland at least. The friction with China which developed in the late fifties and turned into a serious, though still not open, dispute in the early sixties pushed Khrushchev in the same direction. He no longer could count on Chinese support and, indeed, began to look for allies among the Communist leaders who would uphold him in the face of increasing Chinese attacks. In his dealings with Gomułka, therefore, Khrushchev took a conciliatory stand. He seemed to be satisfied with the demonstration by the Polish Communist leader of his loyalty to Moscow.

In resolving the remaining Polish-Russian differences, Khrushchev still expected Gomułka to make an unequivocal stand on those issues that he considered vital to Soviet interest. He did not insist, however, that Gomułka should give in on all controversial points, but was willing to seek some mutually satisfactory compromise. On the other hand the futility of Gomułka's efforts to secure any effective support from the other Communist states, and especially from China, apparently convinced him that a direct understanding with Moscow was the only feasible way to protect Poland's interest. In Gomułka's eyes, among the Soviet leaders, Khrushchev still appeared as a moderate.* Khrushchev's magnanimous stand in negotiations to remove the outstanding Polish-Soviet differences must have only confirmed Gomułka in this belief.

The initial terms of the Polish-Soviet *rapprochement* were worked out during a prolonged visit to the Soviet Union of a Polish delegation headed by Gomułka in October and November of 1958. According to Gomułka, the negotiations dealt with "all the most important questions in relations . . . between the two countries." [37] The agreement reached in Moscow represented a genuine compromise. The Soviets recognized the right of the Polish Communists to participate in formulating policies common for the entire Communist bloc and, within this broad ideological framework, left some room for Poland's internal differences. On the other hand, the Poles, especially in external but also in several domestic policies, accepted the ideological line of the whole socialist camp as binding on Poland.

Apparently both Soviet and Polish Communists found the agreement to their liking. Soon after Gomułka's visit in Moscow, Polish-Soviet relations improved considerably. Both the Poles and the Soviets repeatedly stressed the firm bonds of friendship linking the two countries. They did not try to conceal that there had existed some differences but they emphasized that these were fully overcome. Upon his return home Gomułka declared that "the idea of an alliance and friendship with the Soviet Union . . . cleared from the errors of the period of 'cult of the individual,' acquired new attractiveness and was taken into the hearts of the [Polish] nation." [38]

In July 1959 a Soviet delegation headed by Khrushchev visited Poland. In his speeches on that occasion Khrushchev hailed the closer ties. After

---

* The opponents of Khrushchev in the ranks of the Communist Party of the Soviet Union, and Molotov in particular, clearly were out of sympathy with Gomułka's program. They not only viewed with suspicion Gomułka's return to power, but encouraged the continued factional activity within the Polish United Workers' Party by the remnants of the Natolin faction. For more details see Chapter 10.

returning home he even asserted that Soviet-Polish relations were better than ever in the past. "We consider," he said, "that the relations existing today between the Soviet Union and Poland . . . are at present broader, stronger, and more profound than ever before. There was an incident in 1956 which brought joy to immature people, to people who could not look far ahead. But this was only an incident. Everything that marred our relations, everything that was superficial has been removed." [39]

Gomułka did his best to live up to the letter of the Moscow agreement. Especially in the international sphere he staunchly supported Soviet policies. When the Soviet leaders became convinced that the agreement was genuinely respected by Gomułka, their distrust of him melted away. They endorsed some of his domestic policies to which they had strenuously objected in the past. Beginning in 1959, contact between Polish and Soviet Communist leaders greatly increased. Meetings at various international Communist gatherings were supplemented by a steady exchange of party and governmental delegations at the different levels, including fairly frequent meetings between Gomułka and Khrushchev. Through these contacts the remaining obstacles to harmonious relations between the two countries were removed. The contacts between the two leaders were clearly marked by mutual respect if not cordiality. Thus, what had begun as marriage of convenience gradually turned into a union not devoid of some affection.

Parallel to the Polish-Soviet *rapprochement* and clearly with Moscow's encouragement, the Polish Communists proceeded to mend fences with those Communist governments with which they had been at odds in the past. Especially in the case of East German and Czechoslovak Communists, who had excelled in denouncing various aspects of Poland's policies in 1956–1957, there was marked improvement. This way Poland, thus, became reintegrated into the Soviet bloc not only by the direct cord binding her to Moscow, but also a network of contacts linking Warsaw to the other Communist capitals.

The new pattern of Polish-Soviet relations provided an effective resolution of past conflicts. This resolution was not a matter of Soviet fiat — the Poles and the Soviets alike made concessions and won points. On the issue of defining the Soviet role in the international Communist movement, the Poles eventually won their point. In the declaration adopted by the conference of Communist leaders in Moscow in the fall of 1960, no reference was made to Soviet leadership. Early in 1961 Khrushchev explained that this omission was intentional for "in the Communist movement there are no parties that are superior or subordinate, [but] all are equal and independent."

In defining the position of the Soviet Union in the Communist bloc, Khrushchev adopted terms essentially identical with those which had been used by Gomułka in 1957, namely, "the most powerful country in the world socialist system" and "the first to pave the way to socialism." [40] A few weeks later, in turn, Gomułka hailed the special Soviet role. He referred to the Communist Party of the Soviet Union as "a vanguard — the most experienced and the most tested party of world Communism." Gomułka, however, continued to couple his praise of the Soviet Communist Party with stress on the independence of the Polish party. Only the reactionaries and the enemies of socialism could believe, he declared, "that a single party could determine a political line for the powerful, all-world [Communist] movement . . . Each Communist party . . . expresses the most progressive aspirations of its own workers' class and its own nation." [41]

On the issue of whether the bonds among the Communist parties should be bilateral or multilateral, it was Gomułka who essentially conceded the point. He recognized the need for the regular meetings of representatives of all Communist parties, and their right to formulate policies binding for the entire bloc. Gomułka, however, continued to insist that common policies could no longer be unilaterally imposed by the Russians, but must represent solutions satisfactory to all the parties. "At present," he asserted in 1961, "the theoretical and political thought of the world workers' movement . . . represents a common accomplishment and a common treasure of many parties." On the last controversial issue of 1957, namely the establishing of a new international Communist organization, Gomułka's view prevailed. The Russians apparently shelved this plan indefinitely.

In the conflict over the position of the Polish United Workers' Party vis-à-vis the Communist Party of the Soviet Union, the Polish Communists fared reasonably well. The Soviets did not insist on a formally subordinate status for their Polish comrades, but consented to regard the Poles as junior partners in the international Communist movement. "The representatives of our party led by Comrade Gomułka," claimed the official organ of the Polish Workers' Party in 1961, "made a positive contribution to the deliberations at the international meetings of Communist and workers' parties." [42]

The concessions which the Polish Communists won from the Soviets concerning the methods of interpreting general principles of socialist construction, of course, were not obtained without exchange. Gomułka yielded to Khrushchev on several significant issues regarding the application of these principles in Poland. These concessions involved the recognition of several foreign as well as domestic policies common for the entire bloc as binding on Poland.

The essential condition of the Polish-Soviet *rapprochement* was Poland's accepting restrictions on the independence of its foreign policy. In 1961, Gomułka openly admitted that Polish external policy was guided by the interests of the international Communist movement. "The foreign policy of each socialist country," he asserted,

in order to be correct and effective, must take into account the Marxist-Leninist analysis of the international situation, the position and interests of the socialist camp as a whole . . . In foreign policy each socialist country must be guided by the common and fully coordinated interests of the entire socialist camp.[43]

The subordination of Poland's foreign policy to the interests of the Communist bloc, according to Gomułka, did not exclude the possibility of its undertaking some steps in international affairs on its own initiative. These, however, should be essentially confined to regions of particular interest to Poland, and fully integrated with the general framework of the policies for all Communist states. "Any initiative on the part of a socialist country," Gomułka said, "linked to its particular interests, and its geographic and political location, ought to be subordinated to the general, jointly coordinated direction of activity . . . of the socialist camp." [44]

Since the end of 1958, Poland has faithfully observed these principles. In relations with Yugoslavia, as well as with the West, Poland has strictly adhered to the Soviet line. During his visit in the U.S.S.R., Gomułka stepped up his criticism of Yugoslavia. In a speech in Moscow in November 1958 he assured his audience that the Polish Communists regard the line of the League of the Communists of Yugoslavia as an "erroneous, revisionist path." [45] Yet, Warsaw's relations with Belgrade never deteriorated to the same extent as those between Yugoslavia and other Communist states.[46] In the storm of anti-Yugoslav tirades which in the late fifties came from all corners of the Soviet bloc, Polish newspapers were most restrained. Even at the heights of the dispute, Polish Communists did not give up hope for improved relations with Yugoslavia. "We do not rule out" said Gomułka at the Third Congress, "the prospect of the return of [the League of the Communists of Yugoslavia] to the Communist movement.[47]

During his visit to Moscow in November 1958, Gomułka also sharpened his criticism of the West. He castigated American policy as aimed at "maintaining constant tension in the international sphere," and contrasted it with the Soviet policy which was striving to "bring to an end the armaments race." [48] At the same time, he declared Poland's full support for the Soviet policy toward Germany, including the first demand raised by Khrushchev for a revision of the status of Berlin. Gomułka also upheld the Soviet line in other disputes with the West, which at that time were particularly acute in the Middle East and the Far East.

In subsequent years the Polish Communist government has continued to participate on the Soviet side in the global struggle against the West. It supported the Soviet meddling in the Congo in 1960; it backed the Russian position in the crisis over Berlin in 1961; it upheld Moscow's involvement in Cuba in 1961 and again in 1962. Polish delegates closely followed the Soviet lead in international organizations. In the United Nations, when Khrushchev attended the meeting of the General Assembly in the fall of 1960, Gomułka was there to support the Soviet leader. He ridiculed the references to the Russian domination in East Europe made by the British and Canadian prime ministers. At the same time he came out in favor of the Soviet proposal for the reorganization of the United Nation's Secretariat. Furthermore, the Polish delegation has consistently demanded the admission of Communist China to the United Nations Organization. At the disarmament conference in Geneva the Poles also have adhered to the Russian line. They bitterly denounced all the nuclear tests in the West, but had little to say about the Soviet abandonment of the moratorium on atmospheric tests in 1961. Last but not least, the Rapacki Plan, although never formally abandoned,* became for all practical intents and purposes integrated into Khrushchev's broader disarmament plans. In 1961, Gomułka himself characterized it as merely a "small fragment of the greater problem," namely, carrying out "general and complete disarmament." [49]

The Polish Communists followed the Soviet lead faithfully in periods of crisis and even more enthusiastically in the periods of détente with the West. At times when the international situation took really a dangerous turn, particularly at the climax of the dispute over Berlin and even more so during the confrontation over Cuba in 1962, the Polish government showed signs of anxiety and acted with relative restraint. When international tensions were reduced, the Poles made little effort to conceal their pleasure and strove to preserve the existing atmosphere. When the relations between the Soviet Union and the United States improved in 1959 and early in 1960, the Polish government took a series of steps to cultivate the "Camp David" spirit. In

---

* In fact on two occasions — in the address of Gomułka to the General Assembly of the United Nations in September 1960, and in a memorandum to the Disarmament Committee in Geneva in March 1962 — the plan was formally reiterated.

August 1959, Vice President Richard Nixon, on his way back from Moscow, was invited to stop over in Warsaw for talks with Polish leaders. In September, in his address to the conference of the International Parliamentary Union which took place in Warsaw, Rapacki strongly emphasized Poland's commitment to the cause of peace and cooperation among all nations. In February 1960 the Polish parliament adopted a resolution in which it voiced hopes for the success of the forthcoming summit meeting. In March Gomułka's article concerning the improvement of Poland's relations with the United States was published in *Foreign Affairs*. At this point the optimistic hopes of the Poles were dispelled by the fiasco of the Paris summit conference, only to reappear briefly during the period between the accession of the Democratic administration to office in January 1961, and the meeting of Khrushchev and Kennedy in Vienna a few months later.

Throughout the late fifties and still in the early sixties, Poland's relations with the West were better than those of any other member of the Communist bloc. Poland continued to accept American credits* and developed trade amounting to roughly 40 percent of its total foreign commerce with the West.[50] Next to Yugoslavia, it was the most accessible Communist country in East Europe to Western visitors.

The settlement of the Polish-Soviet controversy over the application of general principles related not only to foreign relations but to Poland's domestic policies as well. The domestic policies of a Communist country, Gomułka declared early in 1961, should follow "the general principles . . . determined at the international conferences." He did not abandon, however, his stress on the existence, parallel to the general principles, of some specific features of socialist construction in each country. "Each Communist party in power," he asserted, "determines its own line of policy — adjusting the general principles to the concrete historical situation as well as the peculiarities of its country." [51]

The issue of the reform of the Polish economic system was resolved by compromise. Gomułka abandoned plans for any drastic changes in industry, and in particular he greatly curtailed the role of workers' councils in industrial enterprises. He gained Soviet endorsement of his policy of indefinitely postponing the collectivization of agriculture. In the industrial sphere, the plans for a far-reaching decentralization of Poland's economy, adopted by

* The total amount of American credits extended to Poland in the years 1957–1963 — the bulk of it for the purchase of agricultural surpluses (wheat) for złotys — amounted to $529.1 millions. *United States Overseas Loans and Grants and Assistance from International Organizations* (Special Report Prepared for the House Foreign Committee), p. 126.

the government in May 1957, were revised early in 1958 by the special commission of the Communist Party. Following its recommendations, instead of delegating broad authority to individual enterprises, an intermediate administrative layer between these enterprises and the central planning authorities, known as the association of enterprises, was created in May 1958. Soon, however, even within this structure the trend toward centralization reasserted itself. In the fall of 1959 when the economic situation in the country temporarily deteriorated, Gomułka called for a "reinforcement of centralized controls." [52] The role of the central planning authorities was once again considerably strengthened.

Parallel to the decline of expectations for genuine decentralization of industrial planning and management, the workers' councils suffered an eclipse. If in the years 1957–1958 the number of the councils rose rapidly to 7,322, in the following year their growth was considerably slowed down, so that at the end of 1961 they numbered 8,698.[53] The plan to integrate all the councils into an organization with its own separate hierarchy never materialized. Instead, in April 1958, Gomułka suggested absorbing the workers' councils in each enterprise into a tripartite industrial self-government, composed of delegates of government-dominated trade unions and representatives of the local cell of the Communist Party, as well as the representatives of the council. In December 1958, the workers' councils legislation of November 1956 was formally revised and the great hopes attached to the emergence of workers' councils as a truly democratic force came to an end.

In the late fifties further expansion of small-scale private enterprise halted. The number of private industrial enterprises reached a peak of about 10,000 in 1959 but by 1960 had declined by 10 percent. The number of artisan workshops began to decrease even earlier. These workshops reached a peak of 135,000 in 1958, but by next year showed a slight decline.[54] Expectations for a broad revival of private enterprise certainly did not materialize; at the same time private trade also declined. In the years 1957–1961 the number of private retailers diminished from 12,800 to 8,900.[55]

In agriculture the changes introduced in 1956–1957 were preserved essentially intact. In 1959, the Polish Communists launched a campaign to promote the so-called agricultural circles, where peasants with active assistance from the state joined in the collective use of agricultural equipment. This was explicitly described by Gomułka as a first step toward realizing socialism in the countryside. At the same time, however, he reasserted his earlier stand that the Communist government would not go against the wishes of "the majority of the peasants who are opposed to collectivization." [56] By mid-1962 there were still less than 2,000 collectives in Poland.[57]

Gomułka's policy toward the Polish peasants was approved by Moscow. During his 1959 visit Khrushchev stressed the superiority of collectivized over privately owned agriculture, but agreed with Gomułka that no one should be compelled to join a collective. The Soviet leader apparently recognized that the resistance of the Polish peasants to collectivization was too strong to be overcome by the Communist government without throwing the whole country into chaos. The Russians, thus, had to console themselves with the program of agricultural circles, taking Gomułka's word for it that their ultimate aim was the socialization of Polish farming. Meanwhile, the structure of Poland's agriculture, different from the rest of the Communist countries, was accepted by them as a feature peculiar to the Polish road to socialism.

The issue of religious freedom was likewise settled by compromise. In the late fifties and early sixties Gomułka moved closer to the policies followed by the rest of the Soviet bloc, but he did not abandon his view that the Catholic Church in Poland must be treated in some special way. Although he accelerated the struggle against the Church, Gomułka refrained from trying to strangle it by persecution. Instead, he resorted to more subtle tactics. The doctrinal incompatibility of Communism and Catholicism was once again strongly stressed by the Polish United Workers' Party. At its Third Congress in 1959, Gomułka explicitly pointed to "the removal of religious superstitions" in the ranks, as one of the urgent tasks of the Communist Party.[58] His directive resulted in a drastic decline of at least the open participation of party members in religious practices.

In 1957 an Association of Atheists and Free Thinkers, designed to spread "the propaganda of the atheist, rationalist outlook; the struggle against clericalism; and the secularization of social life," [59] was established. Also, in 1957, the Society of Secular Schools was founded to promote the secularization of education. In 1958 a Society for the Study of Religion began to publish atheistic journals and books. And along with the intensified atheistic campaign came new attempts to weaken Catholicism from within. An attempt was made to promote a group of dissident priests grouped around the charitable organization Caritas. A new progressive Catholic group, the Christian Social Association, was established in 1957. And, in 1958, Pax once again intensified its activities.

In July 1958, as if deliberately seeking wide publicity, a crude police raid was staged at the Catholic shrine in Czestochowa. In the same month, the theoretical journal of the Polish Communist Party bitterly denounced the Church. It accused the Polish Catholic hierarchy of a reactionary political stand. What we are faced with, claimed the Communist writer,

is a political action which has nothing to do with religion and the Holy Scripture. Its objective is [to establish] an influence of the Church over the government to uphold the reactionary social forces.

[It is a policy] of the Vatican dictated by the interest of an international anti-Communist crusade — the policy of provocation and brinkmanship.[60]

Behind the façade of opposing the political activities of the Church and restricting it to purely spiritual functions, the scope of religious freedom was considerably curtailed. Catholic charitable activities were drastically curbed and severe taxes were imposed on Church institutions. Permission to erect new churches was refused in several cases. The clerical seminaries and the Catholic University of Lublin were deprived of many privileges as institutions of higher learning. Chaplains were limited in performing their spiritual duties in the armed forces as well as in prisons and hospitals. The observance of traditional processions and pilgrimages was often made difficult. Some priests were arrested and sentenced to prison on the far-fetched charges of encroaching on the freedom of conscience of nonbelievers. In defiance of the agreement of 1956, religious instruction in the schools was gradually restricted, and in 1960 formally banned. At the same time an attempt was made to impose governmental control on private religious instruction offered in parishes. The Catholic press was restricted in circulation and subjected to heavy censorship.[61]

However, the attempts of the Communist government to restrict religious freedom met with determined opposition on the part of both the religious hierarchy and the faithful. The spread of atheistic propaganda was countered by an intensified educational effort on the part of the clerical and lay Catholic intellectuals. The dissident priests grouped around Caritas were threatened with disciplinary sanctions and bowed to the will of the Episcopate. Cardinal Wyszyński withheld endorsement of the progressive Catholics.

The government refusal to permit the construction of new churches resulted in violent outbursts by the populace in the cities concerned, notably, in the model socialist city, Nowa Huta. The Catholic University supported by the donations of the Polish Catholics maintained its position. The priests were instructed by the hierarchy not to submit to governmental control over religious instruction offered in the parishes. Cardinal Wyszyński constantly exposed the Communist chicaneries against the Church in episcopal letters and in sermons. On the eve of the elections in the spring of 1961, he intensified his counterattack. In a letter issued in January, he alerted the clergy to be prepared for any sacrifices in defense of the faith, even "punishment, exile, loss of freedom." [62] There are countries, he declared in one of his sermons,

> where nothing is said of freedom, yet people feel free. There can be other countries where newspapers are full of articles and speeches on freedom, but where freedom is absent. People reach out for freedom and other people deprive them of it. Woe to those who seek to deprive others of freedom. Men will hide from them. In defense of his personality and human dignity, man will descend into the catacombs and will begin a life of conspiracy toward the outside world.[63]

The Cardinal's warnings made the Communist authorities proceed cautiously in their campaign against the Church. Freedom of religious practice was preserved largely intact. Control of private religious instruction in the parishes was not enforced. The Communists characterized Cardinal Wyszyński's bold sermons as an attempt to create around himself an aura of "persecution and martyrdom," [64] clearly implying that they would not resort to the direct suppression of the Church. Furthermore, throughout the entire period, relations between the government and the episcopate were never completely severed; even a few meetings between Gomułka and Wyszyński took place. Gomułka kept expounding some of his 1956–57 views on religious freedom. In the fall of 1961, in an interview granted to *Le Monde,* he said:

> Religion in Poland is deeply rooted among a significant part of the population. It would be nonsensical to try to change one's mentality and beliefs through administrative measures.[65]

Gomułka's policies toward the Church apparently met with the approval of Moscow. The Soviet leaders obviously recognized the strength of the Polish Catholic Church and the difficulties it caused the Polish government.* They apparently became reconciled to the fact that this merited the relatively broader scope of religious freedom in Poland, and accepted it as one of the distinctive features of the Polish road to socialism.

Since 1958, control over the press became more acute. Censorship of newspapers was drastically tightened. In 1959 the editorial boards of *Nowa Kultura* and *Przegląd Kulturalny* were purged and their circulation cut by

---

* Speaking to the miners in Sosnowiec, Khrushchev expounded his atheistic views and expressed the hope that they would be adopted in Poland, but at the same time stressed that he would not like to offend anybody's religious feelings. *Trybuna Ludu,* July 17, 1959.

more than half.[66] Surveillance was also increased over the writers. At the Third Congress of the Polish United Workers' Party in March 1959, Gomułka attacked the Union of the Polish Writers for tolerating the publication of books which "smear socialism." [67] In December 1959 Antoni Słonimski, one of the most prominent Polish writers, was replaced as chairman of the Union by a faithful follower of the Communist line, Jarosław Iwaszkiewicz. Writers who had been particularly outspoken critics of the Communist system in 1956–1957, frequently were prevented from publishing their works.

When compared with the 1956–1957 period from 1958 to 1961, Poland's independence from Russia was considerably restricted. For all practical intents and purposes the Polish Communist regime gave up any independent foreign policy. It unmistakably revealed its preference for an East-West détente, but was not prepared to promote it against the wishes of the U.S.S.R. Likewise in a number of internal policies the Polish government followed the Soviet lead. The only two fields in which Poland's right to differ from the U.S.S.R. was explicitly upheld were the Polish position on the collectivization of agriculture and the Catholic Church.

Even Gomułka's success in establishing Poland's right to digress from the line common to the entire Soviet bloc in the policies toward agriculture and religion still could not be regarded as final. Unless the Soviet Union reversed its own course in these matters, Poland was expected eventually to follow the common course. According to Khrushchev, the concept of different roads was not static, but dynamic. It postulated constant changes in all countries in the Soviet orbit toward the ultimate single goal of Communism. Early in 1961, the Soviet leader reminded the Poles that "the Communist parties must synchronize their watches . . . so that the Communist movement . . . keeps in step and makes confident strides toward Communism." [68]

THE EMERGING SPECIAL RELATIONSHIP

In the early sixties dramatic changes took place in the Communist bloc, which greatly improved Gomułka's position vis-à-vis the Soviet leaders. At the Twenty-Second Congress of the Communist Party of the Soviet Union in the fall of 1961, the Sino-Soviet dispute erupted into the open. Arguments between the two Communist parties were exchanged in an overt and acrimonious fashion. Open animosity between the two countries ensued. The clash between Russia and China rocked the entire Communist orbit.

By compromising the universalist pretensions of the Communist ideology, it undermined the very raison d'être of Communist bloc unity. Tha bloc split into two groupings of states centered around Moscow and Peking respectively. Among the Eastern European Communist countries, Albania sided with China. The falling out of the two giants gave the smaller Communist states an opportunity to try to assert their independence from both Russia and China. In East Europe Rumania chose this course. The Twenty-Second Congress of the Soviet Communist Party, however, was not only notable for bringing the Sino-Soviet dispute to a head. The new de-Stalinization campaign was launched on that occasion by Khrushchev. The second wave of de-Stalinization was much more thorough than that of 1956. It affected not only the U.S.S.R. but also some Communist states in Eastern Europe. Hungary and Czechoslovakia, though each in a different way, undertook far-reaching domestic reforms. All in all the trend toward polycentrism was established in the Communist world.

The growth of polycentrism very considerably weakened the Soviet position in the international Communist movement. The nature of multilateral bonds among the Communist countries underwent drastic change. The Chinese and their followers turned from Soviet allies to rivals. The support from the several Communist parties which remained friendly to the Soviets, precisely because the Russians needed so badly to demonstrate a united front against the Chinese, paradoxically could no longer be taken for granted. With the possibility open to them of siding with Peking, the smaller Communist parties gained a bargaining position vis-à-vis Moscow. Several of them were prepared to follow the Soviet course only so far as it suited their own interests. The Russians ran into considerable difficulty in arranging any new multilateral Communist conferences. When, in the fall of 1963, Khrushchev first tried to convene an international Communist meeting, he encountered such strong opposition that he had to abandon it temporarily. When he revived his proposal in the spring of 1964, he still found himself faced with serious obstacles. Several Communist parties stubbornly refused to go along with the scheme.

Khrushchev's ouster in the autumn of 1964 caused no major change in the international Communist movement. Thus, when the international Communist conference finally met in Moscow in March 1965, it proved to be of very little help to the Russians. The Chinese and their allies not only refused to take part in the gathering but bitterly denounced it. The Rumanians, although they refrained from any overt attacks, also did not participate. Several of the parties which were represented at the conference questioned its purpose. In these circumstances all that the meeting achieved was the issuing of a lukewarm communiqué which implicitly confirmed the decline of Moscow's authority in the ranks of international Communism.

With the decline of multilateral contacts the Soviet leaders increasingly turned to cultivating bilateral ties with individual Communist countries. Gomułka's Poland was given special attention. Various facts seemed to have contributed to this development. Poland's location and strategically crucial border with the U.S.S.R. was probably one. Moreover, with the falling out of the Communist giants, the support of the Polish United Workers' Party — which rules the third largest country in the Communist world — was important to Moscow. Last but not least, Gomułka's loyal adherence to the agreement of 1958 inspired confidence in him among the Soviet leaders. In the late stages of his rule Khrushchev went a long way to manifest his confidence in, and indeed, personal friendship toward Gomułka. Contacts between the two leaders have been frequent. On the occasion of the celebration of his seventieth birthday in Moscow in the spring of 1964, Khrushchev treated the Polish leader with special attention. During his visit to Poland the following summer, Khrushchev missed few opportunities to compliment Gomułka.

Following Khrushchev's ouster in the fall of 1964, the new Soviet leaders continued his course toward Poland. Gomułka was given a personal briefing on Khrushchev's fall by Brezhnev and Kosygin, who traveled for that purpose to the Białowieża forest. In the spring of 1965, both Soviet leaders reappeared in Poland to sign the renewal of the Soviet-Polish Friendship Treaty. In his speech in Warsaw, Brezhnev hailed the Soviet-Polish friendship as "a relationship of a new type, without parallel in the past." [69] Clearly the Soviet leaders were offering to Gomułka's Poland a kind of special relationship with the U.S.S.R.

The new turn in Soviet attitude toward Poland was obviously highly pleasing to Gomułka. The stress on bilateral rather than multilateral bonds among the Communist states was what he had always advocated. The Soviet offer of a special relationship was fully in line with his belief that Poland's interests were most effectively protected by direct cooperation with Moscow. Gomułka eagerly seized on this opportunity and went out of his way to repay the Soviet leaders' trust and cordiality. He not only refrained from exploiting Soviet difficulties to improve Poland's position vis-à-vis Russia, but throughout all the stages of the crisis in the Communist ranks he remained firmly on Moscow's side. Moreover, in exchange for his support, Gomułka did not insist on any overt concessions from the Russians. The stand that he took toward the Soviet leaders was that of *noblesse oblige,* the resolving of controversial issues not under pressure, but through mutual forbearance.

Nevertheless, even without an overt effort to take the advantage of the new situation, there is little doubt that it played into Gomułka's hands. The very fact that he supported the Soviet Union against China witnessed to his improved position. It was no longer only Warsaw that needed Moscow, but, *toutes proportions gardées,* Moscow which needed Warsaw. The contrast between Poland's position and the rest of the Communist world was largely eliminated. With the spread of polycentrism the national deviations from the course common to the entire Communist bloc were now widely accepted.

The position of the Polish Workers' Party as a junior, but nevertheless fully-fledged partner of the Communist Party of the Soviet Union was fully affirmed. In a speech after his return from the Twenty-Second Congress in Moscow, Gomułka once again asserted that each Communist party is "fully independent and autonomous, and bears full responsibility for the country where it is in power." At the same time he made it clear that the plan for the restoration of an international Communist organization was for all practical intents and purposes abandoned. Although he cut himself off from what he described as the "vague concept of polycentrism," Gomułka emphasized that "there exists no center which directs the activities of all Communist and workers' parties. It is not needed." [70]

The general course of Poland's foreign policy did not change in any essential way in the sixties. Its external relations remained subordinate to the overall interests of Moscow. "At the foundation of our foreign policy," declared Gomułka in 1965, "there is a close alliance with the Soviet Union and member countries of the Warsaw Pact." [71] Within this general framework, however, in the sixties Poland's foreign policy was adjusted to take into account the changed pattern of Soviet relations with the dissident Communist states and with the West.

Poland sided with the Soviet Union in its quarrel with China. In taking this stand the Polish Communists seemed to have few second thoughts, for ever since 1957 they had been out of sympathy with the policies advocated by the Chinese. In the international sphere they feared that the bellicose Chinese pressure might aggravate tensions between the East and the West beyond the point of no return. In internal policies they resented the Chinese upholding of Stalinism. As a result, at the various crucial stages of the dispute Gomułka stood firmly on the side of Soviet leaders. At the Twenty-Second Congress of the Soviet Communist Party, Gomułka joined Khrushchev in denouncing the Albanians. Soon after the theoretical journal of the Polish United Workers' Party, in thinly veiled terms, criticized the Chinese for upholding the Albanian Workers' Party.[72] When in the summer of 1963 Soviet-Chinese talks in Moscow failed, the Polish Communists promptly launched a direct attack against the Chinese position. In 1964, despite his dislike of multilateral ties among the Communist parties, Gomułka supported Khrushchev's proposals to convene an international conference to deal with the Chinese problem.

While Poland's relations with China deteriorated, her relations with Yugoslavia improved. In the early sixties the Poles clearly welcomed the new *rapprochement* between Moscow and Belgrade. The Poles emphasized that the close Polish-Yugoslav relations were motivated not only by the interests of the two states but also by their common Communist ideology. Polish Deputy Premier, Piotr Jaroszewicz, during his visit to Belgrade early in 1962, explicitly referred to the need for strengthening Poland's bonds with "socialist Yugoslavia." [73] In 1963 Cyrankiewicz visited Yugoslavia and in mid-1964 Tito paid a visit to Poland. In his speech in Warsaw the Yugoslav leader declared that "everything that divided us has disappeared and will never return." [74]

Poland's relations with the West underwent no major change in the sixties. Both in crisis and détente the Poles toed the Soviet line. In 1963, when relations between the U.S.S.R. and the U.S. improved, and especially when the nuclear test-ban treaty was signed in Moscow, the Poles did not conceal their hopes that this time a détente would be permanent. The treaty was characterized as a first step toward further relaxation; possibly to be followed by the establishment of an atom-free zone in Central Europe along the lines proposed by Rapacki.[75] In December, Gomułka advanced a proposal for freezing nuclear armaments at their present level throughout Poland, Czechoslovakia, and the two Germanies. The Gomułka plan, the Poles explained, was not aimed at superseding the Rapacki proposal, but rather it was conceived as the first step leading toward the complete ban of nuclear weapons in Central Europe. As with the Rapacki proposal, however, the Gomułka plan, when formally presented to the Western governments in the spring of 1964, did not seem to interest them.

Early in 1965 the attitude of the Polish government toward the United States once again stiffened as a result of the new deterioration in East-West relations over the conflict in Vietnam. The visit of Polish Deputy Premier,

Stefan Jędrychowski, to the United States was cancelled. In a May Day speech Gomułka bitterly denounced American policies in Vietnam and the Dominican Republic. At the same time, however, Poland's relations with France underwent marked improvement. Since the fall of 1964, diplomatic exchanges between Paris and Warsaw had been considerably stepped up. In September 1964 a French parliamentary delegation visited Poland, clearly with a view to exploring the possibility of establishing close ties between the two countries. The diplomatic overtures of Paris were warmly received in Warsaw. The contacts between the two countries were further enhanced, in a flurry of praise of the traditional Polish bonds with France in the Polish press, and by the visit of Premier Cyrankiewicz to Paris in September 1965.

In the domestic sphere Gomułka abstained from introducing any radical innovations in the sixties. He took advantage of the second wave of de-Stalinization to obtain new Soviet endorsement of his agricultural policy. When Stalin's terror was submitted to open criticism at the Twenty-Second Congress of the Soviet Communist Party, Gomułka immediately broadened it to cover the denunciation of forcible collectivization. In a speech delivered upon his return home from the Congress he offered an interpretation, unique among the Communist leaders, of the origin of Stalin's terror. He traced it to the brutal collectivization campaign in the U.S.S.R. in the early thirties. This apparently drove the point home to the Russians for they soon came out with new approval for his agricultural policy. During a visit to Poland in January 1962, one of the secretaries of the Central Committee of the Soviet Communist Party, Demichev, praised the course of the Polish United Workers' Party, pointedly including agriculture. "We see," he said, "that also in agriculture the policy of your party has brought about good results." [76]

The new de-Stalinization campaign also led to the revival of interests in the reform of Poland's economic system. In the fall of 1961, a senior Polish economist, Professor Oskar Lange, reopened the issue, and an extensive discussion in specialized economic publications followed. Proposals for further decentralization and rationalization of the economic system were obviously resisted by influential segments of the Polish United Workers' Party, for the changes were slow in coming. The proponents of reform, however, persisted in their efforts. They were encouraged by the experiments with reform along the lines advocated by Professor Yevsei Lieberman in the U.S.S.R. And in the spring of 1964 they scored their first victory. The theses prepared for the Fourth Congress of the Communist Party included the proposals for far-reaching economic changes. Although the Congress' resolution considerably narrowed the original propositions, it recognized profit as the main criterion of economic efficiency, and recommended that production should be determined on the basis of market analysis.[77] In the summer of 1964 these recommendations were turned into practice. Following the widespread adoption of Liebermanism in the Soviet Union late in 1964 and the far-reaching economic reforms in some other Eastern European countries, notably in Czechoslovakia, further changes were introduced in Poland. In the summer of 1965 a new reform was undertaken. Not only the principle of the profitability of production was reaffirmed, but the system of planning was revised. Although key decisions remained in the hands of the central authorities, more authority was given to the associations of enterprises and even individual managers. With the recognition by the Russians of the Yugoslav system based on the workers' councils as truly socialist, the Poles decided to put more life into their workers' councils. At the Congress of the Trade Unions in February 1962, the Politburo member, Ignacy Loga-Sowiński, criticized the Communist Party for excessive interference with the workers' councils.

In the realm of relations between the Communist government and the Catholic Church there was little change in the sixties. The tug-of-war between them, which had developed in the late fifties, continued essentially unabated. The Communist Party persisted in its policy of piecemeal undermining the position of the Church, and the Episcopate continued resisting it with all the means at its disposal. Meanwhile, however, both sides watched carefully for signs of change in relations between the U.S.S.R. and the Vatican. When, toward the end of the reign of Pope John XXIII these relations suddenly improved, a marked change also occurred in the attitude of the Polish regime toward the Catholics. It looked as though the deadlock in the relations between the Communists and the Catholics might now be overcome. In his speech at the Peace Congress in Moscow in the fall of 1962, Gomułka approvingly referred to statements of the Pope condemning war. The press praised the Encyclical *Pacem in Terris,* and paid considerable attention to the proceedings of the Ecumenical Council. In November the Catholic representative on the State Council, Jerzy Zawieyski, went to Rome where he personally conveyed to Pope John XXIII the respects of the Polish authorities. The Pope, in turn, expressed his satisfaction at the favorable reception of his statements by Gomułka.

In March 1963, in a speech to parliament, Zawieyski proposed the undertaking of negotiations between the Vatican and Poland, as well as between the Catholic hierarchy and the Communist government.[78] In April a meeting between Cardinal Wyszyński and Gomułka took place, and, throughout April and May, negotiations between the Holy See and Warsaw were clearly under way. Cardinal Koenig, the Pope's representative to the Communist governments in East Europe, visited Warsaw; and soon after Cardinal Wyszyński went to Rome. On May 26, Pope John XXIII, in a special message to the Polish people, pledged that he would do what he could to improve their conditions. His death in June, however, interrupted the negotiations, leaving the major issues between the Vatican and Poland still unresolved. Toward the end of June, the leader of the Catholic group in parliament, Stanisław Stomma, appealed for continued negotiations, but his efforts failed to prevent a worsening of State-Church relations in Poland. At a meeting of the Central Committee in July, Gomułka resumed his attacks on the Church hierarchy.

By the fall of 1964, the Gomułka regime and the Polish Episcopate were once again in the throes of a bitter conflict. Communists, atheists, and progressive Catholics combined forces to render a scathing personal attack on Cardinal Wyszyński. The Primate of Poland was publicly denounced as an opponent of reform in the Church and as a reactionary politician in sympathy with the objectives of the anti-Communist exile groups. The Communist Party organ likened him to the "neo-fascists, French ultramontanists and the Spanish Caudillo." [79] Cardinal Wyszyński did not remain silent in the face of these attacks. In a sermon in Warsaw on January 31, he denounced the government's restriction of religious freedom:

Man is still regarded in many states as the worst enemy of the state, as if the state were meant not for the people, but for itself . . . How long do we have to work until a citizen becomes a citizen in his own country, not a slave, not a prisoner all the time suspected, all the time shadowed, and somehow followed even in his inner-most thoughts? [80]

The Communist youth newspaper, *Sztandar Młodych* retaliated and accused the Cardinal of blocking the improvement in relations between the Polish government and the Vatican and of maintaining contact with emigré political centers. In February, however, the influential Catholic paper, *Tygodnik Powszechny,* called for the resumption of talks between the Communist authorities and the Episcopate with a view to seeking an accommodation.[81] In March Gomułka came out with renewed assurances that he regarded religion as a private matter and promised that the government would treat believers and nonbelievers alike.

The cultural policy of the Gomułka regime continued essentially unchanged. After Khrushchev launched a new de-Stalinization campaign in the fall of 1961, the unrest among the Polish intellectuals once again came into the open. In *Przegląd Kulturalny* a lively debate took place among several leading Polish scholars on the subject of the relationship between ideology and science. In comparison with the blunt criticism of Communism in the Polish press in 1956–1957, the debate in 1961 was restrained, but the political overtones were unmistakable. Law professor Władysław Wolter exclaimed at the climax of the debate that the curtailment of freedom "leads to the extinguishing of the sacred fire of human thought, to the replacement of constructive discussion and polemic from which the truth evolves by the worthless wandering in a prison compound of chained human thought." [82]

Other signs of a new ferment among the writers appeared parallel to the bolder tone of the press. The meeting of the Union of the Polish Writers in Wrocław in December 1961 brought with it demonstrations against Communist restrictions. Early in 1962 the issue of freedom of thought was taken up by the Club of the Crooked Circle. At its meeting of January 18, 1962, the President of the Polish Academy of Sciences, Professor Tadeusz Kotarbiński, reviewed the debate on the relationship of science and ideology. On February 1, the senior Marxist philosopher, Professor Adam Schaff, spoke to the club on the subject of humanism and freedom under socialism. As in 1956, both meetings were very heavily attended; and both resulted in lively and controversial discussions.

The reaction from the Communist Party was swift. The debate on the relationship of ideology and science was brought to an end by Communist academicians. Writing in *Przegląd Kulturalny*, Professor Stefan Żółkiewski declared that scholarly inquiry must be subjected not only to scientific, but also to social discipline — it must be linked to "the process of creating social values chosen by the nation at a given historical stage." [83] Scholarly endeavors in Poland, he declared, cannot be divorced from the process of socialist construction. Soon after the turbulent meeting of February 1, the Club of the Crooked Circle was closed by the authorities. [84]

No drastic steps to restrict the press were taken in Poland, as long as relative journalistic freedom continued in the Soviet Union after the new de-Stalinization campaign. Indeed, throughout 1962, controversial Soviet works were reprinted in Poland. In that year, translations of poems by Akhmadulina, Voznesensky, Evtushenko, the novel of Solzhenitsyn, and the memoirs of Ehrenburg appeared in *Polityka*. However, when Khrushchev ruled that peaceful coexistence does not imply the cessation of ideological struggle with the West, and denounced the "rotten idea of absolute freedom" in creative expression in the spring of 1963,[85] a sharp curtailment of intellectual freedom in Poland soon followed. In June 1963 *Przegląd Kulturalny* and *Nowa Kultura* were shut down. In their place was established a new weekly, *Kultura,* devoted to "the struggle against reactionary ideology" which was spreading to Poland from the West.[86] At a meeting of the Central Committee of the Polish United Workers' Party in July, the issue of ideological influences upon Polish intellectuals again received prominent attention. In his address to that meeting, Gomułka echoed Khrushchev in emphasizing that peaceful coexistence does not represent an "ideological truce" with the West; and castigated journalists, artists, and scholars for seeking inspiration for their activities in the bourgeois notion of "integral freedom." [87]

Gomułka's scathing attack, however, failed to subdue the Polish intellectuals, for early in 1964, they took an even bolder stand. By mid-March a letter of protest against the curtailment of the freedom of expression, signed by thirty-four leading Polish writers, journalists, and scientists, was dispatched to Premier Cyrankiewicz. The letter pointed out that the Communist government's cultural policy creates "a situation which is endangering the development of Polish national culture" and demanded that it be changed "to conform to the spirit of the rights guaranteed by the Polish Constitution and for the good of the nation." [88] The protest was met by the Communist Party leadership with crude repressive measures. The security police arrested for questioning the former secretary of the Club of the Crooked Circle, Jan Józef Lipski, who was suspected of having collected signatures for the letter. The publication of works by the writers who had signed the letter, including those by Antoni Słonimski who had personally delivered it to Premier Cyrankiewicz, was abruptly and drastically curtailed.

The repressive measures against Polish intellectuals evoked strong protest in the West, but the Gomułka regime, still refused to change its course. Instead, it accused some signatories of the letter to Cyrankiewicz of "passing distorted information abroad with a view to instigating a campaign of lies against Poland." [89] At the same time the writers loyal to the regime, led by Iwaszkiewicz and Żółkiewski, came out with a counterprotest, charging the Western press and broadcasts of interference in Poland's "internal problems . . . and cultural policy." [90] An open letter to that effect was signed by some six hundred writers representing, however, only roughly half of the membership of the Writers' Union. Many other writers, again including several well known Communist Party members, failed to join in the counterprotest.

The failure to win to their side even some party-card-carrying writers, undoubtedly represented a heavy blow to the prestige of the Communist leadership. The party leaders did not try to conceal their disappointment. At the Fourth Congress of the Polish United Workers' Party in June 1964, the Secretary of the Warsaw Committee, Walenty Titkow, came out with a bitter criticism of the party organization in the Writers' Union and called for undertaking there the "decisive offensive action." [91] At a meeting of the Writers' Union in Lublin in September 1964, Gomułka himself continued the attack. He accused "many writers of being divorced from the major currents of nation's life" and warned them that the Communist Party "will not resign from putting forward its appraisal, postulates, and demands in the literary sphere." [92] As if to underline the party's determination to stamp out the ferment among intellectuals, early in October 1964, one of the signers of the letter to Cyrankiewicz, the elderly writer Melchior Wańkowicz, was arrested and sentenced to three years of imprisonment on the charges of sending abroad information detrimental to the Communist government. Although the enforcement of Wańkowicz's punishment was left in abeyance, his trial still served its purpose. By staging it, Gomułka gave a warning to the restive intellectuals that he would not hesitate to turn to coercion to keep them in check.*

Compared with the 1958–1961 period, in the midsixties, the scope of Poland's independence from Russia has been somewhat widened. The spread of polycentrism in the Communist world has enhanced the position of the Polish Communist regime vis-à-vis Moscow and enabled it to seek broader authority in internal affairs. Gomułka has availed himself of this opportunity to extract from the Soviets the approval of his agricultural policy; however, he has continued to follow the Soviet lead in the realms of religion and culture.

Gomułka's policies toward the Catholic Church and the intellectuals have been particularly revealing. In the new situation he could have tried to secure greater leeway for Poland also in these two fields. Yet he has not done so, but instead has chosen to follow the Soviet example. In taking this course Gomułka has been no longer motivated by political realism, but by Communist ideology. He has clearly revealed himself to be a Communist first and a political realist second.

---

* The arrest of Wańkowicz, since he is an American citizen, heralded Gomułka's determination to suppress the ferment among intellectuals, all international complications notwithstanding. Wańkowicz, who already before the war had been a writer of considerable repute, left Poland in 1939 and in the postwar years lived in the United States. He returned to Poland only after the upheaval in 1956, but has retained his American citizenship.

9

GOMUŁKA AND THE POLISH PEOPLE

THE HONEYMOON PERIOD

Imbued with the tenets of political realism, the Polish people viewed Gomułka's program as offering them the best chance they had to improve their lot in the existing international situation. They, therefore, threw their support behind it. In the elections of January 1957, they readily responded to Gomułka's appeals to maintain — in order not to prejudice relations with Russia — the Communist government in Poland. The results of the elections, however, were such that they unmistakably indicated the voters' confidence in Gomułka personally, rather than in the Communist Party as a whole.* Apparently misled by his realist arguments, the voters thought of Gomułka first as a political realist and only secondly as a Communist. For in the eyes of the Poles, Communism and political realism were not the same thing. They were willing to support the former only so long as it served the objectives of the latter. As such, the goals of the Polish masses were clearly incompatible with those of Gomułka, for whom political realism was virtually synonymous with Communism.

In the first months after the "Polish October," the different political objectives of Gomułka and the Polish people remained obscured by their common adherence to the slogan of "Poland's own road to socialism." The Poles interpreted this quite broadly. They expected that the acceptance of

---

* In the elections, while Gomułka did quite well, several prominent figures in the party (notably, Ochab and Cyrankiewicz) fared very poorly. Since the multimember constituencies' system was used, they still managed to be elected, but in terms of votes received, they trailed badly behind nonparty candidates.

what they simply called the "Polish Road" would bring about further drastic changes in the country. The spontaneous debate on the program of reform, thus, continued with unabated force. In discussion clubs and in the press, various aspects of the Communist system were submitted to criticism. Particularly bitter attacks appeared in *Po prostu*,* the weekly publication of the students and young intelligentsia. Issue after issue contained shattering reports exposing various dark sides of life in Poland. Although the paper never came out with a cohesive program of reform, its ultimate goal was obvious. It was to "bring about a radical transformation of the Stalinist model of socialism into a Polish model, genuinely socialist." The young writers in *Po prostu* were not unaware that such a development might be opposed by Moscow, but they preferred to ignore this. Carried away by their enthusiasm they wanted to believe that the assertion of "Poland's right to an independent road to socialism" meant virtually a free hand in the domestic sphere.[1]

The difference between Gomułka and the Polish people became obvious by mid-1957. Gomułka's speech in May of that year, defining the limits of Polish autonomy quite narrowly, represented a serious setback to the Poles. The restriction of criticism in the press and, above all, the suspension in July, and then the forced closure in October, of *Po prostu* came as a shock to them. The enthusiasm of the people for Gomułka began to wane.

At this stage some older intellectuals attempted to bridge the widening gap. These men condemned as exaggerated and vague the hopes for reform expounded in *Po prostu* and, instead, tried to advance a more moderate but at the same time more concrete plan of action. Using the Club of the Crooked Circle and the press as a forum, they soon came out with their own program of reform. The new program took Gomułka's difficult position vis-à-vis Moscow into account and, consequently, carefully avoided any overt proposals incompatible with his version of Poland's road to socialism. Within these limits, however, the program still advocated considerable change in the internal political system.

The interdependence of Poland's external policy and internal reforms was succinctly analyzed in an article (written for a confiscated issue of *Po prostu*, but widely circulated in Warsaw in manuscript form) by a well-known economist, Stefan Kurowski.[2] In 1956, he said, the Polish people

---

* Its militant advocacy of a reform program resulted in considerable mass popularity. This was explicitly acknowledged by Gomułka in October 1957. See *6 lat temu: Kulisy polskiego października* (Paris, 1962), p. 187.

expected radical political and economic changes. However, "due to external as well as internal political reasons," the reforms could not be carried out. As a result "apathy, indifference, disillusionment, and boredom" spread throughout the country. Yet, suggested Kurowski, such reaction was not necessary for there existed a way out. "Irrespective of the grave problems flowing from the situation on the larger political plane," he argued (deliberately avoiding explicit mention of Poland's juxtaposition to Russia), "there exist several problems on a local scale." And local problems can be resolved by the Poles alone "without getting involved in larger conflicts." Solving such problems would give the Polish people a chance to improve their life, and thus would check the spread of their frustration. Clearly, what Kurowski was calling for was a tacit agreement between the Communist regime and the masses to carry out reforms in Poland with as little fanfare as possible in order to avoid arousing the wrath of Moscow.

The domestic aspect of reform was advanced in two articles published in *Przegląd Kulturalny* by a prominent sociologist, Professor Jan Szczepański.[3] The writer advocated a broad program of democratization. He denounced the view that only the Communist Party is fit to rule the country. "Political wisdom," he asserted, "is spread across the whole nation . . . and the responsibility for Poland belongs to all citizens without exception." What was needed, then, concluded Szczepański, was not to ignore the people who are not members of the Communist Party, but — for the benefit of the entire nation — to take advantage of their energy and their knowledge through permitting them to participate in the government.

From the proposals of Kurowski, Szczepański, and others there emerged a fairly coherent program of reform designed to promote the broad democratization of political life in Poland within the rigid framework of external circumstances. It advocated several measures which, if carried out, would have substantially transformed the Communist system in Poland without affecting its façade in any important way. In addition to the economic reforms and the widening of religious and cultural freedom, (the approval of which was to be overtly extracted from the Russians as specific features of the Polish road to socialism), the program proposed the following measures: 1) Strict observance of the rule of law in relations between the government and the people, to be safeguarded by some institutional checks; 2) Enhancement of the powers of parliament, both in legislation and supervision of administration; 3) Reorganization of the administration so as to eliminate bureaucracy; 4) Extension of the freedom of voluntary association so as to create an additional outlet for the creative energies of the people.

The program advanced by these Polish intellectuals was realistic par excellence. It took into account the hard facts of Poland's position vis-à-vis Russia. It accepted the necessity of preserving the Communist government in Poland. It did not even postulate any radical internal changes, taking as its point of departure Gomułka's interpretation of Poland's road. Within these limits all it asked for was a certain degree of democratization of Polish life. As such, however, the program presupposed that Gomułka would be free and willing to tacitly cooperate with the Polish people against the wishes of Moscow. In other words, the program of reform was still inspired by the belief that Gomułka was first a political realist and only secondly a convinced Communist.

DISILLUSIONMENT WITH GOMUŁKA

Throughout the remaining fifties the gap between the Communist government and the Polish people widened steadily. Gomułka's falling in line with Moscow in 1958, which resulted in the drastic curtailment of Poland's external as well as internal autonomy, in itself contributed to a widespread disenchantment with his policies. His unequivocal endorsement of Soviet foreign policy and, especially, support of the Russian position in the Berlin crisis dispersed hopes for a gradual widening of Poland's independence through the transformation of the international situation in Central Europe. At the same time, the tightening of Communist controls in the domestic sphere, and especially the resumption of the attacks against the Catholic Church, brought an end to expectations of any major change in the nature of the political system in Poland. Gomułka's cutting himself off from "rightist-nationalist deviation" at the Third Congress of the Polish United Workers' Party in 1959, and his return to the centralized control over the economy in the same year, only accelerated the disillusionment with his course. As a consequence of all these events, Gomułka's popularity in the country declined greatly, although in the late fifties many Poles continued to trust him. Pointing to Poland's difficult situation as the lonely outpost of reform in the Communist bloc, they clung to an image of Gomułka as primarily a political realist and justified most of his retrogressive measures as a response to pressure from Moscow.

As time went on, however, it became increasingly evident that Gomułka's conduct could not be attributed solely to Soviet pressure. On several issues Gomułka turned against the Poles and sided with the Russians — not because he was compelled to do so by the exigencies of Poland's external position, but clearly on his own volition. In doing so, he showed himself to be motivated not by precepts of political realism but by the tenets of Marxism-Leninism.

The differences between Gomułka's objectives and those of the Polish people came to a head over the program of the democratization of Poland's internal political system. Gomułka was clearly out of sympathy with the major proposal advanced by Szczepański, Kurowski, and others,[4] namely, that Communists should share the responsibility for ruling the country with non-Communists. From the beginning, Gomułka made no bones about the fact that he had no intention of restricting the power monopoly of the Polish United Workers' Party in any way. "Poland is engaged in socialist construction," he gave as his reason for taking such a stand, and this task "cannot be accomplished by anybody else but the Communist Party."[5]

Thus, while Gomułka continued to pay lip-service to the principle of democratization, it was obvious that he conceived this process in a way exactly opposite to the view of the masses of Polish people. For if the majority of Poles looked at democratic reforms as a vehicle with which Communism could be weakened, Gomułka regarded such reforms as a tool with which the Communist system could be strengthened. For Gomułka, the progress of democratization in Poland was inseparably linked with the advancement of Communism. Indeed, in his eyes it was the success of Communism which determined the scope of democracy. "The deepening of the influence of the [Communist] Party in all spheres of life," Gomułka declared in 1959, "represents a precondition of socialist democracy . . . When the leading position of the party is weakened . . . the activities of hostile, antisocialist elements are revived . . . Then the [class] struggle is inevitably aggravated and the scope of democratic freedoms must be restricted."[6]

Gomułka's insistence on maintaining strict one-party rule, of course, made it impossible to carry out any genuine democratic reforms. The changes he himself initiated after 1956, thus, represented, at best, half-hearted measures.

The most striking example of the restricted character of these political reforms was provided, perhaps, by feeble attempts to restore the rule of law.

After his return to power, Gomułka strongly condemned the terror which prevailed in Poland during the Stalinist era and solemnly pledged to uphold the observance of legality. He had no intention, however, of dispensing with coercion in dealing with opponents of the Communist regime. Freedom, according to Gomułka, was a class concept subordinate to the exigencies of the dictatorship of the proletariat.[7] There can be no freedom for the opponents of Communism. In line with such views coercion could be restricted but not abandoned. The authority of the organs of justice was enhanced, but by no means freed completely from political control.

In 1956–1957, the activities of the security apparatus were brought under the control of the government and considerably curtailed. In November 1956, the separate Committee of Public Security was abolished and its functions transferred to a special division of the Ministry of Internal Affairs. At the same time, a fairly extensive purge of the entire security apparatus took place.[8] A handful of the top security officials who had been guilty of particularly flagrant abuses were even tried and punished with various prison terms.[9] Other channels of governmental control over the security apparatus were also established. In February 1957, the system of public prosecution was reorganized to strengthen its supervision over all stages of criminal investigation. Since 1957, a parliamentary committee on internal affairs has been conducting a regular review of the activities of security organs.

The above reforms reduced but by no means eliminated police surveillance over certain aspects of life in Poland. The police were kept in the background but they remained very much present. In 1958 the security apparatus once again was reorganized and expanded.[10] "The constant perfecting of the work of . . . the organs of public security," asserted the resolution of the Third Congress of the Polish United Workers' Party in 1959, "is necessary . . . in order to quench all sorts of anti-socialist, anti-state, and espionage activities."[11] Soon the activities of the security police throughout the country visibly intensified. As a whole, they still remained preventive rather than repressive in their nature, but there were at least a few cases in which people were arbitrarily deprived of their freedom.[12] The increase in the activities of the security apparatus were justified in 1961 by the Minister of Internal Affairs, Władysław Wicha, as a response to the alleged revival of "the enemy centers [which] try to instigate . . . the activities of elements hostile" to the Communist regime.[13]

Following Gomułka's return several reforms were also carried out in the execution of justice. In November 1956, the scope of independence of attorneys was widened substantially. The Minister of Justice's supervision over the Bar was curtailed. Attorneys were assured of the same inviolability as judges in performing their functions. In May 1957, the professional qualifications required of judges were considerably increased. At the same time, the principle of appointing and removing judges at all levels not by the Minister of Justice but by the collective head of the state, the State Council, was observed; while the task of overseeing the verdicts of the lower tribunals was shifted from the Ministry of Justice to the Supreme Court.[14]

All of these reforms, however, did not mean that Gomułka desired the court system and the Bar to be independent of political authority. Communist leaders deemed themselves free to rebuke and, indeed, to instruct judges in performing their duties. In the late fifties particularly strong pressure was exerted on the judiciary to punish severely the widespread theft of state property. In 1959, the Minister of Justice, Marian Rybicki, bluntly warned the judges that the Communist Party would not put up with a situation in which people guilty of such crimes received relatively light sentences. The leadership of the Communist Party, he admonished the judiciary, "many times has expressed its anxiety over the [leniency] of the judges . . . We cannot afford . . . to tolerate the lack of determination in punishing the criminals who plunder the socialized property." [15] The reorganization of the Supreme Court in 1962, thus, was exploited for the sake of "deepening of socialist principles of administration of justice." [16] Much as the principle of independence of the judiciary was formally reasserted on that occasion, in fact, by establishing various channels of control by the executive, and particularly by the Minister of Justice, the supremacy of political authority over the judiciary was reaffirmed.

Parallel to reimposing political controls on the courts, the independence of the Bar was once again restricted. By mid-1957, attorneys found themselves under attack by the Communist Party for misconstruing, under the influence of the bourgeois legal tradition, their role in the administration of justice. Soon a campaign against attorneys was mounted in the press, accusing them, in order to justify the revival of governmental supervision over the Bar, of the widespread violation of professional ethics and even of graft and corruption. In March 1958, the autonomy of the Bar was formally circumscribed. The Minister of Justice was provided with "real influence over the selection of a proper attorneys' cadre and real power to interfere in the disciplinary proceedings against the attorneys." [17]

The changes in 1958, however, still failed to bring the attorneys into line with the wishes of the Communist government. As in the case of the judges, especially strong Communist criticism was directed against the attorneys' effective defense of criminals guilty of the theft of state property. In order to prevent criminals from getting away with mild sentences, summary proceedings seriously restricting the right of defense were introduced in trying such cases. The conflict over an attorney's right to defend his clients effectively was brought to a head in December 1960 during the trial of a manager of a tannery who was found guilty of gross corruption. In the course of an argument with the prosecutor, who demanded the death penalty for the defendant, Attorney Michał Brojdes bluntly compared the summary proceedings in the court with Nazi justice. "I see that the Hitler ideology has not been forgotten among us," he exclaimed. "My client is a criminal, yes. But we must defend the individual, corrupt or not," because this is an attorney's duty. The defendant was spared from death, but Brojdes was charged with contempt of court and put on trial in July 1961. His trial, however, provided another occasion for a spirited assertion of the right of defense. Attorney Joachim Markowicz, who defended Brojdes, bitterly denounced the Communist system of justice. "Let us remember," he cried, "the twenty officials doomed in 1953 but exculpated later. Couldn't this sort of injustice be prevented if we had more courageous lawyers as Brojdes? [18] As a result Brojdes was let off with a relatively mild sentence of three months, but for his defense Markowicz was suspended from practice by the Minister of Justice. At the same time a special commission headed by the Deputy Prosecutor, Marian Mazur, was appointed to prepare plans for a general reorganization of the Bar. In December 1961 the commission made public its recommendations. In his report the commission's chairman succinctly defined the rule of an attorney in the Communist system. On the one hand "an attorney has a right and duty to act on behalf of his client. On the other hand, however, he may not undermine the essential objective of a socialist trial . . . [which is] to administer the law in accordance with its social contents — in line with the interest of socialist construction." [19]

Late in 1961 and throughout 1962 an extensive purge of attorneys, especially among those of the prewar generation, was conducted. Under pressure from the Ministry of Justice disciplinary proceedings were undertaken by the Bar against roughly 10 percent of all the attorneys in Poland.[20] At the same time the planned reorganization of the Bar was pushed forward. In 1961 new rates for the services of attorneys were introduced, drastically reducing their incomes. In 1962 — following the Soviet pattern — attorney cooperatives, in which they shared their work and earnings, were introduced in Poland. In addition to the enforcement of professional ethics, a special task of the cooperatives was the improvement of the sociopolitical consciousness of its members. In short, in the words of the Deputy Minister of Justice, the independent legal profession was turned into "one of the elements of the administration of law." [21]

All in all, attempts to restore the rule of law in Poland largely followed those in the Soviet Union after de-Stalinization. The similarity, of course, was not accidental but was brought about by a conscious effort on the part of the Gomułka regime. This was openly admitted in a speech reviewing the changes in this field in the years 1956–1959 by the Chairman of the Association of the Polish Lawyers, Professor Jerzy Jodłowski. The violations of the law of the Stalinist period, he said, have been definitely eliminated. Yet, he emphasized that the reforms "not only preserved the socialist direction of development of People's Poland . . . but in fact contributed to the evolving of more effective forms and methods of socialist construction. The [character of this] transformation has not represented the departure from the general principles followed by all the countries engaged in socialist construction." [22]

The hopes for an essential widening of democracy by enhancing the role of the Polish parliament, the *Sejm,* also did not materialize. True, after his rise to power, Gomułka criticized the situation in which the Sejm had been turned into a rubber stamp of the executive during the Stalinist years, and promised to restore its position as the "highest organ of the state authority." [23] Once again, however, the reforms actually carried out proved to be fainthearted. They stopped short of impairing the power monopoly of the Polish United Workers' Party in any way.

In 1957 several changes designed to enhance the role of the Sejm were introduced. The new parliament elected in January of that year was not really a representative body, for all its members were elected from the single slate of the Front of Nation's Unity which was effectively controlled by the Communist Party. Yet, as a result of liberalized methods of selecting candidates as well as the procedure of appointing more candidates than there were seats to be filled in each constituency (in this way giving the voters a chance to reject the most objectionable individuals) the new Sejm represented a fairly broad cross section of public opinion. Barely more than fifty percent of the seats were held by Communists; the remaining seats were filled by the representatives of the United Peasant Party, the Democratic

Party, and the Catholic Znak group as well as a relatively large number of men not linked to a political movement at all.[24] The standing orders adopted by the new parliament emphasized these lines of political division by establishing a separate caucus for each political group.* Moreover, among the representatives of the Communist Party, there were several men who were known to be ardent supporters of democratic reforms. Indeed, it was the deputy chairman of the caucus of the Polish United Workers' Party, Professor Julian Hochfeld, who in the spring of 1957 came out with a proposal for the autonomy of the caucus from the party leadership. This, in his opinion, would establish within the ruling party a system of checks and balances which would eliminate the danger of an abuse of power.[25]

The role of the new Polish parliament certainly went beyond that which had hitherto been played by the legislature in any Communist state. It far exceeded that of the Supreme Soviet even after the expansion of that body's functions in the post-Stalinist years. The Sejm adopted several practices which brought it closer to the democratic parliaments of the West. Legislation by decree was almost completely discontinued in Poland.[26] In order to give more attention to legislative measures the plenary sessions of the Sejm were considerably extended.[27] The practice of giving each bill two readings was introduced. Fairly exhaustive annual debates took place on the national economic plan and the budget. Legislative measures proposed by the government were sometimes submitted to criticism by nonparty deputies; indeed, occasionally some abstained from voting or even voted against the adoption of bills. The number of parliamentary committees was increased, and they all were quite active. It was in these committees that legislative proposals were scrutinized in detail, occasionally resulting in their modification or even rejection.[28] In addition, parliamentary control over administration was widened. In December 1957 a constitutional amendment was enacted establishing a special auditing commission to broadly supervise the activities of various branches of the executive, responsible to the Sejm. Ministers attended the meetings of parliamentary committees to explain the policies of their departments. Deputies addressed written questions pertaining to different administrative problems to the members of the cabinet. Occasionally, even top Communist political leaders appeared before the Sejm to report the broad lines of the government's policy and ask for approval in the form of a special resolution.

* An attempt to form a separate caucus composed of the nonparty deputies was also made, but it was not allowed by Gomułka on the grounds that it would amount to the forming of a new political party.

There is no doubt that all this amounted to a substantial revival of parliamentary activities in Poland. And, yet, they in no way changed the
essence of the political system in the country, because the Polish United
Workers' Party through its majority (as well as its influence over the
deputies representing the other two political parties), at all times retained
firm control over the Sejm. The proposals of Hochfeld and others to give
Communist deputies the right to a free vote were unequivocally rejected. If
anything, discipline within the parliamentary caucus of the Polish United
Workers' Party was strengthened. At the Third Congress in 1959, its statute
was changed in order to provide explicitly for the subordination of the
caucus to the Central Committee. Moreover, in the elections of 1961 the
number of Communists in the Sejm was increased at the expense of nonparty deputies.[29] At the same time, and again in the elections of 1965, the
most outspoken advocates of further democratization were purged from the
ranks of the deputies, Communist and non-Communist alike. As a result, the
Communists managed to combine effectively the enhanced role of the Sejm
with continued one-party rule. One more level was simply added to the
chain of political command. In terms of the source of all political decisions,
however, there was no essential change. The major political decisions, in
the words of a Catholic deputy, "still are made outside the Sejm in the
Politburo of the Polish United Workers' Party or in the cabinet. When those
decisions need to be translated into law they are passed over [for enactment]
to the Sejm . . . When no such need exists, the Sejm may have nothing to
do with them." [30]

The expectations of a substantial shift toward democracy through the reform of public administration and local government in Poland also were not
realized. As in other spheres of political life, some changes were introduced
here but were ineffective because of the one-party rule. Gomułka's attempts to
curb the power of the bureaucracy and widen local government were of a
threefold nature. First, an effort was made in the late fifties to improve the
qualifications of civil servants. Training in public administration, both at
the university and high school level, was expanded. The recruitment of the
civil servants was liberalized so as to permit more non-Communists with
proper qualifications to join the ranks and even to assume fairly responsible
posts. Secondly, a reorganization of the state apparatus with a view to the
decentralization of authority was undertaken. In the years 1956–1958, the
central administration was considerably streamlined. The number of min-
istries and centralized agencies was reduced from 58 to 35; in the same

years, the number of civil servants employed by these agencies was reduced from 258,000 to 192,000.[31] At the same time, a transfer of administrative authority to local governments took place. In January 1958 the responsibility for various economic and cultural activities was passed downward to the district level. In 1961, a campaign was launched to expand the activities of the local authorities at the town and village level. Last but not least, an attempt was made to improve the position of the public vis-à-vis the state bureaucracy. Thus, in November 1956, the parliament explicitly upheld the right of a citizen to take legal action against any official, even to claim compensation for damages suffered. In January 1961, a code of administrative proceedings, elaborating the channels through which grievances could be corrected, was introduced.

Even though the reforms in public administration were useful, they did not amount to any major change in the relationship between the Communist state and the citizens. They were all, at best, a qualified success. First of all, crucial administration posts from the Council of Ministers down to the local government remained filled by Communists.[32] Indeed, in view of the shortage of loyal party members, many of the men who proved incompetent in one position were given another post in some other part of the country. The failure of the decentralization reform was frankly admitted in 1959 by Premier Józef Cyrankiewicz. "We have not overcome as yet," he said, "the bureaucratic tendencies in the central administrative apparatus." At the same time, he complained that local government "does not take advantage of its newly acquired powers."[33] Finally, the new code of administrative proceedings did not eliminate red tape in relations between the bureaucracy and the people. In accordance with the code's provisions, numerous complaints were filed, only to be ignored by civil servants, without any subsequent recourse to administrative tribunals. "The code has not gotten into the blood of our administration," the Warsaw newspaper conceded in 1962.[34]

The fiasco of administrative reform in Poland was once again the result of an attempt by the Gomułka regime to have its cake and eat it, too: to release greater initiative from below without giving up any real control from above. As such it followed closely the example of similar endeavors in the Soviet Union. Indeed, that the overhaul of the system of public administration in Poland was largely patterned after similar attempts in the U.S.S.R. was acknowledged in 1960 by a Polish specialist in the field. "The profound changes in the realm of reorganization of the state administrative apparatus [in the Soviet Union] exerted a beneficial influence upon the changes taking place in Poland." [35]

Finally, the anticipation that Gomułka would permit a broader democratization of life through expanded activities of voluntary association proved illusory. With regard to organizations of a political character, Gomułka acted quite firmly and swiftly. The revival of the Christian Democratic Party was not allowed. The Alliance of the Democratic Youth, established in 1956, was soon disbanded. Most of the discussion clubs where political topics had been debated were subjected to all sorts of administrative pressures. By 1957 most of these clubs had disappeared. At the same time, the Communists were determined to recover their influence in the professional, cultural and youth organizations where non-Communists had gained ground in 1956. Gomułka's close political associate, Ignacy Loga-Sowiński, was placed at the helm of the trade unions in 1956. The Alliance of the Fighters for Freedom and Democracy, in which many former members of non-Communist forces had assumed responsible posts in 1956, once again became the domain of Communist veterans. In the late fifties the Communists recaptured the key positions in the Union of Polish Writers and most of the other influential cultural associations. The Alliance of Polish Youth, which disintegrated in 1956, was replaced by the Alliance of Socialist Youth, directly subordinate to the Communist Party. The Alliance of Rural Youth, which in 1956 was planned with an exclusive link to the United Peasant Party, was also taken under the wing of the Polish United Workers' Party. The boy scout movement, which in 1956 spontaneously reverted to its prewar traditions, was brought back under Communist influence. Thus, within a few years the great upsurge toward reforging all social bonds in Poland was effectively extinguished; the Communists once again controlled virtually all voluntary associations.

As in other spheres, so in the realm of voluntary association, the policies of the Polish Communist regime were influenced by the Soviet example. There was a growing tendency in Poland to integrate social organizations into the governmental structure by delegating to them functions hitherto performed by the state administration. In the industrial field, the trade unions, which had already been used to that end in the Stalinist years, continued as a virtual arm of Gomułka's government. In the countryside, the agricultural circles increasingly assumed the same character. Also in the early sixties, workers' courts, patterned after similar informal tribunals in the Soviet Union, made their first appearance in Poland.

All the reforms introduced into the political system in Poland by Gomułka, thus, represented merely an *ersatz* democratization. They attempted to mitigate the most oppressive features of Stalinism without, however, striking at the roots of totalitarianism, namely, the power monopoly of the Communist Party. As such they resembled strongly the changes which were carried out in the post-Stalinist years in the U.S.S.R. The resemblance, of course, was not accidental. It was a result of a conscious effort on the part of Gomułka to copy in Poland at least some aspects of what has been described as Khrushchev's "rationalized totalitarianism." [36] This was openly admitted by Polish Communists. The program of reforms followed by the Polish United Workers' Party since 1956, according to a leading Communist specialist on Poland's political institutions, Professor Jerzy Starościak, "did not represent a program of socialist renovation confined within the borders of Poland. It was a reflection in Poland of the new conceptions of democratic socialist construction which were outlined for the entire bloc of socialist states by the Twentieth Congress of the Communist Party of the Soviet Union." [37]

In comparison with the Stalinist years, the changes in Poland introduced by Gomułka undoubtedly represented progress. The very fact, of course, that they were patterned after Khrushchev's "rationalized totalitarianism" precluded the possibility of a return to Stalinist methods. All the essential changes, then, that were introduced in Russia were repeated in Poland. Furthermore, the abandonment of collectivization and the tolerance of relatively broad religious liberty widened the scope of freedom in Poland beyond that of de-Stalinization in the U.S.S.R. The contrast between the situation prior to 1956 and that in the years following was aptly described by a Communist journalist in answer to a Western broadcast's view that there has been a trend toward neo-Stalinism in Poland. "The difference," he exclaimed," is visible everywhere in the way of behavior, in the way of conversation, in the way of entertainment, in the language of the press, in the language of the politicians, in the attitude toward the citizen and his liberties, in legality, in the normal reactions to the knock at the door at five o'clock in the morning." [38]

Still, Gomułka's course came as a bitter disappointment to the Polish people. Above all, his insistence on maintaining the dictatorship of the Communist Party clearly fell short of even the most moderate aspirations of the Poles in the years 1956–1957. Worse than that, his policy brought about the reversal of some reforms which had actually come into existence during the "Polish October." In the eyes of the Polish people, then, Gomułka's course was seen as a step backward. It was generally labeled in Poland as a "retreat from October."

The disillusionment with Gomułka's policies was reflected in a sharp decline in his popularity. In the early sixties the number of people who still refused to see the First Secretary as a convinced Communist had dwindled drastically. Gomułka himself effectively contributed to this process. His persistent playing down of the special characteristics of the Polish road to socialism, and his renewed stress on the copying of aspects of the Soviet political system in Poland, disposed of many illusions about his real beliefs. His failure to take advantage of the spread of polycentrism in the Communist world to change this course — above all manifested in his cultural policy — finally dispelled the myth of Gomułka as a nationalist merely disguised as a Marxist. And, as is frequently the case with frustrated affection, the admiration of many Poles for Gomułka gave way to resentment.*

BACK TO ORGANIC REFORM

The widespread disillusionment with Gomułka's course did not lead to the revival of any overt political opposition in Poland. In accordance with the precepts of political realism, the Poles refrained from resisting the Communist regime by revolutionary means. The tightening of the limits of freedom by the Gomułka regime did not prompt them to revert to any type of organized conspiracy. The occasional anti-regime demonstrations — the strike of electric tram drivers in Łódź in 1957, the student riots in Warsaw after the closing of their newspaper *Po prostu* that same year, or the disorders over the religious issue in Kraśnik Lubelski in 1959, in Nowa Huta and Zielona Góra in 1960, and in Toruń in 1961 — were all spontaneous outbursts and, even more significantly, were all aimed at defending the status quo of the "Polish October" rather than trying to bring about some further revolutionary changes. At the same time, since only extremely limited opportunities existed for legal opposition, the great majority of the Poles withdrew from all politics. They retreated into private life and turned their attention primarily to looking after their own welfare. In Poland, a keen American observer wrote in 1960, "indifference to politics, rejection of any ideology, and retreat into private life dominate the scene." [39]

---

* Gomułka, however, seems to have retained a considerable respect among the Poles for his unassuming way of life. His modesty and his integrity are rarely questioned even by his most bitter political enemies.

The retreat into private life was stimulated by years of tension as well as political frustration. After almost two decades of life in fear and privation, the Polish people were tired. They were anxious, therefore, to take advantage of the absence of terror and the somewhat improved economic conditions. They wanted, above all, to provide themselves and their families with the material amenities of which they had been deprived for so many years. In short, they strove at long last to lead a normal life.*

In the situation of the Poles, however, the very fact of turning away from politics represented a political act. It was the only way available to them, short of conspiracy, to demonstrate disapproval of the policies of the Communist regime. Refusal of popular cooperation was also a partially effective means of thwarting some Communist measures. There is little doubt that the Poles were happy to see their spontaneous withdrawal from political activity in the late fifties achieve either one of these objectives.

The retreat from politics into private life was clearly inspired by the example of positivism. Having followed in the fifties a thoroughly realist program in their foreign policy, the Poles naturally also embraced its tenets in the domestic sphere. "The philosophy which has permeated Poland," observed a visitor from Britain in 1962, "is the nineteenth-century tradition of organic [reform] . . . not resistance . . . but the building up of the cultural and economic happiness of the non-self-governing race." [40]

The old program of organic reform, however, had to be substantially modified to fit the new situation existing in Poland. There is no doubt that it was easier for the Poles to follow the precepts of organic reform under nineteenth-century capitalism than under twentieth-century Communism. The harmony between private and national goals which had existed under the *laissez-faire* system broke down in several respects under Communist totalitarianism. This was manifested both in the economic and political spheres.

In the realm of economic activity the slogan of *enrichissez vous,* of course, was of restricted value in a largely socialized economic system. Turning one's energies into amassing private fortune through building up one's own industrial or commercial enterprise was no longer possible. On a limited scale an outlet for entrepreneurial talent existed, for farmers and for the few remaining owners of small private enterprises. For the bulk of the people

---

* By contrast with the Stalinist period the situation appears almost normal to many Poles. In Poland, a conversant in Warsaw told this writer in 1961: "The war ended only in 1956. Until that time civil strife existed in our country. One could never be quite certain if he would not be the next casualty in it. Nowadays if you mind your own business you can live in peace."

employed in nationalized industry, however, the opportunities for improving their material welfare through intensifying their efforts were greatly limited. This was true because as a whole the level of salaries and wages in Poland remained extremely low. The equalization of income was pushed to the point where it left relatively little room for material incentives. Moreover, the shortages of various consumers' goods, still acute in some spheres, frequently deprived even those individuals who scraped together enough financial means of an opportunity to enjoy a substantially improved standard of living.

The largely socialized and generally planned character of Poland's economy also severely circumscribed the political significance of turning one's attention solely to economic activity. Under the Communist system, unlike the *laissez-faire* system, all crucial areas of economic life were controlled by the government. In such a situation hardly any economic activity independent from the state was possible. Indeed, the most effective way an individual could promote economic progress of the country was by joining the ranks of the state bureaucracy. This represented not an act of defiance but of reconciliation with the government. The aura of political opposition, thus, no longer surrounded turning one's attention solely to economic activity.

The situation was further complicated by the fact that in view of the restricted degree of autonomy of the Polish Communist regime from Moscow, the policies followed by it (as, by the Communists' own admission, was the case prior to 1956) might benefit the Soviet Union rather than Poland. This could deprive organic reform of its patriotic rationale. For by intensifying its economic efforts, the Polish nation might weaken rather than strengthen its relative power position vis-à-vis Russia.

And yet, even though the program of organic reform certainly did not fit their needs as well as it did in the nineteenth century, the Polish people still managed to turn it into a moderately effective instrument with which they tried to advance their economic as well as political goals. This was, above all, due to the fact that in the socioeconomic sphere the objectives of the Polish nation and those of the Communist regime were not incompatible but to a large extent supplementary. The Poles were certainly in agreement with Gomułka's goal of continued industrialization of the country. They might have objected to several means by which the Communist government promoted this end, but they seemed to have approved the generally socialist character of the socioeconomic system in Poland. They were convinced that planned economy was the most effective way to overcome economic backwardness, and that many of the radical social reforms had contributed to the modernization of life in the country.* The majority of the Polish people, thus, regarded turning one's attention to economic activity, even though this necessarily involved active cooperation with the Communist authorities, as essentially in line with Poland's national interests.

Most Poles also appeared to share Gomułka's belief that close economic relations with the Soviet Union were on the whole beneficial to Poland. At least they realized that since Poland was not a self-sufficient country, in order to advance its industrialization, it must simultaneously develop its foreign trade. Because they encountered considerable difficulties in sub-stantially increasing their efforts outside the Soviet bloc, they had to accept the necessity of expanding trade with other Communist states. Well aware of the possible economic as well as political disadvantages inherent in this course, they still seemed to think that on the balance it served their national interests.[41] The Polish people, thus, were not unduly worried about the danger that they would play into Soviet hands by intensifying their economic efforts. On the contrary, they believed that in the end it was the Polish nation which would profit. They recalled that in the long run it was Poland not Russia which had reaped the benefits of industrial expansion in the Polish provinces in the tsarist empire. Indeed, they thought that economic progress was an indispensable precondition to strengthening their position in the international arena. A Polish economist in 1962 expressed the view which appeared to be widely held by the middle-generation of intelligentsia: "Freedom and independence have become economic concepts. One's in-dependence is related to one's economic strength. The stronger is one's economy, the greater is one's independence." [42]

THE "LITTLE STABILITY"

The Polish people, of course, have endorsed the industrialization and mod-ernization of their country not only for nationalistic reasons, but because they expect this also to advance their material well-being. In the existing system,

* The opinions on this subject among Western observers diverge considerably, however. On one side, Professor Calvin B. Hoover, after visiting Poland, arrived at the conclusion that . . . "if the Poles had been entirely free to do so in 1956, they would have tried to revert to some form of capitalism." *The Economy, Liberty, and the State* (Baltimore, 1959), p. 396. On the other side, Professor Richard Hiscocks, after traveling a great deal throughout Poland, voiced exactly the opposite opinion: ". . . The Poles, if not Communists, are convinced socialists. After their past experiences they are enthusiastic supporters of the welfare state." "Social Wel-fare in Poland," *The World Today*, January, 1959, p. 25. The evidence that this writer gathered during his visits to Poland would support the latter view.

not being able to accomplish much in this regard, they content themselves with little. Any small progress toward satisfying their material needs is appreciated. The tendency to strive toward what they call "little stability" pervades the Polish masses.

All existing barriers notwithstanding, some people in Poland still manage to secure at least a modicum of material comfort. Despite a general tendency toward the leveling off of incomes, economists, engineers, managers, scholars, and even some skilled workers are relatively well paid. If necessary, they take on extra employment to supplement their earnings, which in an expanding economy is relatively easy for men with rare skills to find. The shortages of consumer goods, at least to a degree, can be overcome by an individual who has at his disposal sufficient financial means. Certain quantities of Western products, sent to their relatives by Poles living abroad, are usually available on the market. Relative scarcity makes their possession even more desirable. As a result, a new social stratification, determined largely by one's standard of living, seems to have emerged in the country. Men who have some special qualifications, and who thanks to that are relatively well off, also enjoy the highest social prestige.* To join the ranks of these groups is the goal of all ambitious Poles. It is at this point, over their preoccupation with material welfare, that the unity of objectives between the masses and the Gomułka regime largely breaks down. After decades of privations, the Poles are impatient and want to take advantage of the fruits of their work by obtaining immediately even a little increase in their standards of living. The Communist call for even further sacrifices to create conditions of abundance in the remote future has little appeal for them. The Polish people seem to feel that individual and collective goals cannot be separated.

It is precisely the widespread desire for "little stability" which largely immunizes the Polish people against the impact of Communist ideology.**

* The findings of a sociological survey conducted by the Polish radio indicated that in terms of social prestige the most respected professions were those of university professor, medical doctor, and mechanical engineer. The least respected occupations were those of a construction worker and charwoman, and, at the very bottom, a worker on a state farm. *Polityka,* June 13, 1959.

** This was confirmed by the sociological survey conducted in 1961 among the Polish students. In reply to the question if they would risk their lives in the defense of social ideas only 29.5 percent answered in the affirmative. However, 87.4 percent were willing to do so for the sake of their family. Incidentally, it is interesting to observe also that 75.2 percent of the students would also risk their lives in the defense of the country. Anna Pawełczyńska, Stefan Nowak, "Światopogląd studentów w okresie stabilizacji," *Przegląd Kulturalny,* November 14, 1961.

The younger generation in particular, has come down to earth. They measure the achievements of any social system in terms of the welfare it provides for individuals. "The attitude of the youth toward life," observed a Communist writer in 1959, "adheres to the principle of concreteness. Each motive and each action is evaluated in the light of its results. Only the facts count . . . [The youth] is preoccupied with work and studies, television and motorcycle, refrigerator and a snack."[43] Such people, of course, are hardly susceptible to an ideology which offers a panacea for all social ills, and, after the depreciation of its high-sounding slogans in the Stalinist years, to the Communist ideology most of all. Communist attempts to revive an interest in Marxism-Leninism after 1956, therefore, have met with very little response among the masses.

The significance of this repudiation of all ideology and the withdrawal by the Polish people into private life, goes beyond a mere turning away from Communism. The adoption of this posture has brought the Poles nearer to the secular and materialistic outlook dominant in the economically advanced Western societies. There is no question that many people in Poland consciously pattern their way of life after that prevailing in the West. In the words of a Communist critic, their idols are the nations "who are rich . . . who have cars . . . who do not have any ideals but know the taste of [material] satisfaction; who have weekends and refrigerators, a good jazz and colorful labels."[44] In short, the Poles have clearly fallen under the spell of American mass culture. Indeed, especially among the young, the influence of American way of life is easily noticeable. The young men and women in Poland are fond of Hollywood movies, jazz, and night clubs crudely fashioned after New York's Greenwich Village; they frequently try to dress and have haircuts or hairdos like American teenagers; they study English and occasionally even call themselves by English names. They obviously make strenuous attempts to escape from the reality surrounding them in Poland into what they imagine life in America looks like.

The return to organic reform and the resulting widespread adoption of the stance of "little stability" among the Polish people, thus, produces effects deeply damaging to the Communist regime. Above all it has seriously challenged the Communists in the ideological sphere. After two decades of life under Communist rule, the Poles not only fail to derive their ideals from Marxism-Leninism but continue to look for inspiration to the capitalist West. Communism still has little appeal in Poland.

10

THE COMMUNIST PARTY AND ITS ALLIES

The 1956 upheaval brought about a drastic shift in the Polish political scene. After years of lethargy the country abruptly burst into feverish political activity. There was a sudden revival of political parties, groups, and factions of all sorts. In traditional fashion when her external policy is at stake, a major dividing line once again appeared inside the various political movements.

The Polish United Workers' Party was torn into two major wings: the Natolin and Puławska factions. The difference between these groups, in Gomułka's words: "revolved around two essential issues: the conception of Poland's sovereignty and . . . the limits of democratization." [1] The leaders of the Natolin faction — apparently reassured by the Soviet ambassador in Warsaw, Ponomarenko — believed that the Russians would not tolerate an attempt on the part of the Polish Communist Party to regain even a modicum of autonomy, and, if necessary, would restore their influence over Poland through an armed intervention. Consequently, the Natolin faction opposed democratic reforms and instead advocated stern measures to suppress the ferment in the country. When they found that Gomułka was out of sympathy with this program, they tried to block his ascendancy to power.* Indeed, on the eve of the fateful meeting of the Central Committee of October 19, 1956, as if this move were synchronized with the advance of Soviet troops toward Warsaw, the Natolin group was planning to stage a

---

* The Natolin faction at first tried to win Gomułka to their side. They apparently felt that his return to the leadership of the Communist Party (although not to the post of the First Secretary) could strengthen its prestige in the country and, thus, would facilitate suppression of the advocates of genuine reforms.

coup to seize power in the country.* The leaders of the Puławs
took exactly the opposite view to the Natolin group.** They wer
that increasing Poland's autonomy from Russia and carrying out pop.
reforms was the only effective way to avert revolution and to secure the
party's continuation in power. They won to this view the chiefs of the party,
and together they paved the way for adoption of the program of popular
reform and Gomułka's election as the First Secretary.

Soon after Gomułka's return to power, however, a new group appeared
in the ranks of the Polish United Workers' Party. It was not as organiza-
tionally coherent as the Natolin or Puławska factions, but nevertheless its
objectives were quite clear. Its followers were not satisfied with the program
which had been adopted by the party in October 1956, but, with regard to
both Poland's autonomy from Russia and the democratic reforms, they
pressed for further liberal changes. At least some exponents of this view
went so far as to advocate the virtual abdication of the Polish United Workers' Party from power. A few former members of the Polish Socialist Party,
notably Osóbka-Morawski, proposed to revive it as a political organization
independent from the Communist Party.[2] The young writers in *Po prostu*
even suggested replacing the Polish United Workers' Party with a new Communist political movement. "Since the whole party was once Stalinist,"
argued an advocate of such a step, Roman Zimand, and "we are fighting
against Stalinism, would it not be best to liquidate the whole party? Would
it not be better to liquidate the old and start building a new Communist
Party in Poland?"[3]

At that time the feverish political atmosphere was not confined to the

* The hopes of the Natolin faction for the Soviet intervention in Poland were depicted
in no uncertain terms in a speech by Artur Starewicz at the meeting of the Central Committee. "Did we not see how that group of people," he exclaimed, pointing at the Natolin
leaders, behaved at the time when the tension produced by the unexpected arrival of the delegation of the Presidium of the Communist Party of the Soviet Union reached its climax?
[Did we not see how] they tried, one after another, to spread accusations that the Warsaw
party organization was preparing anti-Soviet action . . . [They] announced in the lounge
of this hall that history always starts with little groups, and today the Natolin group is growing." *Nowe Drogi,* October 1956, p. 242.
** The leader of the Puławska group was a veteran Communist, Roman Zambrowski.
Zambrowski, born in 1909, joined the Communist movement in the twenties and even before
World War II had reached some prominence in the ranks. During the war he was in the
U.S.S.R. where he emerged as one of the top leaders of the Polish Workers' Party. Due to
his seniority in the Politburo, after the death of Bierut in 1956, Zambrowski was a strong
contender for the position of First Secretary of the Polish United Workers' Party. Because
of his Jewish background, however — and reportedly at the personal intervention of Khrushchev — he was passed over for Ochab. This apparently embittered Zambrowski toward the
Russians and led him to throw the support of his group behind the reform program.

Communist Party; it spread into the other political movements. The two non-Communist parties which had formally remained in existence but had been largely inactive in the early fifties, the United Peasant Party and the Democratic Party, now showed new signs of life. After toppling their respective leaders, who had been particularly docile toward the Communists, and replacing them with new men, both parties came out in favor of the program of democratization. The President of the United Peasant Party, Władysław Kowalski, resigned in favor of Stefan Ignar, and the Chairman of the Democratic Party, Wacław Barcikowski, was replaced by Stanisław Kulczyński.* The two parties demanded rectification of their subservient position to the Polish United Workers' Party, as one of the reforms in the political system in Poland. Indeed, in each of the parties some groups appeared which pressed for a completely independent line from the Communists. In the United Peasant Party, in some areas, former supporters of Mikołajczyk seized control of the local organization and strove to push it into open opposition to the Polish United Workers' Party. In the Democratic Party similar attempts were made by former Christian Democrats.[4]

The new political climate also affected the Catholics. Internal friction over the attitude to be adopted toward the program of reforms developed among the progressive Catholics. Piasecki's siding in October 1956 with the Natolin faction resulted in the emergence of opposition to his continued leadership among the supporters of democratization. After abortive attempts to seize Pax from within, the dissidents left its ranks and, subsequently, formed their own organization. At the same time, declaring itself firmly in favor of the program of reforms, the Catholic group which had been linked with *Tygodnik Powszechny* resumed its activities. Gathering around itself

---

* Kowalski (1894–1958) was a writer who had been linked with the left-wing peasant movement since the mid-twenties. Early in the postwar period he joined the pro-Communist Peasant Party, and after its merger with the Polish Peasant Party in 1949, he assumed the leadership of the United Peasant Party. Reportedly, he took his demotion in 1956 so badly that after all his efforts to regain the leadership failed, he committed suicide in 1958.

Ignar, born in 1908, joined the peasant movement in the late twenties and soon emerged as one of the leaders of its radical youth organization, "Wici." In the postwar years he led "Wici" into cooperation with the Communists, subsequently emerging as one of the leaders of the United Peasant Party.

Barcikowski, born in 1887, was an attorney in Warsaw in the interwar period. As such, he acted as a defense counsel in the trials of the political leaders who opposed the Piłsudski regime. Toward the end of the war, he emerged as a leader of the Democratic Party, at all times favoring its close alliance with the Communists.

Kulczyński, born in 1895, before the war was a professor of botany at the universities in Cracow and in Lwów. Even at that time he was closely linked with the group of radical intelligentsia who subsequently formed the Democratic Party.

various other Catholic groups, it soon emerged as a considerable political force.

Indeed, in various parts of the country the followers of the prewar rightist parties — the National Democracy and the Piłsudskiite movement — reappeared on the political scene and gained some influence. In 1957, lamented the Communist Party paper in Upper Silesia, "attempts were made in our region to rehabilitate Piłsudskiism . . . and to revive the ideologies of Christian as well as National Democracy." [5]

Soon after his return to power, Gomułka drew a sharp distinction between political movements which he was willing to tolerate and those with which he would not abide. He restricted freedom of political activity to those movements which adhered to the program of Poland's alliance with the Soviet Union in foreign policy and to socialism in the domestic sphere. Gomułka claimed, very much in the vein of a political realist, that no other program would be feasible in contemporary Poland. He admitted that an alternative program did exist — one expounded over Western radio stations by political emigrés — but he denounced it as purely negative. The exiled leaders of the prewar political parties, argued Gomułka,

have no constructive program with which they could oppose ours. Why? . . . Because nobody could put forward an alternative program which would be realistic. It would inevitably lead to trouble. Any other program would lead to one or other variant of the Hungarian situation.[6]

This stand by Gomułka, of course, precluded the possibility of reviving any of the political movements which in the forties had opposed the establishment of a Communist regime in Poland. Not only the prewar rightist political parties, but also the Polish Peasant Party and the Christian Democratic Labor Party remained banned after 1956. The right to undertake open political activity was granted only to those movements which had existed at the time of Gomułka's removal from power. These were the United Peasant Party, the Democratic Party, and various Catholic groups. Furthermore, the role of the non-Communist political movements was to remain subordinate to that of the Polish United Workers' Party. The attempts of former supporters of Mikołajczyk and the Christian Democrats to infiltrate the ranks of the United Peasant Party and the Democratic Party, respectively, with a view to transforming them into genuine opposition, were quickly detected by Gomułka and decisively defeated. The two non-Communist political parties, as well as all the Catholic groups, were obliged to conduct their political activities under the over-all direction of the Front of

Nation's Unity in which, even after 1956, the Communists retained a dominant position. The Polish United Workers' Party, thus, remained very much at the apex of political power.

Having disposed of the opposition outside the Communist Party, Gomułka proceeded to eliminate opposition within its own ranks. He categorically rejected the proposal to dissolve the existing party and replace it with a new one.* On the contrary, he identified himself fully with the Polish United Workers' Party. He left no doubt that, despite the fact that at one time he had been deposed from its leadership, he still considered it as his own party — the same party he had built in the underground and subsequently led to power in the postwar years. He explicitly endorsed the Communist Party merger with the Polish Socialist Party, thus bringing to an end hopes for the revival of the latter as an independent political organization.** Indeed, he went a long way to demonstrate that, all its errors notwithstanding, he viewed the over-all record of the Polish United Workers' Party in 1949–1955 as a favorable one. In short, in a determined effort to recover its influence in the country, Gomułka threw his whole prestige behind the Communist Party. "The Party," he declared in May 1957, "represents the most important instrument for the solution of all problems of our life." [7]

THE POLISH UNITED WORKERS' PARTY (1957–1959)

In order to turn the Communist Party into an effective political force, Gomułka had to restore its internal unity. "To accomplish its tasks," he asserted in his first speech after returning to power, "the party must above all be united and monolithic." [8] Gomułka tried to avoid any harsh measures in achieving this end. He used no drastic sanctions against his former opponents.*** Instead, he simply called for the abandonment of all factional ac-

---

* The advocate of this proposal, Zimand, was branded as a "liquidator" and expelled from the Polish United Workers' Party.

** When Osóbka-Morawski came out with this proposal, he was abruptly dropped as a candidate in the parliamentary elections of 1957.

*** This is well illustrated by Gomułka's magnanimous treatment of the leaders of the party who had been responsible for security activities, and, thus, also for his arrest in the early fifties. A special party commission to investigate the role of these men absolved them of any complicity in the system of terror, but found them guilty of defects in the manner of their supervision of the organs of security. As punishment the former Deputy Minister of Public Security, Mieczysław Mietkowski, was expelled from the Communist Party without any explicit right to seek readmission, while former Deputy Premier Jakub Berman, and the former Minister of Public Security, Stanisław Radkiewicz, were banned from membership in the party for a period of three years. See "Uchwała IX Plenum KC PZPR w sprawie odpowiedzialności za wypaczenia w organach b. Ministerstwa Bezpieczeństwa Publicznego," Nowe Drogi, June 1957, pp. 158–159.

tivity and a closing of the ranks in the party. "It is necessary," he appealed to the Polish Communists, "to eliminate from our vocabulary the terms Natolin or Puławska groups. The members of the party should not be judged by their yesterday's views, but by their today's work." [9]

Gomułka's hopes for immediate cessation of factional activities within the party, however, proved to be unfounded. He apparently grossly underestimated the bitterness of the struggle between its different wings. He must have expected to bring the situation under control within a matter of months, for he originally planned to convene its Third Congress in December 1957. But as it happened, it took Gomułka more than two years to consolidate his position in the Polish United Workers' Party, for the Congress met only in March 1959. In the meantime, to overcome the opposition, he had to carry out an extensive purge in the party ranks.

Throughout 1957 both the Natolin faction and the liberal wing continued to advocate and wherever possible even to push forward their respective programs. "The party has not as yet restored full unity to its ranks," complained Gomułka in May 1957.[10] "In the party there exist various forces which oppose its policies," he cried in October of the same year, admitting that "revisionist" centers, and "dogmatist" groups were still active in the Polish United Workers' Party. "As a result," he continued, "the unity of our party is seriously impaired and the party cannot perform satisfactorily its role as a leader in constructing socialism in Poland. At long last this [situation] must be brought to an end." [11]

Gomułka branded as revisionists those party members who were not satisfied with the reforms which had been introduced in 1956, but who pressed for further democratization of life in Poland. The revisionists by no means constituted a coherent faction. They were mostly Communist intellectuals who shared similar — though not necessarily identical — views, and only in a very loose sense did they act together. Their position in the higher echelon of the Polish United Workers' Party was weak; in fact, they represented only a small minority in the Central Committee. The core of the revisionists gathered around various party periodicals, especially *Po prostu* and *Nowa Kultura*. In these papers they expounded their criticism of Gomułka's line. The most outspoken exponent of their views was Leszek Kołakowski, who, in writings published in 1957, made a blistering attack on some of the fundamental tenets of Communist ideology. The major source of the "revisionists'" strength was that their program for further democratization coincided with the aspirations of the masses and, thus, enjoyed considerable support in the country. The peril of "revisionism" in Gomułka's eyes was of a twofold nature. On the one hand, the sharp criticism of his policies crystallized the objectives of and aggravated the pressure from the Polish people. On the other hand, the penetrating inquiry into the fundamental problems of Marxism-Leninism, especially when expressed in official party publications, met with the disapproval of Moscow and increased tensions in that direction.

It was, therefore, against the revisionists that Gomułka directed his first assault. In May 1957, at a meeting of the Central Committee, Gomułka came out with a sharp attack against the revisionists who "disarm the party in its struggle for socialism." He singled out Kołakowski for criticism, accusing the young philosopher of advocating the restoration of bourgeois democracy.[12] Soon control over the press was greatly tightened, depriving the revisionists of a forum for their views. At the same time, a "verification campaign" aimed at purging the party ranks was undertaken. According to the Chairman of the Control Commission of the Polish United Workers' Party, Roman Nowak, in late 1957 and early 1958, 497 members, most of whom were accused of revisionism, were either expelled or punished for their political activities.[13] Toward the end of 1958 Gomułka bluntly declared that "the party created a climate which prevents the existence of revisionism." [14]

The people whom Gomułka labeled as dogmatists were a group of diehard followers of the Natolin faction who, even after the fiasco of their program in October 1956, continued to oppose Gomułka's course. The defeat which they suffered at that time seriously undermined their strength: their foremost leaders, Franciszek Mazur and Zenon Nowak, forfeited their seats in the Politburo; several other members of the groups were deprived of their posts in the party apparatus and the government. Yet, not all was lost. A considerable number of former Natolin supporters remained well entrenched in the Central Committee and in other high positions in the Polish United Workers' Party. From there, especially since they represented a closely knit group, they could effectively harass if not sabotage Gomułka's policies. Throughout 1957 and even in early 1958, they attacked Gomułka's course on several occasions, denouncing his tolerance of workers' councils, his endorsement of the decline of collective farms, and, above all, his insistence on Poland's right to forge her own road to socialism. The dogmatists, of course, never entertained any illusions about gaining broad support among the Polish people. Their hopes clearly lay in the failure of Gomułka's line, which would bring about direct Soviet intervention in Poland. Indeed, it appears that the dogmatists received some encouragement in their activities from the Russians.* Soon after Gomułka's ascendancy to power, Mazur left on a prolonged visit to the U.S.S.R. In December 1956 a speech by one of the dogmatist leaders, Stanisław Pawlak, bitterly denouncing Zimand and significantly calling for Poland's closer relations with the Soviet Union, was approvingly reported by Radio Moscow.[15] In May 1957 at the meeting of the Central Committee, the general attack against Gomułka's policies launched by another Natolin supporter, Kazimierz Mijał, was reportedly instigated by Maslenikov, a Soviet Embassy official.[16] The Russians apparently were using the dogmatists to bring additional pressure on Gomułka to fall in line with their wishes; or possibly they even viewed the group as an alternative to Gomułka, should he refuse to fall in line and should direct Soviet intervention in Poland prove necessary. Thus, the presence of the dogmatist faction in the ranks of the Polish United Workers' Party constituted a grave potential danger to Gomułka.

Most likely, it was owing to the continued support which they received from Moscow that Gomułka treated the "dogmatists" fairly leniently. They were hardly affected by the general purge of the Polish United Workers' Party; instead, they were dealt with individually, usually by appointment to a post of secondary political importance. Thus, in 1957 Nowak was appointed one of the deputy premiers, and Mazur was despatched later the same year as Polish ambassador to Czechoslovakia. One of the main planners of the abortive coup in October 1956, General Kazimierz Witaszewski, was also removed to Prague as a military attaché. Another prominent dogmatist, Wiktor Kłosiewicz, was expelled from the Central Committee in February 1958, but only after repeated, open criticism of Gomułka's policy.

It was only after he reached an understanding with Khrushchev toward the end of 1958 that Gomułka was able to deal a decisive blow to the dogmatists. At the Third Congress in March 1959, Mazur, Mijał, Pawlak, and a few other former leaders of the Natolin faction, who in the meantime had failed to repent, were dropped from the Central Committee of the Polish United Workers' Party. During his visit to Poland in the summer, Khrushchev explicitly deprived the dogmatists of any further hope of Soviet support. "The dogmatists," he declared,

* The main source of support for the Natolin faction in the Communist Party of the Soviet Union apparently came from the so-called "anti-party" group dispersed by Khrushchev in the summer of 1957.

do not accept the policy of the Central Committee of the Polish United Workers' Party led by Comrade Gomułka. They maintain that they . . . want to improve the policy of your party so that this would be identical with that of the Communist Party of the Soviet Union. In our opinion, one cannot expect that in dealing with the internal problems of Poland the Central Committee of the Polish United Workers' Party should follow a policy which would be identical with that of the Communist Party of the Soviet Union. Each nation should construct socialism and come nearer to Communism while taking into account its own specific national, cultural, and economic features.[17]

The objectives of the purge in the Communist Party which was carried out by Gomułka in 1957–1958, however, were not merely to bring to an end the activities of the revisionist and dogmatist groups. The purge was also aimed at cleansing the party of all sorts of undesirable elements who had made their way into its ranks in the postwar years. The past system of recruitment of party members was blamed for this state of affairs. "Before the unification of the Polish Workers' Party and the Polish Socialist Party," admitted the theoretical journal of the Polish United Workers' Party, "both parties had striven to increase the number of their members, which was reflected in the poor criteria used in selecting their members . . . [Furthermore] purely mechanistic recruitment of party members often was undertaken." [18] As a result of these practices, according to Gomułka, there had entered the Communist Party "men who are corrupt and have no morals . . . drunkards and rowdies . . . all types of speculators, and even criminals." Above all, there had crept into the party the sheer opportunists, the men whom Gomułka characterized as joining "because they hoped that party membership would be beneficial to them . . . [but, who] are indifferent to socialism . . . This group spreads passivity and indifference among other members. It even influences good party members. The size of this group is substantial." [19]

Indeed, judging by scope of the purge in the Polish United Workers' Party, the undesirable elements represented a substantial part of its membership. In the period from November 1957 to May 1958, no less than 206,737 persons, representing 15.5 percent of the total membership, were removed from the party. Of these, 5,584 were expelled explicitly for theft, malversation, speculation, and corruption.[20] Parallel to the cleansing of the ranks, a new recruitment drive, based on the admission regulations set up by Gomułka, was undertaken. In 1958, 23,000, and in 1959, 86,000 new members were admitted to the party.[21] The new acquisitions, however, did not completely offset the losses, and the total membership of the Polish United Workers' Party was reduced from 1,275,957 at the end of 1957 to 1,018,466 at the end of 1959.[22]

The struggle against the revisionist and dogmatist groups, as well as the purge of the corrupt and opportunist elements within the party, were both hailed by Gomułka as highly successful. At the Third Congress of the Polish United Workers' Party in March 1959, he claimed that past difficulties were overcome. He asserted that the party was now "consolidated, united, and monolithic," and that the Congress demonstrated its "ideological strength." [23] To assure the further proper development of the Communist Party, great attention was paid by the Congress to the proper selection and ideological training of party members. The revised party statute increased the requirements for admission to the party, and in particular emphasized the complete adherence of all candidates to the party's ideology.

However, the real situation in the Polish United Workers' Party in the last years of the fifties was not as favorable as Gomułka tried to present it. In fact, neither the factional struggle within the party was over, nor were the opportunistic elements completely eliminated from its ranks. The perennial split in the Polish Communist Party between the supporters of greater autonomy for Poland and the advocates of greater conformity in Poland's policies with those of the Soviet Union persisted even after the Third Congress. Indeed, the Congress was hardly over when, in the fall of 1959, new signs of friction in the party leadership came to the surface. Several former members of the Natolin faction were brought back to influential party and government posts. General Kazimierz Witaszewski returned from Prague to head the important administrative section of the Central Committee. Eugeniusz Szyr and Julian Tokarski were appointed as additional deputy premiers. At the same time two former prominent supporters of Gomułka, with moderate liberal leanings, resigned in disagreement over his policies. Jerzy Morawski stepped down from the Politburo, and Władysław Bieńkowski left the post of Minister of Education.* As Gomułka moved

* Politically Morawski's resignation was particularly serious. Born in 1918, he was one of the ablest Communist leaders of the younger generation. He began his political career in the Communist wartime underground. In the postwar years he led the Communist youth organizations. In the midfifties he emerged as a spokesman of the moderate "liberal" wing in the party, being elevated to the rank of Secretary of the Central Committee and, subsequently, a Politburo member. At the Third Congress of the Polish United Workers' Party in March 1959, he delivered one of the key addresses, being generally regarded as one of the main political figures in Poland, and indeed, a possible heir-apparent to Gomułka.

nearer to the Soviet line in his policies, he clearly began to lean more heavily on the support of the dogmatists.

Nor was there any essential change in the atmosphere permeating the ranks of the Polish United Workers' Party in the late fifties. Gomułka's method of restoring its unity — through applying administrative sanctions against the revisionists and securing Khrushchev's condemnation of the dogmatists, rather than through a genuine exchange of views — did not, of course, revive the party's ideological ardor. Gomułka himself partially acknowledged this fact when, in late 1958, he admitted that during the verification campaign, especially among the intellectuals, the party leadership "failed to create an atmosphere of thorough discussion of ideological problems. Many comrades took a detached stand in defining their ideological and political views." [24] The reasons for the failure of efforts to instill an ideological zeal into the ranks were elaborated with even greater clarity by a writer in the official party organ. "The verification campaign," he observed, "did not manage to overcome passivity among party members." One reason for this, he explained, was that, "after the events of recent years, faith in socialism is weakened among many [party members] and until now their revived doubts have not been removed." [25]

In this respect, the Third Congress made little difference to the situation in the Communist Party. In the fall of 1959, in an article published in the weekly *Polityka,* a member of the Central Committee, Romana Granas, lamented "the fading for some time now of the ideological pulse of the party." Appealing for a revival of ideological zeal, Miss Granas recognized that many Communists were in fact reconciled to the existing state of affairs within the party. Reporting a conversation with an anonymous "senior comrade," she summarized his views as follows: "The period of intense ideological activity, ideological debates, creative thoughts . . . belongs to the past. All attempts to attract broad interest in these matters among party activists are at present doomed to failure." [26]

Miss Granas' article produced a wide response, in the form of letters to the editor of *Polityka,* from party members all over the country. If anything, these letters only confirmed Miss Granas' observations about the thoroughgoing pragmatism of Polish Communists. One writer complained that the activities of local party organizations were reduced to a mere routine. "At the party gatherings," he declared, "there is no political discussion. Everything is clear to everybody." All that was required of party members was purely formal adherence to the organization: "to attend the meetings, to pay the dues, etc." Outside the meetings they did not stand up for Communist ideology, but conformed with the views of the people among whom they lived. The Communists, he claimed, "regard membership in the party merely as a supplement to their professional activities. In private life, then they are not 'on active duty' they are hardly distinguishable from anybody else." [27]

Motives for belonging to the Polish United Workers' Party, according to the writers in *Polityka,* ranged from sheer opportunism to veritable political realism. On the one side there were many party activists, asserted a correspondent from Silesia, "who link their entire work in the party with their own interests. [They show] no enthusiasm for ideological and political activities." [28] On the other side, pointed out a writer from Pomerania, there were people who joined the Communist Party in order "to support Gomułka." They believed that "since no other alternative exists, to cooperate with the U.S.S.R. is the only feasible course." [29]

Tendencies toward "little stability" also appeared in the attitudes of many members of the Polish United Workers' Party. Among the Communists, as among the Poles in general, there existed a widespread disillusionment with all political activity and a retreat into private life. This was well described by the anonymous secretary of a primary party cell in a factory. "We are under pressure not so much from bourgeois as *petit bourgeois* ideology," he said. "This is manifested in a specific mentality and specific attitude toward life: in narrowing one's horizons to the problems of family and housing, in abstaining from the hardships of a struggle, in brushing off any broad social objectives." [30] The spread of such an approach in the ranks of the party members was acknowledged even more explicitly by a woman commentator on Granas' article from Silesia. She admitted that many a Communist strove to pattern his way of life after that prevailing in the West. "Our entire society," she wrote, "is under the strong spell of capitalist ethics. The ambition of everyone is to live in the style of Western Europe. The Communists, perhaps unconsciously, are also affected by this influence." [31]

THE REVIVAL OF THE ROMANTIC TRADITION

The widespread adoption of the attitude of "little stability" among the Polish people, and especially among party members, was a source of grave concern to some Communists. They realized that the attitude of turning away from politics and retreating into private life represented an effective antidote against the spread of Communist ideology and a serious impediment to the program of socialism. Several party activists and intellectuals proceeded to voice their misgivings about this situation. The most articulate attack against the hold of "little stability," came from a young army officer, Colonel Zbigniew Załuski, in a book published in 1962 under the provocative title: "The Polish Seven Deadly Sins." [32]

Załuski expounded his argument in a typical manner of Poland — namely, in the form of a historiographic polemic. The reason for selecting this method of attack was in order to trace the roots of the "little stability" back to the impact of the tradition of political realism, in general, and its highly critical attitude toward Poland's history, in particular. *"Historia est magistra vitae,"* he observed, "it represents a powerful moral weapon." The tendencies in Polish society, continued Załuski, "toward an aversion to ideology, and to social passivity, are undoubtedly stimulated . . . by the activities of the jeerers and scoffers at almost all the more significant patriotic and military episodes of our history." [33]

In order to revive the interest of the Polish people in broad political and social objectives, argued Załuski, they must be presented with a more inspiring picture of their history. "It is essential," he asserted, "not to disparage the role of individual bravery and sacrifice, the boldness of thought and heroism of action." The objective of his book, thus, was to argue with the critics of Poland's past, and, in the author's own words to defend her "romantic history — which was often difficult, stormy, but certainly not stupid." [34]

Załuski's book was not a scholarly study. It was written in a lively but distinctly journalistic style. Its backbone was a lucid and fairly well documented review of seven case studies of the past Polish military undertakings. They were not of any major political or military importance; in fact, they dealt with specific battles rather than campaigns.* The author admitted that he had selected them for discussion merely because of their repeated censuring by the exponents of the critical view of Poland's history — hence, the "Polish seven deadly sins." In reviewing these episodes, Załuski convincingly demonstrated that their critics, guided by the desire to prove that "it all made

---

* For instance, Załuski argued that the charges of Polish cavalrymen against German tanks — which have been so often used as evidence of the futile heroism of the Poles — are in fact a legend. No such suicidal tactic was employed in the entire campaign of 1939. According to Załuski, the sole encounter between the Polish mounted cavalry and the German *panzer* units took place on September 1 in Pomerania when the Poles attacked German infantry, and were attacked in turn by German tanks which suddenly appeared on the scene.

no sense,"[35] frequently went beyond the limits of objectivity — ignoring or even distorting relevant historical evidence.

Having proved his point, the author proceeded to make general observations about Polish historiography. He divided Polish historians into two groups: those in favor of, and those against military action. Załuski, of course, presented himself as belonging to the former group. "In spite of their defects," he wrote, "the positive influence of insurrections** has been conclusively proved long ago. [Insurrections contributed to] the growth of national consciousness, the continuance of the Polish question in the international forum, and the emergence of the . . . modern Polish society."[36]

The division of Polish historians into those who had approved and those who had censured military action, according to Załuski, coincided with their respective political views. In the nineteenth century the critical attitude toward insurrection had been expounded by the conservatives. It had been "raised to the rank of a historiographic school and a political program by the Cracow historians . . . the noblemen who could preserve their social position only by securing support from foreign thrones." This "antiromantic, anti-insurrectionist school of 'realist thought,'" declared Załuski, "survived even longer than the old Poland — it survived until today." At present the critical view of military action, he maintained, is expounded by political bankrupts, "the ideological defenders of 'old Poland' . . . [who] advocate a program of salvation of the nation through small realism, quiet work, the necessity of renunciation of all high ideals and bold undertakings."[37]

In contrast to the conservatives who had been critically disposed toward any military struggle, continued Załuski, there stood the radicals, who placed themselves in the very forefront of the insurrectionist movement. Marx and Engels had sympathized with the Polish uprisings of the nineteenth century; Lenin had defended the revolution of 1905; and the tradition had been ably upheld by the Polish Communists during World War II. In a romantic vein they had undertaken "extremely difficult, and truly gigantic tasks." Against overwhelming odds they had carried out a military struggle in the underground, and side by side with the Soviet army on the Eastern front. Their efforts and sacrifices were not in vain — this time "the madness of the brave ones was crowned with success."[38]

And yet, observed Załuski, today "the history of the Polish workers'

** Załuski's admiration for the Polish insurrections, however, stopped short of approving the Warsaw uprising of 1944. He praised the heroism of its participants, but bitterly questioned the wisdom of the politicians responsible for its outbreak.

movement is not regarded as an object worthy of praise or even ridicule. It is of no interest . . . as if it did not exist." Instead various writers never tired of criticizing Poland's past and propagating as their political program "poor, down to earth, socially useless" goals. The author, thus, made a fervent plea for correction of this situation, for abandonment of the censuring of Poland's past and for revival of the romantic tradition — exemplified in his opinion by the history of the Communist movement. "It is not right," he cried,

to ridicule the nation's past, to present it as a chain of deeds devoid of common sense . . . It is not right to distort in this way the nation's history for it only results . . . in the spreading among the people of contempt for their own nation.

By scoffing at the efforts of all the past generations — even if these were futile . . . one will not educate socialist man — the man who is to be the driving force of history.[39]

The appearance of Załuski's book was something of a sensation in intellectual circles. Its first edition of 10,000 copies was sold out in no time. A lively controversy, lasting for several months, ensued in the press. "The widespread and prolonged concern with this book," exclaimed one of the commentators, "is amazing. It undoubtedly reflects in some way the intellectual and ideological climate of our life." [40] Załuski in his book touched upon the essential issue of Polish politics: the dichotomy between political realism and political idealism. "Despite the prevailing opinion about traditional Polish individualism," declared one of the participants in a debate, "we are actually divided only into two groups: the opponents and supporters of the cult of heroism." [41] The exchange of views over Załuski's book, commented another writer, was a revival of the old argument between the supporters of positivism and those of romanticism. "Ever since World War II," he observed, "the leftist intellectuals have engaged in a continuation of traditional polemics: heroism or organic reform, struggle for independence or the class struggle. It amounts to an extension of the polemics in the workers' movement between the left-wing of Luxemburgism and the right-wing of the Polish Socialist Party and Piłsudskiism. Until today nobody has succeeded in going beyond this." [42]

If Załuski, thus, revived the old arguments of political idealism, his critics retorted with the traditional arguments of political realism. The most articulate denunciation of Załuski's book, carried out in the vein of positivism, was made by the well-known journalist, Kazimierz Koźniewski. In his article "The Eighth Sin: Lack of Objectivity," published in *Polityka*,[43] Koźniewski agreed with Załuski that at least to some extent the spread of social passivity among the people could be attributed to the criticism of Poland's past. "If one demonstrates the senselessness and even the harmful effects of some political and military acts," he wrote, "one must also anticipate that this will bring about certain reactions along the lines of bourgeois materialist egoism." Nevertheless, Koźniewski argued that the continued denunciation of political romanticism was useful and, indeed, necessary. This was because, in his opinion, the major fault of the Poles was not their social passivity but, on the contrary, their predilection for insurrections. "There are some nations," declared Koźniewski, "whose aversion to military action . . . has advanced so far that they need a 'rearmament' treatment; but our nation does not need it. If anything exactly the opposite is true."

Starting from different assumptions, Koźniewski arrived at a view of Polish historiography diametrically opposed to that of Załuski. According to Koźniewski, the uncritical glorification of Poland's past had been linked with rightist political movements. "In the interwar period, as well as today," he argued, "the hagiography of national history was expounded by the right." Consequently, in Koźniewski's opinion, the critical view of the past was associated with leftist political movements. He admitted that some elements on the right, notably the conservatives, had also been critically disposed toward Poland's history; it was the left, however, which had carried out such criticism, "most thoroughly and severely."

The attack against Załuski's book was carried even further by another well-known journalist, Kyzysztof Toeplitz, who also questioned Załuski's thesis that the radicals had been traditionally linked with the insurrectionist movement. Indeed, he pointed out that the Communists had come to power in Poland not through military struggle at all, that their activities during World War II had also been of little practical consequence. It was, according to Toeplitz, "simply the result of the war," [44] which had determined the nature of the political situation in Poland.

Both Koźniewski and Toeplitz, thus, emphatically disagreed with Załuski that, in order to educate a new socialist man, it was necessary to discontinue the criticism of Poland's past. On the contrary, they believed that such a course would be detrimental to the cause of socialism, for it would likely stimulate the resurgence of rightist, nationalist political views. "The uncritical admiration of history of one's own nation," exclaimed Koźniewski, "leads to a nationalistic and chauvinistic education." [45]

Other critics of Załuski's book went still further and accused him of trying to revert to the Piłsudskiite tradition. In an article sarcastically entitled "The Galloping Colonel," Dominik Hordyński asked Załuski if by any chance he did not know who in Poland in the interwar period had spread "militarism, the cult of the armed forces, and superpatriotism?" [46] Another writer, Zygmunt Bukowiński, made this charge even more explicit. He drew a direct parallel between the views advocated by Załuski and those which had been expounded by Piłsudski. "Freedom is won with blood, these are the words of the Marshal himself," he reminded the Poles. "This is formulated clearly enough. The soldiers' blood is to be shed — be it at Monte Cassino or in Warsaw . . . We have been through it all . . . It is for this reason that I declare myself . . . against Załuski." [47]

When he found himself accused of reviving the tradition of Piłsudskiism, Załuski could no longer remain silent. He came out with a lengthy and indignant reply to his critics. [48] Claiming that they had tried to besmirch him, he proceeded to clarify his views. In his reply he succeeded in making his position quite unequivocal. He rejected the conservative tradition, which he still insisted had carried out the "most thorough and severe criticism of Polish history," and declared himself in favor of the radical tradition, which in his opinion had been favorably disposed toward Poland's past. Here, however, he elaborated on his former position. He admitted that at times the left had also indulged in criticism of Polish history — thereby implicitly voicing his disagreement with the program of both the Social-Democracy and the Communist Party of Poland. In this way, Załuski, to all practical intents, reverted to the line which had been espoused by the Polish Workers' Party, led by Gomułka, during the war and immediate postwar years. Indeed, he made it quite explicit. "The line of the Polish Workers' Party," he wrote in the vein of the Gomułka of 1945, "the program of the struggle for Poland and her new social system — for a new Poland in a brotherly family of nations . . . is a continuation of the struggles carried out for one hundred and fifty years by Polish patriots." It is adherence to this tradition which led Załuski to declare, that, ". . . of the two threads of Poland's history — the one associated with the uprising of 1863 and the other with the names of Ksawery Drucki-Lubecki and Aleksander Wielopolski — I choose the former."

Załuski, thus, touched upon a problem of fundamental importance to the Polish United Workers' Party. He came out against the synthesis between Marxism-Leninism and political realism which Gomułka had evolved in 1956–1957. Instead, he proposed a reversion to that peculiar blend of Communism with at least some aspects of political idealism which Gomułka had advanced in 1944–1947. In doing so, however, Załuski failed to take into account that since 1957 Gomułka had not been moving back to the tradition of the Polish Workers' Party but, on the contrary, had come nearer to the tradition of the Communist Party of Poland and the Social Democracy. Consequently, Załuski exposed himself to censure from the leadership of the Communist Party.

In censuring Załuski, however, the leaders of the Polish United Workers' Party were faced with a painful dilemma. On the one hand they were certainly in sympathy with Załuski's goal of overcoming political passivity and arousing some enthusiasm for socialism among the people. On the other hand, they could not agree with Załuski's method of attaining that objective through the revival of political romanticism — a program in several respects in contrast to the official Communist line. They, therefore, tried to take a middle course.

Before the debate on Załuski's book reached a climax, a critical review of it significantly entitled "The Complications of a Certain Subject," appeared in January 1963 in the official organ of the Polish United Workers' Party, *Trybuna Ludu*.[49] The author of the review, Ludwik Krasucki, clearly tried to steer between the Scylla of praising Załuski's end and the Charybdis of denouncing his means. "The aim of the book," he wrote, "to overcome the moral inertia . . . is correct." Załuski's analysis of specific military episodes in the Polish history, he declared convincing. And yet, he continued, "when one deals with the military episodes of a tactical nature, one must not divorce them from the over-all strategic situation. Unfortunately, in his work Załuski in some places confuses . . . tactics and strategy." He underestimated the importance of "sober calculations and wise policy." As a result, concluded Krasucki, Załuski had ignored the most significant thing, namely, that "we owe the victory of People's Poland . . . not so much to romanticism and heroism as to long-term, correct and realistic strategy — to mature political conceptions."

After the polemics over Załuski's book abruptly ended — clearly suggesting an intervention by the leadership of the Communist Party — another piece summing up the results of the entire discussion appeared in April 1963, in the Communist Party organ.[50] The article did not admit that it dealt with a political controversy of major significance. It explicitly denied that the debate over Załuski's book represented a continuation of the arguments between the supporters of romanticism and of positivism. Indeed, *Trybuna Ludu* deliberately strove to present the controversy — as was emphasized in the title of the article, "The Quarrel Over the Educational Ideas of Socialism" — as being concerned with educational rather than political issues. Yet, the fact that the article was not signed, its extensive length, its authoritative tone, and, above all, its content, clearly indicated that it expounded the official views of the leadership of the Polish United Workers' Party.

This April article in *Trybuna Ludu,* as its predecessor of January, drew a distinction between the end and the means advocated by Załuski. It explicitly approved the aim of Załuski's book. The author, the article declared, had rightly recognized "the need for educating society, and especially the younger generation . . . in the spirit of readiness for action and sacrifice in the name of high ideals." These represented "precious values which should be cultivated and propagated." Załuski, the article asserted, had also correctly observed that merely sneering at the nation's history was harmful for this did not assist, but on the contrary hindered, the educating of socialist man. In this respect, it was claimed, Załuski's opponents, and especially Toeplitz and Koźniewski, had gone wrong. Indeed, Koźniewski was accused of carrying out the defense of a critical attitude toward Poland's past to the point where in fact he "agreed with those who impoverish or even completely deny the role of social ideals." Załuski, however, according to *Trybuna Ludu,* had also been carried away by his argument. To prove his thesis he had resorted to improper methods of divorcing "the military struggles from their over-all historical context." As a result, he had reached conclusions which were "superficial and at times false." Above all, while praising heroism, he had failed to provide an answer to the question "why, so frequently, the heroism of a Polish insurgent and soldier proved to be futile, lonely, and tragic." And without answering this crucial question, the article continued, one could hardly expect Poland's "history to become *magistra vitae."*

Having chided, thus, both Załuski and his major opponents, *Trybuna Ludu* proceeded to expound its own version of Polish history — the one that in its opinion was suitable to the contemporary educational needs. This, not surprisingly, came close to the views which had been expounded by Gomułka. "Our beautiful but bloody history," stated the article in realist tones, "was not free from the 'Polish deadly sins' . . . from empty platitudes, from narrow nationalism . . . [and even] from criminal thoughtlessness." The uprising of 1863 was singled out as an example of such a "sin." It was presented as wrongly conceived from the start; it had not been synchronized with the activities of the revolutionary movement in Russia. It had been led by people who were unfavorably disposed toward "the progressive forces in Russia, and who looked for inspiration to the West. And there the insurrection could not find, and in fact did not find, a salvation." The most tragic of the Polish "sins," however, "was the decision of the London reactionary leaders to stage the Warsaw uprising . . . the event for which so many human beings made a futile sacrifice." * All in all, concluded the article, "in one hundred and fifty years of the struggle for liberation . . . many sacrifices were in vain, many insurrections and battles were defeated, many human efforts and lives were lost."

In contrast to the tradition of abortive military struggles adhered to by the bourgeoisie, there had stood, according to *Trybuna Ludu,* the program advocated by the Polish Communists. It was the Communists who had undertaken the "critical review of Polish history," and it was they who had taken this criticism into account in their practical political activities. During World War II, the Polish Workers' Party, "in opposition to the bourgeoisie, pointed out to the nation the only real way to liberation from the Hitlerite occupation . . . [and came out] with a *new* conception of the Polish state, its political system, its borders, and its place in Europe." True, the article conceded, this had required "courage and boundless sacrifice for country, homeland, and the cause of the working people." Just the same it had been an essentially different struggle from those of the past, for:

> It was no longer a struggle in vain. It was no longer a futile sacrifice. It was no more a desperate battle. It was a struggle guided not only by faith, but also by a realistic, sober calculation of the constellation of forces on the international scene. There was a perspective of the liberation of Poland as a socialist state by a victorious Soviet army.

The article in *Trybuna Ludu,* however, was not merely confined to the exposition of Gomułka's own version of political realism. The other essential element of his program — namely, Communist ideology — was also very much present. Indeed, both Załuski and his opponents were criticized for ignoring the precepts of Marxism-Leninism in their analysis. On the one hand, Załuski was rebuked for having reduced the explanation of past events purely to "the *subjective,* moral postures of actors who appeared on the historical scene," and for not having paid sufficient attention to the major factor, "the driving class forces of history." In short, he was charged with failing

* The article acknowledged that Załuski stopped short of endorsing the Warsaw uprising, so the subject was brought merely as an elaboration of the criticism of his book.

to understand the essence of historical materialism. On the other hand, Załuski's opponents were reproached for having fallen victim to the influence of Western bourgeoisie, whose program was well expressed in "the thesis about 'the end of the age of ideology.' " In other words, they were accused of seeking their inspiration from the same sources as the contemporary revisionists: "anti-communist Western propaganda." The shortcomings in their grasp of Marxism-Leninism which had been revealed by the participants in the discussion over Załuski's book, concluded *Trybuna Ludu,* proved that, "the struggle against the alien, bourgeois ideology, the alien, hostile to socialist views and customs . . . is unsatisfactory, not sufficiently vigorous and effective."

The April article in *Trybuna Ludu,* however, still was not the last pronouncement of the leadership of the Communist Party on the controversy which had been stirred up by Załuski's book. In July 1963, in his speech at the meeting of the Central Committee, Gomułka himself elaborated on the official stand of the Polish United Workers' Party in this matter. Without mentioning any names, Gomułka endorsed the criticism of Załuski and his adversaries by *Trybuna Ludu.* He censured both "the abandonment of the Marxist critical analysis of the past," and "the nihilistic attitude toward the patriotic, progressive traditions of the nation." [51] At the same time, Gomułka called on the Communist Party to undertake a broad ideological offensive.

THE POLISH UNITED WORKERS' PARTY IN THE SIXTIES

Gomułka's new ideological offensive was aimed not only at strengthening the Communist influence among the masses, but also at consolidating the ranks of the Communists themselves. For despite all the efforts to overcome them, in the early sixties the Polish United Workers' Party was still faced with considerable internal difficulties. Indeed, the situation in the party was so bad that its Congress had to be postponed once again. While, according to the party's statute, the Fourth Congress should have taken place not later than four years after the preceding one, that is, in March 1963, it was convened only in June 1964. This additional time was needed by Gomułka to try to cure once more the two ills which had plagued the Communist Party ever since 1956: the internal factional struggle and the lack of ideological zeal.

In the early sixties the factional activity in the Polish United Workers' Party did not cease, but indeed once again intensified. At that time a new group appeared in the party ranks which became known, because it was predominantly composed of veterans of the wartime Communist underground, as the "partisans."[52] Because of their background the partisans for years had been fairly close to Gomułka. Some of them had even suffered an eclipse with him in the late forties and had returned to active political life again only after 1956. As the years went by these middle-aged Communists rose to positions of influence in the government and the party, apparently with Gomułka's blessing.

The partisans did not represent a closely-knit faction, but rather a clique bound together by ties of old comradeship. Nevertheless, in their political activities they did adhere to a fairly coherent common political program. They were militant Communists, but with a distinct nationalistic bent. The program which they seemed to espouse — which was quite natural in their position — was the program of the Polish Workers' Party of the war and immediate postwar years. In this sense, they adhered to the brand of Communism expounded by Załuski.* The hard core of the partisans, like Załuski, were senior military figures occupying key posts either in the security apparatus or in the armed forces. The most influential among them were: Generals Mieczysław Moczar,** Ryszard Dobieszak, and Colonel Franciszek Szlachcic (all three Deputy Ministers of Internal Affairs); Generals Zygmunt Duszyński and Wojciech Jaruzelski (Deputy Ministers of National Defense); General Grzegorz Korczyński (Chief of Military Intelligence); and General Aleksander Kokoszyn (Commander of the Military Police). The partisans, like Załuski, emphasized strongly the significance of the Communists' military struggle during World War II. Indeed, arguing both in nationalist and Communist terms, they strove to present it as the true turning point in Poland's history.[53] Last but not least the partisans, again as did Załuski, revealed strong animosity toward the intellectuals. They were scornful of the intellectuals' lack of ideological zeal as well as their critical appraisal of Poland's history.

The major targets of the partisans' attack, thus, were the party leaders who had shown a certain sympathy toward the intellectual revisionist circles. In particular, the partisans turned against the leaders of the Puławska group

---

* Indeed, there seems to be little doubt that Załuski's book represented an attempt to provide a political ideology for this group.

** Moczar commanded one of the largest and most active Communist partisan units during the war. In the postwar years, he served in the security apparatus, being relegated to a minor post after Gomułka's fall and elevated to the post of Deputy Minister of Internal Affairs in 1956. At the same time he entered the Central Committee of the Communist Party.

and, in the interparty struggle which ensued, scored several important successes. In July 1963, they forced out of the Politburo and the secretariat of the Communist Party the leader of the Puławska group, Roman Zambrowski. In November of the same year, they compelled another member of the secretariat, Władysław Matwin, to resign. At the same time, one of the members of the secretariat closely linked with the partisan group, Ryszard Strzelecki* noticeably rose in the party leadership.

On the eve of the Fourth Congress the Polish United Workers' Party found itself again in the throes of a bitter factional struggle. All the different groups were jockeying for position, and at least some of them engaged in a head-on conflict with Gomułka.[54] In the spring of 1964, the die-hards of the Natolin faction once again resumed their attack on Gomułka. They clandestinely distributed a pamphlet in which they charged the party leadership of adhering to a "bourgeois ideology," and indeed, explicitly linked this to Gomułka's "rightist-nationalist deviation." [55] At the same time the Puławska group strove to regain lost ground. At the meeting of the Central Committee in March 1964, pointing to the deteriorating situation in the country, Zambrowski delivered a scathing attack on Gomułka's economic policies. Last but not least, some signs of friction appeared between the influential secretary of the Upper Silesian party organization and Politburo-member, Edward Gierek,** and Gomułka.

Gomułka, however, once again weathered the storm. Cunningly playing one group off against the other, by the time the Fourth Congress met in June, he had brought the situation in the party under control. The Natolin group conspiracy was dispersed by the security apparatus — its top leaders, Kłosiewicz and Mijał, were temporarily placed under arrest and dismissed from their jobs. Central Committee member, Ryszard Nieszporek, who had been implicated in the conspiracy, was dropped from that body at the Fourth

---

* Strzelecki, born in 1907, was chief of staff of the Communist partisan units during the war. As a mechanical engineer by profession, he was Minister of Railroads in 1951–1957 and Minister of Communication in 1957–1960. In 1960 he entered the party secretariat and a year later was elected a member of the State Council.

** Gierek, born in 1913, is a son of a coal miner who was killed in a mine disaster. Early in life Gierek went to France, and subsequently to Belgium, where he worked as a coal miner and participated in the Communist movement. He returned to his native Silesia in 1948 to take part in party work there. He rose swiftly in the ranks of the Polish United Workers' Party — becoming a member of the Central Committee in 1954, one of its secretaries in March 1956 and Politburo member in October of the same year. In the spring of 1964 the rumors in Warsaw had it that Gierek wanted to move Gomułka into the honorific post of Chairman of the State Council (replacing the then ailing Zawadzki) in order to take over the post of the First Secretary himself.

Congress. The Puławska group suffered a debacle, too. At the Fourth Congress, Zambrowski, Morawski, and Matwin all were deprived of their seats in the Central Committee. The partisan group also did not do too well at the Fourth Congress. Strzelecki was elected a candidate-member of the Politburo, and only later in that year, after a vacancy was created in that body by the death of Aleksander Zawadzki, was he elevated to full membership. Moczar did not make it to the Politburo, but toward the end of 1964 was appointed Minister of Internal Affairs. Instead, the former Stalinists, who in the meantime had turned into loyal Gomułka supporters, did well. Eugeniusz Szyr and Franciszek Waniołka both were rewarded with full membership in the Politburo. And Gomułka and Gierek made up: Gierek throwing his support behind the First Secretary, but at the same time increasingly assuming a stance of heir-apparent. All in all the Fourth Congress did not change the situation in the Polish United Workers' Party in any major way.[56] Gomułka retained his over-all dominant position in the party, but he certainly failed to restore its internal unity. The Fourth Congress, it seems, even more than the Third, merely marked a temporary truce among the different factions.

The second chronic illness of the Polish Communist Party, namely the lack of ideological ardor, also persisted into the sixties. As in the past, the swift expansion of the party ranks was partially held responsible for this state of affairs. In the early sixties the recruitment drive not only continued, but was in fact considerably accelerated. By mid-1963 the total membership of the Polish United Workers' Party rose to 1,400,000, and by mid-1964 to 1,568,000, of which roughly half were people who had joined in the preceding four years.[57] This very fact contributed to the decline of ideological standards. "The new cadre of the young party activists," asserted a member of the Central Committee in 1963, "are men who are devoted and eager in their work, but are frequently without training, experience, and Marxist knowledge." [58]

The rapid growth of the party, however, was only one of the reasons for the absence of ideological zeal in its ranks. By the Communists' own admission there were others. A general atmosphere of apathy continued to prevail in the Polish United Workers' Party. At the meeting of the Central Committee in mid-1963, Gomułka complained about the still "weak pulse of ideological work in the party." Indeed, he charged that the least interest in ideological problems was shown by the very members entrusted with the task of ideological indoctrination: "It is paradoxical," he exclaimed, "that in the party organs engaged directly on the ideological front . . . the internal agitation and ideological work is weaker than in the other organs. Ideological discussions there are rare and participation in party indoctrination is regarded as not in *bon ton*." [59]

On the same occasion, the widespread pragmatism among members of the Polish United Workers' Party was vividly described by Cyrankiewicz. There are men, he lamented, "who create an atmosphere of a detached reserve toward the party and the party line — an atmosphere which not infrequently amounts to a terror of active participation [in the party work]. There are also men who carry the party card like a used streetcar ticket. The problem of passivity, the problem of non-engagement, is not as acute as before, but it is still with us." [60]

At the same meeting another Communist leader, Miss Ewa Maleczyńska, in no uncertain terms, affirmed the persistence of an opportunistic attitude on the part of some members of the Polish United Workers' Party. In our life, she asserted, "there is much smartness, egoism, indifference, lack of respect for the law, idleness, snobbery, cliquishness, appropriation or waste of public property . . . these things occur even among the party members." [61] Indeed, judging by the scope of the purge in the party, the opportunistic elements continued to represent a substantial part of its membership. According to the Chairman of the Control Commission, Roman Nowak, in the years 1959–1964, 40,776 members were expelled for the "abuses of financial discipline, immoral behavior, etc." [62]

In midsixties the Communist leaders were faced with a situation which in some respects was even more difficult than that of 1957. They could no longer afford to attribute the shortcomings in the Polish United Workers' Party to their past mistakes. After solemnly pledging to revive the party ideological vigor and to restore the purity of its ranks in 1957 and, furthermore, triumphantly proclaiming that these goals had been achieved in 1959 — they could not admit in the sixties any further errors without risking a serious loss of face. Consequently, they decided to put the blame on outside forces. The old cliché of the bourgeois ideological pressure was revived. Gomułka himself set the tone of debate at the meeting of the Central Committee in July 1963. He charged that the continued ideological chaos in the Polish United Workers' Party was the result of the anti-Communist propaganda spreading into Poland from the West. This theme was eagerly seized upon by other participants in the meeting. "In the imperialist world, and the United States in particular," declared the Chairman of the Association of Polish Journalists, Henryk Korotyński, "an absolutely monstrous apparatus to combat our policy and our ideology has been created . . . The pressure of foreign views has been intensified." [63] The chief of the security apparatus, and one of the partisans' leaders, Mieczysław Moczar, was even more explicit in elaborating the harmful effects of Western propaganda. He bluntly characterized it as the main political danger facing the Polish Communists:

In the historic struggle between the two systems — socialism and capitalism — People's Poland is in an exposed position. The enemy directs special pressure at our country. [The enemy] counts on a split in the unity of our party, on the undermining of faith in socialism among the broad masses, and on a weakening of the ties binding us with the socialist camp and its foremost power, the Soviet Union.[64]

The theme of bourgeois ideological influence was carried to its logical conclusion in a speech to the Fourth Congress by another partisan leader, Ryszard Strzelecki. He virtually equated any deviation from party line with treason. An ideological wavering, Strzelecki asserted, "frequently is the first step in cooperation with the anti-communist ideological subversion. For social facts must be judged by their results, irregardless of subjective intentions." [65]

The invoking of the hackneyed war cry of "bourgeois ideological influence" to explain a continuing crisis in the Polish United Workers' Party, of course, called for stereotyped countermeasures. At the meeting of the Central Committee in July 1963, thus, the party was directed to undertake a broad ideological offensive. The meeting underlined the need to intensify ideological activities within the party and to increase endeavors to spread Communist ideology among the masses. "The idea of Marxism-Leninism," cried Gomułka, "is invincible. Guided by its precepts we should mobilize the whole party in an increased effort on the ideological front — in the struggle for complete victory of socialist consciousness in the hearts and minds of the working class, of all working people, and of the entire nation."

THE DILEMMA OF POLISH COMMUNISM

The Communist Party fell short of what it wished to accomplish both within its own ranks and among the Polish people. The outcome of the meeting of the Central Committee in July 1963, as well as that of the Fourth Congress, clearly pointed out that the leaders of the Polish United Workers' Party did not find the situation existing in the country to their liking, but that they did not really seem to know how to cope with it. As the velvet-gloved rebuke administered to Załuski indicated, Gomułka is not adverse to seeking, within the framework of Communist ideology, some new program which will overcome the political apathy of the masses. At the same time, however, the fact that Załuski's book was after all formally censured, suggests that Gomułka is convinced that the course proposed by its author would not accomplish this objective. On the contrary, it could only add to the problems with which the Communist Party is already saddled.

From Gomułka's point of view, it appears, Załuski's endeavor to bring about a synthesis between political idealism and communism is unsatisfactory because, in the first place, it is very doubtful if it could arouse any enthusiasm among the Polish people. In order to exploit to its advantage the aura of patriotism which surrounds the romantic tradition, any political movement must, of course, genuinely observe its precepts. In the interwar period the Piłsudskiites managed to do so. They exaggerated the political significance of their military struggle during World War I, but they did this with conviction because they truly adhered to the tenets of romanticism. And above all, Piłsudski and his successors upheld Poland's independence, which in the years 1918–1939 was fragile but nevertheless real.

In contrast to the Piłsudskiites the mantle of successors of the romantic tradition ill fits the Polish Communists. The whole history of their movement reveals a commitment to political realism rather than political idealism. The Communist military effort during World War II, especially as compared with that of the anti-Communist forces, was insignificant. It is hardly suitable to be turned into an heroic legend from which political capital can be derived. Last but not least, as every Pole is painfully aware, Poland today is not truly independent. Even since Gomułka's ascendancy to power in 1956, her sovereignty has been seriously circumscribed by Russia. In these circumstances, any attempt to present the policies of the Communist Party as inspired by romanticism would involve such an obvious distortion of widely-known facts that it could not possibly meet with a broad response from the people.

Furthermore, Gomułka seems to be afraid that the linking of the Communist movement to political idealism might produce effects exactly opposite to those desired by the Polish United Workers' Party. In order to legitimize such a step it would be necessary to rehabilitate certain chapters of Poland's romantic history, and this could prove most embarrassing for the Communists. To go back to the program of the Polish Workers' Party from 1943–

1948 would involve rejecting the tradition of the Communist Party of Poland and restoring that of the Polish Socialist Party. From there, as Załuski's critics pointed out, it would be only one short step to rehabilitating Piłsudskiism with its strong pro-Western and anti-Russian overtones. After all, the true romantic program in Poland has always been aimed at shaking off, with the assistance of the West, the yoke from the East. This was the case not only in 1863 and 1905, but — as Załuski failed to mention in his book — in 1920 and still in the midforties. Thus, the leaders of the Polish United Workers' Party could not possibly accept Załuski's proposal to revive the romantic tradition. To do this would mean to open a Pandora's box from which a host of problems, exceeding in their magnitude those with which Załuski tried to cope, could well escape. Returning to political idealism might overcome political apathy among the Polish people, but only at the price of awakening their aspirations for true independence from Russia. Needless to say, this situation could also pose a serious threat to the Polish Communist regime.

It was, above all, the fear that the restoration of political idealism could result in bringing about the reactivation of political opposition, which made Gomułka — much as he might have been in sympathy with the author's goal of overcoming the apathy of the masses — resolve the controversy over Załuski's book in favor of the Communist Party's continued adherence to political realism. Gomułka has apparently decided that if he must choose between the risk of a renewed direct challenge to Communist rule, similar to that which had existed in the late forties, and the widespread indifference to the Communist program which has prevailed since the late fifties, then the latter represents the lesser of two evils. As well as disparaging Załuski's attempted rehabilitation of romanticism, therefore, Gomułka has once again underlined the realist roots of the program of the Polish United Workers' Party. In his speech at the meeting of its Central Committee in July 1963, he rebuked historians who undertake the "criticizing or even condemning of the Communist Party of Poland . . . while simultaneously whitewashing the Polish Socialist Party." [67] On the same occasion the party historian, Daniszewski, emphasized the continuity of tradition between the Communist Party of Poland and the Polish Workers' Party. He denounced as politically harmful "the tendencies to deny continuity in the Polish revolutionary workers' movement [through drawing] an artificial distinction between the Polish Workers' Party and the Communist Party of Poland." [68]

Gomułka, of course, has not lost all hope that he will eventually find a way out of the dilemma with which he is faced. His angry denunciation of Koźniewski's view — that political apathy is an inevitable by-product of political realism — proves that Gomułka is not reconciled to the existing situation. He still wants to have his cake and eat it — to arouse the political interests of the Poles without aggravating their opposition to the Communist regime. The means by which Gomułka expects to achieve both these objectives at once are not particularly novel: he is striving to overcome the existing political apathy by intensifying efforts at Communist indoctrination.

In view of past experience, however, prospects for the success of Gomułka's efforts do not appear too bright. The events of 1956 demonstrated beyond doubt that the repeated Communist endeavors in the Stalinist years to imbue the Poles with an ideological zeal had made very little impact. There is little reason to believe that a similar attempt in the sixties will bring about a different effect. If anything, the memories of the "Polish October" — when the Communist leaders openly admitted that their past methods had been wrong — have hardened the Polish people against the influence of Communist ideology. It is unlikely, thus, that Gomułka's renewed stress on Communist indoctrination will succeed in overcoming the prevailing climate of apathy. Indeed, the artificial whipping up of enthusiasm for Communism might produce exactly the opposite reaction. By adding to their boredom with politics it might well increase the tendencies among the Poles to seek refuge in private life.

The only way the Polish United Workers' Party can arouse the enthusiasm of the people will be by convincing them that it stands for Poland's genuine independence from Russia. It would then have to abandon its extreme political realism and move closer to political idealism. Viewed in this light, some of the ideas advanced in the discussion over Załuski's book — even though they were rejected by Gomułka — might not be lost. They are likely to continue exerting influence upon the minds of many party members. Eventually they might pave the way for the reopening of the perennial split in the ranks of Polish Marxists between the internationalist and patriotic elements.

THE UNITED PEASANT PARTY AND THE DEMOCRATIC PARTY

As with the Polish United Workers' Party, the main task facing the United Peasant Party and the Democratic Party following the events of 1956, was to restore unity in their respective ranks. For the proportionate strength of internal opposition in each of the two non-Marxist political parties probably exceeded even that of the Communist Party. The crisis in the United Peasant Party was quite acute. Especially in the areas where traditions of the prewar peasant movement were still strong, an open rebellion against the party's leadership took place. The objective of the rebels was to free the party from Communist supervision and transform it into a genuine opposition force, patterned after Mikołajczyk's Polish Peasant Party in the middle forties. "In some circles," admitted the resolution of the Supreme Committee of the party early in April 1957, "there appeared reactionary views . . . questioning the leading role of the workers' class and its party in the life of the nation [as well as] rejecting the achievements of the United Peasant Party." [69] By mid-May Gomułka voiced his "deep concern" about the situation in the United Peasant Party. "In some branches of the United Peasant Party," he exclaimed, "there take place openly hostile attacks against the [Communist] Party, against people's government." [70]

Considerable ferment was also revealed in the ranks of the Democratic Party. Several local branches, and notably the Warsaw organization,[71] defied the party's central authorities. The purpose of the rebels, like those of the United Peasant Party, was to push the Democratic Party into opposition against the Polish United Workers' Party. "In the period after October 1956," admitted the Chairman, there appeared in the party "an ideological crisis . . . the rightist centers were revived, and the pressure of reactionary ideology increased." [72]

The restoration of unity absorbed a great deal of the energies of the two non-Marxist parties over a prolonged period of time. In the United Peasant Party internal ferment was suppressed only by resorting to an extensive purge of the rebellious groups. In the fall of 1957 the Supreme Committee of the party in a formal resolution, called for "a struggle against the rightist elements." [73] An extensive purge in the party ranks followed. Its extent was well illustrated by the fact that in October 1957, in one district alone, 44 party cells were disbanded.[74] All in all, in 1958 the United Peasant Party membership dropped by over 16 percent from 264,314 to 217,753.[75] Apparently this still did not eliminate all opposition, because, at the party's Congress in November 1959, the necessity of a continued struggle against the rightist elements was emphasized. In the Democratic Party the restoration of internal unity took a less drastic form. Measures in that direction were undertaken by its Central Committee in May 1957;[76] although, according to the Secretary-General, by the time of its Congress in January 1958, opposition to acceptance of the subordinate status of the Democratic Party was still not "completely overcome." [77]

Parallel to the struggle against internal opposition, the leadership, both of the United Peasant Party and the Democratic Party made considerable efforts to consolidate their respective organizations. The activities of the central authorities of both parties were greatly stepped up. Party congresses and meetings of central committees were convened regularly. Political propaganda in the press was intensified, playing up the traditions of each party. Since 1957 the United Peasant Party, though with the cooperation of the Polish United Workers' Party, has each year commemorated "Peasant Day." In 1958 the Democratic Party celebrated with much fanfare the twentieth anniversary of its foundation. The organizational network of the two parties throughout the country has been considerably expanded. Training centers for the activities of the United Peasant Party and those of the Democratic Party were established in 1958 and 1962 respectively. By 1958 a recruitment campaign was launched by both parties: in the years 1959–1960 the membership of the United Peasant Party rose by almost 20 percent;[78] in 1958–1959 the membership of the Democratic Party increased by 15 percent.[79]

The revival of the activities of the two non-Marxist parties was carried out with the full support of the Polish United Workers' Party. Gomułka himself gave his explicit blessing to such a development. "There is enough room in Poland," he asserted in January 1958, "for the independent activities . . . of the Democratic Party and the United Peasant Party. We support all creative effort and initiative — even if these run along lines of thought different from ours — as long as they enrich the methods and roads of our common task of constructing socialism." [80] Gomułka also encouraged broad participation of the smaller parties as full-fledged partners in the government. The acceptance of the leading role of the Communist Party in the Front of Nation's Unity, he declared in March 1959, "does not mean that the [Communist] Party may issue orders to the allied parties or merely reduce them to transmission belts. [It] assures the independence and initiative of each party, co-responsibility in the realization of the common program, and a share in the government of People's Poland." [81]

In fact, after Gomułka's ascendancy to power, the role of the United Peasant Party and the Democratic Party in the political system in Poland was considerably enhanced. New forms for the direct cooperation of the

Polish United Workers' Party with both of the non-Marxist parties were evolved. In November 1956, the Central Coordinating Commission composed of four delegates from each party was established. Soon analogous coordinating commissions (also based on the principle of parity among all partners), were introduced in all the provinces and most of the districts — the task of these coordinating commissions, at all levels, being to ensure cooperation among the three partners on a day-to-day basis. At the same time the participation of the minor parties in the government was considerably widened. In the parliamentary elections of 1957, out of the 459 seats, 117 were allotted to the United Peasant Party (the Speaker of the Sejm being drawn from their ranks), and 39 to the Democratic Party.[82] In the Council of State, out of 15 members, there were four representatives of the United Peasant Party and two of the Democratic Party. In the Council of Ministers, one of the Deputy-Premiers was from the United Peasant Party, and there were also two ministers from each party. In addition, since the elections in 1958, the two non-Marxist parties have been given generous representation in the local government at all levels.* The position of the United Peasant Party and the Democratic Party in the political system was not changed in any essential way by the parliamentary and local government elections of 1961 and 1965.

And yet, despite the expansion of their organizations and the considerable strengthening of their position in the government, the actual influence of the two non-Marxist parties in the political life in Poland has remained negligible for various reasons. First of all, even after 1956, the scope of organizational work of both the United Peasant Party and the Democratic Party remained seriously circumscribed by the Communists: the two parties were not really national in their character, in the sense that they drew their supporters from among all strata of Polish society. The United Peasant Party was permitted to conduct its activities only among the peasantry, and the Democratic Party among the intelligentsia and the middle class. They were both banned from undertaking any political activities among the workers. Since the Polish United Workers' Party was not subject to any similar limitations, but in addition to its exclusive base among the urban proletariat drew its members from all other social classes — the two non-Marxist parties were from the start handicapped in their relationship with the Communist Party. Their strength was bound to be much less than that

* The proportion of representatives from the United Peasant Party in the local government at all levels rose from 12.1 percent in 1955 to 21.5 percent in 1961, and that of the Democratic Party from 1.0 to 2.0 percent. *Rada Narodowa*, February 16, 1962.

of the Polish United Workers' Party. The striking discrepancy in the membership of the two minor parties as compared to that of the Communist Party, was largely a reflection of this uneven apportionment of their respective spheres of political influence.

Futhermore, the position of the United Peasant Party and the Democratic Party in the government remained formally subordinate to that of the Polish United Workers' Party. Representatives of the two parties who participated in different governmental organs were not regarded as equal but rather as minor partners of the Communists. This was formally confirmed by their explicit acceptance of the role of the Polish United Workers' Party as the "leading" or "foremost" political force in constructing socialism in Poland,* as well as by open repudiation of the principle of coalition government, wherein all parties would cooperate on an equal footing. "The leading role of the Marxist-Leninist party," commented a Communist specialist on political processes in 1958, "both in practice and in theory is incompatible with the nature of a coalition government." [83] The leaders of the two non-Marxist parties, thus, who occupied high posts in the Polish government were reconciled to the fact that they were reduced to the status of junior partners and that all major political decisions would be made by the Communists.

The subordinate position of the two non-Marxist parties to the Communist Party was clearly reflected in their political programs. The Democratic Party in 1956 and the years immediately after, did come out in favor of several constructive reforms generally aimed in the direction of "democratization." At the climax of the ferment in 1956 it even advocated the restoration in the place of the State Council (patterned after the Presidium of the Supreme Soviet) of the office of President of the Republic, the rivival of the activities of the parliament, as well as a general strengthening of the judiciary and the establishment of a state tribunal in particular.[84] It also advanced suggestions that Polish-Soviet relations should follow the example of those between the Soviet Union and Yugoslavia and that Poland should resume her traditional bonds of friendship with France.[85] As late as 1957 the

* It is interesting to observe a parallel in the relationship between the Polish United Workers' Party and the minor political parties in the domestic sphere, and the relationship between the Communist Party of the Soviet Union and the Polish United Workers' Party in the international sphere. In both cases the stress on the "leading" role of a stronger partner is coupled with assurances of respect for the internal independence of a weaker one. Even the terms describing the position of the Polish Workers' Party in the Front of Nation's Unity as "leading," but more frequently as "foremost," are the same as those depicting the role of the Communist Party of the Soviet Union in the international Communist movement.

Democratic Party tried to carry out some of these proposals in practice. It was instrumental, for instance, in revising the parliamentary rules in the new Sejm. By the time of its Congress in January 1958, however, most of these changes were dropped from its program. The United Peasant Party never really put forward any coherent program of reforms. It supported most of the measures for "democratization" of life in Poland, but it revealed little initiative of its own. In the spring of 1957 it called for a thorough ideological discussion in its ranks,[86] but nothing much came out of it.

Once the ferment in the country was over, the two minor parties concentrated their attention on the tasks assigned to them by the Communists, namely, on representing in the government the views of the social groups from which they derived their following. Even within those narrow limits, however, their activities proved to be of little practical consequence. Indeed, each of the two parties endorsed various Communist policies which were objectionable to precisely those segments of Polish society whose interests they were supposed to uphold. Thus, the United Peasant Party adhered to the program of ultimate collectivization of agriculture as well as to the removal of religious instruction from the schools[87] — policies which obviously ran contrary to the wishes of the overwhelming majority of the Polish peasants. The Democratic Party subscribed to restrictions on private, small-scale producers, and circumscription of the freedom of attorneys[88] — measures clearly detrimental to the welfare of the middle class. All in all, after 1958 the two non-Marxist parties followed the Polish United Workers' Party in all its major moves toward narrowing the scope of freedom in Poland. At the closed meetings of the Central Coordinating Commission or in various organs of the government, it seems that the leaders of the United Peasant Party and the Democratic Party occasionally voiced their misgivings about some particularly objectionable features of Communist policies.[89] They certainly did very little, however, to present their objections in the public forum of their respective party gatherings or in the Sejm.

The fact that the non-Marxist parties failed to utilize their position in the government to prevent the Communists from bringing to a halt the policy of "democratization," and, indeed, that they endorsed most of the retrogressive Communist measures, very considerably weakened their appeal to the Polish people. Seeing that, by choice or by necessity, both the United Peasant Party and the Democratic Party were unable to perform effectively even the limited role of quasi-opposition, but trailed the Polish United Workers' Party at every turn, the masses simply lost interest in them. This was well reflected in the meagre success of the efforts by each of the two parties to increase their respective following. The United Peasant Party, after a strenuous recruitment campaign, managed to reach by mid-1962 a membership of 300,000, and by late 1964, 330,000.[90] The failure of the party's policies led to recriminations against some of the leaders. At a meeting of the Supreme Committee in May 1962, Ignar and some of his followers resigned from the leadership of the party. They were replaced by Wycech* and his supporters, who pledged to advance the party's goals more efficaciously. Nor did the Democratic Party fare much better. In the early sixties the membership continued to grow, but at a very slow pace. Early in 1965 the party's strength was only 65,000.[91]

The chances for widening the popular appeal of the two non-Marxist parties appears to be remote. The overwhelming majority of the Poles fail to draw any significant distinction between the program of the Polish United Workers' Party and those of the United Peasant Party and the Democratic Party. Attempts to formulate an independent platform, genuinely representing the views of the masses, were made by the opposition groups in each party in 1956–1957. Yet, at Gomułka's request, the leaders of the two parties suppressed the opposition and in doing so, they let the vicious spiral set in. Deprived of any genuine source of strength of their own, they had to rely increasingly on Communist support, which would be secured only by their meekly following the Communist lead at every turn. This, however, impaired their prestige among the Polish people even further. In the eyes of the Poles — all Gomułka's assurances to the contrary notwithstanding — the United Peasant Party and the Democratic Party have been reduced to mere "transmission belts" for the Communist Party.

* Wycech, born in 1899, was one of the younger leaders of the agrarian movement before the war. During the war he occupied a high position in the underground loyal to the Polish Government-in-Exile, and still in the immediate postwar years he was one of the leaders of the Polish Peasant Party. Early in 1947 he led a splinter group, the Polish Peasant Party-Left, which was in favor of cooperation with the Communists; 1949 he became one of the leaders of the United Peasant Party. Since 1956 he has been the speaker of the Sejm.

II

THE PAX GROUP

The events of October 1956 greatly undermined the position of the progressive Catholics. Indeed, toward the end of 1956, it looked as though the collapse of Pax was imminent. Several developments contributed to this. First of all, Piasecki and his followers were compromised by their alleged connections with the security apparatus. The repeated rumors to that effect in the midfifties, which were stimulated by the revelations of Światło,* now came out into the open. In November 1956, a popular weekly, *Świat,* published an article by a well-known writer, Leopold Tyrmand, which unequivocally accused Piasecki of having been at the disposal of the Polish Ministry of Public Security.[1] Since one of the cardinal reforms pledged by Gomułka was the liquidation of the remnants of "Polish Beriaism," the future of its reputed offspring appeared gloomy.

Moreover, the release from confinement of Cardinal Wyszyński, and the reemergence of the *Tygodnik Powszechny* group, made Pax largely expendable to the Communists. In the turbulent period following October 1956, it was important for Gomułka to obtain the support of genuine Catholic leaders who could exercise an effective influence in appeasing the masses. Needless to say, relations between the hierarchy and the authentic Catholic intellectuals on the one side and the progressivists on the other were anything but affable. Memories of the attitude of Pax toward the Cardinal at the time of his imprisonment could not be obliterated by declarations of loyalty made upon his restoration to office. The affair of *Tygodnik Pow-*

---

* In 1955, and still in the spring of 1956, Światło's account of the Serov-Piasecki deal was widely spread in Poland through Radio Free Europe broadcasts and leaflets.

szechny was well remembered by Catholic writers, who now retrieved their stolen property. Thus, Piasecki could count on little sympathy, either from the Episcopate or the lay Catholic leaders.

Another reason for the weakening of Pax was that the progressivists had never been popular among the rank and file of the Polish United Workers' Party. "The great majority of the Polish Communists had never consented to nor understood this alliance." [2] The quasi-fascist or conservative background of the Pax leaders had been regarded with suspicion, if not enmity, by the genuine proletarian elements in the Communist Party. Their program, aimed at a reconciliation between Catholicism and Marxism, had been treated with reserve and even contempt by the Communist intellectuals. Last but not least, in the intraparty struggle which preceded Gomułka's return to power, Piasecki had openly sided with the Natolin faction. In an article published on the eve of the popular upheaval in October 1956, he threatened resort to force to curb the process of democratization. [3] The article brought a wave of indignation from Communists and Catholics alike. Thus, the rout of the Natolin faction was also a defeat for Pax, and a personal disaster for Piasecki. At last, it seemed, his political career had come to an end.

At the end of 1956 the expectation of Piasecki's imminent fall was widespread in Poland. It was generally believed that the leadership of the Communist Party had decided to dissolve Pax, and to hand over its enterprises to genuine Catholic groups. [4] Apparently this belief was even shared by some of Piasecki's close collaborators. In November 1956, some of the top progressivists, led by Jan Frankowski, seceded from Pax and established an organization of their own. Even those who remained at Piasecki's side expressed misgivings about their leader's attitude toward democratization, an unprecedented step for this strongly authoritarian group. "I would like to make it very clear," wrote the editor-in-chief of Pax's major organ, *Kierunki,* "that from the very outset there existed essential differences among the editorial staff of our newspaper with regard to the theses expounded in the Piasecki article." At the same time, the progressivists took an apologetic stand for their past activities, which they attributed to the pressure of "Beriaism" and for which they promised "to account fully and honestly." [5] As to the future, they declared their unreserved loyalty to the Church and the hierarchy, and pledged their sincere support for the Gomułka program of political reforms.

At this stage Gomułka's attitude toward Pax appeared ambivalent. The cooperation between the Polish United Workers' Party and the genuine

Catholic leaders in the parliamentary elections in January 1957 was generally interpreted as a sign of the political decline of the progressivists. Yet, in none of his public enunciations did Gomułka criticize Piasecki. Nor did the dissolution of Pax take place. Nor, indeed, were the concessions to its commercial enterprises withdrawn by the government. Thus, the very bases of Piasecki's power, indispensable for his political survival, remained intact.

What made Gomułka spare Piasecki from political death? There can be little doubt that had he decided to do so Gomułka could have dealt a *coup de grâce* to Pax. Even if it were true that in 1945 Piasecki had established some direct connections with the Soviet security network and maintained them until 1956 — which in view of the political changes in the Soviet Union alone was highly unlikely — his protectors could not have been so powerful as to restrain Gomułka from exercising his own judgment in this matter. If Gomułka did not hesitate to remove Rokossovsky from command of the Polish forces, he certainly would have had little difficulty in getting rid of Piasecki as well. Thus, the reasons for Piasecki's survival were clearly of a domestic nature. Viewed from this angle, the only political explanation that can be offered is that as early as 1957 Gomułka had decided that in dealing with the Catholics he would follow the maxim of *divide et impera*. He probably felt that Pax's continued existence might be useful to the Communist Party as an instrument with which to split the Catholic political forces.

Another factor, however, seems also to have been involved in Gomułka's decision. Various bonds between Gomułka and Piasecki, at times quite subtle, had existed in the past. It must not be forgotten that Gomułka shared the responsibility for launching Piasecki's postwar political career. After Piasecki's release from imprisonment, it was Gomułka who, at the meeting in Warsaw in September 1945, personally approved the progressive Catholics' initial plan of activity.* In turn, after Gomułka's emergence from arrest, Piasecki was careful not to imperil this valuable connection. In the summer of 1956, even before he joined forces with the Natolin faction, Piasecki established contact with Gomułka, exploring the possibility of their renewed political cooperation. This move, to a very considerable degree, helped him to save Pax from destruction.

Having been assured of their political survival, the progressivists regained their composure and by the spring of 1957 launched a counterattack. In a

---

* In an interview with Mr. Shneiderman, Dr. Jerzy Hagmajer, Vice President of Pax, revealed that at a meeting with Gomułka in January 1957, the progressivist leaders had "reminded Gomułka of his former positive attitude toward [their] movement." S. L. Shneiderman, *The Warsaw Heresy* (New York, 1959), p. 205.

speech immediately preceding the plenary meeting of the Central Committee of the Communist Party — the first since the "Polish October" — Piasecki censored the use of "socialist camouflage" for anti-socialist schemes and appealed for the "liquidation of factions" in the Polish United Workers' Party." [6] His attempt to assume the mantle of the Communist Party's mentor was received with biting sarcasm by Communist writers in *Po prostu* and other newspapers,[7] but it was they, not Piasecki, who in fact were losing ground. A week later Gomułka denounced revisionism and stressed the need for restoring unity in the Polish United Workers' Party.

Soon, there was an even more significant incident. When, in the summer of 1957, Cardinal Wyszyński issued a communiqué forbidding priests to cooperate with the Pax publications, Communist censorship clamped down, preventing its appearance even in *Tygodnik Powszechny*.[8] Thus, the Communist Party not only refrained from turning against the progressivists but it now upheld them in their opposition to the Episcopate. It was around this time that a meeting between Gomułka and Piasecki took place. The odd alliance between the Communist Party and Pax seemed to have been restored.

Encouraged by these developments, the progressivists intensified their activities still more. They made determined efforts to extend their meager influence among the Poles. To gain a broader following, they launched in March 1958 a nationwide campaign of "moral renovation" aimed at coping with the ideological indifference "which undermines the social morality and construction of socialism in Poland." [9] They also tried hard to strengthen their organizational network throughout the country. At a meeting of Pax activists in Opole in June 1960, special attention was given to the recruitment of young people. Parallel to stepping up their activities in Poland, the progressive Catholics eagerly sought to gain some recognition in the international sphere. In June 1960 Piasecki attended the Congress of the East German Christian Democratic Union in Erfurt. In December of the same year the delegates of the Christian Democratic Union appeared at the Pax meeting in Warsaw on the occasion of the fifteenth anniversary of the "progressive Catholic" movement, an event celebrated with much fanfare. In his speech at that meeting, Piasecki stressed that the experience of the progressivists in Poland might prove to be valuable to other countries, not only inside but also outside the Soviet bloc.*

The new expansion of Pax seemed to be carried out with the full approval of the Communist Party. In his speech at the Third Congress of the Polish

* Piasecki singled out India and the Arab states as examples of countries where socialist ideas existed side by side with religious sentiments. *Kierunki*, December 24, 1950.

United Workers' Party in March 1959, although he did not mention Pax by name, Gomułka referred approvingly to Catholics who "explicitly declare themselves in favor of socialism."[10] Concessions to the progressivist enterprises were not only upheld but, in fact, extended to new economic undertakings. In the local government elections in 1958, Pax supporters were allowed to run in three hundred districts and towns.[11] This was generally interpreted as a prelude to their active participation in the next parliamentary elections as well. In the late fifties political prospects once again seemed bright for Piasecki.

THE REVIVAL OF THE WIELOPOLSKI TRADITION

Side by side with the strengthening of their organization, the progressivists elaborated their political program. In a fashion typical of all Polish political movements, the progressive Catholics first of all sought to establish historical roots of their own. To this end they evoked the tradition of political realism as it had been espoused in the nineteenth century by Wielopolski and his succcessors.

In 1957 a new edition of Pruszyński's biography of Wielopolski was published by Pax. Pruszyński having died in the meantime, a new introduction was provided by a well-known political writer, Stanisław Mackiewicz. Mackiewicz, like Pruszyński, was a prewar conservative, although of a somewhat different shade. During the war, however, Mackiewicz had differed radically with Pruszyński. While in exile in London he was one of the staunchest opponents of any compromise with Russia. After the war he remained abroad, and in 1953–1955 even held the post of premier of the Government-in-Exile. At the same time, in his writings, he continued to espouse the traditional conservative line. In 1953, he published a biography of the last king of Poland, Stanislaus Augustus, which conformed quite closely with the precepts of the Cracow historical school.[12] In 1956, completely disillusioned, Mackiewicz returned from exile to Poland. "For many years," he wrote in explaining his decision, "I have fought against Russia as well as against both Russian and Polish Communism . . . Today, however, we cannot count upon the determination of the West to remove Poland from the Soviet orbit. This the emigrés know better than the Poles in Poland . . . In these circumstances, I have decided to return to the homeland."[13] After his return to Poland he joined the Pax group, and became its leading political writer as well as an ardent exponent of political realism.

In his introduction to Pruszyński's book, which amounted to a short biographical essay of the author, Mackiewicz traced the roots of Pruszyński's political outlook. It was "the conservative, conciliatory policies of the old, true conservatives, and especially the Cracow conservatives [which] had an influence on Pruszyński's views." He admitted that from the point of view of historiography, Pruszyński's book was weak, but he praised Pruszyński's political insight during World War II. He characterized Pruszyński as "a man . . . who was irritated by empty slogans. Yet in 1944 . . . we defended our future merely with empty slogans." [14]

The new edition of Pruszyński's book evoked a wide response. A sharp and lively debate, seemingly revolving around the historical events with which the book deals, ensued in the progressivists' weekly, *Kierunki*. But, in fact, the dispute went much further than that. Under the guise of an historical controversy, it provided the participants with an opportunity to expound their political views with regard to the existing political situation in Poland. In summing up its results, one of the writers clearly admitted that "the discussion touched upon broader topics, linking an historical personage with the present currents of our political thought." [15]

The major arguments were presented on the one side by Jerzy Łojek, and on the other side by Aleksander Bocheński.[16] Although Łojek praised Pruszyński as an adherent of political realism, he claimed that in order to advance such views Pruszyński did not need to invoke the ghost of Wielopolski. Indeed, he charged that Pruszyński's book represented the apotheosis of what he labeled as "Quislingism":

Margrave Aleksander Wielopolski, we have to remember, was representative of a phenomenon which today we call . . . Quislingism. Quislingism is the assumption of power in one's own country on behalf and in the interest of a foreign aggressor, occupant, or ruler, under the guise of the hypocritical claim that in view of the existing circumstances this course is beneficial and not detrimental to the nation.

In Łojek's opinion the reason Wielopolski was a quisling and not a political realist was that he tried to achieve the impossible, namely, to cooperate with tsarist Russia. In doing so, by the very logic of his position, Wielopolski was bound to promote Russian rather than Polish objectives. "It is strange," exclaimed Łojek sarcastically,

how naively the supporters of Pruszyński view the tsarist attitude toward Poland. It was nonsensical to count upon Western assistance during the insurrections; but to count upon the Polish-tsarist alliance, wherein Poland would have been an equal partner of the Russian Empire — this was political realism!

By labeling him a traitor, Łojek denied Wielopolski an honorable place in Polish history. For Łojek the true heroes were the nineteenth-century radicals, who repudiated reconciliation with tsarist Russia and stood for Poland's independence. In the last resort, Łojek called to his support the authority of Karl Marx:

> It was not Wielopolski's conciliatory policy, but insurrection which was fervently defended by Marx . . . Both Mackiewicz and Pruszyński in their books assume a strange stand: they look for historical arguments to support the foreign policy of People's Poland in the programs of reactionaries *par excellence*.

In his retort to Łojek, Bocheński denied that Wielopolski could be compared to Quisling. Bocheński did not argue whether cooperation on an equal footing with tsarism was feasible; on the contrary, he implied that it was not. Yet he still maintained that a parallel between Wielopolski and Quisling was unfair, for in 1863 there simply existed no better alternative to Wielopolski's program for Poland. "It is not important," argued Bocheński,

> on whose behalf Wielopolski exercised power. What is important is whether his rule was beneficial or detrimental to Poland . . . Poland had a choice between rule by Wielopolski on behalf of Russia, or rule by Russian governors . . . It is for that reason that Wielopolski's rule on behalf of Russia would have been far more beneficial for Poland than that which had existed before, as well as that which followed afterward.

In accordance with the views which he had expounded in his book, Bocheński went on to justify the principle of reconciliation with a mighty neighbor. In doing so, indeed, he came quite close to providing an excuse for a quisling posture:

> It is quite natural that a weak and dependent nation must eagerly, sincerely, and honestly work in favor of its mighty neighbor. Why? Because then its dependence turns into interdependence. If a weaker partner is really reliable and useful to a stronger one, then it pays for the latter to strengthen and not to weaken the former.

Yet it was clear that Bocheński did not regard surrender to the mighty neighbor as a universally binding principle. For him it was merely a sort of Machiavellian tactic, which it might be desirable to follow when no better alternative existed. In the last analysis, surrender was only a means of promoting the national interest. Nor did Bocheński altogether reject the revolutionary tactic. He recognized that it might have certain advantages, though only when combined with prudent political leadership. "From the insurrectionist tradition," concluded Bocheński, we select only the heroism and willingness to sacrifice, without which no policy whatsoever can be conducted. We reject, however, the "emotional" . . . political decisions. Here we choose the tradition of cool, cautious, responsible and long-term political calculations of . . . Lubecki, Wielopolski, and Dmowski.*

The controversy over Pruszyński's book, and especially the thinly veiled allusions to the present political situation in Poland, brought about a response from the Communist Party. The debate was still going on when the official theoretical organ of the Polish United Workers' Party, *Nowe Drogi*, came out with an article clarifying the Communists' attitude toward the various issues under discussion.

In the opinion of the Communist writer, the underlying assumption in the debate was incorrect for there was no analogy whatsoever between Polish-Russian relations in the nineteenth century and today. In the nineteenth century Poland's eastern neighbor had been the tsarist empire; it was now the Soviet Union. The writer defined, though not without a significant qualification, the nature of Polish-Soviet relations: "The relations between People's Poland and the Soviet Union are based on full respect for Poland's sovereignty and equality — a principle which since October 1956 has been fully observed."

As to the national tradition from which the Communists seek their inspiration, continued the Communist writer, it is broadly the same as that espoused by Łojek:

In our opinion, the true representatives of the nation were those men who stood for a determined struggle against foreign rulers, and who derived their strength from support by the Polish people and the alliance with the people fighting for freedom all over the world.

This did not mean, however, that *Nowe Drogi* disavowed the opinions expounded by Bocheński. On the contrary, with the important reservation that these did not presume to represent the views of the whole nation, they were to a very large extent endorsed by the Communist Party:

* In the course of the controversy revolving around Wielopolski's policies in *Kierunki*, Dmowski's name was prominently mentioned several times. Moreover, early in 1958, an encounter specifically concerning Dmowski's concepts took place in the same newspaper between Stanisław Mackiewicz and a well-known writer, Jan Dobraczyński. In presenting his side of the argument, Dobraczyński pointed out that "Dmowski was the only consistent politician in Poland, who in order to oppose the danger from Germany, put forward a program of seeking alignment with Russia." Dobraczyński also stressed that Dmowski sought understanding with Russia, "not only in the Tsarist period, but also in 1931 when the rumors of a 'crusade' against the U.S.S.R. spread in Europe." Dobraczyński, however, emphasized that his comments were written merely to correct the historical record. He was careful not to create any impression that Dmowski's program could have any political relevance whatsoever in today's Poland. See Jan Dobraczyński, "W stronę Mackiewicza," *Kierunki*, February 2, 1958.

There exist currents of Polish political thought, which, although far removed from any brand of socialism, espouse a loyal attitude toward the People's Government. [Their adherents] in a realistic fashion appreciate fully the potential dangers involved in civil strife and especially civil war. This kind of political realism indicates their political maturity and paves the way for loyal cooperation with them in the camp of democracy. We are not going to argue with the adherents of these currents if, from the rich historical past of our nation, they would choose as their predecessors and patrons politicians of any brand.[17]

THE POLITICAL PROGRAM OF PAX

The debate on Wielopolski served as a starting point for an elaboration of the political ideology of Pax. The direct acknowledgment of the debate by the Communists encouraged Piasecki to pattern his political program after political realism as it had been espoused by Wielopolski and interpreted by Bocheński. Indeed, it appears that Piasecki strove personally to pose as Wielopolski's successor. The mantle of the Margrave — a great patriot and statesman and, yet, a misunderstood and rejected political leader — seemed to suit Piasecki very well. Without retracting anything it absolved the Pax leader of blame for the 1956 fiasco, and thus enabled him to continue his political activity.

Soon after the debate in *Kierunki,* the two major ideological statements of Pax were put forward. In 1958 Piasecki's new book, "Polish Patriotism," was published.[18] Around the same time the "Ideological Guide" for Pax activists was issued.[19] By 1960 it looked as if the progressive Catholics considered their task in this sphere completed. At the close of the year, an editorial article in *Słowo Powszechne,* summing up fifteen years of activities by the progressivists, praised them for evolving a "novel theoretical solution." [20]

The program evolved by the progressive Catholics was indeed a novel one. Their ideology may be readily summarized as Communism without Marxism. In the realm of practical politics the progressivists accepted Communism in its entirety. They stressed the socialist character of their movement; they even regarded themselves as "a socialist ally of the Communist Party." [21] In the theoretical sphere, however, they rejected the fundamental tenet of Communism, that is, its materialistic outlook. They overtly professed their allegiance to Catholicism. Consequently, they denied having derived their political program from Marxism. Instead, they claimed to inherit it from Polish nationalism.

The starting point of Piasecki's political reasoning was undoubtedly his firm belief in the ultimate victory of socialism throughout the world. He did not even argue this point but, not unlike the real Marxists, approached it with an air of inevitability. With such an assumption, it was logical that Piasecki should conceive Polish interests not in the traditional terms of an independent national existence, but, on the contrary, in terms of their fullest identification with the forces of *Zeitgeist*. The weightier Poland's contribution to the international socialist movement, the greater her role in international affairs: "The real sovereignty of Poland," asserted Piasecki, "depends on the objective economic and cultural potential which we represent in the service of the righteous cause of socialism." [22]

In this context Poland's alliance with the Soviet Union would acquire new dimensions. It could be viewed not only as an alignment advantageous from the point of view of Poland's geopolitical position, but also as an indispensable link through which she would participate in the Communist bloc. "The Polish-Soviet alliance," wrote Piasecki, "is not only . . . an expression of the real guarantee of the security of People's Poland, but . . . it is also a vehicle of influence in the socialist camp." [23] Since Polish influence in the socialist camp is exercised through the Soviet Union, "the stronger the Soviet Union is," he declared, "the better it is for our Polish interests." [24] Consequently, Piasecki readily conceded Soviet primacy in the Communist bloc. Indeed, in this respect he went further than Gomułka. While the First Secretary of the Polish Communist Party usually referred to the U.S.S.R. as the "first and mightiest" or the "foremost" socialist country, the chief of the progressive Catholics bluntly stated that "Polish society regards Soviet political leadership in the socialist camp as something fully earned." [25] Poland's cooperation with the other socialist countries, according to Piasecki, came only second to its alliance with the Soviet Union; it was a supplement but by no means a substitute for it.

Although Soviet leadership is concerned with the policies of the bloc as a whole, reasoned Piasecki, and not with internal activities in each country, in fact the alliance with the Soviet Union affected Poland's domestic affairs as well. In the name of this partnership the Soviet Union expected Poland first "to be a morally reliable member of the socialist camp," and, second, to provide "a successful example of socialist construction." [26] Thus, since it was in their national interest to strengthen ties with the Soviet Union, the Poles should regard it as their patriotic duty to engage in the construction of socialism in Poland. The deeper the socialist roots in Poland, the firmer should be her bonds with the Soviet Union. "Polish patriotism demands," exclaimed Piasecki, "that Polish consciousness become more and more a socialist consciousness." [27] Nationalism to all practical intents must become synonymous with socialism:

The history of People's Poland puts an equation mark between the terms: "people's" and "national" . . . At present the terms "people's" and "national" carry the same meaning of Polish patriotism. Poland in the national sense is People's Poland and vice versa.[28]

It was for patriotic reasons that the progressive Catholics claimed to "participate fully in the constructing of the socioeconomic socialist system." Conversely, it was the full participation in this process which in their eyes made them "an authentic socialist" force.[29] Since patriotism and socialism are synonymous, a patriot according to Piasecki's definition would be a socialist and vice versa. Evidently, it would be impossible to be one without at the same time being the other. A patriot who was not a socialist was a "reactionary" opposed to Poland's national interest, a socialist who was not a patriot was a "dogmatist" infected with "inexcusable and ideologically false . . . cosmopolitanism." [30]

The progressivists, however, were not only wholeheartedly committed to the construction of socialism in Poland. They also unreservedly endorsed all the means which the Communists employed to achieve that end. Indeed, the progressive Catholics often outdid the Communists in following the Communist program. In the political sphere, they not only adhered to the principle of Communist Party leadership but urged the party to exercise it in an efficient manner: "We cannot remain passive," cried Piasecki in 1957, "when the party is paralyzed by internal friction . . . The party must rejuvenate itself to perform its leading role." [31] The progressivists' zeal in "constructing socialism" was particularly strongly marked in the economic sphere. It was characteristic that Piasecki viewed the economic changes which were carried out in 1956–1957 merely as a "respite," the purpose of which was "not to stray from the right road, but to be able to march along it even quicker." The "right road" for him was giving priority to investment in heavy industry, tightening the discipline of labor, and accelerating the collectivization of agriculture: "It is imperative," he exclaimed, "for Polish patriotism to show determination in the realization of the economic plan, in order to reach, as soon as possible, the next phase of socialist economy." [32]

Even the progressivists' attitude toward the Church was in line with that of the Communist Party. Here Piasecki's argument rested on a somewhat vague distinction between the apostolic and political functions of the Church.

"One must be ignorant of history," he wrote, "or be dangerously naïve, not to see the political effects of Church activities." The danger that Piasecki saw in the Church was that various forces — such as certain Vatican circles, the conservative elements among the people, and the outright reactionary centers — would try to exploit the influence of the Church for their own political schemes. "Polish patriots," he argued,

Catholics and non-Catholics alike, should decisively reject such attempts, no matter from whence they come . . . With regard to the inevitable by-product of the Church's spiritual activity, which is its socioeconomic influence, Polish patriotism puts forward its demand: we expect that the moral effects of the Church's spiritual activities should be such as to assist — far more than they do at present — both quantitatively and qualitatively in the socioeconomic construction of socialism.[33]

Having accepted in a roundabout way virtually all aspects of the practical Communist program, Piasecki repudiated at least one aspect of Communist theory; namely, the exclusively materialistic character of socialism. "The young Communist camp," said the "Ideological Guide,"

in order to preserve the unity of its ranks has adhered to the principle of an exclusively materialist outlook of the masses, which are liberating themselves from class oppression . . . At present the monistic outlook of the socialist camp no longer serves its unity, but might slacken the dynamics of its growth.[34]

In order to correct this deficiency in the Communist doctrine, Piasecki put forward his own interpretation of the "Polish road to socialism." The specific feature of the situation in Poland in his eyes was that in spite of the progress of socialism, Catholicism remained the predominant faith of the people. "Much as the consciousness of the believers has become more socialistic," he claimed, "it has not ceased to be a Catholic consciousness." As a result, continued Piasecki, the people who participate in the socioeconomic construction of socialism, are barred from sharing the political responsibility which is retained exclusively by the Communist Party. This leads to "restricting the socialist activity of society and . . . the undermining of the party's link to the nation." [35]

Thus, the problem according to Piasecki, was to find some way through which Polish Catholics, alongside the Communists, could participate in the political life of the country. Here he had a readymade formula: in order to achieve that end all that was needed was to broaden the basis of the dictatorship of the proletariat by formally recognizing the progressive Catholic movement as a full-fledged ally of the Communist Party. This, to Piasecki's disappointment, had not been achieved. The progressivists, however, would spare no effort "to attain a formal position as the ally of the workers' party," for they believed "that their official role in the government of People's Poland would represent an objective expression of the specific national conditions in which socialism is constructed in the country." [36] In short, what this interpretation of the "Polish road to socialism" amounted to was that Piasecki should be given a place in the government.

THE PAX FIASCO

Whatever hopes Piasecki might have entertained for putting his program into practice were abruptly dispelled by Gomułka. On January 25, 1961 another meeting between Gomułka and Piasecki took place. This time it was not veiled in secrecy, for an official communiqué on the talks was issued.[37] At the meeting Pax suffered a major reversal. Its economic as well as political activities were drastically curtailed. In the economic sphere tax privileges were withheld from Pax, thus reducing by perhaps more than half the profits of the association. Consequently, in the spring of 1961 there was a sharp reduction in the personnel employed by its various enterprises. Needless to say, depriving the progressivists of their abundant financial means in itself represented a serious political setback. Some direct restrictions of their political activities, however, were also imposed. The progressive Catholics' expectations of broad participation in the parliamentary elections of April 1961 did not materialize. They were allotted three seats in the parliament, as many as the splinter group led by Frankowski, and less than the group linked with *Tygodnik Powszechny,* which got five. Above all, Gomułka expressed his disapproval of the progressivists' ideology and urged them to refrain from expounding it further. Indeed, since January 1961 Pax publications have abstained from discussing their "novel theoretical solution."

What made Gomułka, at this stage, turn against Piasecki? Several reasons seem to have contributed to this development. First, all the objections raised against Piasecki in 1956, of course, remained valid in 1961. Neither the Catholics nor, which is more important, the Communists had changed their opinions of Piasecki. At best they ignored him, his theoretical enunciations being received "in ideological silence with no counteraction and no counterattacks." [38] Behind the scenes, however, a strong group in the Communist Party continued to oppose the expansion, if not the very existence of Pax. Second, the frantic efforts of the progressivists to gain some broader following in Poland proved in vain. Their failure to obtain any endorsement whatsoever from Cardinal Wyszyński alienated them from the overwhelming majority of Polish Catholics. Yet, irrespective of their negligible influence in the country, the progressive Catholics aspired to the role of a full-fledged ally of the Communist Party. Gomułka must have found this irritating. The Communists were prepared to use Piasecki, but certainly not to cooperate with him. When his demands became too arrogant, they quickly put him in his place.

The new reversal, however, did not lead Piasecki to abandon his political activity. He remained at the helm of Pax and preserved its line essentially intact. In fact, the progressivists only intensified their efforts to prove their usefulness to the Communist Party. They increased the harassment of the Catholic hierarchy and of Cardinal Wyszyński personally. In 1963, they hailed the encyclical *Pacem in Terris* as a rehabilitation of their program of ideological reconciliation between the Catholics and the Marxists and contrasted it with the stand of the Polish Episcopate. As did the Communists, the progressive Catholics also blamed the Polish bishops for the failure to establish relations between the Polish Communist regime and the Holy See.*

When the conflict between the Communist government and the Church reached a new acute crisis in the second half of 1964, the progressivists launched an open attack against Cardinal Wyszyński. In an "Open Letter" published in their theoretical organ, *Życie i Myśl,*[39] they accused the Primate of Poland of confusing his "religious authority with the function of political representation of lay Catholics," and they attributed to this the Communists' resort "to the use of the state apparatus to restrict the influence of the Church." However, the progressive Catholics did not call upon both sides, the Catholic hierarchy and the Communist regime, simultaneously to abandon their struggle. Instead, they demanded unilateral concessions from the Church. The hierarchy, in the opinion of the progressivists "should not wait until the Marxists revised their attitude toward religion, but should immediately recognize the good inherent in the socialist socioeconomic system." Until this is done, the Communists will continue to be tempted to "use the state apparatus to support philosophical materialism." **

The strong attack against the Catholic hierarchy apparently helped Pax's

* In the fall of 1963, Piasecki went to Rome to see if there was any way in which he could secure a role for himself in negotiations between Warsaw and the Vatican. Vatican officials, however, flatly refused to have anything to do with him.

** The "Open Letter" was also interesting for in an appendix it publicly refuted the various charges against Pax and Piasecki personally, purporting that they were the tool of the Communists and, indeed, of the security apparatus. However, the progressivists did not go beyond repudiating those charges one by one; they failed to submit any new evidence in support of their case.

position with the Communist Party. In 1965, the progressivists were rewarded for their loyalty with some minor political concessions. In the elections of that year, their representation in the Sejm was increased to five deputies, placing them on a par with the *Tygodnik Powszechny* group. This time Piasecki himself was given a seat in the parliament. The elections, however, once again demonstrated the extreme unpopularity of Pax's leader. He received the least votes among the deputies elected, not only in his own district, but in the country as a whole.

It was Piasecki's own program which brought about his repeated defeats. His program represented an ideological anomaly from the point of view of both Catholicism and Communism. With regard to Catholicism, the progressivists declared their full allegiance to the core of its doctrine. Though purporting to revise merely the social teaching of the Church, in fact, they went far beyond that. If carried to its logical conclusion, their program would have amounted to the complete surrender of Catholicism to Communism. The Church would have become virtually an instrument serving the atheistic state. Even if Piasecki sincerely believed, as he probably did, that this was the only way through which the Church could be raised into a "new epoch," it was a price which Catholicism could not afford to pay. Consequently, the progressivists' program was regarded by Polish Catholics as "an irresponsible piece of trickery aimed at the reconciliation of fire and water." [40]

With respect to Communism, the progressive Catholics took exactly the opposite stand. They accepted *in toto* its socioeconomic policies, but rejected the theoretical foundations upon which they are based. Untrained in dialectical reasoning Piasecki did not realize that such a program would be wholly unacceptable to the Communists for whom it would amount to a revision of the essential tenet of Marxism-Leninism. The crux of the problem was that in their excessive zeal to please the Communists, the progressivists claimed to be a genuine "socialist force." It was by accepting this label that they ruined whatever little chance they might have had to become recognized as a full-fledged ally of the Communist Party. "Perhaps should favorable circumstances develop," commented a keen outside observer of the Polish political scene, Piasecki "could secure the position of a leader of the pro-Russian, yet non-Communist faction. Moscow, however, will never agree to the existence of a non-Marxist socialist party." [41] For approval of the Catholic brand of socialism as an ideological partner of Communism would represent a heresy to the Marxist-Leninists far more grave than the revisionism of Kołakowski.

Blinded by his zest for the paraphernalia of power, Piasecki did not seem to be aware of the delicacy of his position. He was permitted to undertake his political activities only because they weakened the resistance of the Polish Catholics to Communism. Thus, paradoxically, his continued usefulness to the Communist Party depended directly on the persistence of Catholic opposition. Once this could be effectively subdued, Piasecki's services — irrespective of his contribution to their victory — would no longer be needed by the Communists. Conversely, should the Communists decide to seek a genuine compromise with the Catholics, Piasecki — precisely because of his present role — could not be a party to such an agreement.

Piasecki had fallen into the trap that lies in the path of every extreme political realist. He embraced political realism because he believed that in the existing situation this was the most effective way of upholding Poland's national interests vis-à-vis Russia. Yet, he applied the tenets of political realism so consistently, however, that eventually the means defeated the end: in order to secure the confidence of Poland's mighty neighbor, Piasecki proved to be ready to offer Russia several important concessions, asking very little in exchange. In doing so, he endangered the very national interests of Poland which in the first place he set out to uphold. In this respect, Piasecki's experience was not unlike that of Gomułka. Gomułka, however, was not only a political realist, but also a Marxist who believed that Communism was good *per se*. As an avowed Catholic, Piasecki could not admit the same motivation. He had to justify his activities in terms of pure political realism and this he failed to do convincingly. Thus, the Pax leader not only lost his chance to gain political support, but also his integrity. In the eyes of the Poles, Piasecki — as had his idol, Wielopolski, a century before — embraced the position which they labeled "Quislingism."

THE CHRISTIAN SOCIAL ASSOCIATION

After 1956 Pax no longer enjoyed a monopolistic position as the representative of lay Catholics in the Polish political system. In addition to the revival of the *Tygodnik Powszechny* group, another lay Catholic organization called the Christian Social Association came into being in 1957. This Association originated with the former progressivists who had seceded from Pax in November 1956. The ostensible reason for their secession was their disagreement with Piasecki over the theses expounded in his article published on the eve of the "Polish October." After an abortive attempt to take over Pax from within, they publicly denounced the lack of "democratic procedures" in the organization and resigned from its ranks.[42]

The secessionists by no means represented a compact group. Though united in their opposition to Piasecki, they differed with regard to what line of their own they should follow. Some, such as Konstanty Łubieński or Andrzej Micewski, advocated close cooperation with the *Tygodnik Powszechny* group. Others, notably Jan Frankowski, favored taking a separate course aimed at preserving the "permanent values" of the Pax program.[43] Still others, for instance Dominik Horodyński and Wojciech Kętrzyński, apparently disagreed with both views. Throughout most of 1957 the rallying point of the secessionist group was the weekly *Za i Przeciw*, which they had carried away with them from Pax. On its editorial board, however, friction persisted — culminating in the fall of 1957 in an open split. All Frankowski's major opponents, reportedly with the tacit support of the Communists,[44] lost their posts in *Za i Przeciw*.* Soon afterwards the Christian Social Association, under the undisputed leadership of Frankowski, was formally established. In 1961 it was recognized as a separate political group by the allocation of three seats in parliament.

The decision to back up Frankowski's course of preserving the group's independence of both Pax and especially *Tygodnik Powszechny* was a logical one on the part of Gomułka. It certainly was in line with the Communist policy of dividing the Polish lay Catholics from within, since the establishment of the Christian Social Association split them into three groups. Needless to say, this only served to increase the opportunities of manipulating one Catholic group against the other, thus greatly weakening them as a political force.

Among the three Catholic groups the program of "the Christian democratic left,"[45] espoused by Frankowski's faction, came closest to that of Gomułka. The Christian Social Association fully endorsed all the major policies of the Communist regime. In the field of foreign policy its followers subscribed to Poland's close alignment with the Soviet Union and other socialist states. In the domestic sphere, they supported the policy of the transformation of the socioeconomic system in Poland along broad socialist lines. They also declared themselves in favor of the maintenance of personal freedom and democratization of the political system — though barely beyond

---

* The persons dismissed from *Za i Przeciw* did not in turn form a new group, but dispersed in accordance with their individual preferences. Łubieński and Micewski joined the *Tygodnik Powszechny* group; Kętrzyński entered the diplomatic service; Horodyński renounced Catholicism and became a free-lance writer for various Communist periodicals.

the limits determined by Gomułka. This Christian Social Association program was advanced not only as being in Poland's national interest, but also as a rather loosely defined social ideology. "National interests," claimed the theorists of the group, "do not represent a sufficient [political] motivation for all Catholics. Many of them . . . participate in the construction of a new system because of their ideological convictions." [46] The ideology of the Christian Social Association, however, was not as elaborate and coherent as that of Pax. On the contrary, it remained quite vague; almost, it seems, deliberately vague. In this way the association managed to steer clear of the danger of offending either the Catholics or the Communists.

The attitude of the Christian Social Association toward the Catholic Church was also largely in line with that of the Communist Party. Although in religious matters the members were bound to show "full obedience to the Church hierarchy," and publicly declared themselves in favor of "extending the influence of Catholic morality," [47] in the political field their complete independence from the Church was emphasized. In the State-Church dispute the Christian Social Association sided with the former. Early in 1961, the deputies from the Christian Social Association voted in favor of the bill removing the Catholic festivities from the calendar of official state holidays — a measure opposed not only by the deputies from the *Tygodnik Powszechny* group, but even by those from Pax. In a speech in parliament delivered on May 16, 1961, Frankowski in no uncertain terms blamed the Catholic hierarchy, and not the Communist regime, for aggravating the conflict. Indeed, in the vein of a true progressivist, he demanded from the Church proof by deeds that "it accepts the political system of People's Poland." [48] Needless to say, this stand of the Christian Social Association did not endear it to the Church leaders. In fact, owing to their past connections with Pax, the attitude of the Catholic hierarchy toward Frankowski's group from the very outset was quite cool. As the years went by the relations between the two showed no signs of improvement.

Lack of support from the Catholic Church was probably the main reason for the failure of the Christian Social Association to gain any wider following among the people. Apparently the overwhelming majority of the Polish Catholics viewed the association with distrust. The influence of the association was basically restricted to a few urban centers. In fact, its branches existed only in three cities, but a substitute for an organizational network was provided by the editorial offices of the weekly *Za i Przeciw* in four additional towns. All in all, supporters of the Christian Social Association remained confined to a fairly insignificant stratum of Catholic intelligentsia and craftsmen.

The over-all political record of the Christian Social Association indicates that it has followed the program of the progressive Catholics' movement quite closely. Indeed, the group might be labeled as progressivists of Gomułka's brand. Their position vis-à-vis the Communist Party has in no substantial way been different from that of Pax: they owe their existence primarily to Communist support. Also, in the Communists' eyes, their *raison d'être* has been the same as that of Piasecki's group, namely, to split the Polish Catholics. From the point of view of the Communist leadership, however, the Christian Social Association has represented an improved version of Pax. It has not been compromised by cooperation with the Natolin faction, and since 1956 has faithfully followed Gomułka's course. Moreover, the price which the leaders of the Christian Social Association have expected the Communists to pay for their support has not been as high as that requested by Pax. Frankowski, unlike Piasecki, has not been obsessed with zeal for the paraphernalia of power — he seems to have been content with a seat in the parliament and shows no aspiration toward joining the government.

In the political sphere the major contender of the Christian Social Association has no longer been Pax, but the *Tygodnik Powszechny* group, backed by the Church hierarchy. Should relations between the Communist Party and the Church deteriorate even beyond what they are today, it is possible that the Christian Social Association might then be played off by the Communists against *Tygodnik Powszechny*. This could open some fascinating prospects of a political career for Frankowski, but it could also expose him to serious pitfalls. It could result in the overt censuring of the Christian Social Association by the Church authorities, which would certainly ruin whatever little prestige it enjoys among Polish Catholics. It is likely, therefore, that Frankowski, in the future as in the past, will continue his sinuous course, oscillating between loyalty to the Communist government and the Catholic Church but always keeping somewhat closer to the former.

12

THE ZNAK GROUP

One of the most significant changes brought about in Poland by the upheaval of 1956 was the acceptance by the Communists within the political system of at least one genuine Catholic group, namely Znak. In a country which is overwhelmingly Catholic, it is natural that Znak provided a political focus for a large segment of the Polish population, especially in the absence of other political organizations approved by the Church. There seemed to be some truth, therefore, in the claim advanced in 1957 in parliament by one of the Znak leaders, Zbigniew Makarczyk, that the group enjoyed the support of "millions of people in Poland." [1] The position which Znak occupied in the political system did not reflect, however, its actual following in the country. Indeed, the group did not even have the status of a political party.

Strictly speaking, the name Znak described a handful of Catholic deputies in the Sejm who cooperated closely in their parliamentary work. Since the deputies were drawn from several Catholic organizations, they formed a sort of "federation." [2] This did not mean, of course, that the organizations supporting Znak held opinions which were in every respect identical. On the contrary, especially with regard to social problems, considerable differences existed at times. Yet, they also had enough in common to agree on a general platform which, in turn, became the basis for cooperation among their representatives in the parliament.

Among the organizations which adhered to the Znak program, the most important was a group of Catholic intellectuals centered around the weekly,

Tygodnik Powszechny. Between 1953 and 1956, even though this group was formally disbanded, it did not in fact cease to exist. Its members kept closely in touch and, behind the scenes, continued to exert some influence on the currents of cultural and even political life in Poland. Immediately after the "Polish October," the Catholic writers came out into the open. In a statement published on October 23, 1956, they declared their support for the program of reforms advanced by Gomułka and pledged their intention to participate in its realization. "The Polish Catholics," said the declaration,

appreciate the moral significance of a new program of internal policies aimed at the [maintenance of Poland's] sovereignty, departing from Stalinism and deepening democratization in our life . . . All truly progressive and active Catholic elements . . . are willing to participate in creating in Poland a system based on social justice, freedom, truth, and honesty.[3]

Soon after the declaration was issued, a meeting between Gomułka and the leaders of *Tygodnik Powszechny* group took place in Warsaw. Gomułka offered them two concessions. First, the existence of the group was formally recognized and publication of their two periodicals was restored. Second, the group was invited to put up five candidates in the forthcoming parliamentary election, to be held in January 1957. The Catholics did so and their candidates, all running well ahead of the other contenders, were elected. In the Sejm they were joined by four other deputies who had been elected as nonparty candidates. Together they formed their own parliamentary caucus, known as the Znak Circle.

Despite their small number, the Znak deputies occupied a unique position in the parliament of 1957–1961. Since they did not represent a political party, their caucus was not granted full official recognition. Yet, unlike other deputies who did not belong to a political party, they were not treated merely as individuals acting on their own. Their existence as a political group was recognized by extending to them the semiofficial status of a parliamentary circle. In parliamentary practice, in fact, there was little difference between the formal party caucus and the circle. Thus, the Znak group was given the same privileges in proportion to its strength in the Sejm, as the three political parties — the Polish United Workers' Party, the United Peasant Party, and the Democratic Party. The chairman of the circle, Stanisław Stomma,* was a

---

* Stomma, born in 1908, had been a university lecturer in Wilno before the war. At that time he was already linked with the Catholic political movement. During the war, he participated in the non-Communist underground.

member of the Sejm rules committee. One of its deputies, Jerzy Zawieyski,* was appointed a member of the collective "head of state," the State Council.

After the elections in 1961, Znak's position in parliament changed, in that the Communists did not allow the deputies who in 1957 had been elected as nonparty candidates and had subsequently joined the Znak Circle to stand for re-election. In accordance with the terms of the agreement with Gomułka in 1956, however, five candidates, formally sponsored by Znak, and once again running well ahead of their opponents, were reelected. Thus, the Znak Circle, although reduced in number, was reinstated in the new Sejm and Zawieyski remained a member of the State Council. In the 1965 elections, there were no changes in the Znak position.

Since 1956, largely due to the moral credit they gained by their uncompromising stand in the Stalinist years, the Catholic intellectuals from *Tygodnik Powszechny* remained the core of the Znak group. The fact that they had at their disposal two widely circulated and highly respected periodicals** and after 1959, their own publishing house, greatly facilitated their tasks. Throughout these years, however, *Tygodnik Powszechny* was by no means a closed group. On the contrary, there was a deliberate effort to widen and rejuvenate its composition.

At the same time, an important outlet for broader participation by Catholics in the political life was the establishment in Warsaw and four other cities of the Clubs of Catholic Intelligentsia. Formally, each club was independent, but they were all patterned after the Warsaw club (the first to be founded) and they all cooperated quite closely. The primary objective of the Clubs of Catholic Intelligentsia was to create a forum for the discussion of topics ranging from religion and philosophy to social and political problems. As such, the clubs provided a meeting ground for Catholics who held different political opinions. Alongside the supporters of *Tygodnik Powszechny,* former progressive Catholics no less than former members of the prewar Christian Democratic Labor Party participated in the activities of the clubs. The Clubs of Catholic Intelligentsia, of course, were not a mass organization but were restricted to a relatively narrow stratum of intellectual elite.*** Yet, since they

---

* Zawieyski, whose real name is Nowicki, was born in 1902. He did not participate in politics before the war but confined himself to literary activities. In the postwar years, while he continued writing, he joined the *Tygodnik Powszechny* group. In the midfifties, he was largely instrumental in founding Clubs of Catholic Intelligentsia throughout the country.

** The circulation of *Tygodnik Powszechny* was originally 50,000; but in 1951, it was cut down to 40,000, and in 1964 to 30,000, and that of *Znak,* 7,000.

*** For instance, the Warsaw club in 1960 had one hundred ordinary members and seven hundred participating members. "Poland 1960" (Warsaw, 1960), mimeographed, p. 14.

gathered together the most active elements in each locality where they existed, they provided a fairly effective link between the Znak group and the masses of Polish Catholics.

Among the Clubs of Catholic Intelligentsia a somewhat unique position was occupied by a group of young Catholic intellectuals gathered around the monthly *Więź*. The core of this group, centered in Warsaw, was composed of former progressive Catholics who had been disillusioned with the pseudo-Catholic program of that movement and left its ranks in 1955–56.* Subsequently they joined the Clubs of Catholic Intelligentsia but retained a sort of internal autonomy. In 1958 they acquired their own monthly, *Więź*, which was published in Warsaw.** The views expounded by *Więź* differed from those advanced by *Tygodnik Powszechny* chiefly with respect to social problems. The writers in *Więź* as a whole took a somewhat more radical stand on the issue of social reform and looked with more favor on the social aspects of Communist policies than did *Tygodnik Powszechny*. This shade of difference with regard to social problems, of course, was in line with the "federal" character of the entire Catholic political movement. It affected neither the close cooperation between *Więź* and *Tygodnik Powszechny* nor their loyal support of the Znak program. Indeed, to emphasize their unity, in 1961 the editor-in-chief of *Więź*, Tadeusz Mazowiecki, was elected to the Sejm as one of the Znak candidates.

ATTITUDE TOWARD CATHOLICISM AND MARXISM

The cardinal tenet of the Znak program, namely the attitude toward Catholicism and Marxism, has not changed in any essential way since the initial declaration of 1946. The group's unreserved adherence to Catholicism was beyond reproach. At the same time its unconditional rejection of Marxism was in no way modified. "We have never tried to reduce or ignore ideological contradictions [existing] between the Catholic and Marxist outlook," declared one of the Znak leaders, Stanisław Stomma, in 1959. "We also have realized that these [contradictions] have far-reaching, practical consequences." [4] The supporters of Znak, then, unlike the progressive Catholics, never cherished any illusions about the prospects of reconciling Catholic

* The editor-in-chief of *Więź*, Tadeusz Mazowiecki, and some of his friends formed the so-called Fronde group which left the progressive Catholics' movement soon after its condemnation by the Holy Office in 1955.
** The circulation of *Więź* was 4,000.

and Marxist doctrines. They felt that the gap dividing the two philosophies simply could not be bridged.

The existence of an irreconcilable, doctrinal difference between Catholicism and Marxism, argued the supporters of Znak, should not prevent Catholics and Marxists from cooperating on practical matters. Since in Poland Catholics and Communists live side by side and frequently are faced with the same problems, their joint efforts in overcoming obstacles might prove advantageous to both sides. Thus, claimed the Znak followers, without compromising the principles involved in their respective philosophies, some understanding between Catholics and Marxists on a purely pragmatic plane could be reached. That this is feasible was confirmed by actual experience. "In the past years of the so-called 'cult of the individual,'" wrote Stomma in 1957, "we went through the most trying experiences, and today not all difficulties have been eliminated. Yet, despite these, the policy of cooperation [between Catholics and Marxists] has to its credit several significant achievements." [5]

In the practical sphere, but in the practical sphere only, the adherents of Znak were in favor of a modus vivendi between the Catholics and the Marxists in Poland. Their rationalization for taking this stand — in contrast to the progressive Catholics who claimed to deduce their program directly from Polish patriotism — was derived from Catholic teaching. The Znak followers believed that the *sensus catholicus* imposed on them the duty to be concerned with the interests of their nation. In the political sphere, their guiding principle was the "rationally accepted sense of moral obligation flowing from the perception of the nation's needs." [6]

In the last analysis, then, it was their specific interpretation of Polish national interests which made the Znak supporters advocate some accommodation between the Catholics and Communists in Poland. "As Catholics," wrote Stomma, "we must maintain full allegiance to the Church and not depart from its doctrine. Yet, we also have a duty to be concerned with the interests of our nation. These two principles cannot contradict one another. [7] It was because some compromise between Catholics and Communists was the only course compatible with the interests of the Polish nation — and, thus, in line with Catholic morality — that it was adopted by Znak. It was because the other alternatives — to aggravate the conflict between the Catholics and Marxists, or to take a purely passive stand vis-à-vis the Communists — would be harmful to Poland's national interest, and thus contrary to the Catholic ethic, that Znak rejected both of them.

In Poland's political situation, the exponents of the Znak program claimed, increasing friction between Catholics and Marxists in the name of doctrinal incompatibility would be immoral, for it could only worsen and not improve the lot of the Polish people. This perhaps would not be so were there some prospect for changing the political system in the country in the near future. Such a prospect, however, did not exist.* In these circumstances a policy of aggravating the internal conflict would be doomed to defeat. Indeed, from the point of view of the interests of the Polish nation such a policy "in the long run could prove to be suicidal."

The Znak theorists not only rejected the policy of augmenting tensions between Catholics and Communists, but also repudiated the possibility of Catholics assuming a purely passive attitude toward the Marxists. They considered the maximalist position of insisting on everything or nothing as morally wrong. In their opinion adopting the purely negative posture of "internal emigrés" certainly would not help, and often might hurt, the Polish people. "It is possible," exclaimed Stomma,

in the name of maximalist ethics to wash one's hands in order not to stain them with a wrong decision, and thus to pave the way for even greater wrongs. Such alleged maximalism is hypocritical. It is nothing but an easy "angelical" phraseology. In any situation one ought to make a decision instead of trying to escape reality.[8]

The followers of Znak, therefore, in the name of protecting the interests of the Polish nation chose the third alternative. They declared themselves in favor of both reducing the conflict between Catholics and Communists in Poland, and of promoting the broadest possible modus vivendi between the two groups. In line with their underlying belief that there existed many practical problems where cooperation between Catholics and Marxists is possible, they adopted a position which they called "open Catholicism."

The adherents of open Catholicism, without undermining their orthodoxy in any way, took a constructive and not a negative attitude toward the Communists. They did not question a priori all the measures of the Communist regime, but approached them in a purely pragmatic fashion. They judged each policy on its merit: whether it was in harmony or in conflict with what they understood as the interests of the Polish nation. All policies which

* Stomma acknowledged that perhaps the political system in Poland could be changed through war. He felt, however, that in view of the destructive potential inherent in modern warfare, taking such risks would be morally wrong. Indeed, he explicitly branded political calculations based on war as "foolish and criminal." Myśli o polityce i kulturze (Cracow, 1960), p. 76.

passed this test received the Catholics' full support; on those which did not they at least tried to explore all avenues of rational compromise with the Marxists. Since the task of evaluating the policies of the Communist regime in the light of Poland's national interests was a political activity *par excellence,* the natural consequence of adopting open Catholicism was active participation by Polish Catholics in the political life of the country. The Znak group, thus, not only entered the parliament but gradually evolved a distinct political program of its own.

THE REVIVAL OF THE DMOWSKI TRADITION

In evolving its program the Znak group, like Pax, was influenced by the tradition of political realism. Yet the platform put forward by Znak was essentially different from that of Pax, in that it looked for inspiration not only to Wielopolski and the positivists, but also to Dmowski.

Neither of the major theorists of Znak, Stanisław Stomma nor Stefan Kisielewski* could claim any connection with the prewar National Democratic movement. By their own admission, before World War II they both had adhered to political idealism.** They embraced Dmowski's program only as a result of their evaluation of the tragic events in Poland during the war. They simply found it most relevant to the needs of contemporary Poland. Referring to one of the major works of Dmowski published in 1925, in which the policies of National Democracy until the end of World War I are summed up, Kisielewski made the following observation:

Quite a few of our present controversies may be traced, and, incidentally, solved [by consulting] the pages of this encyclopedia of political realism, little known to the younger generation. Often we do not realize that in a new situation history repeats itself, that there are the same political and psychological issues involved.[9]

The Catholic intellectuals, however, did not stop at drawing a parallel between the political situation in Poland in the days of Dmowski and that

* Kisielewski, born in 1911, began his career as a composer, music critic and essayist in the late thirties. Before the war he was loosely linked with the conservative movement, but he really moved into the field of political activity only in the postwar years.

** Before the war, wrote Stomma: "from the emotional point of view I had been close to the people who opposed Russia . . . and who advocated bonds with the West against the East. The tragic events in the years 1939–1944, however, demonstrated that this emotional disposition is incompatible with a rational attitude. As a result of tedious reappraisal, in foreign policy I have declared myself for Dmowski." *Myśli o polityce i kulturze* (Cracow, 1960), p. 18.

after World War II. They adopted several tenets of Dmowski's program as their own. Writing on behalf of the entire Znak group, Stomma clarified their attitude toward Dmowski's program in the following fashion:

We unequivocally reject Dmowski's nationalism; we appraise critically his social program and his leanings, which he revealed toward the end of his life, toward totalitarianism. However, we consider as correct Dmowski's appraisal of Poland's policies in the nineteenth century, as well as his analysis of the position of the Polish nation located between Russia and Germany. We adopt these theses of Dmowski as our own.[10]

The influence of Dmowski's writings was evident in the several aspects of Znak's political program. First of all, the Znak people denied the value of a military struggle for Poland's independence. Especially, they came out against what they labeled the "insane insurrections" which had failed to achieve their political objective and exposed the Polish people to grave loss and suffering. "In the last few centuries," wrote Stomma, the scourge of Poland's fate was that "heroism was always doomed to defeat . . . It led to such events as the uprising in 1863 and the Warsaw uprising." [11]

The Znak people, however, in the tradition of Dmowski, were careful not to indulge in purely negative criticism of the struggle of the Polish nation for independence. They did not even repudiate all military effort, for they realized that at times it is expedient to resort to force. Contemporary positivism, wrote Stomma, "does not deprecate the glorious pages of Poland's past, for it is aware that heroism is the dynamite of history." Indeed, Stomma made it clear that he regarded political realism merely as an alternative method of advancing the same goals as political idealism. "Positivism," he declared, "does not discard idealistic objectives, but strives to promote them so far as historical conditions permit." The Znak theorist, thus, merely rejected the struggle conducted in accordance with Mickiewicz's principle "to measure one's powers by one's purposes." In undertaking military action, asserted Stomma, one must make sure "that there is no discrepancy between the decision and the objective at which it is aimed." [12]

Yet, the Znak group did not completely go back to the Dmowski tradition. They also adopted at least some tenets of the nineteenth-century positivism. Indeed, they oscillated between the two traditions. This was well demonstrated by an argument the group had early in 1963. When Stomma in searching for the reasons of the 1863 uprising, asserted that its outbreak had been caused by the "anti-Russian complex" of the Poles,[13] he was openly criticized by some of his colleagues. One of the younger leaders of Znak, Jacek Woźniakowski, bluntly retorted that the attitude of the Poles toward the Russians in 1863 could not be depicted as a "complex" for it had been "certainly well justified" by the tsarist oppression.[14]

Even more outspoken criticism of Stomma's positivist thesis was voiced on the same occasion by Cardinal Wyszyński. The insurrection of 1863, the Cardinal claimed in a sermon in Warsaw, cannot be explained by an anti-Russian complex,

for a complex represents a disease, while [the Poles] were guided by a healthy striving for freedom which [they] had been denied . . . When a man or a nation is suppressed . . . there is no need to search for complexes. For it suffices to be a decent person, to have honor and dignity to rise against slavery.

Significantly, Cardinal Wyszyński contrasted the position of Stomma with that of Dmowski. One of the positive effects of the uprising of 1863, he said, had been that it paved the way for the search for other ways to improve the lot of the Polish nation. Then there had appeared, he continued, in a direct reference to the major work of Dmowski, "writers of the 'thoughts of modern Poles' who contributed to the strengthening of the bonds of national unity." [15]

ZNAK'S FOREIGN POLICY PROGRAM

Znak's foreign policy program, thus, represents a mixture of the traditions of positivism and those of National Democracy. The Znak group, like the positivists in the past, placed little hope in help coming from the West. The experiences of World War II, no less than those of the postwar years, undermined their faith in the Western democracies. "The West has failed us many times," [16] declared Kisielewski. "The disastrous concept of relying upon the mythical intervention of a 'third power' was at the root of all the tragic cataclysms in Poland from 1939 . . . until the catastrophe of the Warsaw uprising." [17] Consequently, the Znak people ruled out any prospects of effective military or diplomatic Western intervention in East Europe. Instead they sought new ways to improve the lot of the Polish nation within the existing framework of political reality.

In place of a military struggle assisted by the West, the Znak group put forward a program closely resembling that of the nineteenth century's organic reform. Attention was turned from revolutionary activity to peaceful efforts to promote economic and social progress. The new goals of the Poles in the internal sphere were well defined by Kisielewski, in a vein somewhat resembling that of the nineteenth-century positivists:

After bitter experiences, after a sour mixture of disappointments and defeats, after depreciation of slogans and inflation of words, men became austere, critical, difficult and, at times, even cynical; yet in a way more mature. Hamlet-like posture has been abandoned [by them]. Poland gave up her hopes for miracles and severed her addiction to ideology. Today Poland strives to calculate and to gain. Poland wants to live a normal life and enjoy its material rewards.

To overcome . . . the material, technical, and organizational shortcomings of everyday life . . . is the only positive expression of heroism; the only outlet for active patriotism. Patriotism is changing its content; it is less pathetic and less deceptive . . . Its ultimate substance will emerge only with major economic success.[18]

The followers of Znak did not, however, restrict themselves to advocating organic reform, but advanced a concrete program of foreign policy as well. They viewed the present position of Poland vis-à-vis Germany and Russia very much as Dmowski had in the first decade of this century. The analogy between the two was drawn clearly by Kisielewski:

Dmowski based his policy on cooperation with tsarism and pan-Slavism; he was for a united Slavdom as opposed to Germandom. His goal was a united Poland reaching toward the Oder and the Neisse, including Silesia, East Prussia, and Pomerania, allied with tsarism or even, in the first stage, under tsarist rule.

Today, after all the wartime cataclysms and catastrophes a new Poland has emerged with its border along the Oder and the Neisse, allied with the Soviet Union. One could risk a paradoxical statement that nowadays some of Dmowski's conceptions from before World War I have been realized.[19]

Znak followers, like Dmowski, felt that the major danger to Poland came from Germany. They considered the maintenance of Poland's western border along the Oder and the Neisse rivers as, literally, a matter of life and death for the Polish people. Since the chances of recovering Poland's eastern territories lost to the Soviet Union were virtually nonexistent, the loss of the western provinces, they felt, would deprive the Poles of a territorial base essential for the existence of the Polish nation. Thus, the safeguarding of Poland's western frontier was viewed by Znak as the cardinal objective of Polish foreign policy. "In comparison with the necessity of maintaining the territory indispensable for national survival," exclaimed Kazimierz Studentowicz, another exponent of the Znak political program, "all other problems are of secondary importance." [20]

The Znak writers carried their analysis of Polish foreign policy to its logical conclusion. Since, in their eyes, America had failed to disassociate herself from German claims to Poland's territory and had promoted West German rearmament, Poland in this matter could not count upon the West. "Since the United States resumed supporting Germany," wrote Studentowicz, "their foreign policy no longer can be reconciled with our national interests. In spite of the very great sympathy which the Polish people have toward the American nation, it must be remembered that the Americans are indifferent to our fate." [21]

The consequences of American alignment with Germany, argued the Catholic writers, could prove disastrous for Poland. For instance, in the case of a major war in which the West were to emerge victorious, Poland would likely be deprived of her vital western territories. In such a situation, wrote Kisielewski, "the Germans, armed by the Americans, would move into our western territories. Obviously we would not return into the east . . . the Anglo-Saxons have always supported the Curzon line. As a result . . . Poland would become a strange country — poor, overpopulated, not viable, and, indeed, doomed. *Finis Polonia!*" [22]

It was precisely to make sure that such a development could not take place that Znak declared itself in favor of Poland's firm alignment with the Soviet Union. Only the U.S.S.R., asserted Studentowicz, had extended to Poland strong and resolute support with respect "to the maintenance of the [western] territories . . . This is precisely what determines the irrevocability of our political alliance with the Soviet Union." [23]

Znak writers did not try to conceal that the decision to align themselves with the Soviet Union against America was not an easy one for traditionally pro-Western Poles to make. Yet, they believed that this was the only rational choice. As Kisielewski remarked with some resignation, referring to the Polish-Soviet alliance: "a marriage of convenience is often more lasting than a union based on affection." [24]

The adoption of an identical stand with the Communist regime, with respect to the expediency of alignment with the Soviet Union, however, did not mean that the Znak group accepted the Communists' ideological rationale for this alliance. While for the Communists, the reason for close bonds with the U.S.S.R. was principally proletarian internationalism, for the Catholics it was solely Poland's national interests. Here, Znak not only made its position quite clear, but also demanded that the Communists should respect it. Exponents of Znak's program argued that proletarian internationalism was merely one of the links in the Soviet bloc, and that alongside there existed other bonds of a purely pragmatic nature. "The Marxists," wrote Kisielewski,

often regard Marxist internationalism as the only basis for our alignment with the Soviet Union . . . We consider this view incorrect. Although we fully appreciate the importance of ideology, as an element of unity, this is only a part of the problem. One must not disregard the pluralistic nature of any society. What is important is that [the alliance with the U.S.S.R.] should be understood and upheld by the Polish society such as it is at present.[25]

The significance of Poland's siding with the East against the West, moreover, was softened by the fact that (despite the nightmare of war drawn by Kisielewski) the Znak theorists expected the gradual lessening of international tensions. They hoped that this would pave the way for a genuine détente between East and West and, indeed, ultimately lead to a meeting half-way between the two worlds. "Fewer and fewer people in the two hemispheres," wrote one of the younger leaders of Znak, Stefan Wilkanowicz, "believe that one day there is going to be a counterrevolution and a restoration of the private ownership of the means of production in the Soviet Union; or that the councils of the workers and peasants will come into power in the United States. Nothing like that is in view." Instead, reasoned the Catholic writer, the two major contenders in international politics were likely to evolve a compromise, whereby each would profit from the major accomplishments of the other: the West would introduce some socialistic methods of accelerating economic growth, while the East would move closer toward political democracy. Poland, in the opinion of the Znak people, could make a significant contribution to promoting such a development. "Poland," observed Wilkanowicz,

focuses the various paradoxes and contradictions of the contemporary world: Marxism and Catholicism as well as the whole range of existentialist, agnostic, and liberal outlooks; keen interest in the outside world and a passionate devotion to one's own nation; progressiveness and traditionalism; rural patriarchy and rapidly growing cities.

The position of Poland as a meeting ground of ideas from the West and East, continued Wilkanowicz, predestines her to the role of a bridge between the two worlds. Poland, he concluded, is

a strange country . . . "the outpost of Christianity" and the "shop-window of the socialist camp" . . . A country attractive to visitors from both the East and the West . . . A unique position . . . The sole laboratory of some social processes. The slogans repeated a thousand times: rapport, cooperation, coexistence.[26]

The elaborating of Znak's program in *Tygodnik Powszechny* on several occasions produced a vigorous response from the Communists. In particular, the issue of *Tygodnik Powszechny* of September 4, 1960, in which the coherent political program of realist foreign policy was advanced in the articles by Kisielewski, Studentowicz, and Stomma — and, incidentally, where Kisielewski challenged the Communists with his statement regarding the role of their ideology — received prominent attention in the Communist press. On September 19, 1960, the weekly *Polityka* published the lengthy comment of its editor-in-chief, Mieczysław Rakowski, on the theses advanced by *Tygodnik Powszechny*. On September 22, another front-page article dealing with the same subject written by Witold Zalewski, appeared in *Przegląd Kulturalny*.

In both articles, the endorsement by *Tygodnik Powszechny* of Poland's alignment with the Soviet Union was noted with approval, but both took strong exception to the clearcut distinction drawn by Kisielewski between the acceptance of this fact on ideological and on nationalistic grounds. The writers' reactions to this, however (reflecting well the essential ambiguity in Gomułka's program: its peculiar symbiosis between political realism and Marxist ideology), were quite different, Rakowski, while expressing his doubts about the sincerity of the support for the Polish-Soviet alliance on the part of Polish Catholics, strongly underlined the respect felt by Polish Communists for Poland's national interests. "Polish Communists," claimed Rakowski,

as patriots and internationalists, in stressing the significance of friendly relations with the Soviet Union, always have appreciated the two aspects of this problem. They always have combined national interests with internationalist principles . . . The Communists have never thought that the only basis for full acceptance of the alliance with the U.S.S.R. is the adoption of Marxist internationalism.[27]

Zalewski's argument was to some extent the reverse of Rakowski's. Instead of emphasizing the Communists' attachment to Poland's national interest, the latter underlined the importance of ideology. Zalewski argued that in the contemporary world adherence to the Polish-Soviet alignment on the basis of the program advanced by National Democracy, namely, based on strengthening Poland's position vis-à-vis Germany, no longer could be considered satisfactory. Poland's alliance with the U.S.S.R. nowadays was merely a fragment of a broader world conflict and, therefore, might be viewed only through the prism of a universal ideology. "Today," wrote Zalewski, "when universal tendencies prevail, the problem of our survival and our security will depend more and more upon [developments] in the whole world." [28]

ZNAK'S DOMESTIC POLITICAL PROGRAM

In Znak's political program foreign and domestic policies were inextricably linked. Poland's position in the international sphere, argued the Znak theorists, determines not only the course of her external policies, but the major lines of internal development as well. Her political system is inseparably linked with membership in the socialist camp. "It is quite obvious," asserted Stomma, "that from the fact of Poland's participation in the eastern, socialist bloc, the necessity of her having a socialist political system flows logically and irrevocably."

The interdependence of Poland's external policy and her internal political system, according to the Znak leader, also restricts the range of policies available to the Poles in the domestic sphere. Any internal reforms must not be at variance with the general political trend in the Soviet bloc. "Let us talk openly and bluntly," exclaimed Stomma. "We live in an epoch of global solutions. The isolation of particular states is no longer possible." [29]

Znak adherents, however, believed — or at least wanted to believe — that the general direction of political change in the socialist countries was in line with the aspirations of the Poles. They thought that the over-all trend in the Soviet bloc was toward democracy. They seemed to hope that the socioeconomic processes stimulated by industrialization would gradually lead to the democratization of life in Russia and the other Communist states.* "In the socialist world," claimed Stomma, "the main line of development . . . [is] the gradual growth of democratic tendencies." [30] The Znak group did not propose to sit idle and wait until democratization should take place in the Soviet Union, and then eventually spread into Poland. On the contrary, they would have liked Poland, as in 1956–1957, to represent the democratic avant-garde among the Communist countries. "In the new socioeconomic conditions," declared Stomma, "we expect the growth of democracy. We want Poland in her policies to assume the role of spokesman

* In this regard, the views of the exponents of Znak's program are similar to those of some of the Western observers of the Soviet scene. Occasionally they even borrow their arguments from the Western writers. For instance, Studentowicz, in his article mentioned above, explicitly supported his thesis with the view expounded by Walt W. Rostow in his book, *The Stages of Economic Growth* (New York, 1960).

and advocate of these [tendencies]. This is the great cause which over-shadows everything else." [31]

It was the advancement of democracy which from the outset was the central theme of the domestic program of Znak. The attachment of the group to democratic principles was both unequivocal and unconditional. "There are only two methods of governing," asserted Stomma. "One is an authoritarian government. The other is a democratic one. The latter is the method of reaching [political] decisions with the support of the nation . . . and with the approval and cooperation of the whole society.[32] Indeed, promoting democratic reforms was regarded by Znak as its very *raison d'être*. "Should political developments move in the opposite direction [from democracy]," Stomma declared, "our activities would be deprived of their very rationale." [33]

The Znak theorists recognized that ". . . the art of governing Poland is extremely difficult." [34] Long years of foreign rule had deprived the Poles of experience in self-government and made them suspicious of any authority. The exponents of the Znak program, however, denied that these traits provide an excuse for curbing democracy; on the contrary, in their opinion, resorting to authoritarian methods would merely aggravate these sentiments and widen the gap between the people and the government. In Poland, warned Stomma, "it is difficult to govern . . . but is is even more difficult to govern in conflict with the nation." [35] It is only by using democratic methods, he asserted, that the Poles can be ruled. "In order to lead the nation it is necessary to cooperate with it. Such cooperation is possible only when respect is shown for the values which Poles understand and accept. These are democracy and freedom." [36]

It was, thus, the extension of democracy in all spheres of life in Poland which was the main objective of the Znak group. As such its program of internal reforms corresponded closely to that which was advanced by the Polish people in 1956 and, subsequently, elaborated by the Polish intellectuals in 1957. Indeed, with the suppression of the various groups advocating the policy of democratization of life in Poland within the Communist Party, as well as within the two non-Marxist parties, the Znak group has virtually remained the sole heir to the program of "Polish October." In the political field, the concrete measures which Znak followers proposed were manifold. First of all, the group stood for the rule of law. They stressed especially that all branches of the government should act strictly within the limits imposed by law. Secondly, they encouraged strengthening the powers of parliament both with regard to making laws and supervising the administration. Thirdly, they advocated extending the authority of local government at all levels. Last but not least, they supported greater freedom for voluntary associations of all types.

The same democratic principles underlay the Znak program in the socioeconomic sphere. The Znak people were not committed either to the capitalist or the socialist socioeconomic system. They refrained from endorsing socialism on ideological grounds; yet, they did accept on pragmatic grounds some of its specific features, notably, the nationalization of industry. Their reason for doing so was that they felt this step had met with the approval of the Polish people. For the same reason, however, they advocated strongly the principle of private ownership in agriculture, as well as in small-scale manufacturing and trade. Also, because they thought this policy was endorsed by the people, the Znak exponents came out in favor of extensive industrialization. They realized that this would involve considerable sacrifice on the part of the entire nation. Yet, they felt that there was no other way out of Poland's economic difficulties. "Poland is still below the necessary economic level," argued Stomma. "Only through increasing national wealth can the standard of living be improved." [37]

Intensifying the economic efforts of the people, argued the exponents of the Znak program, could be accomplished not through tightening administrative controls but, on the contrary, through the widest possible extension of self-government into the economic sphere. "It would be an illusion to believe," exclaimed Stomma, "that mechanical, administrative rigor, under anti-democratic conditions and without the consent of society can achieve any positive results . . . A dynamic economic policy can be fostered only with the support of the people." [38] The confidence of the Poles in economic policies could be secured only if various changes in the structure of planning and management of industry were carried out. Here the Znak adherents also proposed various concrete steps. First, the entire economic system should be decentralized, giving special attention to workers' self-government. Secondly, more competent people, irrespective of their political affiliation, should be brought into the administration. Finally, economic incentives, particularly among the lowest paid groups of workers, should be used as much as possible.

The problem that received special attention in the Znak program was religious freedom. In line with their conviction that political and religious spheres should not be confused, the Znak people drew a sharp distinction between their stand and that of the Catholic Church in this matter. They emphasized that "Catholicism should not be reduced to a single political program . . . and the Church must not be identified with a single political group." [39] Although as Catholics they pledged in public life to remain faithful to the teaching of the Church — and indeed, it was the Church's teaching which prompted them to participate in the political life of the country — they asserted that they alone assumed responsibility for their political activity. Conversely, they felt that the issue of State-Church relations could be resolved only through bilateral agreement between the Communist government and the Catholic hierarchy.

This did not mean, however, that Znak adherents were not keenly interested in the position of the Catholic Church in Poland. As a political group, however, they viewed this problem not from a narrow denominational position, but within the broader context of democracy. They were in favor of freedom of conscience because they regarded it as good per se. "We consider the matter [of religious freedom] as particularly significant," said an official Znak declaration, "not only because it is supported by Catholics . . . but because freedom is not divisible." [40] Consequently, Znak supporters demanded that in the Church-State dispute the government respect the fundamental rules of political democracy; they simply postulated that "matters of religion and Church be treated in accordance with democratic principles." [41]

DIFFICULTIES AND HOPES

Despite its very modest role in the political system after 1956, Znak has undoubtedly been next to the Polish United Workers' Party the most important political organization in Poland. This is because it has been the only political movement, other than the Communist Party, which has found its own genuine source of strength. If the power of the Polish United Workers' Party, however, has been rooted in its approval by Moscow, the authority of Znak has been derived from within the country. It has been obtained through Znak's endorsement by the Catholic Church which, in turn, command the loyalty of millions of Polish people. The position of Znak, thus between the Communist government and the Catholic masses has clearly reflected the discrepancy that exists between the *pays légal* and *pays réel* in Poland. In Poland's peculiar situation, of course, support from without is more important than that from within, and it is this very fact which has placed the Communist Party in a position superior to that of Znak in the formal political system. Indeed, the disparity in power between the two political movements has been such that the Communists could restrict Znak activities or even suppress them altogether, though they could not liquidate the group without serious consequences. It could be done only at the risk of widening the gap between the *pays légal* and the *pays réel*.

It is only because of Poland's juxtaposition to Russia that Znak has accepted its inferior position to the Polish United Workers' Party. Inspired by the tenets of political realism, the group has recognized the necessity of maintaining a Communist government in Poland. Thus, it has not aspired to win, or even to share power in the country.* Its *raison d'être* has been to articulate the political sentiments of the Polish people and to channel them into the Communist government. "We entered the Sejm," asserted Kisielewski, "in order to transmit the opinions and the demands of the nation to the [Communist] party." [42] The Znak group has performed this function quite effectively. Taking as its starting point the reforms advanced in 1956–57, Znak has continued to set forth its policies as an alternative to those followed by the Gomułka regime. It has expounded its program in the speeches of its representatives in parliament,** in the newspapers, and at meetings of the Clubs of Catholic Intelligentsia.

In this role Znak, of course, frequently has met with the disapproval of the Communist regime, which has led to the restriction of several aspects of Znak's activities. The group has not been allowed to launch its own daily paper. All Znak publications have been subjected to heavy censorship, and in 1961 and again in 1964 the circulation of *Tygodnik Powszechny* was substantially reduced. Out of the more than twenty Clubs of Catholic Intelligentsia established in 1956, only five have been permitted to continue their work. Through Communist refusal in 1961 to approve the reelection of the nonparty deputies who had joined the Znak Circle in 1957, Znak's representation in parliament has been trimmed. Also, relatively few Znak

---

* The Znak leaders emphasized strongly that participation in the legislature did not give them any voice in shaping the policies of the executive. They also underlined that the presence of their representative in the State Council should not be confused with their participation in the government, for the Council is in fact a sort of upper chamber devoid of any real political power. "Rozmowa ze Stefanem Kisielewskim," *Kultura,* June 1957.

** The tactics of the Znak Circle in parliament have been to use persuasion rather than obstruction. Nonetheless, on several occasions it has carried its opposition to a logical conclusion and refused to vote for bills sponsored by the Communist government. In 1957–1961, Znak deputies as a group opposed twelve bills: eight times they abstained from voting, and four times they voted against legislative measures. *Tygodnik Powszechny,* April 2, 1961.

candidates have been permitted to run as candidates in local government elections. Indeed, several times since 1957 it has appeared as if the Communists contemplated liquidating Znak altogether. Moreover, the general retreat of the Gomułka regime from a policy of democratization, has made cooperation between the Communist Party and Znak extremely difficult. In particular, the revival of the State-Church dispute has placed Znak in a precarious position. By sincere conviction, as well as for sound tactical reasons, its members cannot remain neutral in this conflict. They have to side with the Church. In fact, when the controversy between the Communist regime and the Catholic hierarchy became especially acute on the eve of elections in 1961 and again in 1965, some opposition was raised in Znak's ranks against any further participation in the Sejm. However, on both occasions the advocates of a continued attempt at cooperation with the Communists prevailed.

At the same time, however, not all the steps taken by the Communist government toward Znak have been negative. Several concessions extended to it by Gomułka in 1956 have been upheld and even a few new ones have been made. The launching of the monthly *Więź* in 1958 was one of these. The establishment by the Warsaw Club of Catholic Intelligentsia of its own commercial enterprise named "Libella," and Znak's publishing house in Cracow a year later, were others. Thus, as if reflecting the discrepancy in the evaluation of its program between Zalewski and Rakowski, the attitude of the Communists toward Znak as a whole remains ambiguous.

The issue of the State-Church relations is of crucial importance to Znak. Should the dispute between Communist government and the Catholic Church be still further aggravated, it might be that pressure for the withdrawal of Znak representatives from parliament — and from the State Council in particular — would increase greatly. Judging by the past record of Znak leaders, they would be unlikely to make such a decision hastily. Yet, should they be convinced that there is no other way out, there is little reason to suppose that at least the core of *Tygodnik Powszechny* group would refrain from manifesting openly — as they did in 1953 — their disagreement with the policies of the Communist regime. There are signs, indeed, that after the repeated failure of the *rapprochement* between State and Church, a feeling of frustration has been spreading through the ranks of Znak supporters. This mood was well described by Kisielewski in 1963. Declaring that he personally looked forward to the end of the term of the current Sejm in 1965 so that he might retire from political activity (as he incidentally did) he acknowledged that Znak's hope of reaching a modus vivendi with the Communists was diminishing. He attributed this to the quixotic, rationalist optimism of the group which, while advancing its program, had not taken into account

one fundamental difficulty, namely, that in order to effectively persuade there must exist a common language . . . Unfortunately such a language does not exist in our country . . . As a result the efforts of Znak . . . resemble those of Don Quixote . . . The rationalist economic arguments of Łubieński, the rationalist historical arguments of Stomma, the rationalist "ecumenical" arguments of Turowicz, and the rationalist social arguments of Mazowiecki fall upon deaf ears. It is time for the Quixotes to retire.[43]

The difficult position of Znak on the Polish political scene stems largely from the ambiguity inherent in its program. It reflects the incompatibility of the elements derived from the tradition of early twentieth-century National Democracy and that of nineteenth-century organic reform. It is because several tenets of Dmowski's moderate political realism were adopted that the group enjoys the support of the Church hierarchy and the Catholic masses; it is because it endorses some precepts of the positivist extreme political realism that it is tolerated by the Gomułka regime. The resolution of the contradiction inherent in the Znak program can perhaps be postponed for some time, but it cannot be avoided indefinitely. Sooner or later the group, or a part thereof, will have to choose between the two traditions. It will either have to engage in political struggle resembling that of the National Democracy prior to World War I, or it will have to give up its ambition to play a genuine political role as did the nineteenth-century positivists.

Poland will not perish
As long as we are alive.
What the alien power has taken away
We shall regain by the sword.

—Polish national anthem

13

POLITICAL IDEALISM AND
POLITICAL REALISM: THE SYNTHESIS

The fundamental fact of Poland's politics, the split between political idealists and political realists, has persisted now for almost two centuries. This has stemmed from the peculiar situation of that country in the international sphere. The security delemma which plagued the Polish nation at the time of Frederick the Great and Catherine the Great, and again in the eras of Bismarck and Alexander II and of Hitler and Stalin, has not yet been solved. For Poland, the paramount political reality remains its location between Germany and Russia. This is a constant which, as a contemporary German historian observed, "permits but a few ever-repeated combinations."[1] Basically, there are only two combinations possible. These are the programs of either romanticism or positivism.

The equilibrium between political idealism and political realism is preserved in a largely self-regulating manner. The record of Poland's history confirms an observation of a prominent American physiologist that as in a human body also in a nation "hardly any strong tendency . . . continues to the stage of disaster; before the extreme is reached corrective forces arise which check the tendency and they commonly prevail as themselves to cause a reaction."[2] The shifts from romanticism to positivism take place automatically mainly because when pushed to the extreme both programs are self-defeating. Political idealism which, in order to advance national independence, submits a nation to the peril of biological extinction, and political realism which, in order to promote national survival, exposes a nation to the danger of losing its identity — both of these contradict their own goals. Thus, whenever the exponents of romanticism or positivism go too far in their respective directions, they become subjected to an automatic penalty. The people simply refuse to follow their lead.*

Since both political idealism and political realism rarely take an extreme form, the discrepancy between them — all the bitterness which frequently has characterized the political contest between their respective adherents notwithstanding — is considerably narrowed. The end of the moderate versions of both programs is essentially the same: to cope with the security dilemma by advancing Poland's interest vis-à-vis its more powerful neighbors. Even with respect to the means, the gap separating the two approaches to politics is not an unbridgeable one. For each of them represents values which in the long run are indispensable for the survival of a nation — particularly a nation placed in as difficult a position as Poland. Political idealism emphasizes the need for cultivating the high morale of the people, while political realism stresses the necessity of developing the human and material resources of the country. As such, in the long run, romanticism and positivism are not only compatible but actually largely complementary.

The complementary rather than the contradictory nature of the two programs was, in fact, recognized at different periods of Poland's history by political theorists and practitioners alike. Few Polish political leaders have remained consistently faithful to either political idealism or political realism. Most of them openly have changed sides at one stage or the other of their political career, especially at times of national crisis.

The best example of an attempt to combine the moderate versions of the two programs, while rejecting their extremes, may be found in the writings of Roman Dmowski. The leader of National Democracy consciously strove for a synthesis between political idealism and political realism. In 1904 he repudiated the extreme forms of both romanticism and positivism:

In the opinion of some writers our political thought is doomed to shift from one extreme to the other. Either revolution, conspiracy, and seeking independence through military uprising . . . or the abandonment of all aspirations to

* In the twentieth century the tendency toward an alternation between political idealism and political realism in Poland is enhanced by the fact that both programs were tested in the past. There exists strong historicism among the Poles. Especially in times of crisis, they almost instinctively turn to history to look for answers to the problems with which they are faced. This, however, carries with it the danger that, in drawing historical parallels, *comparison n'est pas raison,* the Poles might be overimpressed with the past and ignore the new elements of the situation.

independent existence, the complete acceptance of fate, the unconditional surrender. There is thesis and antithesis, but there is no attempt to seek a synthesis.[3]

In 1908 when the National Democratic movement which he led had made important strides, Dmowski claimed that the synthesis of political idealism and political realism was actually found:

> While in the past, it was understood that the nation had only two alternatives, either military uprising or complete surrender and reconciliation with the existing conditions . . . the Polish nation has found a new way, excluding both of these possibilities . . . It has grasped the importance of political struggle carried out every day and everywhere; a struggle in which its forces gain in enlightenment and strengthen their morale; a struggle which, even if it does not secure gradual successes, at least protects the nation from constant losses.[4]

To refrain from extremes and, instead, to oscillate between moderate versions of political idealism and political realism has served the interests of the Polish nation well. It has not removed the security dilemma which plagues the Poles, but at least it has helped them to cope with their lot. The adverse balance of power between Poland and her neighbors both in the East and the West has remained; but, the Polish nation has survived. If anything, by alternating between romanticism and positivism the Poles have consolidated their strength. Within the last hundred years of their history they have made considerable progress in almost all spheres of national life.

It was in the 1870's that the fortunes of the Polish nation were at their lowest ebb. The Polish state at that time did not appear on the map of Europe. Following the uprising of 1863 the last vestiges of Poland's autonomy had been eradicated. After the Franco-Prussian war of 1870 the Western European powers lost all interest in the Polish question. Poland's territory was torn apart by the three occupying states. In the German and Russian parts, respectively, there were intense efforts at the Germanization and Russification of the Poles — of the younger generation in particular. Especially at the periphery of the country, the Poles were often hopelessly intermingled with national groups of different race, language, and culture. As a whole, national consciousness was confined to the higher strata of Polish society, while most of the peasants were passive. The division into three parts — each incorporated into a separate political unit — hindered the socioeconomic progress of the country. The economic development of the Polish provinces was given low priority by the occupying governments, and when some strides were made, these were primarily directed at complementing the economic development at the center of each of the three foreign empires. The legal system in each part of Poland developed along different lines. In the Russian part, the autocratic nature of the tsarist regime also prevented the most urgent social reforms from being carried out. The educational level of the people was low. In the German and Russian parts of the country there were no Polish universities. All in all, in the last decades of the nineteenth century, the situation of the Polish nation was extremely unfavorable, and the prospects of change seemed to be remote.

Yet within less than a century the Poles have managed to overcome most of the drawbacks with which they were faced at the nadir of their history. The Polish situation today is in striking contrast to that of the 1870's. The right of the Poles to a national existence is generally recognized in the world; it is not openly questioned even by their enemies. All the efforts of the Germans and the Russians alike to destroy the Polish nation have proved futile. The high fertility of the Poles has compensated for heavy war losses. Both in the interwar and the postwar periods Poland's population has grown rapidly; in 1962 it passed the thirty-million mark.[5] All attempts to Germanize or Russify the Poles have failed, and a strong sense of national consciousness permeates all social classes. "Patriotic sentiments in Poland," wrote an astute Western observer of the Polish scene, "are very strong." [6]

Today's Poland also conforms with the requirements of a modern nation-state. The Polish nation occupies a geographically compact territory. The old lines of the three-part division were for all practical purposes already eradicated in the interwar period. The shift of the country to the west at the end of World War II, helped the Poles to consolidate their internal strength. In contemporary Poland there are no significant national minority groups.[7] The mass migration of population during the war years has largely obliterated regional differences among the Polish people. "From the ashes" of World War II, observed a Polish writer in 1961, "there has emerged a truly new, homogeneous, and dynamic nation." [8]

In spite of the devastating effects of the two world wars, Poland also has made considerable economic progress. The first significant efforts toward industrialization were undertaken in different parts of the country in the era of positivism. In the interwar period Poland's economy was effectively integrated into a coherent whole. The major economic advancement, however, took place in the postwar years. Throughout the late forties and the fifties Poland underwent a veritable industrial revolution. Her industrial output, which was about a half that of the world average in the prewar period, rose to more than double the world average in the late fifties.[9] In 1959 almost half of the country's national income came from industrial production. "The present level of industrialization," wrote a Polish economist in 1960, "is still lower than that of the most highly industrialized European countries. But the gap . . . has been greatly reduced." [10]

Economic changes have brought about far-reaching social effects. Urbanization has been rapidly accelerated. In the years 1947–1957 around 2 million peasants moved from the villages to work in the city factories. The present ratio between urban and rural population in Poland is almost at par.[11] And not only was the gap between the cities and the countryside greatly narrowed, but class distinctions in general were largely obliterated. Social status in Poland today is measured primarily by education. Eight-year elementary schooling has been made compulsory, and facilities for secondary and higher education have been considerably expanded.[12] Since the universities have been made accessible to young men from all classes, a very considerable segment of the intelligentsia is composed of people representing a first or second generation of urban proletariat or peasantry. "Poland's social system today," commented a Polish sociologist, "despite inferior economic development is similar and in some respects even superior to that in the rich [western] countries." [13]

The political, economic, and social strides made by the Poles in the last hundred years constitute an impressive record. The internal strength of the Polish nation in this period has steadily increased. In spite of her ordeals, Poland emerged from World War II potentially stronger than she was in the interwar years, and the position of Poland in 1918–1939 already represented a vast improvement over that of the 1870's. Indeed, it seems that Poland today is internally stronger than she has ever been since the eighteenth century.

And yet, from the point of view of her external position, all the strides which the Polish nation has made in the last century have failed to resolve its security dilemma. Although the progress made by the Poles has been swift, the progress of the Germans, and the Russians in particular, has been even faster. Power in international politics being relative, Poland, squeezed between Germany and Russia, has failed to free itself from its small country status. The only alternatives through which the Poles can try to advance their interests remain the programs of either political idealism or political realism.

The Poles seem to be convinced that at present the program of political realism serves their national interests better than that of political idealism. They realize that in the age of totalitarianism a struggle for freedom through insurrectionist means, unless it is supported from without, offers little prospect of success. And the Poles entertain few illusions that, in the event they should rise to arms, any effective outside assistance would be forthcoming. But even if such help were offered to them, in the existing situation the Poles could not accept it. They could not undertake a struggle against Russia, on the side of the West, as long as they were not first assured that this would not prejudice their interests vis-à-vis Germany.

It is over Germany that, in the last century, Poland has won several significant victories. Above all, the Poles thwarted two German attempts to destroy the Polish nation. The first German-Polish contest lasted from the 1870's until World War I, when Bismarck and his successors undertook the Germanization of the Polish provinces within their empire. This German policy, which was carried out vigorously and systematically, threatened the very basis of existence of the Polish nation. It was aimed at the predominantly Polish lands, whose loss would have decisively crippled Poland. Owing to the determined efforts of, at first, the followers of organic reform, and then the National Democrats, the Poles withstood the German assault. With the collapse of the German empire in 1918, most of its ethnically Polish lands joined reborn Poland.

The second major struggle between Poland and Germany came during World War II. Following the crushing of the independent Polish state in 1939, the Nazis incorporated into the *Reich* (the Polish population having been expelled) the Polish territory that stretched far to the east beyond Germany's 1914 border. They also planned, and in fact began to execute in wartime, the wholesale extermination of the Polish nation with a view to the ultimate taking over of all its land. It was only the defeat of Hitler's Germany which rendered these designs inoperative. As a result of World War II, Poland not only recovered all her prewar western territories, but also acquired Prussia's eastern provinces (where, in turn, the German population was expelled), stretching as far west as the Oder and Neisse rivers. The taking over of these territories, from which they had been pushed out by the Germans in the early stages of their history, and which for centuries seemed to be irrevocably lost to them, represented in the eyes of the Poles a decisive reversal of the German *Drang nach Osten*.

The Poles, of course, are anxious to preserve their territorial gains in the west. They feel that pushing their western border to the Oder-Neisse rivers represents a just compensation for the human and material losses which they suffered at the hands of the Germans during World War II. They also think that the new frontier gives them a better chance to cope effectively with the German menace. By generally weakening Germany and strengthening Poland — especially by liquidating the German enclave in East Prussia which has threatened Poland from the north, by taking over from Germany the entire industrial area of Silesia, and by demarcating the Polish-German border along the shortest line from the Baltic Sea to Czechoslovakia — the Poles believe that the shifting of their territory to the west has considerably improved their position vis-à-vis the Germans.

The Poles, thus, are determined to resist any attempt at a revision of their western border. They bitterly resent the claims to their territory which are voiced in West Germany and watch with anxiety the revival of German military power. Since the major Western powers, notably the United States, are closely aligned with the German Federal Republic and refuse to recognize the Polish-German frontiers along the Oder-Neisse rivers as final — while the Soviet Union is antagonistic toward West Germany and strongly upholds Poland's right to her present western border — the Poles feel that in such circumstances it would be incompatible with their national interests to side with the West against Russia. This is the main reason why at present they prefer political realism to political idealism.

If the Poles adhere to political realism, however, the great majority of them refrain from pushing it too far. Political idealism is weakened but certainly not extinguished in Poland. This is because the Poles consider their present position vis-à-vis Russia as hardly satisfactory.

It was Russia that, in the last century, inflicted several significant defeats on Poland. Still the record is not all one-sided, for in their relations with the Russians, the Poles also have scored some successes. In the past hundred years, on three occasions, the Poles have managed to frustrate Russian attempts to rid themselves of the Polish nation by dissolving it in their own empire. The first such trial of strength between the two nations took place after the uprising of 1863 when the tsarist government undertook the Russification of the Polish provinces. However, tsarist Russia was unable to carry out its anti-Polish measures resolutely and consistently. The Russians managed to diminish Polish influence in the Ukraine, Belorussia, and Lithuania, but they made little inroads in central Poland. In the purely Polish territories, the adherents of organic reform effectively opposed the Russification campaign. By the time of the patriotic reaction in the 1890's, it became obvious that the efforts of tsarism to eradicate Poland had been futile.

The second major struggle between the two countries followed shortly after World War I. The advance of the Red Army on Warsaw in the summer of 1920 posed a serious danger to the Polish nation.* The Bolshevik objective was to deprive Poland of its independence and to turn it into a Soviet republic. Had this happened, the chances of the Polish nation retaining its separate identity would have been greatly reduced. In the thirties Poland, too, would have been submitted to Stalin's policy of ruthless supression of Soviet nationalities. By resisting Russia with arms in 1920, however, the Poles managed to escape this fate. The Polish influence in the east was confined to the borders laid down in the Riga Treaty; but beyond this boundary, for close to two decades, the Poles enjoyed complete independence from Moscow.

The third contest between Poland and Russia came after World War II. In 1944 there was a further restriction of Polish influence in the east, this time to the present frontier. Soon after, the Russians had effectively turned all of Poland into a dependency and had embarked on a policy of complete Sovietization. The Polish nation was exposed to a great peril. Russia's might at that time was at its peak. She had emerged from the war as one of the two superpowers in world politics, whose authority in East Europe was beyond any outside challenge; and to deal with internal opposition she had at her disposal the well-tested repressive apparatus of Stalinist totalitarianism. At that stage, however, the strength of the Polish nation had also considerably increased. The recent memory of the independence of their state in the interwar period as well as that of the struggle for freedom during World War II, had greatly intensified the national pride of the Poles, precluding any lasting reconciliation to foreign rule on their part. After overcoming the effects of the war, the Polish nation regained its composure and began to look for means of lessening its dependence on Russia. An opportunity to do this came in 1956. Exploiting the confusion which had been brought about in the Soviet Union by de-Stalinization, the Poles managed to obtain at least partial autonomy from Russia.

Even though in subsequent years the scope of this autonomy was once

* Conversely, Poland's policy earlier in that year had posed a grave threat to Russia. Piłsudski's military venture into the Ukraine was aimed at solving once and for all the Polish security dilemma. It was his intention to tear the western provinces away from Russia and in this way decisively weaken Russia.

again restricted, the significance of the events of 1956 can hardly be over-looked. After the years of humiliation in the Stalinist period, the "Polish October" boosted Polish morale. The Russian retreat under Polish pressure shattered the image, which had been carefully cultivated by Stalin, of the invincible power of the Russians. It also made the Poles aware of their own strength. This new feeling of confidence on the part of the Polish nation was well expressed in 1959 by a Polish historian. "There is no exaggeration," he wrote,

in the assertions about the growth of realism [in Poland] . . . The prospect of our national identity being dissolved in some larger community, however, is probably more distant than ever . . . The nation is determined to preserve its own personality, the same that has been shaped by the course of our history.[14]

The simultaneous existence in contemporary Poland of a strong current of political realism and although weaker now, of political idealism, calls once again for a synthesis of these two political programs. The dilemma with which the Polish nation is faced today is: how to widen the scope of its independence from Russia without acceding to German territorial claims. The Poles seem to think that although these two goals in some aspects might be incompatible, as a whole they are not. Indeed, a great many of them would argue that the retention of its western provinces is indispensable to the gradual improvement of Poland's position vis-à-vis both Germany and Russia.

The reason why the Poles attach such great importance to the maintenance of their western territories is simple. They feel that Poland's present bound-aries make it more viable than it has ever been in recent history and, there-fore, give it a better chance to resist pressure from the east and west alike. Conversely, they believe that Poland, crippled by the loss of its western provinces, would become easy prey for either Germany or Russia. In short, the Poles subscribe to the reasoning of an American historian of modern diplomacy, who appraised the possible consequences of shifting Poland's western borders to the east in the following way: "Poland would have been weaker, perhaps less afraid of future German attempts to regain its territory, but perhaps more dependent than it is on the Soviet Union."[15]

The Poles, of course, are aware that their taking over of a large part of the old Prussian provinces has aggravated their relations with Germany. They feel, however, that this cannot be helped. At the time that the decision was reached to move Poland's border to the Oder-Neisse rivers at the end of World War II, the Poles had every reason to doubt that, if Poland were to satisfy itself with minor border adjustments, or even if it had annexed no German lands at all, the centuries-old Polish-German conflict would have been brought to an end.* They remembered only too well that the interwar border with Poland had never been (even before Hitler's rise to power) really acceptable to Germany; and, indeed, that it had been precisely to carry out a revision of this border that Germany had gone to war in 1939. They had little ground, therefore, for believing that should Germany's power be revived in the postwar years, it would not resume the territorial dispute with Poland. Except that, in such an event, Poland's chances of resisting German pressure along the border of 1939 would have been poorer than along the frontier of 1945. Since in the eyes of the Poles, then, the prospects of completely eliminating the German danger were remote, by shifting borders as far to the west as possible, they at least tried to improve their chances of effectively coping with it.

The Poles think, moreover, that by extending their territory westward they have enhanced their position vis-à-vis Russia. They contend that Poland within its present frontiers is considerably stronger than Poland within its prewar boundaries, not to mention Poland with its western border of 1939 and its eastern border of today, which was the only feasible alternative in 1945. The Poland of today is in a better position than ever in recent history to withstand pressure from Russia.** In effect, the Poles appear to share the opinion of the Russian statesman, Count Witte, who — commenting on the promise which was made to the Poles early in World War I to bring about a unification of all Polish lands under the tsarist rule — summed up the

* The mutual interlocking of the Polish and German territories along the border of 1939 — and particularly the existence of the German enclave in East Prussia — virtually excluded the possibility of adjusting the border in favor of Poland without seriously injuring Germany. The British proposal at the Potsdam conference to move the Polish-German frontier in the south to the east rather than the west Neisse river (leaving within Germany roughly half of the area of lower Silesia) certainly would not have prevented serious resentment of the territorial changes on the part of the Germans.

** Viewed in this light, one of the major concessions extracted by the Poles from the Russians, representing a complete reversal of the Soviet stand from the interwar period, was Stalin's upholding in 1945 the Polish claims to prewar German territories. The credit for winning this concession from Russia, paradoxically, goes as much to Polish political idealists as realists. The loud protest against the seizure of Poland's prewar eastern territories by the Soviet Union, by the Polish Government-in-Exile in London, clearly strengthened the bargaining position of the Polish Communists in their negotiations over the postwar Poland's western borders in Moscow.

prospects of the relationship between viable Poland and Russia in the following fashion:

The moment we annex Austria and Prussia's Polish territories we shall lose the whole of Russian Poland. Don't you make any mistake: when Poland has recovered her territorial integrity she won't be content with the autonomy she's been so stupidly promised. She'll claim — and get — her absolute independence.[16]

Indeed, the significance of Poland's viability in its relations with Russia seems to have been at least partially demonstrated in the postwar years. Poland's internal strength undoubtedly assisted it to cope successfully with Sovietization in the Stalinist years, and to win back from the Soviet Union some of its autonomy in 1956. It is also likely to encourage the Poles to seek even further extension of their independence from Russia in the future.

Poland's chances of gradually improving its position vis-à-vis Russia appear to be enhanced by the declining Soviet influence in world politics. In the early sixties the Soviet Union may well have passed the peak of its power — its global expansionist drive has been losing momentum, and, indeed, it has suffered several serious reversals. The Sino-Soviet split in particular may contribute to the widening of Poland's autonomy from Russia. It is not only that the Chinese defiance of Soviet supreme authority has the general effect of promoting polycentrism in the Communist world. As the third largest country in the Communist orbit, Poland's position is greatly enhanced by the dissension between the two giants. In exchange for Polish support in its ideological dispute with China, the Soviet Union might be amenable to a greater diversity in Poland's domestic policies.

Should the Sino-Soviet conflict continue to the point of a power struggle between the two states, Poland's position vis-à-vis Russia might improve still further. The Soviet Union, threatened in Asia, would be anxious to strengthen the security of its frontiers in Europe. Poland's crucial strategic location in this regard, could make its friendship of considerable importance to Russia. Poland, as a dissatisfied semi-satellite, would not be a reliable ally. Only by giving her complete internal independence, might Russia turn Poland into a trusted partner.

In view of the territorial dispute with Germany, the Poles would welcome the opportunity of entering into a genuine alliance with Russia. Such an alignment — based not on artificial ideological bonds, but on the common interests of the two countries vis-à-vis Germany — would fulfill Polish national aspirations to a high degree. It would simultaneously protect the integrity of Poland's western border and assure the right of the Polish nation to a free internal development. As such a true Polish-Russian alliance would accomplish the objectives of both political realism and political idealism. Indeed, it would represent a practical synthesis of those two programs.

Should a synthesis between the now dominant current of political realism and a weaker but present political idealism fail to materialize, however, in trying to advance their national interests, the Poles might at one stage or another shift back to the romantic program. In the age of nuclear weapons and totalitarianism — and the Poles are well aware of this — the chances of a successful struggle for independence through revolutionary means are restricted. Still, especially at a time when the foreign oppressor is externally or internally weakened, the efficacy of insurrectionist tactics cannot be ruled out. As long as the Russians persist in suppressing their right to free internal development, the Poles will continue to be tempted to try to shake off the yoke from the east through whatever means they have at their disposal. Indeed, the greater the oppression of Poland, the stronger the urge to rise against the Russians with arms.

As always in the past, the prospects for a revival of the romantic tradition in Poland hinge on internal as well as external factors. Domestic developments seem to be working in favor of a gradual advancement of political idealism. Consolidation of the nation's economic and social strength, as in the period of organic reform, is likely to lead to an increase of its political aspirations. With the passage of years, as after the disaster of 1863, the memories of World War II are apt to lose their defeatist impact upon the minds of the Poles. In due time they may be overshadowed by the more encouraging recollections of the "Polish October." Apparently, the very youngest generation, which does not remember the tragic experiences of the war, no longer shares the aversion of the older people toward the insurrectionist tradition. Even Załuski admits that the young boys and girls readily look back to the heroic episodes of Poland's history and "bring flowers to the national cemeteries."[17] There appears to be growing in Poland the general tendency well defined by an American political scientist, that "even if the older generation should some time, as a consequence of its disappointing experience, turn to political realism, the young would always be there to unfold anew the flag of idealism."[18]

In Poland's peculiar position, however, it is not the internal but rather the external factor which traditionally determines shifts from one political program to another. The patriotic reaction in the 1890's which followed the consolidation of the internal strength of the nation alone failed to make the Poles decisively abandon political realism and embrace political idealism. It was only during World War I, when a favorable situation for them developed in the international sphere, that they took such a step. In all likelihood, then, *Primat der Aussenpolitik* would also be of major significance in any new shift from positivism to romanticism. In the fashion of traditional Polish politics, the prospects for a revival of political idealism hinge above all on the Poles securing satisfactory support from without.

Since it is the divergence in the respective objectives of Poland and the West vis-à-vis Germany which in the first place made the Poles embrace political realism, conversely, a major change in the policy of the West toward Germany would make the Poles adopt political idealism once again. By firmly disassociating themselves from the German claims to Poland's western provinces, through recognizing the border along the Oder and the Neisse rivers as final, the Western powers would remove the major obstacle preventing the Poles from seeking cooperation with the West. A solution to the German problem along the broad lines of "disengagement" and restriction of Germany's military might would lift the pressure on Poland's western border, and would enhance the desire among the Poles to renew their close bonds with the West.

A return by the Poles to the romantic program might be impelled by the recent renaissance in world politics of Poland's traditional ally, France. For the national interests of Poland and France are in many respects similar not only vis-à-vis Russia, but also vis-à-vis Germany. If France is to secure her leading position in Europe, she cannot afford to allow Germany's power to grow beyond certain limits. It is for this reason that France to all practical intents already recognizes the Polish border along the Oder and the Neisse rivers as final. It is for the same reason that France can ill-afford to support the reunification of Germany, without at the same time counterbalancing it in the east by promoting Poland's return to free Europe.

The decisive factor in pushing the Poles toward political idealism, of course, would be a major change of policy toward Poland by the German Federal Republic. The sincere abandonment of all claims to Poland's present territory by Germany would bring the centuries-old conflict between the two nations to an end. Assured of the security of their borders in the west, the Poles would no longer be impeded from turning all their efforts toward asserting their right to free internal development. In these circumstances they would probably not fail to exploit the first opportunity — such as, for instance, a Chinese threat to Russia in Asia — to shake off the yoke from the east and to join the community of free European nations. Such a development would fulfill Polish national aspirations to an even higher degree than the attainment of a genuine alliance with Russia. For, in addition to securing Poland's independence, it would restore its traditionally close bonds with the Western world.

There exist, thus, various prospects of gradually resolving Poland's dilemma: of how to widen the scope of her independence from Russia without conceding any territory in the dispute with Germany. Time seems to be on Poland's side. The longer the Poles stay there, the more tenuous the German claims to Poland's western lands become; and the less the pressure from Germany, the better becomes Poland's position vis-à-vis Russia. This trend, of course, could be reversed by some drastic change in the status quo in Central Europe. Such a development, however, appears to be unlikely in the near future. No abrupt shift of the balance of power in that region could be brought about without seriously aggravating the danger of a major conflict, and this is a risk which apparently neither of the two of Poland's powerful neighbors is prepared to take.

Whatever the currents of politics in the Communist orbit and the world at large, one thing seems to be certain: the Polish question will reappear in one form or another in many conflicts, and in many attempts to settle them. Poland's significance in the international sphere comes precisely from the fact which has plagued it for centuries; namely, its crucial geographic location between Germany and Russia. It is also a result of the stand taken by the Polish nation which has proved throughout history that, against all odds, it is not content to leave its fate to others but seeks to shape its own destiny.

NOTES

BIBLIOGRAPHY

INDEX

NOTES

Introduction

1. John H. Herz, *Political Realism and Political Idealism: A Study in Theories and Realities* (Chicago, 1951), p. 3.

2. Wilhelm Feldman, *Dzieje polskiej myśli politycznej,* 2 ed. (Warsaw, 1933), pp. 1–2. Unless otherwise indicated, translations are by the author.

3. Albert Sorel, *L'Europe et la Révolution Française,* p. 474. Quoted by Edward H. Carr in *The Twenty Years' Crisis, 1919–1939: An Introduction to the Study of International Relations,* 2 ed. (New York, 1964), p. 11.

4. Feldman, *Dzieje polskiej myśli politycznej,* pp. 1–2.

Chapter 1. The Early Political Realism

1. "Lettre d'un gentilhomme Polonais au prince de Metternich" in Henryk Lisicki, *Aleksander Wielopolski* (Cracow, 1879), IV, 469.

2. *Ibid.*

3. Jan Friedberg, *Zarys historii Polski* (Hanover, 1946), II, 37.

4. Władysław Pobóg-Malinowski, *Najnowsza historia polityczna Polski* (Paris, 1953), I, 3.

5. H. Wereszycki, *Historia polityczna Polski w dobie popowstaniowej 1864–1918* (Warsaw, 1948), p. 16.

6. *Polska i Rosja w 1872 roku, przez b. członka Rady Stanu* (Dresden, 1872), quoted by Feldman, *Dzieje polskiej myśli politycznej,* p. 137.

7. Michał Bobrzyński, *Dzieje Polski w zarysie* (Jerusalem, 1942), I, 16–17.

8. Marian Henryk Serejski, "Rozwój nauki historycznej," in *Historia Polski,* vol. III, pt. 1 (Warsaw, 1961), p. 690.

9. Quoted from Marian Kukiel, *Dzieje Polski porozbiorowe, 1795–1921* (London, 1961), p. 392.

10. Wereszycki, *Historia polityczna Polski,* p. 71.

11. Antoni Wrotnowski, *Porozbiorowe Aspiracye Polityczne Narodu Polskiego* (Cracow, 1898), pp. 356–357.

12. B. Bolesławita (J. Kraszewski), *Z roku 1869 Rachunki* (Dresden, 1870), p. 38.

13. Anonim, *Nasza polityka wobec Rosji jaka być powinna* (Leipzig, 1865), quoted by Feldman, *Dzieje polskiej myśli politycznej*, p. 42.

14. B. Bolesławita (J. Kraszewski), *Z roku 1868 Rachunki* (Poznań, 1868), pp. 21–22.

15. Based on statistics quoted by Kukiel, *Dzieje Polski porozbiorowe*, p. 400; and Wereszycki, *Historia polityczna Polski*, pp. 78–79.

16. Bronislaw Chlebowski, *Literatura polska* (Warsaw, 1932), p. 446.

17. Wereszycki, *Historia poltiyczna Polski*, p. 251.

18. Roman Dmowski, *Myśli nowoczesnego Polaka*, 7 ed. (London, 1953), p. 78.

19. Ignacy Chrzanowski, "Roman Dmowski," in *Polski Słownik Biograficzny*, V (Cracow, 1939), 215–216.

20. Roman Dmowski, *Niemcy, Rosja i kwestja polska*, 2 ed. (Czestochowa, 1938), p. 238.

21. *Świat powojenny i Polska*, 2 ed. (Warsaw, 1931), p. 139.

22. "Przeciw wojnie," subsequently included in Dmowski's book, *Świat powojenny i Polska*. The articles, with a foreword highly unflattering to the author, were also published in pamphlet form in the U.S.S.R. See Roman Dmowski, *Kommivoyazher v zatrudnenii* (Moscow, 1930).

23. Roman Dmowski, *Pisma*, VIII (Czestochowa, 1938), 407.

Chapter 2. The Decline of Political Realism

1. Feldman, *Dzieje polskiej myśli politycznej*, p. 222.

2. Wereszycki, *Historia polityczna Polski*, p. 90.

3. *Ibid.*, p. 93.

4. The figures in 1870 were 63,892; in 1897, 243,733.

5. Zygmunt Zaremba, *Sześćdziesiąt lat walki i pracy P.P.S.: Szkic historyczny* (London, 1952), p. 5.

6. M. K. Dziewanowski, *The Communist Party of Poland: An Outline of History* (Cambridge, Mass., 1959), p. 39.

7. Resolution of the first congress of the Social Democracy of the Kingdom of Poland held in 1894. Quoted by Wereszycki in *Historia polityczna Polski*, p. 43.

8. Originally written in German as Rosa Luxemburg's doctoral dissertation, and first published in Germany in 1898. For Polish translation, see *Rozwój przemysłu w Polsce* (Warsaw, 1957).

9. Dziewanowski, *The Communist Party of Poland*, p. 32.

10. Wereszycki, *Historia polityczna Polski*, p. 43.

11. *Ibid.*, p. 250.

12. Jósef Piłsudski, *Pisma wybrane* (London, 1943), p. 8.

13. *Ibid.*, p. 330.

14. *Ibid.*, pp. 8, 9.

15. Quoted from Henryk Cepnik, *Józef Piłsudski; Twórca Niepodległego Państwa Polskiego*, 3 ed. (Warsaw, 1935), p. 50.

16. Piłsudski, *Pisma wybrane*, p. 47.

17. Quoted from Pobóg-Malinowski, *Najnowsza historia*, I, 122.

18. Quoted from Cepnik, *Józef Piłsudski*, p. 283.

19. Stanisław Mackiewicz, *Klucz do Piłsudskiego* (London, 1943), p. 59.

20. Piłsudski, *Pisma wybrane*, p. 92.

21. Tytus Filipowicz, *Marzenie polityczne* (Cracow, 1909), pp. 5, 161.

22. Polonus-Viator (W. Jodko-Narkiewicz), *Kwestya Polska wobec zbliżającego się konfliktu Austryi z Rosyą* (Cracow, 1909), p. 44.

23. Brzoza, Jan (Feliks Młynarski), *Do Broni-Prawda o Naczelnym Komitecie Narodowym i Polskich Legionach* (New York, 1915), p. 77.

24. Cepnik, *Józef Piłsudski,* pp. 115, 116.

Chapter 3. Political Idealism

1. Quoted by William L. Shirer, *The Rise and Fall of the Third Reich: A History of Nazi Germany* (New York, 1960), pp. 212.

2. Gustav Stresemann, *Vermächtnis,* vol. II., Henny Bernhard ed. (Berlin, 1932), pp. 236–237. Quoted by Harold von Riekhoff, "Revisionism vs. Reconciliation: Germany's Poland Policy During the Period of the Weimar Republic," unpub. diss. Yale University, 1965.

3. Quoted by Alexander Skrzyński in *Poland and Peace* (London, 1923), p. 78.

4. Głowny Urząd Statystyczny, *Mały Rocznik Statystyczny,* 1939 (Warsaw, 1939), p. 16.

5. According to Polish sources in 1931, 31.1 percent of the population of Poland had a mother tongue other than Polish, *ibid.,* p. 23. At the same time, however, a considerable number of Poles remained outside Polish borders in Germany and the U.S.S.R., as well as in Czechoslovakia and Lithuania. Altogether the number of Poles living in these countries in the interwar period is estimated at about one and a half million. Oscar Halecki, ed., *Poland* (New York, 1957), p. 44.

6. Quoted by Konstanty Wojciechowski in *Dzieje literatury polskiej* (Hanover, 1946), p. 225.

7. *Ibid.,* p. 224.

8. Antoni Chołoniewski, *Duch dziejów Polski* (Cracow, 1918). Also published in a somewhat abbreviated version in English as *The Spirit of Polish History* (New York, 1919). Chołoniewski's book was quite popular in Poland. In the years from 1917 to 1933 it was reprinted four times, and it was widely used as a text for high school students.

9. English edition, p. 59.

10. Polish edition, p. 133.

11. Juliusz Łukasiewicz, *Polska jest Mocarstwem,* 2 ed. (Warsaw, 1939). Łukasiewicz was a high-ranking official in the Polish Ministry of Foreign Affairs. At the time he wrote his pamphlet, in the fall of 1938, he was Poland's ambassador to France.

12. *Ibid.,* pp. 59–62.

13. Komisja Historyczna Polskiego Sztabu Głównego w Londynie, *Polskie Siły Zbrojne w Drugiej Wojnie Światowej: Kampania Wrześniowa,* vol. I, pt. 1: *Polityczne i wojskowe położenie Polski przed wojną* (London, 1951), pp. 462, 463.

14. Piłsudski, *Pisma wybrane,* p. 189.

15. *Polskie Siły Zbrojne w Drugiej Wojnie Światowej,* vol. I, pt. 1, p. 25.

16. Piłsudski, *Pisma wybrane,* p. 196.

17. Stanisław Mackiewicz, *Colonel Beck and His Policy* (London, 1944), p. 77.

18. *Polskie Siły Zbrojne w Drugiej Wojnie Światowej,* vol. I, pt. 1, p. 71.

19. Ludwik Stolarzewicz, *Dzieje i Czyny Nieśmiertelnego Wodza Narodu,* rev. ed. (Warsaw, 1936), pp. 622, 624.

20. Mackiewicz, *Colonel Beck and His Policy*, p. 77.

21. *Ibid.*, p. 108.

22. Quoted by Henryk Frankel, *Poland: The Struggle for Power 1772–1939* (London, 1946), p. 176.

23. Ferdynand Zweig, *Poland Between Two Wars: A Critical Study of Social and Economic Changes* (London, 1944), p. 12.

24. Stolarzewicz, *Dzieje i czyny Nieśmiertelnego Wodza Narodu*, p. 623.

25. Pobóg-Malinowski, *Najnowsza historia*, II, 599.

26. Łukasiewicz, *Polska jest mocarstwem*, pp. 9–10.

27. Shirer, *The Rise and Fall of the Third Reich*, p. 625.

28. Quoted by Shirer, *ibid.*, p. 660.

29. Tadeusz Bór-Komorowski, *Armia Podziemna* (London, 1952), p. 144.

30. Quoted in *The Story of the Warsaw Rising* (Newton, Montgomeryshire, 1945), pp. 47, 49, 72.

31. Halecki, *Poland*, p. 152. This represented almost one percent of the population of Poland which in February 1946 was roughly 23.9 million. *Rocznik Statystyczny, 1956* (Warsaw, 1956), p. 1.

32. Harold Macmillan in the introduction to Władysław Anders, *An Army in Exile* (London, 1949), p. xiv.

33. Ministerstwo Obrony Narodowcj, *Fakty i zagadnienia polskie* (London, 1944), p. 165–166.

34. Quoted by Edward I. Rozek, *Allied Wartime Diplomacy: A Pattern of Poland* (New York, 1958), p. 355.

35. Anders, *An Army in Exile*, p. 305.

36. Halecki, *Poland*, p. 46. This represented about two percent of Poland's population at that time.

37. The Communist source reported that in the years 1945–1948 approximately 240 partisan units fought against the Communist regime, *Żołnierz Polski*, May 27, 1962. The intensity of armed resistance was described in the Parliament by the Minister of Public Security, Stanisław Radkiewicz, who admitted that there were 1,124 encounters with the underground in October 1946 and 463 in March 1947. Stefan Korboński, *W imieniu Kremla* (Paris, 1956), p. 290.

38. Conversation quoted in Rozek, *Allied Wartime Diplomacy*, p. 390.

39. Stanisław Mikołajczyk, *The Rape of Poland: Pattern of Soviet Aggression* (New York, 1948), p. 120.

40. K. S. Karol, *Visa for Poland* (London, 1959), p. 94.

41. The struggle of the Polish Peasant Party against the Communists is described in considerable detail in Mikołajczyk, *The Rape of Poland* and Korboński, *W imieniu Kremla*. See also the memoirs of the American ambassador, Arthur Bliss-Lane, *I Saw Poland Betrayed* (Indianapolis, 1948). For the best scholarly analysis, see Hugh Seton-Watson, *The East European Revolution* (New York, 1951), pp. 171–179.

42. Wydawnictwo Zachodnie, *Straty wojenne Polski w latach 1939–1945* (Warsaw, 1960), pp. 38, 47.

43. *Ibid.*, pp. 107, 111.

44. Figures given by Gomułka in 1959. Władysław Gomułka, *Przemówienia*, 1959 (Warsaw, 1960), p. 421.

45. The expression was used as a title of the book on Poland's diplomatic activities toward the end of the war, by a former Polish Ambassador to the United States, Jan Ciechanowski, *The Defeat in Victory* (New York, 1947).

Chapter 4: The Rise of Communism

1. The exact name adopted in 1918 was the Communist Workers' Party of Poland. This was changed to the Communist Party of Poland only in 1925.

2. According to the Communist sources, the membership of the party, including the affiliated youth organizations, was at most 30,000 to 35,000 people. Józef Kowalczyk in *Trybuna Ludu,* December 16, 1958. According to other sources, however, the party's membership never exceeded 10,000. See Karol, *Visa for Poland,* p. 47.

3. In the two free elections participated in by Communist-front organizations, they received 1.5 percent of the popular vote in 1922 and 7.9 percent in 1928. Dziewanowski, *The Communist Party of Poland,* pp. 101–127.

4. Quoted in Dziewanowski, *The Communist Party of Poland,* p. 78.

5. Quoted by Jan Krzysztof Kwiatkowski (Ren), *Komuniści w Polsce: Rodowód–Taktyka–Ludzie* (Brussels, 1946), p. 14.

6. *Ibid,* p. 13.

7. *Ibid.,* p. 14.

8. Dziewanowski, *The Communist Party of Poland,* p. 96.

9. Zenon Kliszko, *Z problemów historii PPR* (Warsaw, 1958), p. 7.

10. Quoted in Dziewanowski, *The Communist Party of Poland,* p. 158.

11. *The Times,* May 4, 1943.

12. The strength of the Communist underground military units as compared with those of the underground loyal to the Government-in-Exile is well illustrated by the number of freedom fighters representing the two groups who took part in the uprising in Warsaw in 1944. The Communist units numbered 570 men; while the non-Communist formations had 46,000 men. Adam Ciołkosz, "Węzłowe zagadnienia w dziejach kommunizmu polskiego" (London, 1959), p. 13.

13. Władysław Gomułka (Wiesław), *W walce o demokrację ludową,* 2 vols. (Łódź, 1947), II, 219.

14. *Ibid.,* II, 126–127.

15. *Ibid.,* II, 127.

16. *Ibid.,* I, 133.

17. *Ibid.,* II, 220.

18. *Ibid.,* II, 160.

19. *Ibid.,* I, 157.

20. The official sources indicate that in July 1944 the party's membership was around 20,000. See Zakład Historii Partii przy KC PZPR, *PPR VIII, 1944–XII, 1945* (Warsaw, 1959), p. 291.

21. In December 1946 the Polish Workers' Party had 550,000 members; a year later its membership rose to 820,000. Dziewanowski, *The Communist Party of Poland,* p. 347.

22. *For a Lasting Peace: For a People's Democracy,* April 15, 1948.

23. Bernard Newman, *Russia's Neighbour: The New Poland* (London, 1946), p. 95.

24. Adam B. Ulam, *Titoism and the Cominform* (Cambridge, Mass., 1952), p. 159.

25. *Ibid.*

26. Gomułka's fall from power in 1948–49 is described in considerable detail in several books and articles. See Ulam, *Titoism and the Cominform,* pp. 146–188; Dziewa-

nowski, *The Communist Party in Poland*, pp. 208–217; also M. K. Dziewanowski, "Gomulka and Polish National Communism," *Problems of Communism* (January–February 1957); Karol, *Visa for Poland*, pp. 104–115; Zbigniew Brzezinski, *The Soviet Bloc: Unity and Conflict* (Cambridge, Mass., 1960), pp. 71–72; Interesting information was also provided by a well-informed defector to the West, Józef Swiatło, who, as a high-ranking official of the security apparatus, had conducted the investigation of Gomułka's case. See *The Swiatlo Story* (New York, 1955).

27. *Nowe Drogi*, November 1949, p. 144.

28. Dziewanowski, *The Communist Party of Poland*, p. 211.

29. For the split in the ranks of the prewar Polish Socialist Party which gave birth to the left-wing group that assumed the name of the old party and eventually merged with the Communist Party, see Chapter 5.

30. Bolesław Bierut, *O Partii* (Warsaw, 1952), p. 196.

31. *Ibid.*, p. 122.

32. *Ibid.*, p. 197.

33. *Ibid.*, pp. 16, 23, 40.

34. *Ibid.*, p. 197.

35. *Ibid.*, pp. 182, 340, 150.

36. *Ibid.*, p. 323.

37. Bolesław Bierut and Józef Cyrankiewicz, *Podstawy ideologiczne PZPR* (Warsaw, 1952), pp. 53, 54.

38. Bolesław Bierut, *O Konstytucji Polskiej Rzeczypospolitej Ludowej* (Warsaw, 1952), p. 40.

39. Bierut, *O Partii*, p. 74.

40. Oskar Lange, *Some Problems Relating to the Polish Road to Socialism* (Warsaw, 1957), p. 9.

41. Rokossowsky was born in Poland but left for Russia at the age of eighteen and became completely Russified. In 1944 he commanded the Russian armies which abstained from coming to the assistance of the Warsaw uprising. In 1949, however, he was not only elevated to the rank of Politburo member of the Polish United Workers' Party but was also appointed Marshal of Poland.

42. *The Swiatlo Story*, p. 4.

Chapter 5: The Revival of Political Realism

1. *Dzieje głupoty w Polsce: Pamflety dziejopisarskie* (Warsaw, 1947).

2. *Ibid.*, p. 41. Bocheński was particularly harsh in criticizing the views of Chołoniewski which he simply described as nonsensical.

3. *Ibid.*, pp. 17, 41.

4. *Ibid.*, pp. 26, 121, 278.

5. *Ibid.*, pp. 41, 42

6. *Ibid.*, pp. 12, 26.

7. *Margrabia Wielopolski*, 2 ed. (Warsaw, 1957).

8. Pruszyński's political views were expounded more openly and also more forcefully in the political testament which he left with a friend abroad, Professor Edward Rożek, who published it after Pruszyński's death. Rozek, *Allied Wartime Diplomacy*, pp. 413–415.

9. Pruszyński, *Margrabia Wielopolski*, pp. 25, 26.

10. Korboński, *W imieniu Kremla*, p. 252.

11. Zaremba, *Wojna i konspiracja*, pp. 305, 313.

12. Reportedly toward the end of 1943 the group was composed of only five persons. Adam Ciołkosz, "Poland," in Denis Healey, ed., *The Curtain Falls: The Story of the Socialists in Eastern Europe* (London, 1951), p. 39.

13. Bierut and Cyrankiewicz, *Podstawy ideologiczne PZPR*, p. 86.

14. At the Unity Congress there were 1,008 delegates from the Polish Workers' Party, and only 520 from the Polish Socialist Party. Healey, *The Curtain Falls*, p. 56.

15. The fortunes of the Peasant Party in the late forties are ably presented in Andrzej Korbonski, *Politics of Socialist Agriculture in Poland, 1945–1960* (New York, 1965), ch. iv.

16. *Znak*, July 1946.

17. Claude Narois, *Dieu Contre Dieu? Drame des catholiques progressistes dans une église du silence* (Paris, 1956); "Jak Bolesław Piasecki stał się agentem NKWD," *Wolna Europa*, November 1955; Leopold Tyrmand, "Sprawa Piaseckiego," *Świat*, November 18, 1956. Since at the time when the article was published in Poland Serov was in charge of Soviet security apparatus, Tyrmand, although clearly alluding to him, withheld the name.

18. *Wolna Europa*, November 1955. This writer has had an opportunity to interview Światło, and feels that his evidence should not be approached without reservations.

19. Stefan Kisielewski. A letter to the editor of *Kultura*, November 1958.

20. Vincent C. Chrypinski, "The Movement of 'Progressive Catholics' in Poland," unpub. diss. University of Michigan, 1958, p. 13. Chrypinski's study is by far the most systematic and informative review of the activities and ideology of the progressivists in the years 1945–1956. Even the most embittered opponent of Piasecki, Józef Mackiewicz, an emigré political writer, agrees that "the conception underlying the foundation of Pax was of a political character." *Zwycięstwo prowokacji* (Munich, 1962), p. 135.

21. *Świat*, November 18, 1956.

22. *Zagadnienia istotne*, Warsaw, 1954.

23. Chrypinski, "The Movement of 'Progressive Catholics' in Poland," p. 138.

24. *Życie Gospodarcze*, July 7, 1957. Quoted from " 'Non-Communist' Political Organizations," *East Europe*, October 1957, p. 9. Also see M. S., "Bolesław Piasecki," *East Europe*, January 1961, p. 24.

25. *Życie Gospodarcze*, July 7, 1957. This profit of Pax amounted to roughly one and a half million dollars. This money was used partly to employ over 4,000 people. Leonard Barszczewski, "Problemy Gospodarcze Stowarzyszenia 'Pax,' " *Kierunki*, October 6, 1957. Barszczewski rightly points out that Pax, unlike the state enterprises, employed many persons who were regarded as politically unreliable. He fails, however, to explain the reasons why the security authorities tolerated this unique personnel policy of Pax.

26. *Świat*, November 18, 1956.

Chapter 6: The Triumph of Political Realism

1. There is an extensive literature in English on events in Poland in the years 1953–1956. The following books deal with the topic in an analytical fashion: P. Zinner, ed., *National Communism and Popular Revolt in Eastern Europe* (New York, 1956), p. II; Dziewanowski, *The Communist Party of Poland*, chs. xv–xvi; Brzezinski, *The So-*

viet Bloc: Unity and Conflict, especially chs. xi and xiv; Hubert Ripka, *Eastern Europe in the Post-War World* (London, 1961), ch. v; Oscar Halecki, "Poland," in Stephen D. Kertesz, ed., *East and Central Europe and the World: Developments in the Post Stalin Era* (Notre Dame, Ind., 1962), pp. 45–54; Richard Hiscocks, *Poland: Bridge for the Abyss?* (New York, 1963), chs. viii–ix.

2. Światło's information was effectively disseminated in a special series of broadcasts as well as by leaflets carried to Poland by balloons; both were sponsored by the American Free Europe Committee. The importance of Światło's information in promoting ferment in the country was publically confirmed in Poland in 1956. "There is no sense in concealing," asserted an editorial article in a popular weekly, "that Światło's escape and his revelations exerted a certain influence on the development of events in Poland. Światło was an unusual scoundrel even according to the standards of our own Beria's clique. Still, by evading his own responsibility and accusing others, he brought to the surface so much dirt that it accelerated placing certain matters in the daylight." *Przekrój,* December 2, 1956.

3. *Nowa Kultura,* August 19, 1955. For an English translation see Zinner, ed., *National Communism and Popular Revolt in Eastern Europe,* pp. 40–48.

4. *The Soviet–Yugoslav Controversy, 1948–1958: A Documentary Record* (New York, 1959), p. 57.

5. For the text of Moscow declaration, see Vaclav L. Beneš, et al., eds., *The Second Soviet–Yugoslav Dispute* (Bloomington, Ind., 1959), pp. 8–11.

6. "Wzmóżmy wysiłek w pracy ideologicznej," *Nowe Drogi,* October 1955.

7. "Lekcje XX Zjazdu KPZR," *Nowe Drogi,* April 1956.

8. *Trybuna Ludu,* April 7, 1956.

9. Józef Olszewski, *Nowe Drogi,* October 1956, p. 226.

10. Natolin is a fashionable resort near Warsaw, where the group used to hold its meetings.

11. *Trybuna Ludu,* July 31, 1956.

12. Oskar Lange, *Nowe Drogi,* October 1956, p. 203.

13. Jan Szczepański, "Próba diagnozy," *Przegląd Kulturalny,* October 31, 1957.

14. *Pravda,* July 2, 1956.

15. *Trybuna Ludu,* July 22, 1956.

16. Aleksander Zawadzki, *Nowe Drogi,* October 1956, p. 16.

17. *Ibid.*

18. This was publically admitted by Rokossovsky at the meeting of the Central Committee. *Ibid.,* p. 20.

19. Zdzislaw Najder, "Dług i Skarb," *Przegląd Kulturalny,* December 20, 1956.

20. Dziewanowski, *The Communist Party of Poland,* pp. 279–280. A popular jest in Poland to the effect that in 1956 the Hungarians acted like the Poles, and the Poles acted like the Czechs, indicates that the Poles were conscious of the change in their political attitudes.

21. Quoted by Frank Gibney, *The Frozen Revolution in Poland: A Study in Communist Decay* (New York, 1959), p. xiv.

22. B. Heydenkorn, "Obawy przed wojną," *Związkowiec* (Toronto), March 23, 1960.

23. Anna Bratkowska and Ryszard Turski, "Mit na karuzeli," *Przegląd Kulturalny,* October 19, 1959.

24. *Polityka,* June 13, 1959.

25. Paweł Jasienica, "Niektóre z przemian," *Nowa Kultura,* August 16, 1959.

26. Jerzy Kirchmayer, *Powstanie Warszawskie, 1944* (Warsaw, 1958); also *1939 i 1944, Kilka zagadnień polskich* (Warsaw, 1960); Adam Borkiewicz, *Powstanie*

Warszawskie (Warsaw, 1958). Kirchmayer had been largely compromised in the eyes of his former comrades-in-arms by offering his services to the Communist regime as early as 1945. Thus, even though he was later disgraced and imprisoned by the Communists, his works are still treated with some suspicion. Borkiewicz's conduct, however, was beyond reproach. He did not cooperate with the Communists, and, in fact, during the Stalinist years he was exposed to grueling persecution.

27. John K. Galbraith, *Journey to Poland and Yugoslavia* (Cambridge, Mass., 1958), p. 27.

28. A penetrating glimpse at the completely chaotic nature of the demonstrations in Warsaw is provided by a writer who participated in them. Leszek Szymański, "Październik niedyskretny," *Kultura*, November 1960.

29. Zbigniew Stypułkowski, *Polska na progu 1958* (London, 1958), p. 85.

30. George Sherman, "Sputniks Paying Dividends," *The Observer*, December 15, 1957.

31. *Wiadomości o życiu w Polsce*, June 15, 1960.

32. See Adam Bromke, "A Visit to Poland: Impressions of a Political Scientist," Russian Research Center, Harvard University (Cambridge, Mass., 1961), mimeographed, p. 4.

33. Arthur J. Olsen, "Poles Cut Dollar on Black Market," *The New York Times*, November 28, 1960.

34. For a penetrating sociological analysis of the declining role of political emigration by a Polish exile, see Felix Gross, *The Seizure of Political Power* (New York, 1958), pp. 380–384.

35. Londyńczyk (Juliusz Mieroszewski), "Post scriptum," *Kultura*, May 1961, p. 59.

36. Bernard Newman, *Portrait of Poland* (London, 1959), p. 203.

37. The role played by the German problem in shaping up the political outlook of the Poles is focused upon in Adam Bromke, "Nationalism and Communism in Poland," *Foreign Affairs*, July 1962.

38. Heydenkorn, "Niemcy i Niemcy," *Związkowiec*, June 23, 1965.

39. Leslie B. Bain, *The Reluctant Satellites* (New York, 1960), p. 230.

40. Patrick O'Donovan, "Marx Among Angels," *The Observer*, September 2, 1962.

Chapter 7: Gomułka's Political Program

1. *Przemówienia*, 1956–57, p. 315.
2. *Ibid.*, p. 384.
3. *Ibid.*, 1959, p. 416.
4. *Ibid.*, 1962, p. 10.
5. *Ibid.*, 1959, p. 413.
6. *Ibid.*, 1960, p. 97.
7. *Ibid.*, 1962, p. 19.
8. *Ibid.*
9. *Ibid.*, 1957–58, pp. 524, 552.
10. *Ibid.*, 1956–57, pp. 197–198.
11. *Ibid.*, p. 200.
12. *Ibid.*, 1960, p. 409.
13. *Ibid.*, 1959, p. 67.

14. *Ibid.*, p. 404.

15. *Ibid.*, 1956–57, p. 201.

16. *Ibid.*, p. 391.

17. *Ibid.*, 1959, p. 562; 1960, p. 83.

18. *Ibid.*, 1956–57, p. 40.

19. *Ibid.*, 1960, pp. 131, 149.

20. *Ibid.*, p. 134.

21. *Ibid.*, 1959, p. 416.

22. *Ibid.*, p. 418.

23. *Ibid.*, p. 421.

24. *Ibid.*, p. 422.

25. *Ibid.*, 1960, p. 133.

26. *Ibid.*, p. 134.

27. For a stimulating analysis of this aspect of Gomułka's program by a leader of the old Polish Socialist Party, see Adam Ciołkosz, "Partia i rzad," in *Rocznik Spraw Krajowych* (London, 1960), pp. 7–15.

28. *Przemówienia*, 1960, p. 125.

29. *World Marxist Review: Problems of Peace and Socialism*, January 1960, p. 67.

30. *Przemówienia*, 1962, p. 35.

31. *III Zjazd Polskiej Zjednoczonej Partii Robotniczej — Stenogram* (Warsaw, 1959), p. 830.

32. *Ibid.*, p. 831.

33. *Ibid.*, p. 826.

34. *Przemówienia*, 1959, p. 87.

35. Brzezinski, *The Soviet Bloc: Unity and Conflict*, p. 349.

36. *Przemówienia*, 1960, p. 124.

37. *Ibid.*, p. 127.

38. Tadeusz Daniszewski, "Under the Banner of Proletarian Internationalism," *World Marxist Review: Problems of Peace and Socialism*, January 1959, p. 54.

39. For evaluation of Gomułka's statements in a general theoretical debate in the Communist bloc, see A. Bromke and A. N. Pol, "The Concept of People's Democracy in the Post-Stalinist Period," *Revue de l'Université d'Ottawa*, October–December, 1959.

40. *Przemówienia*, 1956–57, p. 269.

41. *Ibid.*, pp. 265, 269.

42. *Ibid.*, p. 269.

43. *Ibid.*, 1957–58, p. 105.

44. *Ibid.*, 1956–57, p. 268. For almost identical statements, see *ibid.*, p. 94; 1957–58, p. 106.

45. *Trybuna Ludu*, June 11, 1964.

46. *Przemówienia*, 1956–57, p. 213.

47. *Ibid.*, 1957–58, p. 532.

Chapter 8: Poland and the Soviet Union

1. An extensive literature exists in English on Polish-Soviet relations and Poland's position in the Soviet bloc since 1956. Among the books which, in the opinion of this writer, particularly deserve attention are the following: Brzezinski, *The Soviet Bloc: Unity and Conflict,* chs. xii, xiii, *passim;* Halecki in Kertesz, ed., *East and Cen-*

tral Europe, pp. 57–63; W. Żurawski, *Poland: The Captive Satellite* (Detroit, 1962), chs. vii, x; Hiscocks, *Poland: Bridge for the Abyss?,* chs. x–xii.

2. *Trybuna Ludu,* November 19, 1956. For full text in English, see Zinner, ed., *National Communism,* pp. 306–314.

3. From 1956 on the pace of the repatriation of Poles from the Soviet Union accelerated. In the years 1956–1958 approximately 217,000 persons returned to Poland from the Soviet Union. *Trybuna Ludu,* January 7, 1959. This, however, is still less than was generally expected both in Poland and abroad. The estimated number of Poles in the Soviet Union varied from 300,000 to several hundred thousand more. For a discussion of this topic, see Józef Poniatowski, "Ludność," in *Rocznik spraw krajowych,* pp. 128–129.

4. *Przemówienia,* 1957–58, p. 112.

5. B. N. Ponomarev et al., *Istoria Kommunisticheskoi Partii Sovietskogo Soyuza* (Moscow, 1959), p. 241.

6. O. V. Kuusinen et al., *Osnovy Marksizma-Leninizma* (Moscow, 1959), p. 533.

7. N. S. Khrushchev, "The Meeting of the Party Organization in the Higher Party School of the Academy of Social Science and the Institute of Marxism-Leninism of the Central Committee of the CPSU," *World Marxist Review: Problems of Peace and Socialism,* January 1961. Excerpts included in Dieter Dux, ed., *Ideology in Conflict: Communist Political Theory* (Princeton, N.J., 1963), p. 154.

8. *Przemówienia,* 1957–58, p. 153.

9. *Ibid.,* pp. 147–148.

10. *Ibid.,* pp. 151–152.

11. *Ibid.,* p. 150.

12. Paweł Jasienica, "Polska i Chiny," *Po prostu,* January 7, 1957.

13. Juliusz Burgin, "Chiny 1949–1957," *Świat i Polska,* September 26, 1957.

14. Zofia Artymowska, "Po rozmowach w Belgradzie," *Świat i Polska,* September 19, 1957.

15. *Przemówienia,* 1957–58, p. 152.

16. *Pravda,* April 23, 1957.

17. *Przemówienia,* 1957–58, p. 135. In this speech, Gomułka openly noted that "some capitalist circles . . . attempted to exploit granting credits [by the United States] to weaken Poland's bonds with the camp of socialist states."

18. Hansjakob Stehle, *The Independent Satellite* (New York, 1965), p. 222. Dr. Stehle's book contains a detailed and extremely informative study of the Rapacki Plan.

19. *Przemówienia,* 1957–58, p. 138.

20. *The Rapacki Plan: Documents* (Warsaw, 1961), p. 18.

21. *Trybuna Ludu,* November 5, 1958.

22. The changes in the Polish economic system since 1956 are reviewed in English in the following penetrating articles: Alexander Erlich, "The Polish Economy After October: Background and Outlook," *The American Economic Review,* May 1959; J. M. Montias, "The Polish Economic Model," *Problems of Communism,* March–April, 1960; and "New Models and Old Dilemmas," *Survey,* January–March, 1961.

23. "Rady robotnicze w ofensywie," *Trybuna Ludu,* November 4, 1956. The influence of the Yugoslav example on the Polish workers' councils is discussed in Adam Bromke, "The Workers' Councils in Poland," *Slavic and East European Studies,* Winter 1956–1957.

24. *Mały Rocznik Statystyczny, 1958* (Warsaw, 1958), p. 46.

25. *Trybuna Ludu,* May 21, 1957.

26. *Mały Rocznik Statystyczny, 1958,* p. 51.

27. *Przemówienia,* 1956–57, pp. 304, 305.

28. Tadeusz Mrówczyński, "Uwagi na temat religii," *Nowe Drogi*, May 1957, p. 63.

29. "Trwałe i przejściowe wartości marksizmu," *Nowa Kultura*, January 27, 1957; "Odpowiedzialność i historia," *Nowa Kultura*, September 1–22, 1957. For the full English texts, see Paweł Mayewski, ed., *The Broken Mirror* (New York, 1958), pp. 157–174, and Edmund Stillman, ed., *Bitter Harvest* (New York, 1959), pp. 94–125.

30. See, for instance, A. Azizian, "O proletarskom internatsionalisme," *Pravda*, December 23, 1956. For highlights of the attacks against the Polish writers by foreign Communists, see Brzezinski, *The Soviet Bloc*, pp. 270–282.

31. S. I. Mikhailov and K. A. Komarov, "Starye pagubki na noviy lad," *Voprosy Filosofii*, September 1957, p. 112.

32. *Trybuna Ludu*, January 27, 1958.

33. Radio Moscow, April 28, 1958. For excerpts in English, see *East Europe*, June 1958.

34. *Pravda*, May 8, 1958.

35. Brzezinski, *The Soviet Bloc*, p. 330.

36. *Przemówienia*, 1957–58, pp. 261–264. For the full text in English, see Beneš, *The Second Soviet-Yugoslav Dispute*, pp. 157–160.

37. *Przemówienia*, 1957–58, p. 443.

38. *Ibid.*

39. *Pravda*, September 5, 1959.

40. Khrushchev, in Dux, ed. *Ideology in Conflict*, p. 153.

41. *Przemówienia*, 1961, pp. 78, 79.

42. *Trybuna Ludu*, November 15, 1961.

43. *Przemówienia*, 1961, pp. 77, 78.

44. *Ibid.*, p. 78.

45. *Ibid.*, 1957–58, p. 418. For an English translation of Gomułka's speech in Moscow, see *The Current Digest of the Soviet Press*, December 17, 1958.

46. A chronological survey of contacts between Yugoslavia and the Soviet bloc countries prepared by Radio Free Europe in Munich shows that in the period from January 1, 1959, to May 15, 1960, Poland was the first in the number of contacts and only second in trade with Yugoslavia.

47. *Przemówienia*, 1959, p. 85.

48. *Ibid.*, p. 424.

49. *Ibid.*, 1961, p. 464.

50. *Concise Statistical Yearbook of Polish People's Republic, 1960* (Warsaw, 1961), pp. 122–123.

51. *Przemówienia*, 1961, p. 77.

52. *Ibid.*, 1959, p. 545.

53. *Rocznik polityczny i gospodarczy, 1959* (Warsaw, 1959), p. 386; *Rocznik polityczny i gospodarczy, 1961* (Warsaw, 1961), p. 224. The changing role of the workers' councils is described in detail in the two papers by Kazimierz Grzybowski: "Workers' Self-Government in Poland," and "Workers' Self-Government in Poland a Year After," published in *The Polish Review* of Winter–Spring 1958 and Autumn 1959, respectively. See also Janina Miedzinska, "Social Policy under Gomulka," *Soviet Survey*, January–March, 1961.

54. *Rocznik polityczny i gospodarczy, 1959*, p. 499; *Rocznik polityczny i gospodarczy, 1960* (Warsaw, 1960), pp. 475–476; *Rocznik polityczny i gospodarczy, 1961*, p. 548.

55. Stehle, *The Independent Satellite*, p. 172.

56. *Przemówienia*, 1959, p. 476.

57. On August 31, 1962, there were exactly 1,669 collective farms in Poland. *Biuletyn Statystyczny*, October 1962.

58. *Przemówienia*, 1959, p. 182.

59. *Rocznik polityczny i gospodarczy, 1960*, p. 220.

60. Józef Siemek, "O współpracę wierzących i niewierzących," *Nowe Drogi*, July 1957, pp. 59, 60.

61. In 1961 the circulation of *Tygodnik Powszechny* was reduced from 50,000 to 40,000. At the same time on the average of 10 percent of the contents of each issue of this weekly, usually the most important political items, was struck out by the censors. Significantly, there also existed a ban on distributing the paper in the other Communist countries.

62. *The New York Times*, March 4, 1961.

63. Quoted in *Polish Affairs*, April 1961, p. 12.

64. "Na marginesie rekolekcyjnych wypowiedzi," *Życie Warszawy*, April 28, 1962.

65. *Przemówienia*, 1961, p. 473.

66. In 1957 *Nowa Kultura* had a circulation of 75,300 and *Przegląd Kulturalny* had 52,000, while by early 1959 this was reduced to 22,600 and 25,900, respectively. *Express Wieczorny*, May 22, 1959.

67. *Przemówienia*, 1959, p. 165. For an interesting report on the intellectual scene in Poland in the late fifties. See Leopold Labedz, "The Polish Intellectual Climate," *Survey*, January–March, 1961.

68. Khrushchev, in Dux, ed., *Ideology in Conflict*, p. 155.

69. *Trybuna Ludu*, April, 1965.

70. *Przemówienia*, 1961, pp. 517, 518.

71. *Trybuna Ludu*, March 29, 1965.

72. Mieczysław Rakowski, "Treści i formy jedności," *Nowe Drogi*, January, 1962. For a more detailed account of Poland's stand in the Sino-Soviet dispute, see Adam Bromke, "Poland: A Matter of Timing," *Problems of Communism*, May–June 1962. See also M. K. Dziewanowski, "Poland," in Adam Bromke, ed., *The Communist States at the Crossroads: Between Moscow and Peking* (New York, 1965).

73. *Trybuna Ludu*, January 31, 1962.

74. Quoted in *East Europe*, August 1964, p. 41.

75. Michal Hofman, "Układ moskiewski," *Nowe Drogi*, September 1963, p. 40.

76. *Trybuna Ludu*, January 27, 1962.

77. *IV Zjazd Polskiej Zjednoczonej Partii Robotniczej* (Worsaw, 1964), pp. 320–326. For an excellent review of the subject, see Michael Gamarnikow "Economic Reform in Poland," *East Europe*, July 1965.

78. "Przemówienie Sejmowe Jerzego Zawieyskiego wygłoszone w dniu 29 marca b.r.," *Tygodnik Powszechny*, May 5, 1963.

79. *Trybuna Ludu*, November 10, 1964.

80. *The New York Times*, February 2, 1965.

81. "Konsekwencje i cierpliwość," *Tygodnik Powszechny*, February 21, 1965.

82. "Ryzyko wolności," *Przegląd Kulturalny*, December 14, 1961.

83. "Swoboda i wybór," *Przegląd Kulturalny*, January 11, 1962.

84. On the closing down of the Club, see Witold Jedlicki, "The Death of the Crooked Circle Club," *East Europe*, August 1963.

85. *Pravda*, March 9, 1963.

86. *Kultura* (Warsaw), June 16, 1963.

87. *Nowe Drogi*, August 1963, pp. 9, 38.

88. For the entire text in English, see *East Europe,* May 1964, p. 48.

89. "Nie uda się przeciwstawić," *Polityka,* April 25, 1964.

90. *Życie Warszawy,* May 10, 1964.

91. *Trybuna Ludu,* June 19, 1964.

92. *Trybuna Ludu,* September 19, 1964.

Chapter 9: Gomułka and the Polish People

1. Ryszard Turski and Eligiusz Lasota, "Polski październik," *Po prostu,* October 28, 1956.

2. Stefan Kurowski, "Apatia — czyli poszukiwanie celu," in *6 lat temu: Kulisy polskiego października* (Paris, 1962), p. 162.

3. "Próba diagnozy," *Przegląd Kulturalny,* August 22, 1957; "Próba diagnozy — uzupełnienie," *Przegląd Kulturalny,* October 31, 1957.

4. Already in October 1957, Gomułka had explicitly repudiated Kurowski's proposals, denouncing them as essentially a continuation of the political line of *Po prostu. 6 lat temu,* p. 86.

5. *Przemówienia,* 1957–58, pp. 22–23.

6. *Ibid.,* 1959, pp. 134–135.

7. *Nowe Drogi,* August 1963, p. 38.

8. It is estimated that late in 1956 and early in 1957 roughly 25 to 30 percent of the security personnel were dismissed. Jan Nowak, "Analysis of Developments in Poland" (Munich, 1957), p. 17.

9. In the fall of 1957, three top officials of the former investigation section of the Ministry of Public Security received sentences ranging from twelve to fifteen years; in February 1958, four other officers of the security apparatus were tried but the court's verdict was not made public. For an interesting first-hand report on the first trial, see S. L. Shneiderman, *The Warsaw Heresy* (New York, 1959), pp. 91–100.

10. Reportedly by 1958 the security division of the Ministry of Internal Affairs employed 18,000 men. Their tasks varied from counter-intelligence and uncovering illegal political organizations to a surveillance of the contacts between Poles and Westerners and of the individuals suspected of the anti-regime sympathies. *Dziennik Polski i Dziennik Żołnierza,* July 4, 1958.

11. *III Zjazd Polskiej Zjednoczonej Partii Robotniczej,* p. 1055. In 1960, 0.8 percent of all prisoners in Poland were serving sentences for "anti-state" activities (Ludwik Krasucki and Henryk Werner, eds., *100 Pytań i odpowiedzi,* Warsaw, 1961, p. 69). Since the total number of prisoners at the end of 1959 was 92,597 (*Rocznik Statystyczny, 1960,* p. 448), this would indicate that the total number of political prisoners was well below 1,000. Taking into account that among the prisoners sentenced for "anti-state" activities there were the persons guilty of war crimes, collaborating with the Nazis, and cooperation with the West German organizations striving for the return of Poland's western territories to Germany — the activities which in the eyes of all Poles call for the punishment by the deprivation of freedom — the number of people imprisoned specifically for opposing the Gomułka regime seemed to be actually much smaller.

12. For instance, the detention in 1960 of a Canadian citizen of Polish descent, Tadeusz Koyer, suspected of working for Polish exile centers; the arrest of a young sociologist, Hanna Rudzińska, accused of cooperation with the emigré journal *Kultura;*

also in 1961 the mysterious death (while in the hands of the security apparatus) of a journalist, Henryk Holland, charged with passing information to the correspondent of *Le Monde* in Warsaw; and in 1964 the arraignment of an elderly writer, Melchior Wańkowicz, described in Chapter 8.

13. *Trybuna Ludu,* December 7, 1961.

14. For a detailed account of the changes in the Polish Bar by a specialist in the field, see Zygmunt Nagórski, Sr., "The Legislation of the Polish People's Republic 1958–1959," in Z. Szirmai, ed., *Law in Eastern Europe* (London, 1962), pp. 88–90. For an interesting comment on the reform of the judiciary in Poland by an impartial observer, see Jules Wolf, "L'organisation judiciare en Pologne," in *Le régime et les institutions de la république populaire de Pologne* (Brussels, 1959), pp. 108–112.

15. *III Zjazd Polskiej Zjednoczonej Partii Robotniczej,* p. 893.

16. "Projekt ustawy o Sądzie Najwyższym," *Prawo i Życie,* December 10, 1961.

17. Zdzisław Sachnowski, "O co ta burza?" *Głos Pracy,* October 1, 1958.

18. George Weller, "Polish Lawyers Block the Red Purge," *The Boston Globe,* October 27, 1961. For other reports on the Brojdes case, see "Lawyers in the 'New Society,'" *East Europe,* December 1961, pp. 34–35; also *The New York Times,* April 22 and October 7, 1961.

19. *Prawo i Życie,* December 1, 1961.

20. At the end of 1961, out of a total of approximately 6,000 attorneys in Poland, almost 100 were accused of violations of the law of a criminal nature, and 500 were charged with breaking the code of professional ethics. Radio Warsaw, December 5, 1961.

21. K. Zawadzki, "U progu reformy adwokatury," *Prawo i Życie,* May 26, 1963.

22. *Prawo i Życie,* May 31, 1959.

23. *Przemówienia,* 1956–57, p. 49.

24. There were 459 seats in the parliament, which were distributed as follows: the Polish United Workers' Party — 237; the United Peasant Party — 120; the Democratic Party — 39; non-party — 62, out of which 11 formed the Catholic Znak group.

25. Julian Hochfeld, "Z zagadnień parlamentaryzmu w warunkach demokracji ludowej," *Nowe Drogi,* April 1957. Although Hochfeld is a Communist, this proposal was not startling in the light of his background. Hochfeld is a former socialist who spent the war years in England and also a prominent authority on political sociology.

26. In the years 1957–1961, the Sejm passed 174 bills; in the same period the State Council issued only 2 decrees.

27. In the first two years of its existence, the plenary meetings of the Sejm lasted 46 days. A. G., "Kadencja Sejmu Polskiej Rzeczypospolitiej Ludowej," in *Rocznik polityczny i gospodarczy, 1959,* p. 93. For an interesting analysis of the activities of the Sejm in the early stages of 1957, see Zbigniew Pelczynski, "Parliamentarism in Poland," *Parliamentary Affairs,* Summer 1957.

28. In 1957–1959 the committees held 695 meetings. A. G., *Rocznik polityczny i gospodarczy, 1959,* p. 59. For a detailed analysis of the activities of parliamentary committees, see Vincent C. Chrypinski, "Legislative Committees in Poland" (Windsor, Ontario, 1963).

29. The distribution of the seats in the parliament elected in 1961 was as follows: the Polish United Workers' Party — 255; the United Peasant Party — 117; the Democratic Party — 39; non-party — 49, out of which 5 joined the Catholic group Znak. In the elections of 1965 this distribution was preserved with only very minor changes.

30. Konstanty Łubieński, "Kilka refleksji o Sejmie P.R.L.," *Tygodnik Powszechny,* June 2, 1963.

31. Sylwester Zawadzki, "Państwo Demokracji Ludowej," *Węzłowe zagadnienia budownictwa socjalizmu w Polsce,* p. 215. Those reforms were partially linked with the decentralization of economic planning and management discussed in Chapter 8.

32. In the State Council in 1957, out of 15 members elected, 8 were Communists; and in 1961, out of 17 members, 9 were Communists. In the Presidium of the Council of Ministers in 1957, out of 4 members appointed, 3 were Communists; and in 1961, out of 6 members, 5 were Communists. In the Council of Ministers in 1957, out of 27 members, 16; and in 1961 out of 29 members, 24, respectively, were members of the Polish United Workers' Party. In the local government in 1958, 40.5 percent, and in 1961, 45.3 percent of all officials were Communists.

33. *III Zjazd Polskiej Zjednoczonej Partii Robotniczej,* pp. 944–945.

34. *Życie Warszawy,* January 11, 1962.

35. Mieczysław Kowalik, "Preobrazovaniya apparata gosudarstvennogo uprovleniya Pol'shi v 1955–1957 gg.," in *Voprosy gosudarstva i prava stran narodnoi demokratii* (Moscow, 1960), p. 157.

36. Merle Fainsod, *How Russia Is Ruled,* rev. ed. (Cambridge, Mass., 1963), p. 580.

37. Jerzy Starościak, *Decentralizacja administracji* (Warsaw, 1960), p. 135.

38. Janusz Wlihelmi, "Skoro jest to juz historia," *Kultura,* July 14, 1963.

39. W. E. Griffith, "Warsaw Notebook," *Soviet Survey,* January–March, 1961, p. 26.

40. P. O'Donovan, "Marx Among Angels," *The Observer,* September 2, 1962. Mr. O'Donovan uses in his report the literal translation from Polish of the expression "organic work," rather than the one adopted by this writer: "organic reform."

41. This was bluntly stated by a Polish economist in a conversation with an emigré political writer. The economist admitted that in its trade with Poland Russia derives certain economic benefits, but he minimized Poland's losses (estimating them at less than 4 percent of the total volume of trade), and firmly supported Poland's continued close economic bonds with the Soviet Union. Juliusz Mieroszewski, "Rozmowa z anonimem," *Kultura,* November 1962, p. 53. This view seems to be shared by Western economists. In the words of a noted Western observer, "a large share of [Polish-Soviet] trade follows the lines of natural economic advantage." J. M. Montias, "Unbinding the Polish Economy," *Foreign Affairs,* July 1957. For a similar opinion see V. Winston, "The Soviet Satellites — Economic Liability?" *Problems of Communism,* January–February, 1958.

42. *Ibid.*

43. Zbigniew Załuski, *Siedem polskich grzechów głównych* (Warsaw, 1962), pp. 190–192.

44. *Ibid.*

Chapter 10: The Communist Party and Its Allies

1. *Przemówienia,* 1956–57, p. 71.

2. Gomułka explicitly acknowledged these proposals in his speech at the meeting of the secretaries of the Provincial Committees on November 23, 1956. *6 lat temu,* p. 79.

3. R. Zimand, "Parę zwykłych dni we Wrocławiu," *Po prostu,* December 9, 1956.

4. These attempts were acknowledged by Morawski as early as February 1957. *6 lat temu,* p. 141.

5. S. Migdał, "Nasi rewizjoniści," *Trybuna Robotnicza,* December 3, 1957.
6. *6 lat temu,* pp. 79–80.
7. *Przemówienia,* 1956–57, p. 307.
8. *Ibid.,* p. 46.
9. *Ibid.,* p. 73.
10. *Ibid.,* p. 316.
11. *Ibid.,* 1957–58, pp. 32, 35.
12. *Ibid.,* 1956–57, pp. 321, 327.
13. *III Zjazd Polskiej Zjednoczonej Partii Robotniczej,* p. 856. In addition, according to Gomułka, "some revisionists resigned from the party fearing that they would share the same fate." *Przemówienia,* 1957–58, p. 338.
14. *Ibid.,* p. 327.
15. Radio Moscow, December 22, 1956.
16. Shneiderman, *The Warsaw Heresy,* p. 62.
17. *Trybuna Ludu,* July 22, 1957.
18. "Partia po X Plenum," *Nowe Drogi,* December 1957, p. 43.
19. *Przemówienia,* 1957–58, pp. 45, 46, 50. In addition, Gomułka pointed out that the past system of recruitment had been responsible for the faulty social composition of the Polish United Workers' Party. He was particularly worried about the decreasing number of workers in the Communist Party. Their percentage in the years 1954–1959 dropped from 48.3 to 41.8. *Ibid.,* 1959, p. 186.
20. *Ibid.,* 1957–58, pp. 342–343.
21. Julian Andrzejewski, "Polska Zjednoczona Partia Robotnicza," *Rocznik polityczny i gospodarczy, 1961,* p. 182. The figures include the close to 8,000 men who had been expelled from the Polish United Workers' Party in the Stalinist years and rehabilitated after Gomułka's return to power. *III Zjazd Polskiej Zjednoczonej Partii Robotniczej,* p. 855.
22. *Rocznik polityczny i gospodarczy, 1958,* p. 314.
23. *Przemówienia,* 1959, pp. 209, 214. At the same time, Gomułka pointed to the improvement in the social structure of the Polish United Workers' Party. He stressed that among the new recruits the proportion of workers was on the increase. *Ibid.,* p. 186.
24. *Ibid.,* 1957–58, p. 347.
25. J. Wacławek, "Przyczynek do spraw biernych," *Trybuna Ludu,* October 31, 1958.
26. "Gdzie jest szkoła komunizmu?" *Polityka,* September 26, 1959.
27. Zdzisław Dąbrowski, "Gorąco popieram," *Polityka,* October 10, 1959.
28. Mieczysław Lipiec, "Ideowość na codzień," *Polityka,* October 10, 1959.
29. Dąbrowski, *Polityka,* October 10, 1959.
30. Quoted by J. Wacławek, *Trybuna Ludu,* October 31, 1958.
31. Bronisława Erenbrod, "Młodzi są mało krytyczni," *Polityka,* October 24, 1959.
32. *Siedem polskich grzechów głównych* (Warsaw, 1962).
33. *Ibid.,* pp. 214–215.
34. *Ibid.,* pp. 7, 103.
35. *Ibid.,* p. 31.
36. *Ibid.,* p. 32.
37. *Ibid.,* pp. 32, 33, 154.
38. *Ibid.,* pp. 123, 125.
39. *Ibid.,* pp. 101, 210–212.
40. Teodor Toepliz Krzysztof, "Tradycja za tradycję," *Przegląd Kulturalny,* January 30, 1963.

41. Zygmunt Bukowiński, "Hej, kto Polak na bagnety," *Polityka,* February 9, 1963.

42. Andrzej Kijowski, "Pokłońmy się ideom martwym," *Przegląd Kulturalny,* February 6, 1963.

43. "Grzech ósmy: bezkrytycyzm," *Polityka,* December 8, 1962.

44. Toeplitz, *Przegląd Kulturalny,* January 30, 1963.

45. Koźniewski, *Polityka,* December 8, 1962.

46. "Galopujący pułkownik," *Nowa Kultura,* September 30, 1962.

47. Bukowiński, *Polityka,* February 9, 1963.

48. "Spór o polskie grzechy," *Polityka,* February 16, 1963.

49. "Komplikacje pewnego tematu," *Trybuna Ludu,* January 13, 1963.

50. "Spór o ideały wychowawcze socjalizmu," *Trybuna Ludu,* April 26, 1963. Also published in May under the same title as a separate pamphlet.

51. *Ibid.,* p. 32.

52. For information on the rise and activities of the "partisans" group, see W. Jedlicki, *Klub Krzywego Koła* (Paris, 1963), ch. 1; Jerzy Ptakowski, "Politics in Poland," *East Europe,* December 1962; S. L. Shneiderman, "Eclipse of the Polish October," *Problems of Communism,* September–October, 1963.

53. The twentieth anniversary of the existence of the "people's armed forces," celebrated with much fanfare in Poland, provided a suitable occasion for publishing several articles along these lines. In particular, the article written by one of the "partisans'" leaders, General Duszyński, was close in tone to Załuski's book. See "Historia i dzień dzisiejszy," *Tygodnik Demokratyczny,* October 10, 1963.

54. For an interesting analysis of factional struggle in the Polish United Workers' Party on the eve of the Fourth Congress, see Jerzy Ptakowski, "Political Maneuvers in Warsaw," *East Europe,* April, 1964.

55. "W walce zwyciestwo! Milczenie i bierność to zguba!" For the English text, see Jan Nowak, "The Stalinist Underground in Poland," *East Europe,* March 1965.

56. For the analysis of the Fourth Congress, see Richard F. Staar, "Warsaw's Quiet Congress," *East Europe,* August 1964.

57. *Trybuna Ludu,* July 7, 1963 and June 18, 1964.

58. Jan Ptasiński, *Trybuna Ludu,* July 11, 1963.

59. *Nowe Drogi,* August 1963, p. 39.

60. *Trybuna Ludu,* July 11, 1963.

61. *Trybuna Ludu,* July 10, 1963.

62. *Trybuna Ludu,* June 21, 1964.

63. *Ibid.*

64. *Ibid.*

65. *Trybuna Ludu,* June 18, 1964.

66. *Nowe Drogi,* August 16, 1963, p. 42.

67. *Nowe Drogi,* August 1963, p. 18.

68. *Trybuna Ludu,* July 10, 1963.

69. "Uchwała Naczelnego Komitetu ZSL przyjęta na VI Plenarnym Posiedzeniu," *Wieś Współczesna,* April–May, 1957, p. 7.

70. *Przemówienia,* 1956–57, p. 303.

71. *Polityka,* May 22, 1957.

72. Stanisław Kulczyński, "Referat polityczno-sprawozdawczy," *VI Kongres Stronnictwa Demokratycznego* (Warsaw, 1958), pp. 48–49.

73. "O konieczności wzmożenia walki z prawicą i umocnienia współpracy z PZPR," *Trybuna Ludu,* October 11, 1957.

74. "Rozbijacze jedności," *Trybuna Ludu,* October 27, 1957.

75. *Rocznik polityczny i gospodarczy, 1958,* p. 357.
76. Kulczyński, *VI Kongres Stronnictwa Demokratycznego,* p. 48.
77. Leon Chajn, "Referat Statutowo-Organizacyjny," *ibid.,* p. 101.
78. *Rocznik polityczny i gospodarczy, 1961,* p. 198.
79. *Referat statutowo-organizacyjny, VII Kongres Stronnictwa Demokratycznego* (Warsaw, 1961), p. 5.
80. *Przemówienia,* 1957–58, p. 186.
81. *Ibid.,* 1959, p. 136.
82. In the practice of the United Peasant Party a considerable number of members were drawn from the intelligentsia. In fact, at the end of 1958, the peasants represented only 77 percent of the party's total membership. *Rocznik polityczny i gospodarczy, 1958,* p. 357. The Democratic Party, however, is almost solely confined to its assigned social base. In 1958 workers and peasants (who retained party cards from the period when they had still been accepted into its ranks) represented less than 1 percent of its total membership. Chajn, *VI Kongres Stronnictwa Demokratycznego,* p. 95.
83. Wiesław Skrzydło, "Z problematyki i genezy istoty partii politycznych," *Annales Universitatis Mariae Curie-Skłodowska,* vol. V, no. 3, 1958.
84. Centralyn Komitet Stronnictwa Demokratycznego, *Wytyczne działalności Stronnictwa Demokratycznego (Projekt)* (Warsaw, 1956), pp. 15–16, 18–19.
85. Centralny Komitet, *Wytyczne . . . (Projekt),* p. 13; also Centralny Komitet, *Wytyczne . . . (Uchwała),* pp. 20, 21.
86. "O konieczności dyskusji ideologicznej w ZSL," *Wieś Współczesna,* April–May, 1957, pp. 11–14.
87. Stefan Ignar, "ZSL wspólnie z PZPR będzie realizować program rozwoju rolnictwa i przebudowy wsi," *Trybuna Ludu,* November 28, 1959; "Uchwała polityczna III Kongresu ZSL," *Trybuna Ludu,* December 1, 1959.
88. *"Referat Polityczno-Sprawozdawczy," VII Kongres Stronnictwa Demokratycznego* (Warsaw, 1961), pp. 14–15; *Projekt Uchwały VII Kongresu Stronnictwa Demokratycznego* (Warsaw, 1961), p. 43.
89. There is evidence that the deputies from the two parties objected to some legislative measures proposed by the Communists at meetings of parliamentary committees. See Tadeusz Orlewicz, "Klub Poselski ZSL w Sejmie II kadencji (1957–1961)," *Wieś Współczesna,* February 1961, pp. 17–21.
90. *Trybuna Ludu,* May 29, 1962 and November 26, 1964.
91. Radio Warsaw, February 12, 1965.

Chapter 11: The Pax Group

1. *Świat,* November 18, 1956.
2. *Ibid.*
3. Bolesław Piasecki, "Instynkt Państwowy," *Słowo Powszechne,* October 16, 1956; also *Kierunki,* October 21, 1956.
4. Indeed, in his article, Tyrmand speaks of the "fall of Piasecki" as if this were an accomplished fact. *Świat,* November 18, 1956.
5. Mikołaj Rostworowski, "O własny profil 'Kierunków,'" *Kierunki,* November 25, 1956.
6. Bolesław Piasecki, "O socjalistycznym zangażowaniu narodu," *Słowo Powszechne,* May 10, 1957.

7. Jerzy Kossak, "Semper fidelis," *Po prostu,* May 19, 1957.

8. The significance of this event is evaluated by Alexander Korab in "Strange Alliance: Piasecki and the Polish Communists," *Problems of Communism,* November–December, 1957.

9. Zygmunt Przetakiewicz, "Przeciw Indyferentyzmowi," *Kierunki,* March 23, 1958. To settle accounts with Tyrmand, his books were singled out by Przetakiewicz for attack. Przetakiewicz's views were ridiculed by the Catholic and Communist intellectuals alike. See Kisiel, "Sprawy poważne i djablik w ornacie," *Tygodnik Powszechny,* April 13, 1958; Teodor Krzysztof Toeplitz, "Nie dopuść aby miecz nieprawy . . ." *Nowa Kultura,* March 30, 1958. Toeplitz sarcastically observed that the slogan of moral renovation "is not new, and at one time was employed by the Piłsudskiites."

10. *Przemówienia,* 1959, p. 138.

11. Nowak, *Analysis of Developments in Poland,* p. 22.

12. Stanisław Mackiewicz, *Stanisław August* (London, 1953).

13. Stanisław Mackiewicz, *Zielone oczy* (Warsaw, 1958), pp. 325–326.

14. *Margrabia Wielopolski,* pp. 18–19.

15. Zygmunt Komorowski, "Konsekwencje realizmu," *Kierunki,* February 15, 1958.

16. Jerzy Łojek, "Apoteoza Quislingizmu," and Aleksander Bocheński, "Analiza polityczna artykułu Jerzego Łojka," *Kierunki,* January 5, 1958.

17. R.K.M., "Nasza tradycja," *Nowe Drogi,* February 1958, pp. 151–152.

18. Bolesław Piasecki, *Patriotyzm polski* (Warsaw, 1958). Piasecki's book is a collection of articles written by him in 1955–1958. Significantly, it includes the controversial article published on the eve of the upheaval in 1956. It does not, however, include the article in which Piasecki discussed State-Church relations, which could possibly once again have put his book on the Vatican Index. For a penetrating review of Piasecki's book by one of his former close associates, see Andrzej Micewski, "Nad 'Patriotyzmem polskim' B. Piaseckiego," *Więź,* September 1959.

19. "Wytyczne Ideologiczne," quoted and discussed extensively in two articles by Juliusz Mieroszewski: " 'Rewizjoniści' których popiera Moskwa," *Kultura,* December 1958; and "Powrót na punkt startu," *Kultura,* October 1960. Mieroszewski's articles provide a penetrating analysis of the progressivists program and political calculations. Although the assumption at least in the first article, that Piasecki enjoyed support from Moscow is disputable, in all other respects the articles are written with unusual insight.

20. "Wchodząc w Nowy Rok 1961," *Słowo Powszechne,* December 31, 1960.

21. "Wytyczne Ideologiczne," quoted by Mieroszewski, *Kultura,* October 1960, p. 57.

22. Bolesław Piasecki, "Patriotyzm polski," *Kierunki,* Christmas 1958.

23. Bolesław Piasecki, "Patriotyzm a miejsce Polski w świecie," *Kierunki,* November 9, 1958. Significantly this article on Polish-Soviet relations was published during the friendship visit of Gomułka to the U.S.S.R.

24. *Słowo Powszechne,* May 10, 1957.

25. *Kierunki,* November 9, 1958.

26. *Ibid.*

27. Bolesław Piasecki, "Postawa społeczna a funkcja społeczna katolicyzmu," *Kierunki,* January 6, 1957.

28. *Kierunki,* Christmas 1958.

29. Bolesław Piasecki, "Tło ideowe polskiej drogi do socjalizmu," *Kierunki,* January 6, 1957.

30. *Słowo Powszechne,* May 10, 1957.

31. *Ibid.*

32. *Kierunki,* Christmas 1958.

33. *Kierunki,* October 26, 1958.

34. Quoted by Mieroszewski in *Kultura,* October 1960, p. 57.

35. *Ibid.*

36. *Ibid.*

37. *Trybuna Ludu,* January 26, 1961. In addition to Gomułka and Piasecki, three members of the Central Committee participated in the meeting on the Communist side, and for Pax, its Vice President and Secretary General.

38. Dominik Horodyński, "Dobrze jest być generałem," *Nowa Kultura,* October 18, 1959.

39. August 4, 1964.

40. Kisiel, "Socjalista z 'Kierunków,'" *Tygodnik Powszechny,* February 28, 1960.

41. Mieroszewski, *Kultura,* October 1960, pp. 76–77.

42. Jan Frankowski, "W związku z artykułem B. Piaseckiego," *Trybuna Ludu,* November 12, 1956.

43. *Ibid.*

44. J. B., "Polityczne grupy katolickie w Polsce," *Dziennik Polski i Dziennik Żołnierza,* November 4, 1957.

45. *Za i Przeciw,* August 28, 1957.

46. Jan Majdecki, "O właściwą postawę obywatelską," *Biuletyn Informacyjny: Chrześcijańskie Stowarzyszenie Społeczne,* April 1961, p. 20.

47. *Ibid.,* September 1960, p. 64.

48. *Ibid.,* May–June, 1961, p. 15.

Chapter 12: The Znak Group

1. "Sprawozdanie stenograficzne z 8 posiedzenia Sejmu Polskiej Rzeczypospolitej Ludowej od 11 do 13 lipca 1957," p. 202.

2. Tadeusz Mazowiecki, "Pozycja i praca środowiska 'Więź,'" *Więź,* March 1961, p. 15.

3. "Oświadczenie pisarzy i działaczy katolickich," *Życie Warszawy,* October 23, 1956.

4. Stanisław Stomma, *Myśli o polityce i kulturze* (Cracow, 1960), p. 73. Stomma's book is a collection of his articles on various political and cultural problems which had been previously published in *Tygodnik Powszechny.* In view of the influential position which Stomma occupied in the Znak group, the book might be viewed as an attempt at a coherent exposition of the political philosophy underlying the activities of the entire group.

5. *Myśli o polityce i kulturze,* p. 16.

6. *Ibid.,* p. 81.

7. *Ibid.,* p. 73.

8. *Ibid.,* p. 24.

9. Kisielewski, "Wigilia polityczna," *Tygodnik Powszechny,* December 28, 1958.

10. *Myśli o polityce i kulturze,* p. 18.

11. *Ibid.,* pp. 71, 56.

12. *Ibid.,* pp. 32, 30.

13. "Z kurzem krwi bratniej," *Tygodnik Powszechny,* January 20, 1963.

14. "Inni szatani byli tam czynni," *Tygodnik Powszechny,* February 3, 1963.

15. *Myśl Polska,* May 15, 1963.
16. Kisiel, "Nie, tak, czy jak?" *Tygodnik Powszechny,* May 7, 1961.
17. "W tym miejscu Europy," *Tygodnik Powszechny,* September 4, 1960.
18. "Polska nowego klimatu," *Tygodnik Powszechny,* April 26, 1959.
19. *Tygodnik Powszechny,* September 4, 1960.
20. Kazimierz Studentowicz, "Polska racja stanu," *Tygodnik Powszechny,* September 4, 1960. Studentowicz did not, strictly, belong to the Znak group. He was a former Christian Democrat — incidentally, imprisoned for his political views during the Stalinist years — and his connection with the Catholic intellectuals gathered around *Znak* came only after 1956. Yet since his article appeared alongside those by Kisielewski and Stomma in the issue of *Tygodnik Powszechny* clarifying the political program of the entire group, it must be taken as expressing their common viewpoint.
21. *Ibid.*
22. Kisiel, "Głos przerażonego minimalisty," *Tygodnik Powszechny,* November 19, 1961. The date of this article is significant. The author admitted it was written under the impact of the war scare when the crisis over Berlin reached its climax.
23. *Tygodnik Powszechny,* September 4, 1960.
24. Stefan Kisielewski, letter to the editor, *Kultura,* November 1958, p. 152.
25. *Tygodnik Powszechny,* September 4, 1960.
26. "Notatki o strategii pokoju," *Znak,* December 1962, pp. 1801, 1814, 1813.
27. " 'Znak' i zapytania," *Polityka,* September 17, 1960.
28. "Raison d'etat," *Przegląd Kulturalny,* September 22, 1960.
29. *Myśli o polityce i kulturze,* p. 82.
30. Stanisław Stomma, "Na co liczymy?" *Tygodnik Powszechny,* June 18, 1961.
31. *Ibid.*
32. "Trudności i nadzieje," *Tygodnik Powszechny,* December 6, 1959. The crucial passages of this piece were published in English in *East Europe,* February 1960, pp. 11, 55.
33. *Tygodnik Powszechny,* June 18, 1961.
34. *Myśli o polityce i kulturze,* p. 58.
35. *Tygodnik Powszechny,* December 6, 1959.
36. *Myśli o polityce i kulturze,* p. 58.
37. *Ibid.,* pp. 84–85.
38. *Tygodnik Powszechny,* December 6, 1959.
39. "Czym jest Koło Poselskie 'Znak,' " *Tygodnik Powszechny,* May 28, 1961.
40. *Ibid.*
41. *Tygodnik Powszechny,* June 18, 1961.
42. "Rozmowa ze Stefanem Kisielewskim," *Kultura,* June 1957, p. 32.
43. "Głupstwo rozum zjadło (felieton pesymistyczny)," *Tygodnik Powszechny,* September 29, 1963.

Chapter 13: Political Idealism and Political Realism: The Synthesis

1. Golo Mann, "Rapallo: The Vanishing Dream," *Survey,* October 1962, p. 74.
2. Walter B. Cannon, *The Wisdom of the Body,* rev. ed. (New York, 1939), p. 312.
3. *Niemcy, Rosja i kwestja polska,* p. 227.

4. *Przegląd Wszechpolski*, August 1904. Quoted by Tadeusz Bielecki, "Wyprawa do Japonii," *Myśl Polska*, August 1, 1964.

5. The rate of growth of Poland's population in the interwar and the postwar periods alike was one of the highest in the Western world. The net annual increase per 1,000 inhabitants in the years 1930–35 was 14; and in the years 1950–1955, around 19. *Rocznik Statystyczny, 1956*, p. 415.

6. B. Heydenkorn, "Charakterystyczne znamiona," *Związkowiec*, July 14, 1965.

7. In 1956, all the national minority groups amounted to a half million people, representing 1.8 percent of Poland's total population. *Życie Warszawy*, July 11, 1957.

8. Kisiel (Stefan Kisielewski), "Polska rzeczwiście nowa," *Tygodnik Powszechny*, November 11, 1961.

9. Andrzej Karpiński, *Poland and the World Economy* (Warsaw, 1960), p. 32. In the years 1937–1959, the output of some principal products increased as follows: coal, 36.2 to 99.1 million tons; steel, 1,468 to 6,150 thousand tons; electricity, 3,628 to 26,379 million kwn. *Poland: Facts and Figures* (Warsaw, 1960), p. 77.

10. Karpiński, *Poland and the World Economy*, p. 33.

11. The exact figures are as follows: urban population, 47.3 percent and rural population, 52.7 percent. *Concise Statistical Yearbook of Polish People's Republic, 1960*, p. 10. The number of workers employed in industry and construction increased in that decade from 1,162,000 to 3,627,000. Jan Danecki, "Przemiany klasowe i walka klasowa we współczesnej Polsce," *Węzłowe zagadnienia budownictwa socjalizmu w Polsce*, p. 80.

12. In the academic year 1958–1959 there were 53 university students per 10,000 inhabitants. The Central Statistical Office, *Poland in Figures* (Warsaw, 1959), p. 65.

13. Aleksander Małachowski, *Rzeczniepospolita* (Warsaw, 1964), p. 240.

14. Paweł Jasienica, "Niektóre z przemian," *Nowa Kultura*, August 16, 1959.

15. Herbert Feis, *Between War and Peace: the Potsdam Conference* (Princeton, N.J., 1960), p. 268.

16. Maurice Paleologue, *An Ambassador's Memoirs*, 6 ed. (London, 1925), I, 123.

17. Załuski, *Siedem polskich grzechów głównych*, p. 222.

18. Herz, *Political Idealism and Political Realism*, p. 42.

BIBLIOGRAPHY

I. BOOKS

Alton, Thad P., *Polish Postwar Economy*, New York, 1955.

Anders, Władysław, *An Army in Exile*, London, 1949.

Andrzejewski, Jerzy, *Popiół i Diament* (Ashes and Diamonds), Warsaw, 1949.

Anonim (Anonymous), *Nasza polityka wobec Rosji jaka być powinna* (Our Policy Toward Russia As It Ought to Be), Leipzig, 1865.

Arski, Stefan, *My pierwsza Brygada* (We, the First Brigade), Warsaw, 1963.

Bain, Leslie B., *The Reluctant Satellites*, New York, 1960.

Barnett, S. R., et al., *Poland, Its People, Its Society, Its Culture*, New Haven, 1958.

Bass, R., and E. Marbury, eds., *The Soviet-Yugoslav Controversy, 1948–1958: A Documentary Record*, New York, 1959.

Baume, Wolfgang la, et al., *The German East*, Berlin, 1954.

Beck, Józef, *Dernier Rapport: Politique Polonaise, 1926–1939*, Paris, 1951.

Beneš, Vaclav L., et al., eds., *The Second Soviet-Yugoslav Dispute*, Bloomington, Ind., 1959.

Bialer, Seweryn, *Wybrałem prawdę* (I Choose the Truth), New York, 1956.

Bierut, Bolesław, *O Konstytucji Polskiej Rzeczypospolitej Ludowej* (On the Constitution of the Polish People's Republic), Warsaw, 1952.

——— *O Partii* (On the Party), Warsaw, 1952.

Bierut, Bolesław, and Józef Cyrankiewicz, *Podstawy ideologiczne PZPR* (The Ideological Basis of the Polish United Workers' Party), Warsaw, 1952.

Bliss-Lane, Arthur, *I Saw Poland Betrayed*, Indianapolis, 1948.

Blit, Lucjan, *Gomulka's Poland*, London, 1959.

——— *The Eastern Pretender*, London, 1965.

Bobrzyński, Michał, *Dzieje Polski w zarysie* (Poland's History in Outline), vol. I, Jerusalem, 1942.

Bocheński, Aleksander, *Dzieje głupoty w Polsce: Pamflety dziejopisarskie* (The History of Stupidity in Poland: Historiographic Essays), Warsaw, 1947.

Bocheński, Jacek, *Boski Juliusz* (Divine Julius), 2 ed., Warsaw, 1962.

Bolesławita (Kraszewski, Ignacy), *Z roku 1868 Rachunki* (An Account of 1868), Poznań, 1868.

——— *Z roku 1869 Rachunki* (An Account of 1869), Dresden, 1869.

Borkiewicz, Adam, *Powstanie Warszawskie* (The Warsaw Uprising), Warsaw, 1958.

Bór-Komorowski, Tadeusz, *Armia Podziemna*, London, 1952. Translated as *The Secret Army*, London, 1957.

Brandys, Kazimierz, *Obywatele* (The Citizens), Warsaw, 1951.

Braun, Joachim F. von, ed., *German Eastern Territories*, Berlin, 1957.

Bromke, Adam, "A Visit to Poland: Impressions of a Political Scientist," Russian Research Center, Harvard University, 1961. Mimeographed.

——— *Eastern Europe in a Depolarized World*, Toronto, 1965.

Bromke, Adam, ed., *The Communist States at the Crossroads: Between Moscow and Peking*, New York, 1965.

Brown, J. F., *The New Eastern Europe*, New York, 1965.

Brzezinski, Zbigniew, *The Soviet Bloc: Unity and Conflict*, Cambridge, Mass., 1960.

——— *Alternative to Partition*, New York, 1965.

Brzoza, Jan (Młynarski, Feliks), *Do Broni — Prawda o Naczelnym Komitecie Narodowym i Polskich Legionach* (To Arms! The Truth about the Supreme National Committee and the Polish Legions), New York, 1915.

Budurowicz, Bohdan B., *Polish-Soviet Relations, 1932–1939*, New York, 1963.

Burks, R. V., *The Dynamics of Communism in Eastern Europe*, Princeton, N.J., 1961.

Campbell, John C., *American Policy Toward Communist Eastern Europe: The Choices Ahead*, Minneapolis, Minn., 1965.

Cannon, Walter B., *The Wisdom of the Body*, rev. ed., New York, 1939.

Carr, Edward H., *International Relations between the Two World Wars, 1919–1939*, New York, 1963.

——— *The Twenty Years' Crisis, 1919–1939: An Introduction to the Study of International Relations*, 2 ed., New York, 1964.

Centralny Komitet Stronnictwa Demokratycznego (The Central Committee of the Democratic Party), *Wytyczne działalności Stronnictwa Demokratycznego (Projekt)* (The Main Lines of Activity of the Democratic Party: Proposals), Warsaw, 1956.

——— *Wytyczne działalnosci politycznej, ekonomicznej i organizacyjnej Stronnictwa Demokratycznego (Uchwała z dn. 10. X.1956)* (The Main Lines of Political, Economic and Organizational Activity of the Democratic Party: Resolution of October 10, 1956), Warsaw, 1956.

——— *VII Kongress Stronnictwa Demokratycznego* (The 7th Congress of the Democratic Party), Warsaw, 1956.

——— *Referet Polityczno-Sprawozdawczy, VII Kongres Stronnictwa Demokratycznego* (The Political Report, 7th Congress of the Democratic Party), Warsaw, 1961.

——— *Projekt Uchwały VII Kongresu Stronnictwa Demokratycznego* (The Draft Resolution of the 7th Congress of the Democratic Party), Warsaw, 1961.

Cepnik, Henryk, *Józef Piłsudski: Twórca Niepodległego Państwa Polskiego* (Józef Piłsudski: The Creator of an Independent Polish State), Warsaw, 1935.

Chlebowski, Bronisław, *Literatura polska* (Polish Literature), Warsaw, 1932.

Chołoniewski, Antoni, *Duch dziejów Polski*, Cracow, 1918. Translated in an abbreviated version as *The Spirit of Polish History*, New York, 1919.

Chrypinski, Vincent C., "The Movement of 'Progressive Catholics' in Poland," unpub. diss. University of Michigan, 1958.

——— "Legislative Committees in Poland," University of Windsor, Windsor, Ont., 1963. Mimeographed.

Churchill, Winston S., *The Second World War*, Vol. VI: *Triumph and Tragedy*, Boston, 1953.

Ciechanowski, Jan, *The Defeat in Victory*, New York, 1947.

Cienciala, Anna M., "Polish Foreign Policy and the Western Powers, January 1938– April 1939," unpub. diss. Indiana University, 1962.

Ciołkosz, Adam, "Węzłowe zagadnienia w dziejach kommunizmu polskiego" (The Crucial Problems in the History of Polish Communism), London, 1959. Mimeographed.

Colier, David S., and Kurt Glaser, eds., *Berlin and the Future of Eastern Europe*, Chicago, 1963.

Czapski, Józef, *Terre inhumaine*, Paris, 1949.

Czwarty Zjazd Polskiej Zjednoczonej Partii Robotniczej, 15–20 Czerwca, 1964 (IV Congress of the Polish United Workers' Party, June 15–20, 1964), Warsaw, 1964.

Dallin, Alexander, ed., *Diversity in International Communism: A Documentary Record, 1961–1963*, New York, 1963.

Dallin, Alexander, et al., *Russian Diplomacy and Western Europe, 1914–1917*, New York, 1963.

Debicki, Roman, *Poland's Foreign Policy, 1919–1939*, New York, 1962.

Deutscher, I., *Stalin: A Political Biography*, London, 1949.

Dmowski, Roman, *Kommivoyazher v zatrudnenii* (Salesman in Trouble), Moscow, 1930.

⸺ *Świat powojenny i Polska* (The Postwar World and Poland), Warsaw, 1931.

⸺ *Niemcy, Rosja i kwestja polska* (Germany, Russia, and the Polish Question), 2 ed., Częstochowa, 1938.

⸺ *Pisma* (Works), vol. VIII, Częstochowa, 1938.

⸺ *Polityka polska i odbudowanie państwa* (Poland's Policy and the Restoration of the State), Hanover, 1947.

⸺ *Myśli nowoczesnego Polaka* (The Thoughts of a Modern Pole), 7 ed., London, 1953.

Drzewieniecki, W. M., *The German and Polish Frontiers*, Chicago, 1959.

Dux, Dieter, ed., *Ideology in Conflict: Communist Political Theory*, Princeton, N.J., 1963.

Dyskusja o polskim modelu gospodarczym (Discussion of the Polish Economic Model), Warsaw, 1957.

Dyskusji o prawie wartości ciąg dalszy (Discussion of the Theory of Value Continued), Warsaw, 1957.

Dziewanowski, M. K., *The Communist Party of Poland: An Outline of History*, Cambridge, Mass., 1959.

Fainsod, Merle, *How Russia Is Ruled*, rev. ed., Cambridge, Mass., 1963.

Fallenbuchl, Zbigniew M., *Zagadnienia gospodarcze ziem odzyskanych* (The Economic Problems of the Recovered Territories), London, 1956.

Feiss, Herbert, *Between War and Peace: The Potsdam Conference*, Princeton, N.J., 1960.

Feldman, Józef, *Problem polsko–niemiecki w dziejach* (The Polish–German Problem in History), Katowice, 1946.

Feldman, Wilhelm, *Dzieje polskiej myśli politycznej* (The History of Polish Political Thought), 2 ed., Warsaw, 1933.

Filipowicz, Tytus, *Marzenie polityczne* (The Political Dream), Cracow, 1909.

Fischer-Galati, Stephen, ed., *Eastern Europe in the Sixties*, New York, 1963.

Frankel, Henryk, *Poland: The Struggle for Power, 1772–1939*, London, 1946.

Friedberg, Jan, *Zarys historii Polski* (An Outline of Poland's History), vol. II, Hanover, 1946.

Galbraith, John K., *Journey to Poland and Yugoslavia*, Cambridge, Mass., 1958.

Gibney, Frank, *The Frozen Revolution in Poland: A Study in Communist Decay*, New York, 1959.

Giertych, Jędrzej, *Pół wieku polskiej polityki* (Half a Century of Polish Politics), London, 1947.

Główny Urząd Statystyczny (The Central Statistical Office), *Mały Rocznik Statystyczny, 1939* (Concise Statistical Yearbook, 1939), Warsaw, 1939.

——— *Rocznik Statystyczny, 1956* (Statistical Yearbook, 1956), Warsaw, 1956.

——— *Mały Rocznik Statystyczny, 1958* (Concise Statistical Yearbook, 1958), Warsaw, 1958.

——— *Poland in Figures, 1959*, Warsaw, 1959.

——— *Concise Statistical Yearbook, 1959*, Warsaw, 1959.

——— *Concise Statistical Yearbook*, 1960, Warsaw, 1960.

——— *Rocznik Statystyczny, 1960* (Statistical Yearbook, 1960), Warsaw, 1960.

Golachowski, St., et al., *Polska Zachodnia i Północna* (Western and Northern Poland), Poznań, 1961.

Gomułka, Władysław, (Wiesław), *W walce o demokrację ludową* (In the Struggle for the People's Democracy), 2 vols., Łódź, 1947.

——— *Przemówienia* (Speeches). Published on an annual basis, Warsaw, 1956–1962, 1957–1963.

——— *Artukuły i przemówienia, styczeń 1943–grudzień 1945* (Articles and Speeches, January 1943–December 1945), vol. I, Warsaw, 1962.

Grabski, Stanisław, *Myśli o dziejowej drodze Polski* (Thoughts on Poland's Historical Road), Glasgow, 1944.

Griffis, Stanton, *Lying in State*, New York, 1952.

Griffith, William E., "Thaw and Frost in Eastern Europe," Cambridge, Mass., 1960. Mimeographed.

Griffith, William E., ed., *Communism in Europe: Continuity, Change and the Sino-Soviet Dispute*, vol. I, Cambridge, Mass., 1964.

Gross, Felix, *The Seizure of Political Power*, New York, 1958.

Gruchman, Bohdan, et al., *Polish Western Territories*, Poznań, 1959.

Grzybowski, Kazimierz, *The Socialist Commonwealth of Nations: Organizations and Institutions*, New Haven, 1964.

Gwiżdż, Andrzej, and Janina Zakrzewska, eds., *Konstytucja i Podstawowe Akty Ustawodawcze Polskiej Rzeczypospolitej Ludowej* (The Constitution and the Essential Legislative Acts of the Polish People's Republic), 3 ed. rev., Warsaw, 1958.

Halecki, Oscar, ed., *Poland*, New York, 1957.

Healey, Denis, ed., *The Curtain Falls: The Story of the Socialists in Eastern Europe*, London, 1951.

Herz, John H., *Political Realism and Political Idealism: A Study in Theories and Realities*, Chicago, 1951.

Hiscocks, Richard. *Poland: Bridge for the Abyss?*, New York, 1963.

Hłasko, Marek, *The Eighth Day of the Week*, London, 1959.

Hoover, Calvin B., *The Economy, Liberty and State*, Baltimore, 1959.

Instytut Badania Zagadnień Krajowych (Research Institute for the Homeland's Affairs), *Rocznik spraw krajowych — Okres 1958–1959* (The Annals of the Homeland's Affairs, 1958–1959), London, 1960.

——— *Październik 1956* (October 1956), London, 1963.

Ionescu, Ghita, *The Break-up of the Soviet Empire in Eastern Europe*, London, 1965.

Jabłoński, H., *Polityka Polskiej Partii Socjalistycznej w czasie wojny 1914–1918* (The Policy of the Polish Socialist Party during the War of 1914–1918), Warsaw, 1958.

—— *Narodziny Drugiej Rzeczypospolitej, 1918–1919* (The Birth of the Second Republic), Warsaw, 1963.

Jaksch, Wenzel, *Germany and Eastern Europe,* Bonn, 1962.

Jaroszyński, Maurycy, *Zagadnienia Rad Narodowych* (The Problems of National Councils), Warsaw, 1961.

Jedlicki, Witold, *Klub Krzywego Koła* (The Club of the Crooked Circle), Paris, 1963.

Jordan, Z. A., *Philosophy and Ideology,* Dodrecht and Stuttgart, 1963.

Karol, K. S., *Visa for Poland,* London, 1959.

Karpiński, Andrzej, *Poland and the World Economy,* Warsaw, 1960.

Karski, Jan, *Story of a Secret State,* Boston, 1944.

Katelbach, Tadeusz, *Rok złych wróżb (1943)* (A Year of Bad Signs, 1943), Paris, 1959.

Kennan, George F., *Russia and the West under Lenin and Stalin,* Boston, 1961.

Kertesz, Stephen O., ed., *East and Central Europe and the World: Developments in the Post-Stalin Era,* Notre Dame, Ind., 1962.

Kirchmayer, Jerzy, *Powstanie Warszawskie, 1944* (The Warsaw Uprising, 1944), Warsaw, 1958.

—— *Kilka zagadnień polskich 1933–1944* (Some Polish Problems 1933–1944), Warsaw, 1959.

Kliszko, Zenon, *Z problemów historii PPR* (Some Historical Problems of the Polish Workers' Party), Warsaw, 1958.

Kokot, Józef, *The Logic of the Oder-Neisse Line,* Poznań, 1959.

Kolaja, Jiri, *A Polish Factory: A Case Study of Workers' Participation in Decision Making,* Lexington, Ky., 1960.

Komarnicki, Tytus, *Rebirth of the Polish Republic: A Study in the Diplomatic History of Europe, 1914–1920,* London, 1957.

Komisja Historyczna Polskiego Sztabu Głównego w Londynie (The Historical Commission of the Polish General Staff in London), Vol. I: *Polskie Siły Zbrojne w Drugiej Wojnie Światowej: Kampania Wrześniowa* (Polish Armed Forces in World War II: The September Campaign), London, 1951. Vol. III: *Polskie Siły Zbrojne w Drugiej Wojnie Światowej: Armia Krajowa* (Polish Armed Forces in World War II: The Home Army), London, 1953.

Konstantinov, F. T., ed., *O narodnoi demokratii v strankakh Evropy* (On People's Democracies in the European Countries), Moscow, 1956.

Kopański, Stanisław, *Wspomnienia wojenne* (War Reminiscences), London, 1961.

Korab, Alexander, *Die Entwicklung der kommunistischen Parteien in Ost-Mitteleuropa,* Hamburg, 1962.

Korbel, Josef, *Poland Between East and West: Soviet-German Diplomacy Toward Poland, 1919–1939,* Princeton, N.J., 1963.

Korbonski, Andrzej, *Politics of Socialist Agriculture in Poland, 1945–1960,* New York, 1960.

Korboński, Stefan, *W imieniu Rzeczypospolitej,* Paris, 1954. Translated as *Fighting Warsaw,* New York, 1956.

—— *W imieniu Kremla,* Paris, 1956. Translated as *Warsaw in Chains,* New York, 1959.

—— *W imieniu Polski Walczącej* (In the Name of Fighting Poland), London, 1963.

Korowicz, Marek, *Polska pod jarzmem sowieckim* (Poland under the Soviet Yoke), London, 1954.

Kostuch, Tomasz, ed., *Fifteen Years of People's Poland,* Warsaw, 1959.

Kot, Stanisław, *Listy z Rosji do gen. Sikorskiego* (The Letters from Russia to General Sikorski), London, 1956.

Kotok, V. F., and N. P. Faberov, eds., *Voprosy gosudarstva i prava stran narodnoi demokratii* (The Problems of Government and Law in People's Democracies), Moscow, 1960.

Kozicki, Stanisław, *Historia Ligi Narodowej* (History of the National League), London, 1964.

Krasucki, Ludwik, and Henryk Werner, eds., *100 Pytań i odpowiedzi* (100 Questions and Answers), Warsaw, 1961.

Kridl, M., J. Wittlin, and W. Malinowski, *The Democratic Heritage of Poland,* London, 1944.

Kukiel, Marian, *Dzieje Polski porozbiorowe, 1795–1921* (Poland's History in the Post-Partition Period, 1795–1921), London, 1961.

Kuśnierz, Bolesław, *Stalin and the Poles: An Indictment of the Soviet Leaders,* London, 1949.

Kuusinen, O. V., et al., *Osnovy Marksizma-Leninizma* (The Fundamentals of Marxism-Leninism), Moscow, 1959.

Kwiatkowski, Jan K. (Ren), *Komuniści w Polsce, Rodowód-Taktyka-Ludzie* (The Communists in Poland: Origin, Tactics, Personalities), Brussels, 1946.

Lange, Oskar, *Some Problems Relating to the Polish Road to Socialism,* Warsaw, 1957.

Lange, Oskar, et al., *Węzłowe zagadnienia budownictwa socjalizmu w Polsce* (The Crucial Problems of Socialist Construction in Poland), Warsaw, 1960.

Laqueur, Walter, and Leopold Labedz, eds., *Polycentrism,* New York, 1962.

Lenin, V. I., *Sochineniya* (Collected Works), vol. XXIX, Moscow, 1950.

Lewis, Flora, *A Case History of Hope: The Story of Poland's Peaceful Revolution,* New York, 1958.

Lisicki, Henryk, *Aleksander Wielopolski,* vol. IV, Cracow, 1879.

Lowenthal, Richard, *World Communism: The Disintegration of a Secular Faith,* New York, 1964.

Luxemburg, Rosa, *Rozwój przemysłu w Polsce* (The Development of Industry in Poland), Warsaw, 1957.

Łukasiewicz, Juliusz, *Polska jest mocarstwem* (Poland Is a Great Power), 2 ed., Warsaw, 1939.

Mackiewicz, Józef, *The Katyń-Wood Murders,* London, 1951.

——— *Zwycięstwo prowokacji* (A Victory of the Provocation), Munich, 1962.

Mackiewicz, Stanisław, *Historia Polski od 11 listopada 1918 r. do 17 września 1939 r.* (History of Poland from November 11, 1918 to September 17, 1939), London, 1941.

——— *Klucz do Piłsudskiego* (The Key to Piłsudski), London, 1943.

——— *Colonel Beck and His Policy,* London, 1944.

——— *Stanisław August* (Stanislaus Augustus), London, 1953.

——— *Zielone oczy* (The Green Eyes), Warsaw, 1958.

Makarczyk, Wacław, *Czynniki stabilizacji w zawodzie rolnika i motywy migracji do miast* (Factors Affecting Stability with Occupation of Farmer and Motives Underlying Migration to Towns), Wrocław, 1964.

Mała Encyklopedia Powszechna (The Little Popular Encyclopedia), Warsaw, 1959.

Małachowski, Aleksander, *Rzeczniepospolita* (Not an Ordinary Thing), Warsaw, 1964.

Małcużyński, Karol, *The Gomułka Plan,* Warsaw, 1964.

Mayewski, Pawel, ed., *The Broken Mirror,* New York, 1958.

Micewski, Andrzej, *Z geografii politycznej II Rzeczypospolitej* (From the Political Geography of the 2nd Republic), Cracow, 1965.

Mieroszewski, Juliusz, *Ewolucjonizm* (Evolutionism), Paris, 1964.

Mikołajczyk, Stanisław, *The Rape of Poland: Pattern of Soviet Aggression,* New York, 1948.

Mills, C. Wright, *The Marxists,* New York, 1962.

Miłosz, Czesław, *The Captive Mind,* London, 1953.

Ministerstwo Obrony Narodowej (The Ministry of National Defence), *Fakty i zagadnienia polskie* (Polish Facts and Problems), London, 1944.

Montias, John M., *Central Planning in Poland,* New Haven, Conn., 1962.

Morgenthau, Hans, *Politics Among Nations,* 2 ed., New York, 1956.

Mosley, Philip E., *The Kremlin and World Politics,* New York, 1960.

Nagórski, W., J. Sztucki, and M. Tomala, eds., *Strefa ograniczonych zbrojeń w Europie Środkowej: Dokumenty i materiały* (The Zone of Limited Armaments in Central Europe: Documents and Materials), Warsaw, 1959.

Narois, Claude, *Dieu Contre Dieu? Drame des catholiques progressistes dans une église su silence,* Paris, 1956.

Newman, Bernard, *Russia's Neighbour: The New Poland,* London, 1946.

────── *Portrait of Poland,* London, 1959.

Nowak, Jan, "Analysis of Developments in Poland," Munich, 1957. Mimeographed.

Osmańczyk, Edmund, *Sprawy Polaków* (The Affairs of the Poles), Katowice, 1948.

Paleologue, Maurice, *An Ambassador's Memoirs,* vol. I, London, 1925.

Piasecki, Bolesław, *Zagadnienia istotne* (The Vital Problems), Warsaw, 1954.

────── *Patriotyzm polski* (Polish Patriotism), Warsaw, 1958.

Piłsudski, Józef, *Pisma zbiorowe* (Collected Works), vols. I–IV, Warsaw, 1937.

────── *Pisma Wybrane* (Selected Works), London, 1943.

Pobóg-Malinowski, Władysław, *Józef Piłsudski, 1867–1901: W podziemiu i konspiracji* (Józef Piłsudski, 1867–1901: In the Underground and Conspiracy), Warsaw, 1935.

────── *Najnowsza historia polityczna Polski* (The Recent Political History of Poland), vol. I, Paris, 1935; vol. II, London, 1957.

────── *Józef Piłsudski, 1867–1914,* London, 1964.

Pogodin, Alexander L., *Glavnyia techeniia polskoi politicheskoi mysli (1863–1907)* (Main Currents of Polish Political Thought, 1863–1907), St. Petersburg, 1908.

"Poland, 1960," Warsaw, 1960. Mimeographed.

Poland, Facts and Figures, Warsaw, 1960.

Pologne 1919–1939, vol. I: *Vie politique et sociale;* vol. II: *Vie economique,* Neuchatel, 1946–1947.

Polonus-Viator (Jodko-Narkiewicz, W.), *Kwestja Polska wobec zbliżającego się konfliktu Austryi z Rosyą* (The Polish Question in the Light of an Approaching Conflict between Austria and Russia), Cracow, 1909.

Polska Akademia Nauk, Instytut Historii (Polish Academy of Sciences, Institute of History), *Najnowsze dzieje Polski, Materiały i Studia* (The Recent History of Poland, Documents, and Studies), vol. I, Warsaw, 1957.

Polska Akademia Umiejętności, *Polski Słownik Biograficzny* (Polish Biographical Dictionary), vol. V, Cracow, 1939.

Ponomarev, B. N., et al., *Istoria Kommunisticheskoi Partii Sovietskogo Soyuza* (The History of the Communist Party of the Soviet Union), Moscow, 1959.

Pounds, Norman J. G., *Poland Between East and West,* Princeton, N.J., 1964.
Pragier, Adam, *Cele wojenne Polski* (Poland's War Objectives), Glasgow, 1944.
Pruszyński, Ksawery, *Margrabia Wielopolski* (Margrave Wielopolski), 2 ed., Warsaw, 1957.
Raczyński, Edward, *W sojuszniczym Londynie* (In Allied London), London, 1959.
Riekhoff, Harald von, "Revisionism vs. Reconciliation: Germany's Poland Policy During the Period of the Weimar Republic," unpub. diss. Yale University, 1965.
Ripka, Hubert, *Eastern Europe in the Post-War World,* London, 1961.
Rocznik Polityczny i Gospodarczy (Political and Economic Yearbook), published on an annual basis. Warsaw, 1958–1964.
Rose, William J., *The Rise of Polish Democracy,* London, 1944.
—— *Poland Old and New,* London, 1948.
Rozek, Edward I., *Allied Wartime Diplomacy: A Pattern of Poland,* New York, 1958.
Rozmaryn, Stefan, *La Diète et les conseils du peuple dans la republique populaire de Pologne,* Warsaw, 1958.
—— *Konstytucja jako ustawa zasadnicza P.R.L.* (The Constitution as a Fundamental Law of the Polish People's Republic), Warsaw, 1961.
Russian Institute, Columbia University, *The Anti-Stalin Campaign and International Communism,* New York, 1956.
Seton-Watson, Hugh, *The East European Revolution,* New York, 1951.
—— *From Lenin to Khrushchev,* New York, 1960.
Sharp, Samuel L., *Poland: White Eagle on Red Field,* Cambridge, Mass., 1953.
Shirer, William L., *The Rise and Fall of the Third Reich: A History of Nazi Germany,* New York, 1960.
Shneiderman, S. L., *The Warsaw Heresy,* New York, 1959.
Skarżyński, A., *Polityczne przyczyny Powstania Warszawskiego* (Political Background of the Warsaw Uprising), Warsaw, 1964.
Skilling, H. Gordon, *Communism National and International: Eastern Europe after Stalin,* Toronto, 1964.
—— *The Governments of Communist Eastern Europe,* New York, 1966.
Skrzyński, Alexander, *Poland and Peace,* London, 1923.
Sławoj-Składkowski, Felicjan, *Kwiatuszki administracyjne* (The Administrative Mélange), London, 1959.
Sliwiński, Artur, *Powstanie Styczniowe* (The Uprising of 1863), London, 1945.
Snell, John L., *Illusion and Necessity: The Diplomacy of Global War, 1939–1945,* Boston, 1963.
Staar, Richard F., *Poland, 1944–1962: The Sovietization of a Captive People,* New Orleans, La., 1962.
Stahl, Walter, *The Politics of Postwar Germany,* New York, 1963.
Stankiewicz, W. J., and J. M. Montias, *Institutional Changes in the Postwar Economy of Poland,* New York, 1955.
Starościak, Jerzy, *Decentralizacja administracji* (The Decentralization of Administration), Warsaw, 1960.
Stawar, Andrzej, *Pisma ostatnie* (Last Writings), Paris, 1961.
Stehle, Hansjacob, *Nachbar Polen,* Frankfurt, 1963. Translated as *The Independent Satellite,* New York, 1965.
Stillman, Edmund, ed., *Bitter Harvest,* New York, 1959.
Stolarzewicz, Ludwik, *Dzieje i czyny Nieśmiertelnego Wodza Narodu* (The Story and the Deeds of an Immortal Leader of the Nation), rev. ed., Warsaw, 1936.

Stomma, Stanisław, *Myśli o polityce i kulturze* (Thoughts on Politics and Culture), Cracow, 1960.

The Story of the Warsaw Rising, Newton, Montgomeryshire, 1945.

Strumph-Wojtkiewicz, Stanisław, *Sikorski i jego żołnierze* (Sikorski and His Soldiers), Łódź, 1946.

Stryszowski, Bronisław, *Zarys dziejów narodu i państwa polskiego w latach 1914–1939* (An Outline of the History of the Polish Nation in the Years 1914–1939), London, 1947.

Stypułkowski, Zbigniew, *Invitation to Moscow,* London, 1952.

—— *Polska na progu 1958 r.* (Poland at the Beginning of 1958), London, 1958.

Sulimirski, Tadeusz, *Poland and Germany: Past and Future,* London, 1942.

The Swiatlo Story, New York, 1956.

Syrop, Konrad, *Spring in October: The Story of the Polish Revolution of 1956,* London, 1958.

6 lat temu: Kulisy polskiego października (Six Years Ago: Behind the Scenes of the Polish October), Paris, 1962.

Szirmai, Z., ed., *Law in Eastern Europe,* London, 1962.

Szyr, Eugeniusz, et al., *Twenty Years of the Polish People's Republic,* Warsaw, 1964.

III Zjazd Polskiej Partii Robotniczej: Stenogram (The 3rd Congress of the Polish United Workers' Party: Stenographic Record), Warsaw, 1959.

Ulam, Adam, *Titoism and the Cominform,* Cambridge, Mass., 1952.

Uniwersytet im. Adama Mickiewicza w Poznaniu. Prace Wydziału Filozoficzno-Historycznego. Seria Historia, Nr. II (University of A. Mickiewicz in Poznań. The works of the Faculty of Philosophy and History), *XX Rocznica powstania Polskiej Partii Robotniczej* (The 20th Anniversary of the Foundation of the Polish Workers' Party), Poznań, 1962.

Wagner, Wolfgang, *The Genesis of the Oder-Neisse Line,* Stuttgart, 1957.

Wandycz, P. S., *Czechoslovak-Polish Confederation,* Bloomington, Ind., 1956.

—— *France and Her Eastern Allies: French-Czechoslovak-Polish Relations from the Paris Conference to Locarno,* Minneapolis, Minn., 1962.

Wereszycki, Henryk, *Historia polityczna Polski w dobie popowstaniowej 1864–1918* (Poland's Political History in the Post-Insurrectionist Period, 1864–1918), Warsaw, 1948.

Wiskeman, Elizabeth, *Germany's Eastern Neighbours,* London, 1956.

Wojciechowski, Konstanty, *Dzieje literatury polskiej* (The History of Polish Literature), Hanover, 1946.

Wojciechowski, Zygmunt, ed., *Polska — Niemcy, dziesięć wieków zmagania* (Poland and Germany: Ten Centuries of Struggle), Poznań, 1945.

—— *Poland's Place in Europe,* Poznań, 1947.

Wolikowska, Izabella, *Roman Dmowski: Człowiek, Polak, Przyjaciel* (Roman Dmowski: A Person, a Pole, and a Friend), Chicago, 1961.

Wrotnowski, Antoni, *Porozbiorowe Aspiracye Polityczne Narodu Polskiego* (Post-Partition Political Aspirations of the Polish Nation), Cracow, 1898.

Wydawnictwa Zachodnie (Western Publications), *Straty wojenne Polski w latach 1939–1945* (Poland's War Losses in the Years 1939–1945), Warsaw, 1960.

Zakład Historii przy KC PZPR (Institute of History, Attached to the Central Committee of the Polish United Workers' Party), *PPR VIII, 1944-XII, 1945* (Polish Workers' Party, August 1944–December 1945), Warsaw, 1959.

Załuski, Zbigniew, *Siedem polskich grzechów głównych* (The Polish Seven Deadly Sins), Warsaw, 1962.

Zaremba, Zygmunt, *Sześcdziesiąt lat walki i pracy P.P.S. Szkic historyczny* (Sixty Years of the Struggle and Work of the Polish Socialist Party: An Outline of History), London, 1952.

Zawodny, J. K., *Death in the Forest,* Notre Dame, Ind., 1962.

Zbrodnia Katyńska w Świetle Dokumentów (The Katyn Crime in the Light of Documents), London, 1962.

Zinner, Paul, ed., *National Communism and Popular Revolt in Eastern Europe,* New York, 1956.

Żółtowski, Adam, *Border of Europe: A Study of the Polish Eastern Provinces,* London, 1950.

Zurawski, Joseph W., *Poland: The Captive Satellite,* Detroit, 1962.

Zweig, Ferdynand, *Poland Between Two Wars: A Critical Study of Social and Economic Change,* London, 1944.

Zych, J., *Rosja wobec Powstania Warszawskiego* (Russia's Attitude Toward the Warsaw Uprising), London, 1947.

II. NEWSPAPERS AND PERIODICALS

1. *Polish*

Annales Universitatis Mariae Curie-Skłodowska (The Annals of the University of Mariae Curie-Skłodowska). Quarterly.

Argumenty (The Arguments). Weekly. Organ of the Association of Atheists and Free Thinkers.

Biuletyn Informacyjny-Chrześciańskie Stowarzyszenie Społeczne (Information Bulletin of the Christian-Social Association). Monthly.

Biuletyn Statystyczny (Statistical Bulletin). Monthly. Published by the Central Statistical Office.

Dziś i Jutro (Today and Tomorrow). Weekly. Organ of Pax. Discontinued in 1955.

Express Wieczorny (Evening Express), Daily.

Głos Ludu (The Voice of the People). Daily. Organ of the Polish Workers' Party. Discontinued in 1948.

Głos Pracy (The Voice of Labor). Published every other day. Organ of the Central Council of Trade Unions.

Kierunki. Weekly. Organ of Pax.

Krajowa Agencja Informacyjna (The Homeland Information Agency). Weekly.

Kultura (Culture). Weekly.

Kultura i Społeczeństwo (Culture and Society). Quarterly. Published by the Sociological and Cultural Division of the Polish Academy of Sciences.

Nowa Kultura (New Culture). Weekly. Discontinued in 1963.

Nowe Drogi (New Roads). Monthly. Theoretical organ of the Central Committee of the Polish United Workers' Party.

Polish Western Affairs. Quarterly. Published by the Western Institute in Poznań.

The Polish Sociological Bulletin. Semi-annual publication of the Polish Sociology Association.

Polityka (Politics). Weekly.

Po Prostu (Speaking Frankly). Weekly. Discontinued in 1957.

Prawo i Życie (Law and Life). Bi-weekly. Organ of the Association of Polish Lawyers.
Przegląd Kulturalny (Cultural Review). Weekly. Discontinued in 1963.
Przekrój (Cross Section). Weekly.
Słowo Powszechne (Popular Word). Daily. Organ of Pax.
Sprawy Międzynarodowe (International Affairs). Monthly. Published by the Polish Institute of International Affairs.
Świat (The World). Weekly.
Świat i Polska (The World and Poland). Weekly. Discontinued in 1958.
Sztandar Młodych (The Flag of Youth). Daily. Organ of the Socialist Youth Alliance.
Trybuna Ludu (The People's Tribune). Daily. Organ of the Polish United Workers' Party.
Tygodnik Powszechny (Popular Weekly). Weekly. Catholic organ.
Wieś Współczesna (Contemporary Village). Monthly. Theoretical organ of the United Peasant Party.
Więź (Link). Monthly. Catholic organ.
Za i Przeciw (Pro and Contra). Weekly. Organ of the Christian-Social Association.
Zeszyty Naukowe Uniwersytetu Jagiellońskiego: Seria Nauk Społecznych (The Scholarly Papers of the Jagiellonian University: Social Science Series). Quarterly.
Zeszyty Naukowe Uniwersytetu im. A. Mickiewicza w Poznaniu: Prawo (The Scholarly Papers of the University of A. Mickiewicz in Poznań: Law). Quarterly.
Zielony Sztandar (The Green Flag). Weekly. Organ of the United Peasant Party.
Znak (Sign). Monthly. Catholic Organ.
Życie Gospodarcze (Economic Life). Bi-weekly.
Życie Literackie (Literary Life). Weekly.
Życie Warszawy (Warsaw's Life). Daily.

2. *Emigré*

Cahiers Pologne-Allemagne. Quarterly published in Paris. Discontinued in 1964.
The Central European Federalist. Published semi-annually by the Czechoslovak-Hungarian-Polish Committee in New York.
Dziennik Polski i Dziennik Żołnierza (Polish Daily and Soldier's Daily). Daily published in London.
Kultura (Culture). Monthly published in Paris.
Myśl Polska (Polish Thought). Bi-weekly. Organ of the emigré National Democratic Party in London.
Nowy Świat (The New World). Daily published in New York.
Poland and Germany. Quarterly published by the Centre on Polish-German Affairs in London.
Polemiki (Polemics). Quarterly published in London.
Polish Affairs. Monthly published by the Council of National Unity in London.
The Polish Review. Quarterly published by the Polish Institute of Arts and Sciences in America in New York.
Wiadomości (The News). Weekly published in London.
"Wiadomości o życiu w Polsce" (The News from Poland). Mimeographed weekly. Published by the Free Europe Committee in New York.
Związkowiec (The Alliance). Semi-weekly published in Toronto.

3. *Foreign*

The American Economic Review
The Annals of the American Academy of Political and Social Science

Canadian Journal of Economics and Political Science
Canadian Slavonic Papers
The China Quarterly
The Current Digest of the Soviet Press
Current History
East Europe (formerly News from Behind the Iron Curtain)
The Economist
Encounter
For a Lasting Peace: for a People's Democracy (discontinued in 1956)
Foreign Affairs
Frankfurter Allegemeine Zeitung
International Affairs
International Journal
Journal of Central European Affairs (discontinued in 1964)
Journal of International Affairs
Kommunist
Der Monat
Mezhdunarodnaya Zhizn
Neuen Zurcher Zeitung
The New Leader
The New York Times
The Observer
Orbis
Ost-Europa
Ost-Probleme
Parliamentary Affairs
Peking Review
Politique étrangère
Pravda
Problems of Communism
Queen's Quarterly
Revue de Défense Nationale
Revue de l'Université d'Ottawa
Revue du Droit Public et de la Science Politique en France et à l'Etranger
Slavic and East European Studies
Slavic Review (formerly The American Slavic and East European Review)
Sunday Times
Survey: A Journal of Soviet and East European Affairs
Die Welt
World Marxist Review: Problems of Peace and Socialism
World Politics
The World Today
Voprosy Filosofi
Yugoslav Review

INDEX

Russian Research Center Studies